*f*ado Resounding

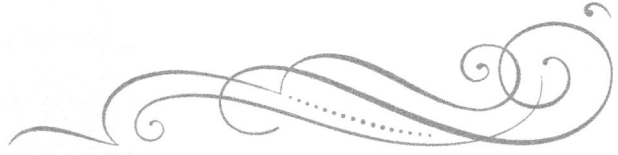

*f*ado Resounding

AFFECTIVE POLITICS AND URBAN LIFE

Lila Ellen Gray

Duke University Press • Durham and London • 2013

Library of Congress Cataloging-in-Publication Data
Gray, Lila Ellen
Fado resounding : affective politics and urban life / Lila Ellen Gray.
pages cm
Includes bibliographical references and index.
ISBN 978-0-8223-5459-8 (cloth : alk. paper)
ISBN 978-0-8223-5471-0 (pbk. : alk. paper)
1. Fados—Portugal—History and criticism. I. Title.
ML3718.F3G73 2013
781.62'691—dc23
2013018963

Duke University Press gratefully acknowledges the support of the AMS 75 PAYS Endowment of the American Musicological Society, funded in part by the National Endowment for the Humanities and the Andrew W. Mellon Foundation, which provided funds toward the publication of this book.

Frontispiece: A guitarrista and viola player in Alfama on the way to a shift . Lisbon, July 2008. Photograph by the author.

To
JOHN BARBOUR GRAY and NANCY ORSAGE MORLEY

and to
JOSÉ MANUEL OSÓRIO
in memoriam

CONTENTS

ILLUSTRATIONS

Figures

Musical Examples

ACKNOWLEDGMENTS

To the *fadistas*, instrumentalists, aficionados, and fado listeners in Lisbon who shared with me their voices, their friendship, and patience, I thank you. I first learned how to listen to fado and how to value it in Lisbon's Tasca do Jaime. I did so through the assistance of so many there, but I am particularly grateful to Fátima Fernandes, Maria José Melo, Fernanda Proença (Pimpona), Olga Rosa de Sousa, and Álvaro Rodrigues.

I gratefully acknowledge the institutions and organizations that made long-term ethnographic research financially possible. The International Dissertation Field Research Fellowship Program of the Social Science Research Council, with funds provided by the Andrew W. Mellon Foundation; the Luso-American Development Foundation, in conjunction with the Council for European Studies; the U.S. Department of Education's Foreign Language and Area Studies program; and Duke University (Department of Cultural Anthropology, Center for European Studies, Center for Latin American and Caribbean Studies, and Center for International Studies) supported field research and language study conducted in Lisbon between 2000 and 2003. Subsequent follow-up research (2006–10) was supported by two Columbia University faculty summer research awards, a grant by the Luso-American Foundation for Development, and funding from the Center for Race and Ethnicity, and from the Center for Ethnomusicology at Columbia University.

Numerous fadistas, instrumentalists, fans, and music industry professionals participated in recorded interviews during 2001–2003 and in informal conversation and dialogue over the past decade; I am grateful for their generosity. My research was facilitated by the goodwill of multiple proprietors of *casas de fado* and fado venues in Lisbon. Jaime and Laura Candeias, owners of the Tasca do Jaime, graciously accommodated my regular presence and welcomed me warmly when I returned. In addition, I am grateful to the following venues that opened their doors to me: A Baiuca, Bacalhau de Molho, Café Luso, Tasca do Careca, Taverna do Embuçado, and the Grupo Excursionista Vai Tu. The Associação Cultural o Fado in Marvila encouraged me to participate as a member and as a singer and allowed me to record rehearsals. António Rocha permitted me to record the series of fado "lessons" I took with him at Lisbon's Fado Museum. Sebastião de Jesus accommodated my research within the spaces of Vai Tu and Tasca do Careca and, through conversation and his artful presentation of the fado, helped to teach me what it means to respect it.

Numerous institutions in Lisbon granted me access to their collections and assisted me with multiple queries. I am indebted to José Carlos Alvarez, the director of the Museu Nacional do Teatro, and his staff; to Alda Gomes of the Fonoteca Municipal de Lisboa; to Sara Pereira at the Museu do Fado; to Maria do Carmo Pacheco at Rádio Difusão Portuguesa; to José Jorge Letria and his staff at the Sociedade Portuguesa de Autores; and to Carmo Gregório and João Pimentel of the bookstore Fabula Urbis.

I am appreciative of the academics and writers in Lisbon who met with me to discuss this project in its earliest stage: Salwa El-Shawan Castelo-Branco, Rui Vieira Nery, José Moças, António Firmino da Costa, Joaquim Pais de Brito, Rui Mota, and Ruben de Carvalho. I thank K. David Jackson for his initial encouragement. Virgílio Santiago helped to teach me Portuguese. Ana Gonçalves carefully transcribed some of my earliest taped interviews. Helena Correia and Ana Gonçalves assisted with the Portuguese orthography for this book.

This project began while I was in the Department of Cultural Anthropology at Duke University, where I had wonderful mentors and colleagues. I am particularly grateful to Louise Meintjes, Charles Piot, Kathy Ewing, Ralph Litzinger, and Sarah Beckwith for their feedback. To Louise Meintjes I owe a tremendous debt for her mentoring and her friendship, and for the exceedingly high bar she sets through her own ethnographic commitments, inspiring through fearless example.

At Columbia University, I have been grateful for the intellectual community that my colleagues Aaron Fox, Ana Maria Ochoa-Gautier, and Chris Washburne, and our graduate students in the ethnomusicology program, have provided. James Napoli and Melissa Gonzalez assisted with the digital transfer of my field recordings from digital audio tape. The composer Yoshiaki Onishi brought his sharp ears and a meticulous eye to his labor on the musical transcriptions for this book.

Two residencies—one at the John Hope Franklin Center for International and Interdisciplinary Studies at Duke University during 2004–2005 ("Knowledge and Its Institutions") and the other at the Rutgers Center for Historical Analysis during 2009–10 ("Vernacular Epistemologies")—provided me with invaluable writing time and energetic intellectual communities with whom to think through some of the project's central questions as they evolved. I thank Julie Livingston and Indrani Chatterjee at Rutgers for their support and dialogue. The seminar participants at Rutgers, the Ethnomusicology Working Group at Duke in the summer of 2008 (Alessandra Ciucci, Louise Meintjes, Amanda Minks, and Jenny Woodruff), Paul Berliner, Virginia Danielson, Ana Maria Ochoa-Gautier, and Christine Yano offered insightful critiques on earlier versions (spoken and written) of some portions of this book. Audiences at presentations I gave at Harvard University and Wesleyan University and at panels on musical celebrity I organized for the American Anthropological Association (2007) and the Society for Ethnomusicology (2008) meetings helped me sharpen my arguments in chapter 6. The book has benefited from the attentiveness and insights of my readers from Duke University Press: Kimberly DaCosta Holton, who read the first version; Steven Feld, who read the second; and an anonymous reader who read them both. Working with Ken Wissoker and the staff at Duke University Press, particularly Jade Brooks, Liz Smith, Susan Deeks, Courtney Baker, and Bea Jackson, on this book has been a great pleasure and privilege.

Stephen Miles introduced me to the tools through which to think politics and music in the same frame, and Robert Knox introduced me to the tools through which to understand narrative and poetics. Kató Havas, my former violin teacher, taught me about the power of the voice and about multiple pedagogies of the soulful in sound. My gratitude to her exceeds all efforts to write it on the page.

I thank Christina Gier, Jennifer Fitzgerald, Jessica Wood, Kelley Tatro, and Netta Van Vliet for intellectual debate and sustaining grace. Matt Goodrich, Davida Singer, Isabelle Deconinck, Iris Zmorah, Nuno Morais, and Ana Rosenheim Rodrigues, through the generosity of their friendship and the exuberance of their play, kept me writing. Julie Kline sent me my first cassette tape of fado that got the project going. Wim Jurg has lent his ears and eyes to my stories since this project's earliest beginnings and steadfastly kept the faith. I thank my parents, John Gray and Nancy Morley, and my sister, Rebecca Gray, for their boundless love. The fado researcher and performer José Manuel Osório shared with me his knowledge, his friendship, and his fados. The memory of his voice continues to remind me what is possible.

AN EARLIER VERSION of chapter 3 appeared in *Anthropology and Humanism* 36, no. 2 (2011). Portions of the introduction and chapters 1 and 2 appeared in earlier form in *Ethnomusicology* 51, no. 1 (2007). I thank the American Anthropological Association and the Society of Ethnomusicology for permission to include this work in *Fado Resounding*. The Sociedade Portuguesa de Autores kindly granted me permission to include the fado lyrics that appear in excerpt. I am grateful to the Museu do Fado and to Rui Pimentel for permission to publish my photograph of Pimentel's "Vielas"; to the street artist MrDheo for permission to publish my photograph of his mural "Amália Rodrigues"; to Editorial Avante! for granting me permission to publish "Alfama" by Ary dos Santos; to the poet José Luís Gordo for permission to include his poem "Fado da Meia Laranja"; to the poet Álvaro Rodrigues for permission to include the lyrics to "Alfama Eterna"; and to Edite B. de Medeiros Tomé for permission to publish the lyrics to the fado "Lisboa Não Mudes Assim" by her late husband, Manuel Calado Tomé. The musical transcriptions in chapter 4 and in the appendixes are by Yoshiaki Onishi, and the layout and design are by W R Music Service. Scott Smiley made the index. All translations are mine. I made every effort to fairly represent the communities and people with whom I worked. I have changed the names of some of my interlocutors in order to respect their privacy. Any errors or misrepresentations in this book lie in the challenges of ethnographic writing and are fully my responsibility.

Placing Fado Resounding

In the city of Lisbon, there are stories built upon stories about what fado is, is not, was, should be. Urban legends, official and unofficial histories, vestiges of totalitarian regime-making propaganda, and academic discourse come together in the fado origin tales and variants I hear on the ground.[1] *It came from the troubadours. No, it began in the 1800s and was influenced by European salon music. Or, It came from the Moors; it is Arab. The Moors were so far from their home and they felt* saudade. *That feeling, that feeling of saudade is where fado comes from. Or, Fado came from the streets, from the brothels of Lisbon, from the bars or tascas; it started with the working class. It has always been a revolutionary song. Or, Fado came from the sung voices of homesick sailors on boats during the Discoveries. (The Portuguese discovered the world, you know.)[2] Those sailors made the sea salty with their tears. Or, Fado came from Africa, then from Brazil, and it used to be a lascivious dance.* But almost always, *Fado is from Lisbon; fado is sung with a Portuguese soul (alma); fado is ours and is about the longing of saudade, expressing what is lost and might never be found, what never has been but might be.*

In the city of Lisbon, *fadistas* (fado singers) sing fado in out-of-the-way clubs, on concert-hall stages, in tourist-oriented restaurants and in professional *casas de fado* (lit., fado houses), in neighborhood recreation centers, and in small neighborhood bars. Fado can be heard as ambient sound in many restaurants, and through loudspeakers on city streets, and can sometimes be heard on television commercials that promote

Portuguese products. A fadista might sing until *her throat hurts*, the voice hovering on the break of a sob; the accompanying *guitarra* (Portuguese guitar) might vibrate a note thus making it weep (*gemer*); in moments of sung beauty, listeners sometimes cry.[3] Fado gathers stories and feelings about histories and places in its movement and charges scenes with affect.[4] One feels how to sing based on a personal experience of history and locality, as felt in relation to neighborhood, to the city of Lisbon, and to a sense of Portugal's past and to its place in the rest of the world. Fado travels the world on internationally marketed recordings by star figures as the sound and "soul" of Lisbon, as the voice of Portugal, circulating sonic imaginaries of a soulful periphery.

Fado Resounding argues for the power of a musical genre to sediment, circulate, and transform affect, sonorously rendering history and place as soulful and feeling as public. Its ethnographic focus is on the social life of the sung poetic genre of fado, and some of its listeners, singers, instrumentalists, and cultural brokers in the city of Lisbon during the first decade of the 2000s, concentrating primarily on the years of sustained ethnographic research I conducted between 2001 and 2003.[5] While the research for this book spanned diverse and overlapping Lisbon sites and social worlds, including museums and archives, professional fado venues and small amateur bars, neighborhood fado associations, Amalianos (fans of the fado diva Amália Rodrigues), recording studios, and the day to day on Lisbon's streets, it is primarily grounded in ethnographic work on *fado amador*, or amateur fado practice.

Fado Resounding foregrounds the knowledge embedded in and transmitted by the expressive performing body and musical sound, knowledge that simultaneously engages habits of memory alongside inventive improvisation; knowledge that often opens fissures in narratives of history as officially told and ruptures the order of things; knowledge that is transmitted from one body to another via aesthetic power and that in making itself heard is felt. It asks questions about the affective labors of forms in circulation, the intertwining of genre and feeling, senses of place and history; it works with a popular song genre as a form of possibility for ways of being in the world. It locates these questions ethnographically in a time that both European "belonging" (through the practical instantiation of a common currency) and belonging writ large (via the attacks of September 11, 2001) were buzzwords both in international media and in Lisbon's bars. It situates these questions in a place on Europe's farthest southwestern margins, a place that for centuries has been cast from the perspective of Europe's North as "the South," as peripheral to the kinds of access to resources and power that count, with laments simultaneously resounding from within, already for centuries, about the waning of Portugal's own centrality as *center of the world that discovered the world*, laments for an empire lost, about being "behind," while at the same time spectacular projects of urban development and renewal beckoned optimistically toward the future. In narratives cast from Europe's North and in identity-making discourses from "within," one resource abundant in this periphery is sentiment. Sonorously, in these discourses, this capacity for feeling, this abundance of the soulful, takes persuasive form in the genre of fado.

Fado developed in Lisbon in the early 1800s as a sung poetic genre voiced from the city's socioeconomic margins, with originary narratives linked to prostitution, criminality, Portuguese colonial expansion, and a musical legacy of the "Moors." It was later embraced by the upper classes (Brito 1999; Nery 2004). During Portugal's dictatorship (1926–74), the state's role in the development of casas de fado facilitated fado censorship, sanitization, and professionalization. Meanwhile, some singers sang revolutionary lyrics behind closed doors. Following the revolution in 1974, there was a backlash against fado due to its supposed relation to the dictatorship; many fado venues shut down. Fado's success on the international "world music" market over the past two decades, a newly thriving Lisbon fado scene, recently increased attention to fado by international media, and a globally realigned music and heritage industry (Ochoa-Gautier 2006) have recast the political stakes attached to fado from a genre of "deviance" and protest to a "national" genre of the late dictatorship, then to an underdog genre of the post-dictatorship era, and now to an "expedient" cultural resource (Yúdice 2003). In November 2011, the United Nations Educational, Scientific, and Cultural Organization declared fado an "Intangible Cultural Heritage of Humanity."

Lisbon is a place with a dynamic and rich history of cross-cultural encounter and influence. As the point from which the first colonizing expeditions departed and returned; as a formerly active site for slave trade; and as a place to which immigrants from former Portuguese colonies (particularly Angola, Mozambique, and Cape Verde) now come to inhabit, Lisbon is a place of gathering and convergence for multiple sounds, performance styles, and histories. Fado style and talk engage with a re-presentation of a history that is hybrid, gendered, illicit, and raced. In contemporary Lisbon, fado is performed and enjoyed by local actors from diverse socioeconomic backgrounds, although particular venues and styles may be marked by class, with the distinguishing characteristic that in a city with a large and ever-growing immigrant population, the majority of participants continue to be white Portuguese.

For those who sing and listen to fado, the polemic around origins is charged. This history is often foregrounded in fado lore—for example, in pamphlets distributed in tourist clubs—yet fado has come to represent quintessential Portugueseness. Simultaneously, alternative histories, particularly those of Africans and Muslims in relation to Portugal, are increasingly voiced after years of repression under the dictatorship. Amateur singers sometimes claim that fado's improvisatory vocal turns (*voltinhas*) were inherited from the Moorish "occupation" centuries ago; others argue that fado is "uncontaminated" and belongs to Portugal. I take the charged nature of discourse on fado's origins as one point of departure for theorizing relationships between musical experience and the shaping of the ideas about history on which belonging and locality are often predicated in postcolonial Portugal (Gray 2007).

How might fado shape the ways in which Lisbon places are felt and imagined in relation to the vestigial burdens of Portugal's long-standing dictatorial regime and colonial past? How does fado figure affective geographies of Lisbon and Portugal in a contemporary dialectics of North and South? From the perspective of the listener or the performer, might musical experience accumulate history in ways different from other expressive aesthetic forms? From the perspective of an anthropology of the senses, what might a "musical" history mean? In tracking articulations of these questions through the poetics and politics of ethnography, I put in conversation theoretical work from across the social sciences and the humanities that grapples with relations between sound, listening, and vocality to social life; aesthetic form to feeling; genre to affect; music to language; performance to politics; and, finally, memory, history, and place to the senses. I gloss briefly here some of the most salient arguments and theoretical approaches that in turn scaffold or provoke those in this book.

Fado Resounding is premised on a dynamic model of genre. It is a social analysis through the prism of musical genre; it examines the socio-aesthetic labors of fado *as genre*. Thus, I follow the lead of recent scholarship in the humanities and social sciences that argues for the need to take seriously the power of aesthetic form or genre in rendering communicative and affective the implicit narratives that shape one's sense of self and place in the world (Berlant 2008; Frow 2005; Holt 2007; Ramaswamy 2010). Arguing for genre as sociohistorically contingent (Bakhtin 1986: 12) and against a notion of genre as formally fixed is not to undermine the importance of formal features to what defines genre; rather, it is to understand form itself as at once socially shaped and emergent (Bauman and Briggs 1992). It is to understand the labor of shaping and contesting genre's formal characteristics as undergirded by questions of value, ethics, and personal reputation (Meintjes 2003); it is also to locate some of the social power of genre in its "porosity" and intertextuality (Bauman and Briggs 1992; Berlant 2008).[6] Finally, it is to be attentive to genre in relation to the "cultures of circulation" (Lee and LiPuma 2002) through which it moves and in which it thrives, both as it is transformed along and by the circuits through which it travels and as it shapes them in turn.[7]

Throughout the text, I grant genre a certain agency, a circulatory power. Fado as genre is *sticky*; unofficial and official histories, rituals, sounds, styles, affects, memories, and biographies attach to it, circulate, morph.[8] Fado as genre is reflexive; its own lyrics comment back on it, endlessly remaking it as object. Fado as genre is a flashpoint, a catchment of affect and of story: of affect that binds people to place and to one another, and a sounding board through which actors hear their own voices and are heard.

Lauren Berlant (2008) has written about ways in which affect nests within genre and circulates, providing forms for belonging. I work with fado as genre as a nexus of gathering, as an affective aesthetic force field, as a scene of engagement and attention (Berlant 2008) through which listeners, musicians, and policymakers play "serious games" (Ortner 1996: 12).[9] I cast fado as genre in a wide net to include both its formal aesthetic features as practiced and talked about and its scenes, its places, its iconographies, its aesthetic forms, its poetics, its meta-discourses, its repertoires of feeling, and most of all, its sounds.

Sound and hearing are powerfully linked to the experience of emotion (Feld 1996b).[10] The ways in which one makes emotional sense of sound (I refer specifically to para-linguistic features of vocal sound and to instrumental sound more broadly) are at once shaped socially and physiologically. By virtue of being musical, fado as genre foregrounds the significations that accrue and circulate that are sensuous, pleasurable, and embodied as they are felt and heard, meanings that actors often have a hard time pinning down exactly in words. Fado as genre, as a prism for analysis, also foregrounds how any given musical moment or genre "makes sense" to listeners, in part by its capacity to point to diverse memories, places, and histories while saturating these memories, places, these histories, with feeling and with sound.

MUSIC, LANGUAGE, AND VOICE

Fado Resounding works from a premise that poetics about music making are inseparable from music's social life. It draws on approaches to musical signification in recent scholarship in musical-sociolinguistic anthropology that argue for music and language as co-constitutive domains of meaning (Feld and Fox 1994; Feld et al. 2004; Fox 2004; Meintjes 2003; Samuels 2004). This research foregrounds some of the productive ambiguities in how music "makes sense" to listeners. One of the ways in which it does so is by taking seriously the poetics practitioners and listeners use when talking about music—for example, when describing (often in highly metaphoric language) the notoriously ineffable and affect-laden modality of timbre (or "tone color"). Another is by attending to indexical relations with respect to how musical meaning is made in relation to any given listener or community of listeners (Samuels 2004; Turino 1999). In other words, in the ears of one person, one musical moment might simultaneously point to multiple memories or feelings, senses of place or of history. Among a group of listeners, the same musical moment might accrue indexical meanings grounded in shared histories of listening while at the same time have other meanings specific to the individual.[11] In the case of fado performance in Lisbon, one musical moment might simultaneously index multiple meanings for the same listener or performer; a fado style that some listeners might point to as proof of fado's "African" origins might, for others, unequivocally index "Portugueseness." Attention to music's indexical relations opens up possibilities for thinking about relationships between aesthetic forms, practices, and social belonging that complicate identity-based analyses of expressive culture (Samuels 2004) and a homologous mapping of musical genre onto identity or belonging (national or otherwise).

Fado Resounding thus works from an understanding of both music and language as essentially interconnected domains of signification and along these lines is attentive to speech and song as residing on a continuum of expression rather than as two distinct modes of communication (see Feld 1982; Feld and Fox 1994; Feld et al. 2004; Fox 2004; List 1963; Samuels 1999, 2004). Likewise, it works with an idea of performance as existing on a rich and often intertextual continuum (Bauman and Briggs 1990), with performances of the everyday at one end (Frith 1996; Goffman 1959) and highly framed, formal, or staged performances at the other. In fado's worlds, speech and song, performances of the everyday (such as telling a story), heightened performances (such as getting up to sing a fado during an amateur fado session), and mediatized performances (such as sound and audiovisual recordings via multiple forms of circulation and playback) interanimate one another. Listening can also be considered as a type of performance (Frith 1996; Hirschkind 2006; Valverde 1999), signaled on its own continuum of markedness, by its own rituals and repetitions. For many participants, the term "fadista" refers to both one who sings and one who knows how to listen; through listening, one enters into the affective, poetic, and performative sound world of fado, mind, body, and *soul*. This continuum of the fado voice sounding (and re-sounding), and the ways in which people listen, forms a central analytic of this book.

As the voice resonates within the body, it is experienced as intensely personal, its timbre marking the "uniqueness" (Cavarero 2004) of an individual. Yet as a primary vehicle for expression, voice is intrinsically linked to both subjectivity and sociality. To focus on the voice is to be attuned to the ear, to listening: "the voice is always *for* the ear, it is always relational" (Cavarero 2004: 169). The sounded voice might be understood as a juncture at which "nature" meets "culture" (Dolar 1996, 2006), at which physiology meets sociality (Feld et al. 2004); the voice might be thought of all at once as index of an interior self, a physical self, and a social self, standing in for a trope of both agency and social power. I privilege the voice, sound, and listening as key sites through which to understand the shaping of the subjective and the intersubjective, the intimate and the public.[12] By analyzing specific instances of the fado voice as both collectively and singularly inflected, as both rhetorical and expressive, I connect theorizations of the voice as trope to the voice as embodied foregrounding their co-production. Recent anthropological and historical scholarship on vocality emphasizes the role that technologies and ideologies of the voice play in shaping notions of "tradition" and "modernity" (Bauman and Briggs 2003; Sterne 2003; Weidman 2006). Indeed, particular ideologies of "voice" have been critical to shaping the "interior" of a subject, and an "essence" of a collectivity of subjects, on which some modernities (or alternative modernities) have relied (Fox 2004; Ivy 1995; Weidman 2006). I track both technologies and ideologies of voicing, examining how through genre they are given form; circulate; spin out into story; shape senses of self, place, and history; and render particular ways of feeling public.

FEELING FADO: AFFECTIVE MUSICAL SUBJECTS

Fado provides both a form for feeling and a form for its contagion.[13] For some practitioners and aficionados, fado is also a form for living (*uma forma de vida, a vida fadista*), a way of being (*uma maneira de ser*), a cosmology with a distinct ontology to which the word "music" fails to do justice. Many described fado to me as a faith, as a religion. Fado listeners, musicians, and fans talk about being "caught by the fado" (*apanhados pelo fado*); one world music fado diva told me that fado has a will. Seven months or so into my field research, people began telling me, "You are completely caught by the fado." "Fate" and "destiny," the literal meanings of "fado" in these usages, blur with fado's designation as a musical/poetic genre. Aesthetic form provides a framework for feeling— literally, a structure *for* feeling—conditioning expectations, teaching one how and when to feel in relation to gesture, to style, and to ritual (Cumming 2000). One of fado's primary labors as a genre is *affective* (Hardt 1999).[14] *Fado Resounding* takes a cue from recent Americanist work in literary and cultural studies on affect that extends Raymond Williams's (1977) "structures of feeling" into the domain of "public feeling" and intimacy, arguing for the sociopolitical shape to the forms feelings take and how they move through worlds, often in ways that are mercurial and difficult to map.[15] In other words, "We find ourselves in moods that have already been inhabited by others, that have already been shaped or put into circulation, and that are already there around us" (Flatley 2008: 5). Sara Ahmed (2004: 11) works with a concept of "stickiness" for theorizing the circulation of emotions as social: "It is the objects of emotion that circulate, rather than emotion as such. . . . Such objects become sticky, or saturated with affect, as sites of personal and social tension." I argue here for the stickiness of fado as a genre in circulation and for genre as an object around which affects, histories, life worlds, and social practices coalesce. I use the term "affect" to foreground the social, historical, and corporeal (sensed) dynamics of feelings.[16] I work with feeling in this book as affect communicated through musical and sonic form. The genre of fado forms the object around which are shaped communities that involve particular kinds and ways of feeling (Rofel 2007; K. Stewart 2007) and of being "soulful," ways of feeling that are simultaneously locally, geopolitically, and historically situated. I treat the interanimation between different registers of feeling that fado accrues—feeling as embodied, feeling as simultaneously of the social and of the subject, and feeling as discursive trope.

A "HISTORY OF THE PRESENT" BY WAY OF THE SENSES

Fado listeners told me how sometimes when moved by a particular performance, goose bumps might rise on the flesh, the skin might vibrate (*vibrar*), how one might tremble or cry. "History" in these moments gains coherence, is organized via its affective mediation by the sensuous palpability of music as genre, as voice, as sung story. And both history and place, through fado, in being given sound, are granted "soul." *Fado Resounding* argues for fado's work as a genre in circulating and transforming official and unofficial historical narratives and for the ways in which in moments of fado listening, history is rendered as a feeling. In these moments, tidy chronologies and official historical narratives are sometimes displaced, giving way to a version of history that is such because it *feels* so. History in these moments also becomes entangled with personal memories lodged in habits of the body (Connerton 1989; Gil 2007; Taylor 2003; Trouillot 1995), memories connected to the specificity of places (Feld and Basso 1996; K. Stewart 1996; Tsing 1993, 2005).[17] Memory and history might come together, rising to the surface, as in a taste (Seremetakis 1996) or as evoked by a fragrance, a streetscape, a photograph on the wall, in a phrase of music sounded. Memory and history as felt through fado often come together in the aesthetic poetic ethos of saudade, a nostalgia that is one of fado's most pervasive tropes. Literature on the Black Atlantic has emphasized the ways in which memories and histories accrue and circulate through embodied ritual and cultural performance; in one performance lies always the potential to evoke residues of performances that preceded it, harkening back to an ever elusive point of origin (Gilroy 1993; Matory 2005; Roach 1996). Any given fado performance bears historical traces of contact between cultures, traces of prior performances. It has the potential to evoke memories of places, people, of situations long gone, and bring them sensuously to the present.

Fadistas and fado aficionados note that no one performance of the same fado is ever identical to another, even when sung and played by the same musicians. They credit this endless variation to both singing with soul (*com alma*), and to a highly valued act of creative improvisation, or "composition in performance" (Lord 2003 [1960]), which they call "styling" (*estilar*). While in traversing the international stage through industries of "world music" and in locally inflected discourses of "cultural patrimony," the metaphor of soul may link fado to a timeless essence, the climactic moments of the performance of soul are anything but unchanging. Rather, the music and lyrics contain inventive improvisations and new compositional twists. If each moment of performance contains the embodied traces of history, a study of these soulful stylized moments, precisely because they mark the convergence of heightened creativity and feeling, can help us to understand the shaping of the contemporary historical imaginary as registered in relation to a sense of place in which place is continuously imagined, transformed, and produced. Yet I was often cautioned by fans and singers to respect the mystery of fado and fado's origins.

This book is attentive to the productive power of that mystery, to music's embodied pleasures and meanings, while at the same time unsettling the "secret of sound" (Taussig 1999: 183). *Fado Resounding* unsettles relationships of musical genre, music, and the singing voice to "identity," to interiority, to place, and to "soul." Through an ethnography of listening and voicing—an ethnography of the sonorous—it also "unsettles" (Lubkemann 2005) the former colonial metropole of Lisbon.[18]

I work with contemporary actors' sentient and discursive making and remaking of a musical genre in light of memories and imaginaries of a history of a recent past in which relations between the genre of fado and the long-standing Portuguese dictatorship were ambivalently fraught, a regime that relied on the colonial—as myth, as reality, as episteme—

for its maintenance. I posit that there is rarely a one-to-one relationship between musical performance/genre and political resistance or domination and argue that what makes a musical genre such as fado so compelling as a prism for an analysis of the social is precisely its power to reveal relations of ambivalence (Berlant 2008) through which abstractions like "nation," "history," and "soul" are figured and felt by both individuals and publics. Finally, I argue for this "soulful" as never reducible to the "purely" local (Matory 2005) but, rather, as always, in any given historical moment, entangled in and shaped by more widely circulating cultural forms that inform what it might mean to be "social," what it might mean to feel "human," and what it might feel like to belong.[19]

Placing Genre: Origins, Forms, Histories

Perhaps because of fado's power, its beauty, or its ritualized repeated forms; perhaps because of its importance in shaping the life worlds of my interlocutors; perhaps because it makes and remakes itself as object through the stories it tells about itself; or perhaps because it is "music," people often assumed that my goal as a researcher was to learn and to write about what fado is and where it came from—its forms, its histories, its origins.[20] For many, fado had that kind of agency and presence, that kind of omnipresent and weighty "thingness." *You will never get to the bottom of it, you know! Fado is endless. It is a universe; it is the world. It is a mystery.* Or, *It is good that you are studying our music. All they do around here is disrespect the fado.* Or, *Academics don't understand anything about fado; fado is something you sing, you feel.* Or, *Let me tell you about fado: this is its story, and this is my life.* It was never my plan to chart what fado "is," not only because I did not wish to chase the ghost of an immutable aesthetic form outside of the realm of the emergent that is social life, but also because I was interested initially in questions I believed were more directly related to fado as social practice: questions about memory and history, affect and belonging, place and corporeality. But it was precisely through chasing the "object" as practiced—the formal, musical, aesthetic, stylistic, and historical parameters of the constitution of the genre for different actors in multiple scenes—that the social and affective life of fado as genre made itself heard: the "law of genre"; the play of genre; the elusivity of genre. Affect moves through form. Genre opens into stories.

Alberto Pimentel (1989 [1904]: 66), in his classic text, *A Triste Canção do Sul* (A Sad Song of the South), writes, "Fado is perhaps the bastard son of the *landum*, but is many times more beautiful.[21] Bastard children, I don't know why, are almost always more beautiful than legitimate ones." Pinto de Carvalho (1992 [1903]: 42), in *História do Fado* (History of Fado), claims, "For us, fado has a maritime origin. . . . Fado was born on board [on ships] to the infinite rhythms of the sea, in the convulsions of this soul of the world, in the murmuring intoxication of this eternity of water." Finally, Luiz Moita (1936: 195), quoting the French critic Emílio Vuillermoz in *O Fado: Canção de Vencidos* (Fado: Song of the Vanquished), states, "A wise Portuguese musicologist affirmed that fado was of Afro-Brazilian origin. But many of his compatriots rebel against this explanation, as it lends an undesirable pigment to an eminently national genre.[22] I confess that, for a foreigner, an African [*negra*] origin in fado is entirely credible."

Why is it that musical performance and experience often elicit such impassioned and polemical claims to origin? Polemic surrounding origins has been central to published fado discourse at least since the beginning of the twentieth century (Carvalho 1992 [1903]; Pimentel 1989 [1904]). While the main strains of this polemic argue for African-influenced derivations via the black slave trade and Lisbon's positioning as port city vis-à-vis colonial contact and expansion, Arab derivations due to the long-standing presence of the Moors in Portugal, or a combination of the two, others link fado to the music of the medieval troubadours, to expressive traditions from rural Portugal, to the Celts, or to the "gypsies." The theory of origins granted the most currency by contemporary academics situates fado's "birth" in the first half of the nineteenth century and locates its primary influences as Afro-Brazilian. These influences were heightened by the flight of the Portuguese court to Brazil during the Napoleonic invasions and the court's subsequent return to Lisbon (Nery 2004; Tinhorão 1994), bringing back to the metropole dances, sounds, styles, and songs from Brazil. The Brazilian historian José Ramos Tinhorão (1994) links the evolution of the sung fado in Lisbon to a confluence of Afro-Brazilian and Iberian influences in relation to the traffic in African slaves; colonial relationships between Portugal and Brazil; and intercultural exchange via the port cities of Lisbon, Seville, Rio de Janeiro, and Salvador. According to this thesis, the sung fado emerged in Lisbon in the 1800s from the fandango, an Afro-Spanish popular dance genre; from the Afro-Brazilian dance forms the *lundum* and the *fofa*; and later from a fado that was danced in Brazil. Scholars have also argued for the influence of eighteenth-century European urban song forms (Nery 2004: 51) and of the *modinha*, a melancholic improvised vocal genre accompanied by the guitarra that circulated via Brazil (Castelo-Branco 1994; Moita 1936; Nery 2004) and was popular in the late 1700s to early 1800s in Lisbon, where it was performed in the streets, in homes, and in upper-class salons. Scholars widely agree that fado initially thrived in the early decades of the 1800s among Lisbon's dispossessed, at the social margins—particularly in Lisbon's brothels, cafés, and prisons—but then socially "ascended" early in its "development" to salons and bullfights frequented by the aristocracy.[23] To this day, fado bears traces, in its performance practices, repertoires, venues, and discourses, of these earlier class and political histories.

Discourse on fado's origins from a range of sources, historical and contemporary, as well as from actors from varying subject positions, is marked by its excess. This excess makes itself felt in the continuous production of new variations on originary themes, in the affective energy with which actors stake their claims and with which these claims circulate, and in the frequency in which origin themes serve as the subject of fado lyrics themselves.[24] Music is made in movement. It is shaped in its circulations and performative iterations, emergent. The performance theorist Joseph Roach reminds us that remembering necessitates forgetting. "The relentless search for the purity of origins is a voyage not of discovery but of erasure," and that performance—particularly the type of performance he labels "circum-Atlantic"—is a "monumental study in the pleasures and torments of incomplete forgetting" (Roach 1996: 6–7).[25] From a scholarly perspective, some theories regarding fado's early histories have more credence than others. Yet rather than be concerned with the veracity of these multiple claims, this book focuses on the *excess* of originary discourses attached to fado and on the passion through which those discourses are voiced as objects of critical analysis.

ORDERING GENRE

Among the fado listeners and musicians with whom I worked, fado as genre was argued, debated, defended, embellished, made affective, and also historicized by reference to fadistas, recordings, and fado locales of the past. Fado genre in these discussions had dimensions that were performative, qualitative, ritualized, localized in terms of space and place, and temporalized. Fado genre talk included discussions about form (e.g., the number of syllables per line or number of lines per strophe for a specific traditional fado; harmonic and melodic parameters); discussions about how a particular fado had been named or the subgenre into which it fit; about the authorship of both music and lyrics; and about the words to fado poems. Fado lyrics also often comment meta-discursively on fado itself; these poetics in turn sometimes elicit musical commentary, such as text "painting," ornamentation, or musical citation. Keeping in mind genre's flexibility and porosity, particularly at its fringes (Bauman and Briggs 1992), and also that "center" and "margin" are relative categories, I sketch in broad strokes some of the key contours that shape definitions of fado form for practitioners, listeners, and researchers.

Lisbon fado is performed most often with one vocalist (fadista), male or female, and accompanied by one or two guitarras, a *viola* (Spanish six-string acoustic guitar), and sometimes a *viola baixo* (acoustic bass guitar) or, as is becoming more common, a stand-up acoustic bass.[26] The instrumentalists are almost always male. Generally, the guitarras figure the harmonic counterpoint while the viola rhythmically marks the bass and outlines the harmonic progressions. The instrumentalists and the fadista, in the most skilled performances of fado, perform in improvised "dialogue" with one another (Castelo-Branco 1994).

In terms of its musical parameters as practiced, fado to the present day has been largely an oral/aural tradition and does not depend on musical notation for its transmission. Yet fado practice and transmission, in terms of both music and poetry, foreground intricate interrelations and histories between orality and literacy in Portugal, or the "archive and the repertoire" (Taylor 2003), with respect to both musical notation and written language. While most fadistas and fado instrumentalists I met did not read music, musical notation has played some role in fado transmission since at least the mid-nineteenth century. Notated fado songs circulated in scores for nineteenth-century and early twentieth-century *revistas* (musical theater or vaudeville revues). Sheet music versions of fados for piano, often with elaborately designed covers, circulated in the early twentieth century to be played and sung in well-to-do Portuguese homes. A musically notated fado can be submitted to the Sociedade Portuguesa de Autores (Portuguese Society of Authors, SPA) as proof of intellectual ownership of the musical composition (although in popular musical practice, this notation is not consulted when performing the fado in question, and the musical parameters of a given fado in practice may differ substantially from what is officially notated and registered at the society). Fado lyrics are almost always written down. They circulate on paper and online. They might be handed over in person by a poet to a fadista or by one fadista to another; they are also found in old fado serials and in some liner notes that accompany compact discs (CDs). Both lyrics and music are fixed in sound on recordings. Some practitioners identify specifically as fado poets, and poets may submit their work for registration with the SPA. Yet fadistas, in performance, sometimes substitute words or phrases of a poem with their own. These substitutions or variations can subsequently take on lives of their own and come to be popularly identified with the poem as "correctly" interpreted. Fadistas and instrumentalists sometimes also write fado lyrics, and on occasion, fadistas choose to set poetry not initially intended for fado, to fado musical forms or styles.

Fado lyrics are extraordinarily rich in expressive scope. Some common themes include heterosexual romantic love in multiple manifestations (e.g., betrayal, lost love, death of a loved one, unrequited love), loss, saudade, love for the figure of the mother, Marian themes, politics, the city of Lisbon and its neighborhoods, the Tagus River, the "nation" of Portugal, the Portuguese colonial Discoveries, fado itself (venues, sounds, forms, histories, biographies), and fadistas. Fado as genre foregrounds story and feeling, the telling of stories rendered affective through musical performance and poetic form. Fadistas, instrumentalists, aficionados, and scholars generally break the fado repertoire into two categories: fado tradicional (traditional fado) and fado canção (fado song).[27] I found these classifications to be commonly used among listeners and singers in both amateur and professional contexts and to be widely referred to in the discourse of fans.

Traditional fado is strophic and follows a variety of set poetic forms with regard to the number of stanzas and lines (Carvalho 1999). It can be set to an infinite number of lyrics and foregrounds the inventive styling and improvisation of the fadista and the guitarra over a relatively fixed harmonic and metrical base. Thus, it is the base musical (musical "base") that differentiates one traditional fado from another; the lyrics are unfixed. The fado researcher José Manuel Osório estimates that over four hundred traditional fados exist.[28] Yet the standard performed repertoire is in practice substantially smaller.[29]

The three fados of Fado Menor, Fado Corrido, and Fado Mouraria are commonly cited as being the oldest, are of anonymous authorship, follow a basic I-V harmonic scheme, and use stock instrumental figurations; the vocal line is highly improvised. Some also refer to these three fados as the *raízes do fado* ("roots of fado") (Castelo-Branco 1994: 134). Fado Menor, which is in a minor key and is often performed at a slow tempo, is considered by many instrumentalists, singers, and fans to be the oldest fado, the saddest fado, and the most affectively charged. Many of my interlocutors cited the twentieth-century fado diva Amália Rodrigues for naming the Fado Menor "the mother and father of fado." Thus, the fetishization of origins found in discourse about fado's history is also manifest in relation to fado form. In the discourse on Fado Menor, the saddest, the most highly improvised, and the most authentic merge in the concept of the original, in affect as embodied in sonic form.

Fado practitioners discuss the musical bases, and sometimes the melodies, of traditional fados (with the exception of the three root fados) as "authored" or "composed" by an individual. However, in practice the ascribing of rights and authorship to some of these fados can be ambiguous. There is often substantial variation in the names practitioners give to particular traditional fados. The name of a traditional fado (again, with the exception of the three root fados) generally refers to its musical/poetic structure, and sometimes refers to the person who is believed to have "composed" the harmonic/melodic base. However, the name of well-known lyrics might supplant the name of the "composer" of the musical base or a name for a traditional fado might be linked to a place name. Alternatively, the name of a fado might refer to the person to whom it was originally dedicated (Castelo-Branco 1994: 135). Names indexically connect the form to social relationships, memories, places, and histories.[30]

Many practitioners differentiate *fado canção* (lit., fado song) from traditional fado by noting that rather than being strophic in form, it contains stanzas juxtaposed with refrains and that each fado song has set lyrics.[31] Researchers point to the influence of the revistas that came into vogue in Lisbon in the mid- to late 1800s as playing a central role in the development of fado canção (Castelo-Branco 1994; Nery 2004). The voice and career of Amália Rodrigues (referred to by some as the "Queen of Fado") also had an impact on the recognition and consolidation of fado canção as a form. A number of fado songs were written specifically for her; many circulated via films in which she starred.

Salwa El-Shawan Castelo-Branco (1994: 133), on the basis of her study conducted primarily with professional instrumentalists, suggests that traditional fado and fado canção might be understood on a continuum on which the former represents the "minimum of fixed elements," thus allowing for the most flexibility and improvisation in performance, and the latter represents "maximum fixity." The discourse my interlocutors used when referring to these two fado subgenres generally followed that understanding. Both musicians and listeners generally drew sharp evaluative and affective distinctions between the two categories that went beyond explications of musical, harmonic, or poetic form.[32] Singers and instrumentalists commonly spoke to me about traditional fado as both enabling and demanding more improvisation, and I often heard fado canção referred to as musically "scored" or marked as "less" fado, farther from the "soulfulness" of lived story and more "musical" (see chapter 1). Yet in sung practice, particularly in amateur performance, I also often heard creatively improvised and dramatically reconfigured performances of what might be generally classified as fado canção and fados canção set to new lyrics; I also heard particular traditional fados to which multiple fadistas set the same lyrics. Thus, the continuum as practiced was fluid.

Throughout this book, I argue that an accretion of memory and affect occurs in the practices of listeners which is linked to fado form. The syncretic, reiterative form of traditional fado (which, to some extent, fado canção shares) allows for hearings and musical experiences that become saturated by past renderings yet that are always newly inflected through individual improvisation. Fado form works as a ground upon which affect and memory accrue and are figured, one performance stacked upon another, one listening overlapping with a previous listening of the same fado. One fado becomes multiply populated with memories of people, of places, of stories, of histories, but these are all grounded in and facilitated by musical form. Certain traditional fados are often thought to convey particular affective states, and poets or singers sometimes use these associations when deciding on which fado to set their text to. In traditional fado, the hearing of one story set to music potentially indexes previous hearings of different stories set to the same musical base; it might remind one of different singers, voices, contexts, and locales in such a way that histories, places, and voices become stacked one upon another, this excess made emotionally salient through musical sound and aesthetic form.

The relationships between fado's forms and the affects they transmit to communities of listeners are always in process; these relationships are at once socially and historically contingent (Bakhtin 1986). An amateur fado aficionado, a man in his sixties, lamented to me in 2001 that "there is not much sad fado, the real fado, the *fado fado* these days. The tourists don't like it." At the same time, a heightened affect of sadness, of saudade, a sentimentality, became attached to certain fado forms and practices in particular ways throughout the Estado Novo (New State) as a result of censorship, of cultural policy, the cultivation of fado tourism in the late dictatorship, and of shifting approaches of the state to an unruly genre (Côrte-Real 2001; Leal 2000b; Nery 2004). Fado's soundings in the present circulate affective traces of these histories in its forms. At the same time, fado's forms are continuously repurposed in official and unofficial discourses and practices to respond to a dynamic politics of the present.

NETWORKS, VENUES, AND PRACTICES:
AMATEUR–PROFESSIONAL DISTINCTIONS

Fado performance in contemporary Lisbon moves through interrelated sites and social networks that mutually inform and influence one another.[33] The density of tourist-oriented professional fado venues, both *casas típicas* (lit., "typical houses") and casas de fado, in the "traditional" Lisbon neighborhoods of Bairro Alto and Alfama delimit and mark spaces of the "real Portugal" for an international tourist market; some of these sites also feature performances of "folkloric" dancing.[34] Elite fado art-house venues, which cater to tourists and to "in-the-know" aficionados who can afford to pay steep prices, boast fine dining and professional fado, often sung by fadistas who have international careers and recording contracts with multinational labels. Both types of venue have contracted instrumentalists and an *elenco* (group of contracted professional fadistas) and almost always require minimum consumption or cover charges from audience members. Simultaneously, fado lovers and musicians continue to imagine and reproduce their everyday lived neighborhoods and social networks through engaging with fado, often within the context of "amateur" fado. Amateur fado sessions occur in a handful of *tascas* (small neighborhood bars), in some restaurants that are not classified as official fado houses, at neighborhood associations, and at private functions.

Distinctions between *fado amador* (amateur fado) and *fado profissional* (professional fado) are central to how people navigate and participate in Lisbon's fado networks; these distinctions are myriad and are made by practitioners, aficionados (tourists and locals), venue owners, and policymakers. In the most general sense, the amateur–professional distinction with respect to fadistas refers to those who are paid to sing and those who are not. (Instrumentalists are almost always paid, regardless of the type of venue or performance context.) But the distinction as practiced is equivocal. Actors might invoke the amateur–professional distinction to mark aesthetic standards, singing style, performance practices, political histories, repertoire, class positioning, and differences in neighborhoods with respect to fado venues; to police the limits of genre; to stake claims to authenticity; and to argue for affective power. *You know, fado amador is where only drunks go to sing. That is not fado. All they do is scream!* Or, *Yes, I have sung professionally for many years, but at heart I am an amateur. I feel most at home when I am singing fado amador, unwinding with friends.* Or, *Fado amador has the most soul; the rest is just for tourists.* Or, *Fado amador is about the working class; fado began that way—in the brothels, in the taverns.*

The distinction has ramifications for the required licenses and the fees owners of venues pay to municipal entities and to the SPA. Some commercial establishments host amateur fado "unofficially" to avoid having to pay the fees; when this is discovered, they might be closed down. As fado has gained increasing recognition internationally over the past decade, the venues themselves have become increasingly diverse and hybrid in the types of fado they claim to offer, and the economics at work, particularly in relation to the compensation of fadistas in the so-called amateur venues, is increasingly difficult to parse. A venue might hire a few regulars but still encourage participation by amateurs. Or a restaurant might have a group of unpaid regulars who sing almost every night of the week, generally to tourist audiences, but charge food prices on par with professional venues. By hosting so-called "amateur" fado, these venues substantially lower their operating costs and also capitalize on tourists' desire for authenticity (see also Klein and Alves 1994). Some professionals participate (without pay) in fado amador in their leisure time, yet many who identify as *amador* do not have access to the opportunities and social networks that would enable them to participate as professionals at the elite venues. Many stars of Lisbon's amateur circuit are semiprofessionals who earn a portion of their income by singing fado for payment at parties, charity events, and neighborhood fundraising events and by selling their recordings, often between sets of performance, at the unpaid amateur venues. These recordings are often produced at one of the few studios on Lisbon's periphery that cater to fado's semiprofessionals.

Within communities of fadistas who identify as amateur, and among fadistas who primarily identify as professional, exist diverse social networks. Among elite professionals, I heard sharp evaluative distinctions voiced regarding different styles and venues for professional fado. In the early 2000s, I met amateurs who sang aristocratic fado who boasted hereditary descent from the old monarchy and were still lamenting the loss of the dictator Salazar. At the same time, I met amateurs who participated in completely separate social networks, many working class, those of the older generations claiming Communist Party alliances during the Estado Novo. I also attended single amateur venues that were regularly frequented by listeners and fadistas from strikingly diverse socioeconomic backgrounds. Both amateur fado and professional fado (as venues; as practices; as categories for social and aesthetic evaluation; as social networks; and as relations to labor, consumption, and pleasure) carry with them tangled, and often differing, sociopolitical histories (see chapter 2). Within the amateur communities in which I spent the most time in the early 2000s—whose participants were predominantly working class, older than fifty, and strongly tied to Lisbon's historic core neighborhoods—actors sometimes called forth aspects of these perceived political histories and distinctions of genre to mark their own relationships to the past, to ethics, to solidarity, and to the future.

POLITICAL HISTORIES, POLICIES OF CULTURE (1926–1974)

The Portuguese totalitarian regime, the Estado Novo (New State), began in 1926 and ended with a bloodless military coup on April 25, 1974 (*25 de Abril*). António de Oliveira Salazar was the dictator from 1932 to 1968; in 1968, Marcelo Caetano took his place. The coup was given impetus by desperately failing colonial wars in Africa, the 1968 protests in Paris, international pressure calling for Portuguese decolonization, and extensive mobilization within Portugal through clandestine communist networks with international ties, particularly to Portuguese in exile abroad. The revolution signified the end—at least in practical terms—of the Portuguese empire and the beginning of a wave of immigration from the former colonies to Lisbon, significantly altering racial dynamics in the metropole.[35]

Portuguese totalitarianism, particularly in its first few decades, shared many ideologies and practices with other, coterminous European forms of totalitarianism (e.g., with respect to the formation of youth movements, the "disciplining" of the mind and the body through organized expressive cultural practices, state censorship, state corporatism, and a powerful secret police force). While it is beyond the scope of this book to enumerate in detail the differences and similarities of these regimes, I note some key facets that marked the Portuguese dictatorship: (1) the Catholic church played a fundamental role in its institutions of power and in shaping and disseminating ideologies of the regime to "the people"; (2) the Estado Novo was excessively focused on an idealized past, particularly in relation to the glorification of the Portuguese Discoveries and with respect to sentiments of anti-industrialization (evident in a celebration of rurality, as contrasted with the "degeneracy" of the urban; see Castelo 1998; Holton 2005; Melo 2001); (3) Portugal remained neutral during the Second World War; and (4) Portuguese colonialism was essential to the maintenance of the regime.

Many of my interlocutors were hesitant to call the Estado Novo "fascist." Some referred to it as a "light" dictatorship (compared with those of Germany, Italy, and Spain) and lauded Salazar for keeping order and peace in the country. Yet many spoke to me about the final decades of the Estado Novo as being marked by brutal censorship, panoptic police surveillance, increasing imprisonment of political activists, and the deployment of sophisticated techniques of torture by the state. Some of my interlocutors were imprisoned during that time, and many had family members or friends who were.

Cultural policy with respect to expressive culture—and to fado in particular—underwent multiple shifts during the course of the dictatorship.[36] During the first decades of the Estado Novo, the state played a key role in the professionalization, codification, and censorship of fado through the creation of official professional venues, but the state did not explicitly appropriate fado in the service of the nation during that time.

In fact, in official discourses, fado was often considered inappropriate as a national form because of its "illicit" origins, its dolorous tenor (it was not a "fighting" song; see Moita 1936), and its urban degeneracy (Melo 2001; see also chapter 2). At the same time, during the first Portuguese Republic (1910–26)—the period that immediately predated the Estado Novo—anarchist and workers' movements sang fado (*fado anarquista* and *fado operário*) as a means of social protest. The formation of official fado venues, fado censorship, and professionalization thus worked as ways for the state to take some control of what was perceived to be a potentially disruptive expressive form (Nery 2004). The beginnings of the Estado Novo coincided with the era of sound reproduction and radio; fado circulated on the radio, on Portugal's first sound films, and on recordings.[37] By the 1950s, the Estado Novo was increasingly marshaling what by then had become a highly sentimentalized practice of fado in the service of a burgeoning international tourist industry in Lisbon (Côrte-Real 2001; Nery 2004) and as an ideological force on state-controlled radio. Luxurious casas de fado became meeting places for senior state officials, visiting foreign dignitaries, and members of the ruling elite. Through the voice of Amália Rodrigues, the state channeled fado as an international export as the sound and soul of Portugal. At the same time, in many parts of Lisbon and in the towns across the Tagus river, people performed fado behind closed doors, singing lyrics that otherwise would have been censored. *Fado Resounding* attends to some of the stories, affects, and silences of the Estado Novo that accrue around fado as genre within a sociopolitical context marked by post-colonization, Portugal's accession to the European Union (1986), and economic crisis. It argues neither for fado as a "national" or as a "revolutionary" genre; rather it foregrounds the ambiguity of these distinctions as practiced, as remembered, as sung, as felt.

Fado Resounding: *Method and Form*

I worked in the present, documenting acts, sounds, performances, social formations, and stories. Grounding myself primarily in Lisbon's amateur fado scenes, I traced fado networks outward from the Tasca do Jaime, a small, primarily working-class bar that held amateur fado sessions during weekends, in the neighborhood of Graça, in which I lived in 2001–2003. I interviewed fadistas and instrumentalists, ranging from singers on the street and amateur musicians to world music divas and venerated professionals of the older generation. I spoke with fans, listeners, policymakers, club owners, and sound engineers. I attended and recorded a wide range of performances that took place in a rich variety of contexts and scenes, from hidden-away word-of-mouth-only amateur sessions to the most touristic fado and folklore restaurants and elite professional venues. I studied fado institutionalization and pedagogy by taking "lessons" at a museum and at a neighborhood association and by attending and documenting fado coaching sessions and rehearsals. I used my singing to elicit feedback about genre, style, and the parameters of the soulful sung. I came to "history" and memory initially through the traces left in bodies, in the sounds of voices, in the fragments of story told between sets of singing, in the expressions of feelings about the past, and in the cityscape of Lisbon itself. I mapped correspondences and discontinuities with traces in the archive, in work by Lisbon's "organic intellectuals," by Portuguese academics, in films, and in the popular press.

The chapters of *Fado Resounding* ethnographically track the flourishing and genealogies of the soulful in interconnected fado worlds and forms. They move from an amateur fado venue and institutionalized sites of learning in relation to poetics and pedagogies of soulfulness in sound of chapter 1 to fado's "affects of history" with respect to histories of Portuguese nationalism, colonialism, and the Estado Novo (chapter 2); the interanimation of place, sound, and genre in Lisbon as "fado's city" (chapter 3); the "style of the soulful" through a musical explication of fado's sonic structure and vocal styling in performance (chapter 4); the "gender of genre" in relation to fado's affective labors of the feminine (chapter 5); and, finally, the multiple forms of the soulful manifest in the early twenty-first century afterlife of the voice of fado's greatest diva, Amália Rodrigues, who admirers told me had a "throat of silver" (chapter 6).

LISBON. I AM in the vestiges of an empire long gone on the far fringe of western Europe, in the capital city of a country that hosted Europe's longest dictatorship, a place where modernity and expansion have run amok and often collide with the material and not-so-material stuff of history. It is 2001. European Union money has come and gone. A taxi driver tells me, "Portugal is in a sad state (*é uma tristeza*)! No, it is in a tragic state! Go home, girl. Go home. Portugal has no future." Art deco buildings fall to ruins. Trees grow from rooftops. Graffiti referring to the 1974 revolution is still visible on walls, fading: "Liberdade! Viva o 25 de Abril!" The current rate of the euro flashes neon in the financial district. Electric trolleys covered with Coca-Cola advertisements heave up steep inclines, getting stuck behind badly parked suvs. Beggars sit still, with withered faces, holding out hands. Tourists wander, carrying the same guidebook in different languages. *Look, there we can see old-timers playing cards!* Old theaters are knocked down to build new shopping malls where people buy on credit. Another theater is restored to become the Hard Rock Café. One of Europe's largest shopping malls, Colombo, stretches out on Lisbon's periphery, with "streets" named for former colonies and with a chapel of Nossa Senhora das Descobertas (Our Lady of the Discoveries) in its basement, its glass windows facing a wall on which is painted a mural-size map of Africa. Displaced and hard-up eastern European immigrants with advanced degrees do manual labor, working to restore decaying city buildings. Black men from former African colonies and Islamic immigrants hang out smoking and talking in the square outside the former Church of the Holy Inquisition. Immigrants from former colonies sell their wares in a cement four-story mall structure built into the side of a sixteenth-century chapel, while drug dealers make fast transactions outside in the neighborhood of Mouraria, the neighborhood at the bottom of the hill beneath the castle to which the Moors were banished after the Christian Reconquest, the neighborhood that, according to one legend, gave birth to the music of fado in the voice of the first fadista/prostitute, Maria Severa, in the early 1800s.

On the swank shopping street Rua Garrett, a woman stands begging, with a green towel wrapped around her shoulders, in place of a shawl, singing fado. She holds out her cup, singing to the accompaniment of a boom box. Just down the street, on Rua do Carmo, fado sounds pour out of speakers attached to a green cart that sells fado CDs to tourists. Around the corner, tourists line up for a ride on Lisbon's famous art deco elevator, the Elevador de Santa Justa; as one rides upward, the wailing of the beggar singing fado is overlaid by the voice of Amália Rodrigues, Portugal's most celebrated fado diva, blaring from the fado cart. A sign on the outside of the cart reads, "Lisbon, the City of Fado." As I approach the Moorish castle, O Castelo de São Jorge, on the hill above the neighborhood of Alfama, on a Sunday afternoon, one star fado voice bleeds into another, one historical moment into the next, as fado recordings sound from small souvenir shops with open doors, the sounds bouncing off high stone walls on narrow cobbled streets. On the castle's grounds on a stone bench with a panoramic view of Lisbon sits a middle-age woman singing Amália's fados off-key and out of meter, sometimes mixing one melody up with another. She takes song requests and collects coins from Japanese tourists. She tells me the story of her life, narrating it in a script that fado as genre has over and over again inscribed and inflected, in an endless dialogue between life stories of its protagonists and the mythological biography of a genre. *A life of suffering. I sing with the voice that God gave me.* Across the hill in the neighborhood of Bairro Alto, the waiters in fado's prime tourist restaurant destination fold cloth napkins, set the tables, and ready the wines. "Why should I go pay money to hear fado to cry and be sad?" asks the woman in her mid-fifties who sells me my groceries each day. A middle-class Portuguese man in his forties complains to me, "Fado, all of this saudade, I don't like it."

A chilly Saturday afternoon in the winter of 2003, as dusk turns to dark. A small, densely packed Lisbon bar on the bustling main street of the neighborhood of Graça, standing-room only on the narrow sidewalk outside the front door. Those passing by might stop, crane their necks toward the darkened interior when they hear the sound of a strident female voice singing fado way in the back pouring through the open door, or when they hear the entire group inside burst forth singing a refrain, or when they hear the distinctive steel string twang of the guitarra. A car speeds down the street blasting hip-hop. An electric trolley clanks past. The singing stops. Someone turns on the lights inside. Men come outside, stand near the door, and smoke and talk. The lights dim. The men go back in, a hush falls, the fado starts up again. Inside, we close our eyes and we listen.

ONE

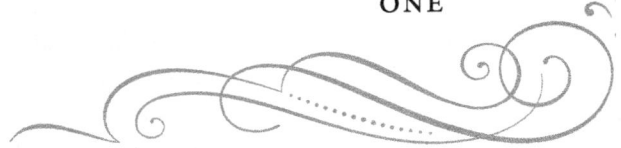

Pedagogies of the Soulful in Sound

Não é fadista quem quer mas sim quem nasceu fadista. (A fadista is not
someone who wants to be fadista but one who was born fadista.)
—FADO EPITHET

There are places in Lisbon that gather fado and fadistas: places where the
talk of fans and singers, the photographs on the walls, and the songs
and the stories told through singing merge and spin off of one another,
teaching and reinscribing what fado is and its relation to history—both
its own history as a genre and Portuguese history writ large.[1] These
places teach one how to listen to fado, how to feel *saudade*, and teach one
how to have a soul.

It is a Saturday afternoon in 2002 at the bar, or *tasca*, O Jaime, in the
Lisbon neighborhood of Graça, which hosts amateur fado on weekend
afternoons.[2] There is an interval, the lights come on; people talk, get up
to stretch their legs, greet one another, and order new rounds of food,
wine, and beer. I sit across the table from a fadista named Olga, singing
to her under my breath, trying out a fado I am learning for my upcoming audition for fado lessons at Lisbon's Museu do Fado (Fado Museum).
Interrupting my singing, she says, "I could hit you, I could kill you, but
you will never have a Portuguese soul." "But we have souls, too," I say.
(*Since when have the Portuguese had a monopoly on soulfulness?*) I try
again and ham it up by singing extended *voltinhas* (improvisatory melismatic vocal turns) and drawing out the phrase "cantando dou brado"

(singing I cry) with a rubato. She says, "Now you are *beginning* to have some soul."

As a central ethnographic trope, learning for the ethnographer is often to move from "outside" to "in," with the knowledge that belonging risks a partial blindness and deafness to a world gradually rendered natural through the quotidian. I wanted to study how people learn to sing, play, and listen to fado as a way to understand how particular affects become linked to expressive styles and sounds, how these sounds become aesthetically and socially salient, and how in learning to sing or to listen one might be learning how to feel, developing a sonic repertoire for emotional expression (Cumming 2000). Yet for most fadistas and listeners, an idea of learning had nothing to do with fado. For many, the concept of learning was anathema to fado, canceled it out; either one is born with *fado na alma* (fado in the soul) or one is not. *Ser fadista não se ensina, não se aprende, nasce logo quando nasce uma pessoa* (One is not taught, nor does one learn to be a fadista; one is born a fadista). I heard variations on this fado epithet from singers, listeners, instrumentalists, the general public, and in fado lyrics, and even saw it printed on tiles covering a building in an alleyway in the Lisbon neighborhood of Alfama. To admit to learning might be to reveal an essential lack, to *não ser fadista* (to not be fadista), as singing with *sentimento* (feeling) is widely understood as something that cannot be learned. For Olga, my voice and performance lacked soulful signifiers. The soul, in this case, resides in a musical, stylistic, and performative semiotics of the voice. An explicit culture of non-learning with respect to fado seals "the secret of sound" (Taussig 1999: 183) upon which is writ fado's "soul."[3]

Fado discourse shapes the stuff of a subjectivity predicated on binaries of interior and exterior. The fado voice is often spoken and sung about by listeners as revelatory of a deep embodied inside, an inside that runs "in one's veins" (*veias*). One fan explained fado to me as the "DNA" of Portugueseness; many listeners and fadistas told me (in some form), "Fado é nossa canção portuguesa e vem de dentro da alma" (Fado is our Portuguese song and comes from inside the soul). This "inside" full of feeling, *um estado de alma* (a state of the soul, of being), is one that listeners often talk about as unique to the person who sings, yet also as part of a certain way of being Portuguese. Fadistas talk about singing their lives and their stories as individuals, in their own style, with singularly marked voices. One of the most severe critiques possible to level at a fadista is that she or he is imitating the vocal style or repertoire of another. At the same time, fadistas' life stories often share similar biographical narratives and trajectories, while timbral and stylistic characteristics of individual fado voices (both of which are externalized indices of the soulful) are shaped in processes of learning that are necessarily social. This chapter flips over the story of non-learning that binds fado as sound, fado as music, to fado as "a state of the soul." How are soulfulness and interiority in fado learned, ritualized, talked about, instituted, improvised, performed, listened to, and heard?[4] At the same time, this chapter understands fado's ideologies of the "unlearned" voice to align with widespread metacultural tropes about musical expression, voicing, and emotion where they are understood to reflect an "interior self" or "essence." What kinds of selfhood and socialities might practices of fado shape? What are the stakes of the soulful sung?

A Tasca do Jaime

It is a late Saturday afternoon in February 2002 at the Tasca do Jaime in Graça. Men line up along the bar drinking; women sit at tiny tables with their girlfriends or husbands; people sitting on milk crates squeeze between chairs; two tourists stand tentatively in the entrance. Photographs of fadistas, living and dead, vie for space on the walls. In the back of the room, under a guitarra hanging on the wall and an illuminated framed photograph of Portugal's twentieth-century fado icon, Amália Rodrigues, sit two or three male instrumentalists, one playing the guitarra and another the acoustic guitar (viola). In front of them, or sometimes behind, stands the fadista. People sitting at the tables get up and take turns singing. While fado is in session, the lights are turned off, and the owner of the bar and listeners enforce strict silence, hissing, glaring, or shouting to demand "Silêncio!" from anyone who as much as tries to whisper. When a fadista starts singing, particularly if a song is a sad one, people listening sometimes close their eyes and silently move their lips in the shapes of the words. The fadista often sings the more melancholic songs with eyes closed, with her head thrown back, her hands at times interlocked in front of her and at others gesturing expressively, the torso in a stillness rapt with a focus that directs all attention to the sound and expression of her voice.

During a break, the lights are switched on, and a woman in her early fifties sitting near me, wearing a black dress (Olga) softly sings a fado, looking into my eyes. She turns around and announces, "We have an *americana* here who likes fado!" When the fado is back in session with a male fadista singing, a listener mutters under his breath, "Bom" (Good), nodding his head, positively appraising. The fadista suddenly stops; a man behind the bar calls out "Baixinho!" (A little lower!), and the fadista sings again at a lower pitch. He still cannot sing the high part; appearing shamed, he turns his back to us, and listeners fill in the melody and the words with their voices. He resumes singing, and when he finishes, listeners applaud. An older woman sitting with Olga tells me, "Her family wouldn't let her be a fadista, but it has always been her dream, and she has the voice. Today is only her second time singing in public." Olga talks to the viola player about a way of singing a vocal line in the style of Argentina Santos (a famous fadista of the older generation who is known in some circles in Lisbon for her "authentic" singing style) and demonstrates. They go to the back corner, and Olga sings quietly, experimenting. I hear strong opinions from everyone about how to sing: what is right, what is beautiful. I am in a place where people love what they are doing. I am in a place where people are also allowed to fail. I return again and again to this tasca that has fado in the light of the afternoon. The Tasca do Jaime gives me a base to learn how learning happens in a fado enclave, which somehow becomes the whole of a particular world writ small. One man says about me as I am leaving after my first visit, "She is studying the fado, and she likes this atmosphere the best."

Performance Practices of the Soulful

Some people acknowledge fado venues as places where singers learn from one another in the acts of both singing and listening. The fadista and fado researcher José Manuel Osório claimed that *casas de fado* are "the only schools fado has."[5] In the words of one of Lisbon's most revered presenters of amateur fado, Sebastião de Jesus (1930–2005), "Eighty percent of professionals come out of the context of amateur fado; *fado vadio* (amateur fado) was a great school."[6] Certainly, within the networks of fans and singers who participate in the amateur fado scene in Lisbon, places like O Jaime—places of dense sociality centered on music making and listening—function implicitly as schools for the performance of "soulful" listening, playing, and singing.

The tasca, or small neighborhood bar, is one type of venue where "amateur" fado performance traditionally has taken place. The tasca is reified through ongoing and multiple discourses—urban legends and fado origin myths, song lyrics, fado marketing, international media—as the space of authentic social and musical practice and contrasted with official casas de fado where professionals regularly perform under contract for predominantly tourist audiences.[7] In the presentation of fado outside Portugal to international audiences, in the narratives that often circulate with recordings by elite fado celebrities, an invocation of *fado amador* can do the work of bolstering multiple authenticity claims (for the genre, for the city of Lisbon, for international stars). *I grew up singing fado in the tascas in Lisbon's traditional neighborhoods.* Participants in Lisbon's amateur fado scene (including some professional fadistas) told me about how the routine and the contracts associated with casas de fado lead to repetitive, "soulless" singing and playing. "I would never say this to a journalist," a famous guitarra player, who had traveled the world with Amália Rodrigues, says to me after I switched off my tape recorder, "but you know these little tascas where there is amateur fado, this is where there is the most fado." A professional fadista who sings at O Jaime for fun before his nighttime gig tells me, "The Tasca do Jaime has a different kind of soul (*alma*); it is not like the professional places where the singer sells his voice."[8]

The boundaries between sites of official fado and places that host so-called amateur fado—fado amador or fado vadio—are in many ways porous; along with the recording and media industries, "amateur" and "professional" fado shape interdependent discourses and practices. I focus here on performance practice within amateur sites because venues like O Jaime offered me the greatest scope to bear witness to failures, risks, and dreams amid audiences whose ways of listening shape aesthetic style and the learning of the soulful. Fado singing at O Jaime, and in amateur fado practice in general, depends on numerous codified ritual practices; the exact details of rituals vary depending on the venue, but many aspects are the same.[9] The ways in which I came to understand individual variation and development; the shaping of an aesthetic; and ways of listening, feeling, and expressing the soulful in sound figure against a ground of ritual's weekly repetitions.

It is 3 PM on a Saturday in June 2002. I walk up the series of steep cobblestone streets that connect my apartment building on the Rua da

Bela Vista à Graça to the Tasca do Jaime on the Rua da Graça. When I arrive, a few men are standing outside the door smoking. We exchange kisses of greeting. Smells of frying fish and potatoes mingle with tobacco as I walk in and my eyes adjust to the darkness. A few men alone sit at tables finishing their lunches with hard liquor. A dapper man in his seventies wearing a suit jacket with a pin of a guitarra on his lapel sits drinking water and humming to himself as he looks at a folded list of all of the fados he sings and the keys in which he sings them, which he keeps in his breast pocket.[10] A middle-age couple sits in the back chatting with the proprietor, Jaime Candeias, who eats before the fado starts at 4 PM. I say hello to everyone individually with a kiss on each cheek. "Ah, Elena, the *americana*," someone says. Laura, Jaime's wife, chides me for coming so late but takes my lunch order anyway (see figure 1.1). The instrumentalists occasionally come early to eat a meal before playing; sometimes they bring their wives, who sit patiently through the entire afternoon. Gradually, more people come in, many claiming regular tables. After attending O Jaime for many months, I have a sense of which people arrive and when; I know who are singers and who come to listen—and those who come to do both. People banter, ask about one another's lives, children, illnesses. I learn about their families, their jobs, their relationships to fado, to Graça and other Lisbon neighborhoods, to other fadistas, and to other venues in which fado is performed.

The place begins to buzz with the activities of fado about to happen and sounds of fado conversation. "Did you know that that fado was first sung by Maria Teresa de Noronha? A *grande senhora* of fado she was." Someone else chimes in, "Well, her voice was too lyrical for me, but yes, a *grande senhora* she was." "Yes, she had a clear voice (*uma voz limpa*)." "*What key do you sing 'Lágrima' in?*"[11] "I sing it in G." "*I have always sung it in F. Are you coming tonight to the fado night at Boa Vista?*" "No, we are going to Tasca do Careca." "*But they can bring the van by and pick you up later. They need fadistas.*" A poet arrives with sheets of paper containing drafts of a fado poem, hoping to get a fadista to try it out for him. A fadista begins the fado halfheartedly, then stops because she does not like the flow of the words. The guitarra player unpacks his instrument and takes out his *unhas* (fingernail extensions)—which lend brilliance to the sound and are sometimes made from pieces of plastic or old credit cards—carefully taping them to his fingers, and begins to tune. The viola player comes in and greets everyone then opens his case.

FIGURE 1.1 • Laura Candeias during an interval at the Tasca do Jaime. Lisbon, July 2006. Photograph by the author.

It is 3:55 PM.[12] Jaime switches off the television set. He plugs in the light that illuminates Amália's portrait and connects the cord to light a diorama that hangs in the center of the back wall in a glass-covered wooden box framed with dominoes. A group of cardboard cut-out men in suits stand around a domino table in a miniature bar. Jaime long ago altered the diorama by adding a viola and a guitarra to the picture and pasting a tiny photo of Amália Rodrigues singing, taken from a post-card, in the back and surrounding it with a cardboard stage (plate 1).[13] Jaime turns on a dim red light and switches off the main lighting. This is the signal that the session is about to begin.

Jaime walks to the back of the bar where the instrumentalists are po-sitioned and in a resonant bass voice gives a general welcome that goes something like this: *Welcome to my humble tasca, to yet another after-noon of fado, another afternoon of tradition* (see figure 1.2). *I am proud that so many good people and fadistas come here every week. I am sorry that the place is not more comfortable. We are all like family here* (em família), *so feel at home.* He introduces the instrumentalists with great flourish. The guitarra and viola play a *guitarrada*.[14] Jaime then often sings the first three fados of the afternoon, sometimes dedicating them to specific

Pedagogies of the Soulful in Sound • 33

FIGURE 1.2 • Jaime Candeias in front of the Tasca do Jaime. Lisbon, June 2002. Photograph by the author.

people in the room, before introducing the first fadista: *And now I wish to present our friend, eighty-three years old and still going strong, the great fadista and popular poet of Alfama: Senhor Álvaro Rodrigues! Or, Ladies and gentleman, the sun is setting, and as it begins to gets dark, the atmosphere becomes even more special. So listen with great* silêncio *and attention to the voice of this fadista who has sung fado all over Europe. She is also a fadista of the neighborhood* (bairro) *and lives here in Graça: Fátima Fernandes. Or, We're going to play around a little* (vamos brincar). *This girl* (menina) *has come all the way from the United States to study our music. Now she is going to try to sing a bit: Elena! Or, This gentleman never sings the same way twice. This is a great interpreter of fado*

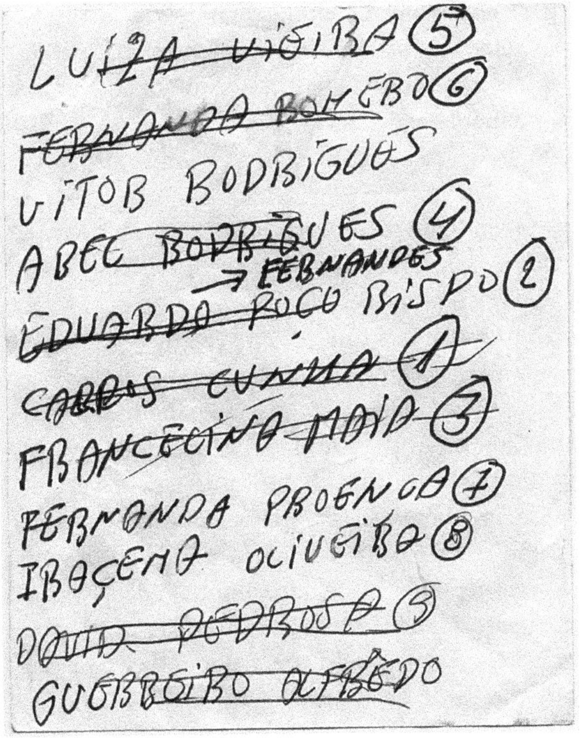

FIGURE 1.3 • List of fadistas to sing at a fado session at O Jaime, June 2002. Photograph by the author.

you are about to hear. Or, *This young man has been waiting all of these hours just to sing, and no, I will not turn him away. After all, this is a place where everyone is allowed to sing.* The order in which people sing follows strict guidelines. The general rule is that the presenter of the fado session (in this case, Jaime) writes down the names of singers as they arrive, and fadistas are called to sing in this order (see figure 1.3). But exceptions are sometimes made depending on someone's status as a fadista, schedule, or condition of health.

The presentation of fado is in itself a form of verbal performance and art that speaks to the expertise of the presenter, his taste in fado, and the fado social milieu in which he travels.[15] In the early 2000s, aficionados and singers told me that fado presentation was a dying art and that good presenters were hard to come by.[16] The responsibility of presenting can involve teaching the audience something about fado in addition to maintaining the proper atmosphere in the audience of silence and "respect for the fado."[17] In an amateur fado session, the presenter plays a role in shaping the audience's reception and opinion of individual fadistas, as well as in teaching the audience "proper" listening and participation practices, through the ways that he enforces silence or might encourage participation at strategic moments.

PERFORMING

She has only just begun singing fado, and she is a little shy, but we all agree that this senhora *really carries fado in her voice* (traga fado na voz). *I would like to present Olga de Sousa!* There is the squeak of chair legs against the tile floor, the shuffling of feet, and the movement of bodies as Olga, dressed completely in black and wearing a black shawl, makes her way to the instrumentalists. They ask her what she will sing first and if she knows the key. She does not know the key but tells them the name of the fado. They have her hum the beginning, and the guitarra player decides on a key for her. As she is about to start, there is still whispering in the house and some outright talking near the door. Laura, who is busy trying to serve a group of four a platter of shrimp, shouts, "Silêncio, por favor! Silêncio!" A woman sitting at the table closest to the musicians whispers a piercing hiss, with a well-aimed glare at the talkers. At the last minute, a woman at the same table, one of the star fadistas at O Jaime, pulls a black lace shawl from her bag, puts it around Olga's shoulders, and adjusts it, saying, "Now you will be more fadista." The instrumentalists begin to play, the guitarra elaborating the harmony of the melody and the viola marking the bass line. Olga nervously fingers the edges of her shawl, closes her eyes, tilts her head back, takes a breath, and begins to sing in a low, husky voice the first lines to the fado "Que Deus Me Perdoe" (May God Forgive Me [for loving the fado]), "If my closed soul could show / If it could tell how I suffer in silence." Her body sways slightly from side to side; her fingers twist the edges of her shawl; and her voice gains momentum as she moves further into the song. She begins to fall slightly out of sync with the viola player, to lose the beat (compasso). I hear the instrumentalists mark the rhythm more strongly, and she gets back on track. The entire house bursts forth singing the refrain, in tune, out of tune, some in time, some lagging behind, but all with tremendous energy. After the refrain, Olga's voice picks up the next verse with extra vigor, and as she moves into the finale, there are shouts of "Lindo!" (Beautiful!), "Bem!" (Well done!), from listeners as they break into applause. Olga has a tremor in her voice. She sometimes sings off pitch and she cannot get the rhythm, but her eyes are luminous and her body alive with this new excitement of singing in public. The instrumentalists have a few words with her and give her tips for the next time. Almost immediately the house fills with waves of talk.

In a photo portrait shop up the street, a framed photograph of Fátima Fernandes, a stately woman in her fifties, sits in the window. The same photo also hangs prominently on the wall at O Jaime. Once, during a slow non-fado afternoon, Laura leaned toward me and softly said, "Have you heard the voice of Fátima Fernandes? For me, she is the very best that there is. Fátima, she is special, she really knows the fado." Fátima makes rare appearances at O Jaime, although she is a regular at Friday night fado sessions a few miles up the road at the Jardim do Poço do Bispo and appears often as a hired fadista at special fado gala nights throughout the city.

This Saturday, Fátima arrives late, during a set between songs, to whispered fanfare as people move out of the way to let her by. She walks heavily, holding a cane, leaning on Laura's arm. From head to toe she is dressed in black; her eyes sparkle as she greets friends and settles down in the back corner at a table near the instrumentalists. "I leave my bed only to sing fado," she later told me. "Fado keeps me alive. I am passionate for life and for fado. Fado—I can't explain it. Fado makes me very happy. Sometimes I sing and the tears fall, because what I sing is the truth. I have sung in many foreign countries and I have also sung up the street at O Jaime."[18] When it is Fátima's turn to sing, she does not walk to the instrumentalists. Instead, she stands near her chair, propping herself up with her cane, her eyes closed, her head tilted back, and sings three melancholy fados to an almost absolute silence that is broken only by the audience singing the refrain and by whispered gasps of "Ah fadista!" "Lindo!" or "Bem!" After she finishes singing three, choruses of voices cry, "Mais um! Mais um!" (One more!). Jaime walks in front of the instrumentalists and makes a formal plea for Fátima to sing, and she acquiesces: *Só um* (Just one).

Amateur venues have different rules concerning the number of fados one can sing consecutively, but all venues I attended strived for an egalitarian policy so that no one singer would be favored over another. At the Tasca do Jaime, three is the customary number, but that can change to two (or even one) if many singers are present. When a fadista is asked to exceed three, it is a sure signal that both Jaime and the audience endorse her or his quality. There is an unspoken rule, which held at all of the amateur venues I attended, that if one person had already sung a particular fado (i.e., lyrics for *fado tradicional*, or a particular coupling of lyrics to a specific traditional fado form, or both music and lyrics for *fado canção*), no one else should repeat it during the course of the session. At intimately small venues such as O Jaime that have a number of faithful regulars, most singers and audience members know which repertoires "belong" to particular singers, as there is great deal of repetition from week to week. Yet repertoires inevitably overlap. I have heard fadistas asking what has already been sung to avoid the embarrassment of singing the same thing. I have also heard fadistas begin a fado only to be told by a listener that it had already been sung earlier in the session. These practices fit into a discourse on fado performance that places high value not only on the uniqueness of individual style but also on the relationship between the fadista's repertoire and biography; the words of a song should be applicable to one's life and be sung as one feels them.

SILENCE

Silence, like sound, can be affectively charged, bearing multiple nuances of attention and feeling. My eyes are closed and I am listening. The person next to me whispers to her friend across the table, "Look how she is *feeling* the fado." A four-year-old boy sits with his mother for an entire afternoon session. When he starts to talk, she gently places a finger on his lips, teaching him silence. Silence in the performance space of fado can be filled with the raptness of the listening that is feeling; it can direct all attention to the voice and expressive movements of the fadista, sounds of the instruments, the meanings of sung words. For some, "fadista" refers both to one who sings fado and to one who knows how to listen. A listener passes me a fado epithet scribbled on a piece of torn paper tablecloth during a fado afternoon at O Jaime, "É fadista quem canta como quem sabe ouvir em silêncio" (A fadista is one who sings like one who knows how to listen in silence). A fadista must sing showing she can also listen.

Silence can be qualitative; singers and fans might speak of a venue in terms of the quality of its silence, where an audience who knows how to be silent is one that knows how to listen with the same intensity with which the fadista is singing, thus entering into the fado and thus into feeling. Silences may be enforced: a hiss, a glare, a shout for silence, or before a set or when things get really out of hand, a short speech from the presenter to the house about how *fado tem um outro sabor com silêncio* (fado has a different taste/flavor/quality with silence), or "Silêncio! Que se vai cantar o fado" (Silence! Fado is going to be sung).

There are decorous silences, bored but respectful silences, or silences of laughter held in, just about to break when people tell jokes written on napkin scraps or catch someone's glance across the room. It is often the singers recognized as most powerful (as house "stars") who are given more leeway in causing disruption during their "off-stage" listening. Distraction during a less than optimal performance may give way to whispers and nudges. Then there are the feeling-filled silences that fall upon a room as a deep hush, a collective transfixion commanded by the sheer affective force of a singer's voice. One way in which a masterful performance is acknowledged is by the quality of silence it elicits and another by the way in which this silence is broken.

In the space of silence, a listener might perform her soulfulness or interiority by the way she closes her eyes and utters the words to the fado being sung in soundless incantation. The silent intonation of lyrics is common practice among many listeners in amateur venues and blurs the line between the fadista's performance of interiority and the listener's interiorized hearing. An entire audience may collectively burst into song during a refrain of a fado canção; in traditional fados (they do not have refrains), the instrumentalists often play one strophe or a portion of a strophe alone. In amateur fado, both of these instances present opportunities for the listeners to sing. The way in which an audience sings the refrain or strophe often depends on the fadista who is singing. If she or he is a beginner or someone whom the listeners sense needs help, they may sing the refrain with added energy and volume.

There are moments in fado, particularly in the last strophe during the finale on a key utterance, when the instruments might pause, and in this space of silence, the voice might hover on the break of a cry; it might become almost impossibly soft (or, for a man, impossibly high); the voice might tremble and turn upon itself in ornamentation. These are moments at which listeners sometimes cry out "Bem!" (Good!). "Boca linda!" (Beautiful mouth!), "Fadista!" In amateur fado, listeners often voice exclamations of approval at moments of heightened emotion, particularly immediately before the finale or during the finale on the final repetition of a key poetic utterance. In amateur fado, the unspoken rules for understanding how and when to exclaim vary depending on the venue. In some cases, even in places where exclaiming is common practice, absolute silence may be the highest accolade or the most "appropriate" response.

These moments are often stylistically signaled by shifts in vocal register or dynamic; heightened improvisation; use of rubato, melisma; or vocal ornamentations (voltinhas). In practical terms, when executed near the end of a fado, these heightened moments of fadista styling can serve to give the instrumentalists an auditory cue that the fado is drawing to a close. In a performance of traditional fado, strophes often accrue amplified emotional significance and more marked improvisation as the singer progresses through the poetic narrative of the fado—that is, they accrue *mais fado* (more fado). When I asked fadistas whether this stylistic moment of heightened expression had a name, some said that it did not, and others had various ways of describing it. One older professional male singer called it "fado," using the generic term qualitatively, implying that within one fado song, certain parts could have "more fado" than others; he also used the phrase *dar sentimento* (to give feeling). Other words and phrases that fadistas used to describe what happens during this stylistic moment included *fazer um bonito* (to make a beauty), *dar expressão* (to give expression), *baixar a voz* (to lower the voice), and *pianinho* (very quiet). ("Baixar a voz" and "pianinho" generally refer to the voice singing unaccompanied during a critical moment in the musical structure and in the lyrics at a lowered volume or at higher pitch.) Fátima Fernandes spoke about this moment for the listener as one that "gives people goose bumps" (*arrepia as pessoas*), "where people vibrate/ feel more" (*a gente vibra mais*), and "where it seems like everything is going to explode" (*parece que tudo vai explodir*) and concluded with "Language doesn't do it justice."[19]

The ways in which audience silence is enforced differs at amateur venues like O Jaime, tourist-oriented casas de fado, and elite "art" fado venues. Individual venues have distinct soundscapes based on listening histories and means of maintaining silence (see chapter 2). Audience participation by singing refrains and voicing exclamations is often discouraged or considered in bad taste at elite professional venues. One listener who favored elite venues told me that exclaiming was usually practiced only where people go "para brincar" (to play around) or to relax. A professional fado star of the past referred to the practice of exclaiming as *ordinário* (vulgar) and noted that listeners did not exclaim when she sang because they knew she did not like it. At the most elite venues, an employee or audience member most likely would not hiss or call for silence. At times, the physical space of some of the elite venues (architectural patrimony with material signifiers of an ancient Lisbon, heavy and low arched stone ceilings, the look and feel of wealth and exclusivity) helps to maintain a quiet and subdued public.

Silence in fado listening practice was one type of behavior encouraged by the new professionalization of fado during the early years of the Estado Novo: "The real fadista must refuse to sing when there is the least noise in the café or place of performance. Silence while the fado is sung—that is the notice to be posted, in a clearly visible position, above the stage" (the fado serial Canção do Sul, n. 197, 1938, quoted in Jerónimo and Fradique 1994: 105). Yet it is probable that the insistence on silence was part of fado listening practice much earlier.[20] Today, mandates for silence continue in full force, and it is common to see a posted sign in some amateur venues proclaiming, "Silêncio! Que se vai cantar o fado" (Silence! Fado is going to be sung). In performances I witnessed at O Jaime and many other amateur venues, silence figured as a poetics and aesthetics of soulful listening and singing and as a structure of aurality that enabled the forging of a collective intimacy. Silence in fado performance is sometimes charged with an overdetermined poetics that surges, is heard, precisely at a juncture of an aesthetics of the present and a politics of the past, where residues of enforced silences in place during the long dictatorship flash for a moment to the fore, where a capacity for keeping silent might be read by some as a particular way of being Portuguese (a point I develop in chapter 2). "Tourists: Respect the Portuguese Silence or Go to Spain!" read graffiti in English in stencils stamped along the walls in Alfama in 2007 near a popular *miradouro* (viewpoint) over the Tagus River.

TEARS

Stylistically, the fado voice and its accompanying instruments evoke sadness by employing multiple "icons of crying" (Urban 1991: 156).[21] To vibrate a note while playing the guitarra is to weep (*gemer*). The voice of a singer during a moment of heightened feeling often hovers on the break of a sob; the fadista might employ downward glissandi or extended melismas in expressing intense emotion; the singer might sing until her voice hurts. While singing may elicit tears; while many lyrics refer to tears, crying, sobbing, and melancholy and contain reflexive discourse that links both fado and fado sound to crying; and while singers and instrumentalists often stylistically employ codified "icons of crying," actual crying by the singer would threaten the rupture of form, loss of control, making it impossible to continue to sing. I witnessed one episode in which a woman was singing a sad fado at O Jaime and her voice suddenly broke, faltered, stopped. She walked away mid-song in tears, later explaining that the fado reminded her of her father who had recently died. The contrary also occurs. I also saw a woman standing up to sing already tearful, explaining that she was distraught and was not sure she would be able to make it through one fado. After receiving support from the audience to go ahead—*You must sing!*—she collected herself, singing through the fado with no tears. Fadistas do speak of the release they achieve through singing fado (often in therapeutic terms or as the exorcism of emotional demons), but in sung performance, this is a highly stylized release executed and sustained within the strict confines of form. The voice can tremble upon a cry but must not break sobbing. Guitarras also "weep" within the confines of form. The venerated guitarrista José Fontes Rocha, one of Amália Rodrigues's primary accompanists, explained to me that if one is excessive in executing *gemido* (weeping, vibrato) on the guitarra, one risks pulling the note out of tune.[22]

Soulful exclamation may take the form of tears silently passed. A listener wipes the tears from the corners of her eyes and expresses not only that she has been moved but also that she knows how to listen with feeling.[23] The singer might brush the tears from her eyes after she has finished the finale, expressing that she has sung authentically, with feeling, with soul. These tears index both a private emotional and aesthetic experience and a moment of shared sociality (see Feld 1982; Urban 1991); they point to the power of musical experience to be felt simultaneously as intensely subjective and social. Aesthetic appreciation merges with heightened feeling in a moment of sound, and the soulfulness of the aural is made visibly public, thus social, in the form of the tear. In this context, the tear can be read as a socially salient indexical icon of soul. Talk of tearfulness ("Your singing made me cry," "I had tears in my eyes when you sang," "Your singing made the stones on the street cry") is heard as praise. A listener rarely tears up or talks about tears if the fadista performing is not technically competent (in terms of pronunciation and diction, pitch, and rhythmic coordination) or is far outside of timbral norms. But technical virtuosity does not necessarily translate into tears; virtuosity perceived as gratuitous, that calls attention to itself, almost certainly will not evoke tears from a listener.

One learns the visual icons of soulful singing (the head is thrown back, the throat strained, the eyes closed, the body still) and the embodied aural icons (the raspy vocal timbre of a fado voice that has "suffered," or a voice whose timbre breaks up during a climax as if on the verge of tears, or the sound of a long-held rubato coupled with voltinhas sung during the last verse). People learn to perform their souls in the way in which they listen: in silence, attentively, eyes closed, words uttered inaudibly like an incantation and maybe with tears. In amateur practice, the singing of refrains, the silent incantation of lyrics and the voicing of exclamations, the evaluative silence of listening, and tearfulness or talk of crying shape and frame an aesthetic of soulful listening and singing. Exclamations, and sometimes tears, provide markers that set moments of heightened feeling and virtuosity apart. In other words, they help shape *structures of listening.*

Listening in the context of amateur fado is structured in relation to the performative, musical, and stylistic shifts employed by the fadista and instrumentalists, which are enabled by the musical and poetic forms undergirding the fados themselves (including the tacit forms that scaffold processes of vocal improvisation). Arjun Appadurai (1996) suggests that performance might play a critical role in articulating the "structures of feeling" (Williams 1977) on which the production of locality depends. With "structures of listening" I play with common tropes of hearing and of listening—where they are linked to interiority, to feeling, to subjectivity—while foregrounding the sociability of listening, the sociality of hearing, and their emergent qualities. Fado's "structures of listening" also depend on maintaining the collective conceit that the fadista's emotionality springs from a soul/self that is indexed by the sound of her singing voice and that this "self" bears an intrinsic relation to the fado narratives she sings. Yet this is a relation that demands communicative performance, a relation of "sincerity" (Jackson 2005).[24]

Instituting the Soulful

Attention to how fadistas learned to sing, and learning to sing fado my-self, became critical to my understanding of relationships between mu-sical and poetic form and feeling, between a semiotics of vocal expression and the transmission of affect within the context of fado performance. A focus on learning shed light on the socio-aesthetic parameters of fado form, of genrefication, of classification, on questions of value. However, I was uneasily positioned on a number of counts to employ musical par-ticipant observation, historically one of ethnomusicology's key method-ologies, in which the process of gaining "emic" musical competence (often by entering into a master–disciple relationship) serves as an ethnographic "window" into understanding something about "culture" or social life.[25] The mythos of the impossibility of learning to be a fadista was directed at me full force when I spoke to people about my desire to learn how to sing fado, exacerbated by my subject positioning as an American and an academic—and, to some extent, as a musician trained in the Western art music tradition.

In 2002, I approached two female fadistas whose voices I admired—one an amateur and the other a professional with an illustrious career—about the possibility of learning how to sing with them. Both deflected me, my amateur fadista friend by claiming that she would not take money from me. (I had offered it when she suggested she would not have time, as she worked multiple jobs to make ends meet.) The professional fadista brusquely pointed me to the famous elderly guitarrista at her side, saying, "I am no professor of fado. Talk to the guitarrista!" Both reactions point to wider phenomena related to learning and the respon-sibility for knowledge that traverses both amateur and professional worlds. Fadistas often regard instrumentalists, particularly guitarristas, as more competent when it comes to transmitting "official" knowledge about fado (see Castelo-Branco 1994). Women often conceded authority for the transmission of knowledge, particularly when I made formal re-quests, to men (see chapter 5). Both male and female fadistas, along with instrumentalists, participate in discourses that reinforce the idea that the singing of fado itself cannot be taught.

While the first part of this chapter ethnographically invoked *implicit* practices of learning fado performance and aesthetics, embedded within rituals of listening, singing, and socializing in the context of amateur fado, I now examine how *explicit* or marked discourses about learning figure in practice against the ubiquitous imaginary of the essentially unlearnable. The three ethnographic contexts for this discussion are situated along different points on a continuum of institutionality as unmarked to formally marked in relation to pedagogy: amateur fado venues as "informal" schools, the "fado school" at Lisbon's Fado Museum, and a fado association on Lisbon's periphery that offered weekly fado coaching sessions. In all three contexts, I used my participation as a singer as the means to elicit feedback about vocal aesthetics.

INFORMAL PEDAGOGIES: FADO VENUE AS SCHOOL

After about thirty minutes of performance during a fado afternoon at the Tasca do Jaime, Jaime indicates the beginning of an interval by switching on the lights. People get up and move around; some go outside to talk on their cell phones or order more food. The space is filled with the dense, overlapping texture of voices in which can often be heard fragments of songs half sung. Fado style, aesthetic, and learning are shaped just as much during these intervals as during performances themselves. The novice fadista, in the best of situations, is taken under the wing of audience and instrumentalists.[26] After the performance, or during the interval, fadistas or instrumentalists may approach the new singer and offer commentary or feedback; if the singer returns in following weeks, this feedback may continue. I heard various types of such commentary addressed to less experienced fadistas at O Jaime, including tips on breathing; coaching on rhythm that involved singing along; feedback on the choice of key in relation to the tessitura of an individual's voice; advice on repertoire, which sometimes included a reference to a particular recording; and the correction of lyrics or pronunciation of specific words.[27] The last two types of feedback might be given regardless of whether the singer is a novice or experienced. Heated conversations often take place about the correctness of lyrics (when the lyrics are old or common), the authorship of lyrics, and correct pronunciation.

Sometimes a fadista will refer to the fadista who has provided him or her with guidance (e.g., by providing performance tips, moral support, leads on gigs, help in obtaining a recording contract) as "madrinha" (godmother) or "padrinho" (godfather) of fado. In these cases, fictive kin terms sediment social relations and can serve to index status and reputation in relation to musical lineages.[28] In interviews with me, some fadistas (amateur and professional) provided meta-commentary on feedback within the context of fado performance. Fernanda Proença (b. 1946), a star fadista at O Jaime, told me that she is grateful for feedback and that Fátima Fernandes helped her in the beginning by telling her when she was not singing something correctly. She referred to a famous professional fadista as her "madrinha do fado," telling me how the fadista had placed a shawl around her shoulders[29]—sometimes a charged symbolic act by a more experienced female fadista that serves partly to sanction and "intitiate" a less experienced singer. Fátima Fernandes explained to me that she had benefited early on from guidance of Hermínia Silva, one of fado's most celebrated female icons of the past, from whom she learned good diction, and from being taken under the wing of Martinho de Assunção, a legendary viola player of the twentieth century. Her father, who also sang fado, always corrected her pronunciation. Fátima explained, "While there are many who are singing well, there are also many who are singing and saying the words (dizer) poorly. But when we older people tell them about it, they don't like it. Some of the young people say thank you, but others, I see that they don't like it."[30] Sebastião de Jesus mentioned a session he had recently presided over where a fadista sang with blatantly incorrect grammar and he chose not to intervene. "Some accept criticism with humility, but there are [also] people who think they know everything," he told me. Sebastião had hoped that the instrumentalists might say something to her, but they didn't. (Instrumentalists, particularly guitarristas, often have the social sanction to give corrective feedback and sometimes function unofficially as "coaches.") He criticized some instrumentalists who accompany amateur fado who, rather than take on pedagogical roles, complain about the quality of the singers (behind their backs).[31]

Older singers and instrumentalists sometimes nostalgically turn their ears to a past when they claim standards were higher, "styling" (estilar) was more developed, and individual repertoire and interpretation more marked. Undergirding this claim is the belief that young fadistas today learn primarily by imitating recordings and that they do not necessarily want to hear critiques from more experienced fadistas and instrumentalists. Yet many young singers with whom I spoke told me that while they sought feedback from their elders, obtaining it was not always easy. I interviewed a novice fadista in her early thirties who had been singing fado for a few years, had some training in Western art music, and regularly participated in amateur fado. By the time we met, she appeared to be well accepted by numerous experienced fadistas in the amateur fado circuit. She told me:

> The older people don't want to teach us anything. They think we don't want to know. They are very closed. They say we [the younger generation] only imitate. But they forget that they learned in the past from each other, that there were no recordings or cassettes. But we aren't obliged to follow the same path they followed; luckily, we don't have to. We follow a different trajectory. But they are also capable of teaching us a lot when they are in the mood. . . . When you enter into fado and you are new, you have to be careful, because one is entering into a closed milieu. It is very closed. If we understand this, we are very careful. This was my case. I entered very slowly to understand what kinds of people were there. In fado vadio, you have to be careful. People have to like us. When they like us, they help us. When I sing something poorly, they correct me right away. "You're singing too high." "You're screaming (*gritar*) too much. Don't scream!" When I started singing, I sang too high (*em cima*) a lot. We need feedback. We then manage to reach a balance between what they tell us and what we feel.[32]

Thus, giving and receiving feedback often involves delicate social maneuvering and can have much to do with generation; gender; fadista status; whether the commentator is an instrumentalist, a fadista, or a presenter; and the depth and kinds of social ties that bind commentator and fadista and the fadista and the public present. If one attempts to give feedback without taking implicit but highly nuanced social codes into consideration, it most likely will not be well received. And even in the most tightly knit circles of amateur fado, there is rivalry (*rivalidade*), as well as petty and not-so-petty jealousy or envy (*inveja*), among fadistas. Even when no one criticizes a singer overtly, evaluations might be whispered to one's companions at the table right after someone has sung. A fadista might catch the eyes of a friend, another listener, raising an eyebrow to express, "Why can't this guy sing in tune?" At the same time, within the specific performance context of amateur fado and at the venue of O Jaime in particular, an operative ideology of "democracy" is at play. Jaime tries to give every person who wishes to sing the opportunity to do so.

While some people might perceive amateur fado venues and casas de fado as functioning as informal schools for fado, encouraging a kind of "organic" learning tied to fado social praxis, institutionalized formal contexts for the "schooling" of fado singing, emergent during my research in the early 2000s, were sometimes dismissed by practitioners for the very reason that "one does not learn to be a fadista; one is born a fadista." In this model, a popular culture of oral/aural learning is taken on with pride, in contrast to the "artificiality" of institutionalized schooling; the only *real* school is the school of hard knocks. I heard older singers talk dismissively about the phenomenon of young fadistas receiving formal musical training as part of "the modernization of fado." They sometimes contrasted "modernization" in this context to "soulfulness": for *in the past, fado had more soul* (a popular sentiment that recurs in numerous fado lyrics).

INSTITUTING PEDAGOGY I

Lisbon's city-sponsored Museu do Fado opened in Alfama in 1998. By the early 2000s, the museum had begun a small *escola de fado* (fado school) that offered individual instruction in both the guitarra and fado singing by two "master" teachers. In 2002, over a seven-month period, I took twelve fado lessons at the school. The opportunity to participate in a series of lessons enabled me to learn something about the formal institutionalization of fado pedagogy at the moment of its emergence. What kind of pedagogy would be foregrounded or made explicit outside the social and performance contexts within which teaching and learning were usually covertly embedded? What might my experience with formal pedagogical situations reveal about fado's socio-aesthetic fault lines, the evaluative markers that in the most general terms might distinguish a "good" performance from a "bad" one? When I spoke to people about my desire to sing fado, most responded with variations on the authenticity-place-nation-genre-soul theme, which ran like this: *You are not Portuguese. Fado is our music, just like the flamenco is from Spain and the samba is from Brazil—just like you need to be American to sing country or the blues. To sing fado you must be from here.* If a foreigner could never really sing fado, and if fado itself could not be taught (both owing to issues of "the soul"), then what would they teach me?[33]

When I inquired about lessons, a museum employee informed me another foreign woman was already enrolled; that I could participate after passing an audition in which my ability to sing on pitch and in time would be evaluated; and that the cost of the lessons would be seventy-five euros per month, with an initial inscription fee of fifty euros.[34] She counseled me to learn a fado "by heart," advising me against anything from Amália's repertoire (*They don't like that*), and told me to call her to set up the audition when I had my fado ready. In the amateur fado scenes like the one at O Jaime, access and belonging were largely predicated on forging, or already being part of, specific fado social networks. At the museum school, exclusivity in terms of access to training was maintained through prohibitively high fees and the requirement of an entrance audition.[35]

In preparing for my audition, I disregarded the employee's advice and learned a fado from Amália's repertoire. I approached the learning of my first fado much in same the way that I knew some fadistas initially learned a fado they did not know: I began with a recording. I started by intentionally imitating an imitation of Amália—the rendition of the fado canção "Que Deus Me Perdoe" (May God Forgive Me) interpreted by an up-and-coming international fado diva, Mariza, on her first CD, *Fado em Mim* (2001).[36] A few weeks later, I arrived for my audition.

An hour after I arrive, the fadista António Rocha, a venerated professional fadista in his sixties, known in fado circles as a master stylist (estilista) and as the "Rei do Fado Menor" (King of Fado Menor), emerges and leads me to a small basement room, where two men—a guitarra and a viola player, both of whom I recognize from amateur fado venues—are sitting. Rocha comments, "This is not a school (escola) for fado." "Amália is in style now," exclaims the guitarrista when I tell them what I will sing. "You probably don't know what key you want to sing in," says Rocha. I ask the musicians, "Can you play this in C minor?" Rocha replies, "They can play in any key you like." I take a deep breath and start to sing, experimenting with closing my eyes and then try to make eye contact with the viola player, who never looks up. I forget some of the words at the end of the fado, and Rocha starts singing with me. "Open your mouth more! Your As need to be different!" Gesturing to my diaphragm, I tell him that maybe I need to breath more. "We don't teach any of that here. We just guide you. If you like, we can proceed, learn some fados. We don't teach you fados here, either." I leave wondering what they do teach, and what might constitute "guidance."[37]

Rocha verbally reframed "lessons" (*This is not a school; we just guide you*) as if to render the incongruous pedagogical practice in which we were engaging (i.e., school) more in line with the explicit ideology of non-learning prevalent in fado. He later told me that he would have preferred the phrase "Gabinete de Ensaios" (Department of Rehearsals) to "escola" (school).[38] Fadistas and instrumentalists sometimes use the verb *ensaiar* (to rehearse, to practice) or the noun *ensaio* (rehearsal) to describe the moments of collective working out between singer and instrumentalists or the coaching of the fadista by the instrumentalists (usually the guitarrista) that occurs in the shadows of sessions of formally marked performance. In a professional casa de fado, ensaios sometimes take place in a back room between sets or before the fado night officially begins. In amateur fado, these rehearsals take place quietly during intervals between sets, and also in highly condensed form, rendering a fraction of a fado in an instant, in stolen moments between performances of consecutive fados within a set. In one of these "mini" rehearsals that occur during a performance, the fadista and instrumentalists implicitly signal the rehearsal mode (as opposed to the "performance" mode), singing and playing sotto voce and speaking to each other in whispers, the fadista turning her back to the listeners and inclining her body toward the seated instrumentalists, marking off an intimate communicative space that excludes the public. Rocha's preference for the word "ensaio" to frame the practice of lessons at the museum school was also shared with participants and instructors at coaching sessions I attended at a fado association in the Lisbon neighborhood of Marvila (Associação Cultural o Fado, ACOF). The practice and idea of ensaios in both cases is recontextualized from fado performance venues to sites of more formally institutionalized pedagogy, foregrounding the idea of working out a knowledge that to some extent is already present, as opposed to the teaching and learning of something new.

These lessons constituted a kind of ethnography under a looking glass: the micro-dynamics of social interactions intensified in the compressed time, the small and enclosed space, and the sounds of my singing voice the material through which we negotiated our difference (musical, aesthetic, linguistic, cultural, generational, gendered), the act of performance magnifying my difference, my digital recorder running, a microphone propped up on a chair. When I sang something for the first time, particularly if it was an infrequently performed fado canção, Rocha occasionally had to guide the instrumentalists. Sometimes I played a recording or had to hum the melody for them. Rocha and I usually discussed my choice of key; the instrumentalists sometimes chimed in with their opinions. I stopped singing when I had a question or a technical problem (missing an entrance, running out of breath in the wrong place, or forgetting the words), and Rocha stopped me when he had a correction. Sometimes he sang for me to demonstrate a point; sometimes he sang with me (in a lowered voice in register and volume); and sometimes he used a "problem" with my performance as an opportunity to talk to me about fado aesthetics or fado history.

My subject positioning as an academic and as a violinist formally trained in the European art music tradition put me squarely at odds with fado's ethos of non-learning and with fado's vocal aesthetics. But this was a good position from which to learn; the sound of my voice and my subject positioning seemed to represent much that fado *was not*. Thus, my singing elicited feedback during my lessons at the museum, the coaching sessions in Marvila, and sometimes when I sang publicly in amateur fado venues about what fado "is" or should be in relation to technical details of singing. My pronunciation and breathing, my vocal timbre and register, my repertoire and choices of key were all discussed or critiqued.

I might assume that my foreign status (particularly my pronunciation), my status as a researcher and as a fado "beginner," might call forth different kinds of pedagogy from those I would have received had I been Portuguese, a non-researcher, or experienced in singing fado. Yet the pedagogy employed during my lessons with Rocha and the technical aspects of performance that he stressed were similar to those I observed at coaching sessions in the fado association in Marvila and congruous with what I witnessed more generally in relation to implicit pedagogies and aesthetics of evaluation in the context of performance in amateur fado venues. With me, particular critiques and pedagogies were merely amplified.

LESSON 1 (APRIL 19, 2002)
I walk in, and everyone shakes my hand. I ask if I may record, and
Rocha agrees. An old cassette recorder with a built-in microphone
is already sitting on the chair. I set up my recorder, and the surly

guitarrista, who the other night had directed anti-American jokes at me at a fado venue down the street, asks if I am using a Shure microphone. It's a Sony, I say. I explain that I am ready with two new fados and have prepared a third, "Lisboa Casta Princesa," which I was not able to learn properly because the words are very old and are not so comfortable for me to sing. (The lyrics tell a fado origin story of a "royal" Lisbon whose colonies are her offspring nourished at her breast, the fado born in her womb.)

I say that I have learned "Perseguição" (Pursuit) because it is a traditional fado, and I think the melody is straightforward.[39] They decide after I sing a bit that the key in which I am singing is too low. We raise the key twice until I feel I am singing higher than I am used to. Rocha stops me and tells me to anticipate my entrance more; I am late coming in. He admonishes the instrumentalists for talking during their introduction and not giving me a clear enough beat. I try again, but it doesn't feel right. Rocha stops me and says, "Last week, you sang a fado here, 'Que Deus Me Perdoe,' with melody. Today, you are singing this fado dry (seco); but this fado has a sweet melody (doce)." He tells me I am rushing the melody. He demonstrates, luxuriating in the melody and stretching the meter. He notes that I am still having trouble with the language. I don't always sound confident of the next phrase.

He asks if I know Amália's recordings of "Perseguição" and is surprised when I say that I don't. At home, I had learned the fado from a recording by the fadista Maria Alice, singing in the 1920s. Rocha demonstrates his version of the way Amália sang it, replete with ample rubato and use of vocal ornamentation. I comment that it is interesting that this interpretation of the melody has changed so much over the years. He says, "Fado is not a fixed, rigid form. It is about individual style, which is always changing." He tells me that Amália substituted different words for one of the verses I am singing. (The phrase under question is "I am a vigilant sentinel, night and day, always alert, preserving my husband's honor.") Rocha sings a version into my microphone so I can practice with it later.

He tells a story about the history of fado performance practice: how one hundred years ago, all men sang in D major or D minor, and fado was somewhere between speech and song. Each person had *to improvise a vocal style within the constraints of that key and his or her tessitura, and the accompaniment was much simpler. He asks, "Do you know the voice of Ercília Costa [a fadista who began recording in the late 1920s]?" I say I do—she sang like this (I imitate a nasalized head voice). "Yes," Rocha says, "they sang much more nasal, up there."[40] He tells me that we don't have to spend time talking about all of this, but he has a feeling that I am interested. Perhaps Rocha has decided that if I am going to tell a story about fado, he might as well take on the responsibility of teaching me the right one.*

I try without much success to sing the second fado I have prepared, a version of a Fado Menor, widely considered the "origin" fado, the most improvisatory fado, with the simplest harmonic base, and affectively the most melancholic. But I had chosen to learn from a recording of a highly complex vocal rendition from a new "world music" release by the fadista Cristina Branco, and it threw us all off. When we continue to have trouble getting it together, the guitarrista asks, "Is that an American song?" We then listen to an excerpt of the fado from the CD I brought with me. We try again, but to no avail. Rocha tells me not to abandon the Fado Menor but to start by learning other things—that before attempting a Menor, one needs to have listened to and sung thousands of fados. He tells me to learn the fados of Amália and says that she always sings with good rhythm. Afterward, I rush upstairs to the museum's store. I search for Amalia's versions of "Perseguição," find one recorded live in the 1970s, and put the CD into the CD player. No wonder I shocked them, modeling my performance on a recording from the 1920s. Amália bends almost all of the notes; some words are impossible almost to decipher; she sensuously stretches out time. The night watchman, the bookstore manager, a museum employee, and I listen to the recording six times before we are able to determine the exact lyrics of the new verse.[41]

This lesson reveals the multiple uses and invocations of recording technology in the learning of fado, heightened in this particular pedagogical context: the cassette recorder already in the room, my digital audiotape (DAT) recorder and microphone running, the CD player I bring to demonstrate versions from which I have learned, and the references by Rocha and me to recordings from different decades of the twentieth century to negotiate understandings of historically situated interpretive, stylistic, and timbral differences. The lesson context foregrounds and makes explicit sound technology as a salient component of fado learning. I often heard older practitioners blame "learning from recordings" for what they spoke about as a diminishing of individual interpretation and repertoire among fadistas and the widespread prevalence of "imitation," a lament about a perception of modernity that includes a consequent loss of a fado sociality that fosters "organic" learning. Yet recording technology has been a (perhaps *the*) driving force in shifting fado aesthetics and performance practice since the early twentieth century.[42] Many fadistas I knew—professional and amateur, young and old—used commercial recordings in some way as part of the process of learning to perform fados new to their repertoire. The use of recordings for the explicit purpose of learning new fados might range from confirming the contours of a melody, catching the timing of vocal entrances, or learning lyrics, to sophisticated uses of the recorded archive of the fado past as a resource for the fashioning of individuality in repertoire and interpretation. The latter sometimes included passing sung citation to a voice of the past through imitation (through performative reference to vocal timbre, bodily gesture, or manner of "styling" of another) that was "keyed" and "framed" as intentional through the manner of performance (see Bauman and Briggs 1990; Goffman 1959). All of these fadistas emphasized that they always sang with their own voices, in their own manner (*à sua própria maneira*), with their own style, that they did not *imitate*.

In this first lesson, I sang a traditional fado that I had heard previously in a live context set to different lyrics. To internalize the details, I worked from the only recording I owned and the oldest available version of the fado, a digital transfer of a recording from 1924 rereleased commercially on CD. In line with singing styles on other fado recordings from that time period, the fadista, Maria Alice, sings "straight," with minimal pitch inflections or use of rubato. For pedagogical purposes, Rocha rejected this version in favor of Amália's recordings of this fado and her stylistic and interpretive legacy, a style much more fluid; replete with ample vocal ornamentation, stretching of the meter; with much more room for individual interpretation. Some critics derided this style at the beginning of Amália's recording career, for sounding "Spanish," but it is a style that is now "classic" and widely imitated. I know that Rocha does not want me to imitate Amália verbatim from her recordings. Rather, through listening to Amália's versions, I am to learn about ways of making my interpretation of this fado "sweeter" (*mais doce*), with "sweetness" referring to a particular stylistic fluidity of interpretation. Thus, in this example, Amália's recordings, even though they are not the oldest, serve pedagogically as points of *stylistic origin*, as Ur-texts. When during my audition I sang a fado Amália had made famous (and that while learning I had modeled on a cover version sung by the young fadista Mariza, whom people were talking about as potentially becoming "the next Amália"), my interpretation was deemed more acceptable (i.e., I sang with "melody").

LESSON 3 (MAY 10, 2002)

We spend almost an entire lesson on my pronunciation and singing of the nasalized diphthong "ão." Following various attempts to sing "ão," I suggest that this is one of the most difficult sounds for foreigners to make, and Rocha works to convince the incredulous instrumentalists that the sound does not exist in my native language. "She is American," says the guitarrista. The work with "ão" sparks heated conversation between the two instrumentalists concerning regional differences in pronunciation, and this moves to talk concerning language facility. "Even for the Portuguese this is a difficult sound! She doesn't have this sound in her language, but if you hear a group of Russians or eastern Europeans speaking from far away, you might think they are speaking Portuguese. It sounds like Portuguese because of the sonority of their language, and they learn Portuguese so easily. Same with the Germans—[they learn] much more easily than Americans."

While timbre in the fado voice is almost always completely naturalized for fadistas, listeners, and instrumentalists, by critiquing the pronunciation of my vowel sounds, Rocha implicitly critiqued my timbre, as vowel sounds are important variables that control timbral variation in singing. Pronunciation and accent in fado are important even among native speakers; they sometimes serve to mark class and, in a capital city populated by multiple generations of migrants from rural Portugal, can index regional belonging. I heard tips on pronunciation passed between fadistas in amateur venues and changes in pronunciation insisted on by a recording engineer during a studio session. In the studio, the engineer demanded that some amateur singers from O Jaime change the pronunciation of final consonants of specific words, thus shifting a pronunciation associated with the working class to a more "standard" sound.[43]

Accent localizes, emplaces, and marks class and thus can add to or detract from place-based and class-based authenticity in a performance (Feld et al. 2004). In fado, where a rhetoric of soulfulness is so often bound to the specificity of Lisbon places, Lisbon or Portuguese belonging, pronunciation can function as one index of the soulful. Given my status as a non-native speaker, it makes sense that when I sang fado, people would notice and critique my pronunciation, heightened performance magnifying my difference. There is no nasal diphthong "ão" in German. In the context of my lesson, Europeanness was marked in contrast to "Americanness" as an ideological position. I did not "sound" European.

Rocha often stressed the importance of "saying the words well" (*dizer bem as palavras*). This phrase, along with the importance of singing *com alma* (with soul), figures as one of the key tropes undergirding fado performance aesthetics for many actors. "Saying the words well" ranges from clear annunciation, pronunciation, and diction to the division of syllables (*dividir*) in relation to the breath and the quality of feeling (*sentimento*) with which one conveys the words of the story. Breathing, diction, rhythm (in relation to syllabic and word stress), the use of rubato, the manner of styling the melody, and even soulfulness potentially all fall in line if one "says the words well."[44] The emphasis here is very much on "saying" (*dizer*) rather than on "singing" (*cantar*), aligning fado on a continuum of speech and song on which "saying" and "singing" and "story" and "music" are sometimes used as evaluative descriptors in relation to fado aesthetics and generic taxonomies.

In my twelve lessons at the museum, I worked on a repertoire that included five *fados canção* (fado songs) and two *fados tradicionais* (traditional fados).[45] Rocha guided me in finessing my pronunciation, phrasing, and breathing, and in some aspects of saying the words well while at the same time giving me his perspectives on fado history and form. But we never explicitly worked on the styling of a melody of traditional fado, and after my first lesson, I never again attempted to sing a Fado Menor, which is melodically completely unscripted, during a lesson. Almost everyone encouraged me to sing the subgenre of fado canção—fados that were considered *mais musicados* (more "musical") than traditional fados. While I was taking lessons at the museum, I also began to sing the repertoire I was learning publicly at other sites, putting the feedback I was getting from Rocha and the instrumentalists in dialogue with commentary from friends in the amateur fado world and from the participants and instrumentalists at the fado association in Marvila.

INSTITUTING PEDAGOGY II

An eleven-year-old boy with a pierced ear and wearing a surfer T-shirt sings a fado, week after week, about a boy from Alfama, from the "old Lisbon of the past" (velha Lisboa do passado), continuously off-pitch and with no sense of meter. Nothing the guitarrista has him do seems to help. A twelve-year-old girl with glasses wearing a black cape around her shoulders sings fados from Amália's repertoire, and the instrumentalists help her get her entrances right. Maria, a stylishly dressed nine-year-old girl with a blonde streak in her dark hair sings "Que Deus Me Perdoe" full of confidence, with a wide vibrato, her head thrown back, with all of the bodily and vocal gestures of a woman singing tragic fado but with the vocal timbre of a girl. The guitarrista tapes her performance using a minidisc recorder, and her parents watch and listen, attentively taking notes, telling me that their daughter will be auditioning for the television show Academia de Estrelas (Academy of the Stars). An eight-year-old boy gets up to sing for the first time. His five-year-old sister and two nine-year-old girls crowd around him, silently mouthing the words to the lyrics and bursting forth on the refrains.

A taxi driver and I ride the dark back roads, along the river, that connect Graça to the neighborhood of Marvila on the outskirts of Lisbon in March 2002, winding our way past boarded-up factories, abandoned ripped-open buildings, construction projects half-finished, and high-rise apartment buildings. We get lost. We finally find the small public library where I have heard that fado coaching sessions take place on Thursday nights. It is at the bottom of a long, hilly road; the building is covered in black graffiti, the windows broken.

People inside sit at plastic tables on white plastic lawn chairs, smoking and whispering in a large auditorium adjacent to the one-room library.

There is a stage at the far end; silver balls hang from the ceiling, a Portuguese flag hangs on the wall. Children run around, playing. In the corner, a guitarrista and viola player have set up, and people age four to eighty take turns singing fado. Outside the back door, kids kick a ball around; men drink beer and smoke, standing near a small kitchen. Sometimes the guitarrista stops the singer, interjecting critique, pointing out a missed entrance, bad timing, a wrong word, a phrase sung not quite right.[46] Sometimes he sings and plays an excerpt for the fadista, demonstrating how he thinks it should go—or how it should not. Sometimes the singer stops in mid-song, asking a question or wanting to try the fado in a different key. Sometimes there are arguments. A small group clusters around and behind the singer and the instrumentalists: maybe another guitarrista, playing along trying to improve his skills and expand his repertoire (playing "second" guitarra to a "first" is a common form of apprenticeship for guitarristas); maybe a girlfriend or a boyfriend or family members. Some offer advice. From the tables where most onlookers sit, it is difficult to hear what is going on in the coaching sessions as the adults gossip and children run playing, often shouting. Contrary to a formal fado session where silence is strictly enforced, the scene alternates between shouts for silence, some active participation (the silent intoning of lyrics and the singing of refrains), and the privileging of sociality with talk, smoking, and light drinking. Some children hover close to the instrumentalists, observing the sessions, watching the musicians play or standing near a friend, while he or she is singing, mouthing the lyrics, singing the refrains, or offering words of encouragement. A big book sits on a table near the instrumentalists where members who want to sing sign in. Although the sessions run for three hours, there sometimes is not enough time for everyone to sing. The instrumentalists go over time, play past midnight. Or there is grumbling and arguing amongst the members as the instrumentalists (who are paid per session) pack up to go home, people still waiting their turn to sing.

For much of the twentieth century, Marvila boomed with art deco store fronts, riverside industry, and thriving factories; but by the early 2000s, most of the factories had been abandoned and new social housing projects had sprung up in pockets, some along the highway. Some of the participants in the fado coaching sessions and the sócios (dues-paying members) of the ACOF did live in Marvila, but many others did not. In addition to holding weekly fado coaching sessions, the association put on fado gala dinners to raise money for charity; sponsored annual amateur fado competitions; and occasionally arranged tours for its fadistas within Portugal. Every Friday, the same instrumentalists and many of the same singers who attended the coaching sessions, including the children, participated in an amateur session at a restaurant down the road.[47] The association had gained some notoriety for sending top singers to compete in Lisbon's fabled annual fado competition A Grande Noite do Fado (The Grand Night of Fado), and knowledge of the Thursday night coaching sessions spread through the amateur fado community by word of mouth, although some spoke disparagingly of the sessions insofar as they functioned as a so-called school for fado.[48] Membership was obtainable for a very small monthly fee.[49] Occasionally, people from outside of the association dropped in for coaching, and on the few instances when a fadista I knew from O Jaime appeared, we were both surprised, an unexpected overlap of worlds.

People participated in the sessions for different reasons. Some were trying to place in the Grande Noite do Fado. One stage mother was trying to launch her daughter's career. Others did not feel ready to sing in formal contexts but harbored dreams of singing and came to learn away from the pressure of formal performance in amateur fado venues. As with the lessons I took at the Fado Museum, participants framed the Thursday night activities in Marvila not as lessons or as a school but as rehearsals (ensaios). Yet someone who came to "sing" rather than to "rehearse" might be frowned on by the instrumentalists. As the viola player said to me as he gave me a ride home after a session, "That fadista who was arguing with us at the end, he just comes here to *sing*, not to rehearse."

The Thursday night sessions were remarkable in terms of the amount of intergenerational participation they engendered; the children and teenage singers sometimes outnumbered the adult fadistas. It is rare to see many children at late-night fado events and venues. At O Jaime, where the fado happens in the afternoon and where children are sometimes present, it is still rare for young children to sing (although if a young child wants to sing, she or he is encouraged). In terms of the formalized institutionalization of fado learning, within an association focused explicitly on fado, the Marvila "school" revealed an emergent pedagogical and social context for the learning of fado singing. What was emergent here was not the participation of children as fado singers but, rather, a sociality between the children—and between the children, adolescents, and adults—that was negotiated partly through the learning, or the "rehearsing," of fado in an institutionalized context.

> Nine-year-old Carla starts to sing a fado but is unsure about the key. She runs back to a table to retrieve a notebook from her bag, finds a page on which she has noted the key, then says confidently to the instrumentalists that she sings the fado in B. She begins singing again, and her mother shouts from the back of the room, coming forward, "That's too low. It should be in C." She then sings loudly a part of a phrase Carla has been struggling with. "Abre a voz" (open the voice) admonishes the mother, demonstrating. The instrumentalists second the mother's opinion, and Carla tries again. When Carla begins her next fado and tries without success to sing a melody correctly (she is consistently flat), the instrumentalists call Carla's friend Maria to sing the first verse. Maria sings, then turns to Carla, asking, "Are you nervous? Is that why you're having trouble?" Carla shakes her head and sings once more. Then the two girls run to a back table where they are involved in a project with paper and magic markers.[50]

Young children almost always had parents who participated, standing up to take their own lessons with the instrumentalists later in the evening. Sometimes a mother and a daughter would sing the same fado. Children learned in this context from the explicit coaching by the instrumentalists and their parent's interjections, but also by modeling other children (e.g., when the guitarrista called on a more skilled child to demonstrate). Children informally offered advice to other children, and when I sang, Carla, Maria, and a few of the teenage girls advised me on both my choice of repertoire and my pronunciation. Olga showed up one night to sing at Marvila; afterward, nine-year-old Maria said to me, "The repertoire she sings won't work for you. It is too heavy for your voice."

It was in this context in which I participated in my second series of fado "rehearsals" as a singer; in terms of my novice status, I was perhaps more aligned with the children than with most of the adults. The guitarrista, José, encouraged my participation and egged me on with mischievous feedback. Like most everyone else there, we worked on the basics, mostly getting entrances in sync with the instrumentalists and determining choice of key; we did not work on the styling of traditional fado; nor did the other singers. The first time I sang, I overheard an older woman in the back of the room saying, "That voice has nothing to do with fado." Following what seemed like an initial shock after the first time I sang in Marvila (even the children playing soccer outside came inside to listen), almost everyone was supportive of my singing, but it was clear that it was a novelty and that the listeners in Marvila were not always quite sure how to evaluate it. Listeners tried to help me with my pronunciation and some commented, along with José, on my "lyric" voice; the term "lyric" for some placed the sound of my voice and its significations distant from multiple fado authenticities. "You sing with the voice of a foreigner," the viola player tells me, "but you have to just keep singing and learn more fados."

More than a year after my first Thursday night session, and after a hiatus of many months during which I gained more experience singing fado in public and increased fluency in Portuguese, I returned to Marvila. I sang a fado canção from an old *revista* and could feel that I was in a groove with musicians. When I finished, exclamations and applause broke out around the room. "Bonito!" says the viola player. "Uma voz lírica, que bonita, uma maravilha" (A lyric voice, a marvel!), exclaims José. "She is a musician," says the viola player. José agrees: "she has a sense of music; she has the rubatos." A woman next to us says, "It is much better. Down to the pronunciation, it is all better." José jumps in, "It's wonderful, even the way you are saying the words. You are feeling the words, but sometimes you are feeling the fado and forget you are singing. Let the voice come out. You need to exteriorize more. You are singing too much for yourself." The viola player agrees: "Send your voice outward." A man asks, "Are you feeling the words? Do you know the meaning of all the words?" "She is feeling the words, she is feeling them," a woman interjects. José says, "She is singing *à americana* but she feels them." Another man looks at me, saying, "You sang with feeling, you sang with soul" (*cantaste com sentimento, cantaste com alma*).[51]

I include this example to underscore once again that listeners' perceptions of "soulfulness" and feeling in fado are intimately linked to the performer's level of mastery of multiple sonic communicative codes that come into play when one "says the words well," and that "saying the words well" is a composite of learned skills. Even though most people I spoke with held the opinion that a foreigner, especially an American, could never really sing fado with the requisite "soul," occasionally listeners attributed soulfulness to my singing. More than a year after I started attending the coaching sessions at Marvila, I was able to transmit a certain "soulfulness" to this group of listeners even while singing "*à americana*," and with a timbre and tessitura that they heard as "lyric." My increased mastery of word placement, Lisbon-inflected pronunciation, phrasing, breathing, and use of rubato and vocal ornamentation in relation to fado form constituted a grammar that rendered "feeling" communicable to this public and my "interiority" translatable. Yet José also advises me that I need to "exteriorize more" (*exteriorizar mais*), that in some places I sing too much "for myself." In doing so, he points to a process of learning, moments of sonic and performative betwixt and between-ness, moments that reveal the porosity between inner ear and outer voice. The "interior" of self revealed through musical performance, which vocality in this instance foregrounds, does not exist a priori waiting to be "expressed." Through the process of musical learning—through listening, performance, and reiteration—an "interior" is shaped in relation to aesthetic form and social affect, and this is an interior always already under construction.

Limits of the Learnable

The majority of amateur fadistas I knew voiced antagonism toward the emergent institutions focused on the teaching and learning of fado in Lisbon in the early 2000s. Many expressed hostility toward *any* kind of institutionalization explicitly linked to fado. Over the decade from 2000 to 2010, as fado became much more visible (and profitable) locally and on an international stage, the institutionalization of fado increased. This was perhaps most evident in relation to a long-term, high-profile, and ultimately successful bid by a Lisbon based committee for status from UNESCO for fado as "intangible heritage," granted in 2011, and the remodeling of the Fado Museum in Alfama, which was completed in 2008. For many practitioners, formal institutionalization, particularly related to issues of pedagogy and of government policy or intervention, cuts against the grain of passionately held ideas about fado's organic link to the "unlearned" soul, to its "origin" in the popular, arising from the "dispossessed" and working class. Ultimately, these are ideologies about voicing, about what kinds of fado voices are privileged and for whom and about whose voices grant access to particular kinds of capital (social, cultural, financial). Antagonism toward the idea of formal learning in relation to fado might also be understood in relation to historical questions of literacy and educational opportunities in dictatorship-era Portugal. Many of my fadista interlocutors from O Jaime, who were in their early fifties and older in the early 2000s, had not had the opportunity to pursue formal schooling beyond age eleven. They grew up in a Portugal in which formal education beyond that point was accessible primarily to a small percentage of elites. But perhaps more fundamental, and cutting across class, generation, venue, and professional–amateur and class distinctions, are the enduring aspects of fado's origin stories that proudly situate fadistas, fado lyrics, and fado sociality as rebelliously outside institutionality (see chapter 2) and that maintain the idea that fado's essence is an "unlearned" soul or a "feeling" that is given voice.

When I asked fadistas about their processes of learning, the majority repeated almost verbatim the epithet cited earlier in this chapter, "One is not taught, nor does one learn to be a fadista; one is born a fadista." But fadistas who were more inclined to think analytically about fado performance gave me more nuanced responses. Fátima Fernandes told me that she thought fado was being somewhat "mistreated" (*o nosso fado é um pouco maltratado*); that some people were singing with bad diction, with no sense of rhythm (*sem compasso*); and that one could learn diction, rhythm, and how to place the vocal chords. Yet later in our conversation, she commented that "fado is born with people, not learned. Now they are starting to have school for fado. What school? If it doesn't come from here inside, genuinely, it isn't fado" (*O fado nasce com as pessoas. Não se aprende nada. Venha de lá a escola, qual escola? Se não for de cá dentro, genuíno, não é fado*). Fátima's first commentary does not necessarily contradict her second. Fátima and others stressed that certain aspects of fado singing could be learned while simultaneously emphasizing some idea of an essential "soulfulness" (*com alma*), "interior" (*vem cá de dentro*), or "intuition" (*é intuitiva*). For some, learnable aspects of fado included diction and pronunciation (*dizer bem as palavras*), timing (*ter compasso*), comportment (*o comportamento, a maneira de ser*), and the placement of the vocal chords (*colocar as cordas vocais*).[52] "We are born with this intention, this love, this vocation [to sing fado]," Sebastião de

Jesus told me, "it is not only about opening one's mouth and singing (*fazer trinados*)."[53]

To style well (*estilar*), or to improvise artfully, is considered one of the most important features of good singing. As one of the primary signs of authenticity or soulfulness (along with vocal timbre), it is one of fado's most naturalized characteristics. With improvisation (as with timbre), you either have it or you don't. António Rocha believed that some characteristics of fado singing could be learned. However, he marked as natural and intuitive acts of styling a melody and ornamenting the vocal line (*modulações da voz*).[54] As one fadista at O Jaime explained, "One is already born with voltinhas" (*as voltinhas já nascem com a gente*).

These are ideologies of voicing that link styling to a feeling that resides at the core of self, to one's own uniqueness, to an essence that enables one to "be fadista" (*ser fadista*). These are also ideologies of voicing that maintain exclusivity among fadistas, that help to shape fado worlds that are perceived from the outside as "closed" (*fechado*). But "soulfulness" cannot be exteriorized or rendered communicative without learned technical chops, no matter the energy with which this discourse of non-learning is invested and maintained. Through the manner in which one styles and ornaments, along with the timbre with which one sings, one is in an essential sense heard and granted "soul," the "inside," upon which an imaginary of both the singular subject and the social subject are sustained.

The Soul in the Throat

Por isso nós dizemos que fado não se canta com a voz, canta-se com a alma, canta-se com o coração. (We say that fado is not sung with the voice, it is sung with the soul, it is sung with the heart.) —ANTÓNIO ROCHA, June 5, 2002

Genre is made, felt, experienced, and defined in relation to other genres; one socio-aesthetic universe is given definition in reference to others. It is a Saturday afternoon during an interval at O Jaime and Olga is telling me about her opera collection, her visits to the Opera House of São Carlos in Lisbon as a child; she sings me an excerpt from Puccini. I sit at the fadistas' table at an elite professional fado venue in Alfama in September 2002. During the interval, a young fadista reads a biography of Maria Callas. "Callas was a fadista," she says. "She led the life of a fadista; she suffered like a fadista." Yet more often, I heard opera invoked to explain what fado most emphatically is *not*. Another fadista at the table says, "Fadistas can sing music from all over the place, many genres. But only the Portuguese, only a fadista, can sing fado. Maria Callas and [Luciano] Pavarotti could not sing fado." While fado might be about melodrama, tragedy, its divas, and, most certainly, is about story, it is not, as many of my interlocutors positioned "opera," about privileging the voice *as* voice, the voice for the sake of voice, a pretty voice, a beautiful voice, or a voice of gratuitous ornamentation that obscures the word, the story, the poetry. Talk about "true" fado—*fado fado*—often marks it as opera's antithesis. Such talk might run like this: "In fado, the music is only a support for the story, the poem, the words, whereas in opera, the words are there just to enable the music." Sometimes this narrative was demonstrated with sung vocables imitating operatic style (*la, la, la*). In this model, opera is a conceit, it is about musical complexity, whereas fado involves a "naturalness" and "simplicity" as lived story.

In Marvila, at O Jaime, and in my lessons at the Fado Museum, listeners often called attention to the "lyric" nature of my voice while mentioning that I had formal musical training. Comments about the "lyric" quality of my voice not only potentially negate the authenticity of my lived experience in relation to fado, but they also fit into a way of delimiting fado as a genre, where ideas about Western art music, particularly opera, and fado are contrasted. The lyric voice, or a bel canto voice, or "clean voice" (*uma voz limpa*), although not without place in fado, for some listeners carried classed associations with vocal training and with learnedness.[55] In the contemporary world music market, "cleaner" voices tend to circulate most successfully outside Portugal. While there is not necessarily one "typical" fado timbre, a voice that listeners in the milieu of amateur fado might mark as carrying the "most fado," or as being "the voice of the neighborhood" (*voz do bairro*), is often marked by a pronounced nasality, a texture that might occasionally break into roughness, and sometimes a vocal placement that falls between speaking and singing.

"Cantarei Até Que a Voz Me Doa" (I Will Sing until My Voice Hurts) proclaims the title of a popular fado canção sung by women whose lyrics dramatize the aesthetic of the injured voice.[56] The injured "grain" (Barthes 1977) of the fado voice might be understood as iconic for soulfulness, living the life of a fadista (*a vida fadista*), the lived experience of suffering and the particularities of place. Some fadistas talked to me about how the very posture of singing fado, with the neck thrown back, puts undue pressure on the vocal chords, compressing them, making them prone to injury. One professional singer told me in confidence about an operation she had on her vocal chords to heal them. Another told me that some young professional fadistas were taking singing lessons, many from the same teacher. "My teacher works with my voice so I won't strain it," a fadista in her early twenties told me, "but he doesn't ever teach me how to sing fado." Here fado features again as unlearnable. Incongruously, in the statement by this young fadista, vocal technique is severed from "fado" itself; but this statement can also be understood as a way of "saving face," of keeping her discourse in line with fado's maxims of unlearnability. In 2002, the manager of one of Lisbon's most elite venues told me, "Sometimes we go to hear amateur fado [and] look out for good fadistas, singers who have something special. We hire them, then immediately we pay for them to take singing lessons." This gestures to one way in which Lisbon's professional fado world mines amateur fado for *soul*, but then refines this "something special" through formal training of the voice.

The fado voice is often fetishized in discourse and practices pertaining to the throat (*garganta*). In amateur fado sessions, common disclaimers used by fadistas before singing refer to the state of one's throat: "My throat is not doing so well today" (*Estou um pouco mal da garganta hoje*); "I [my throat] am [is] rough" (*Estou rouca*). Fado talk abounds with fadista folk wisdom regarding the care of the throat, from imperatives regarding beverage choices to ideas about air circulation: red wine, water at room temperature, and particular herbal teas are good, while cold water and icy drinks are bad; air conditioning and drafts must be avoided, no matter how extreme the heat. At the same time, "garganta" features in discourses about authenticity and the aesthetic, where the very soul (sometimes both as individual and as collective) is lodged in the throat. "In the crystal of the throat lives the soul of the country" (*No cristal de uma garganta vive a alma de um país*), we chant during a refrain of a fado that Fernanda Proença sings at O Jaime.[57] "Young fadistas today lack throat (*falta garganta*)," a viola player in his sixties tells me. "Garganta linda!" (Beautiful throat!) shouts a man during a moment of heightened sung emotion. "They say Amália had *uma garganta de prata* (a throat of silver)," said one amateur fadista as together we looked over old newspaper photos of Amália Rodrigues with Fernanda at her home.

"Garganta" grounds the voice and the soul unequivocally in the body, in its fragility and in its power, in the imprint that living leaves upon it, and in inscriptions of place, of memory, of history in the corporeal.

Fado's generic distinctions fracture in talk and practice along binaries of "nature" and "artifice," "story" and "music." Fado canção is sometimes spoken of as *musicado* (musical) in the same contexts in which some fans and practitioners devalue it as less authentic, less fado than traditional fado. The critique sounds like this, "Fado canção has a musical score. All of the notes are there. It is not improvised. It is not as sad as *fado fado*, which has more soul." But the argument about the musical score is tenuous, at best, for in practices of singing, playing, and learning, scores are not used, and not every fado canção can be traced back to an "originary" score. The overt "musicalness" of fado canção moves it closer to artifice, or what is considered "studied." I was often told that I should sing fado canção. *A foreigner can sing fado canção but not fado fado. It is easier to start with fado canção; traditional fado is much more difficult.* Some fados recommended as "suited" to my voice were those considered the most "musical." In the most extreme presentation of this continuum, traditional fado is at one end, indicating unschooled, natural, improvised, soulful, and lived, and opera is at the other, associated with artifice, privilege, training, erudition, and high culture. One guitarrista argued at length that fado isn't music at all; rather, it is a "story" or "poetry that is sung," as if music itself were a contaminating element.[58] In the discourse of natural, unlearned soulfulness that surrounds some of these distinctions between *fado fado* and "music," traditional fado is marked as embodied, as closer to the speaking voice and lived stories, and as more reflective of sincerity of feeling.

Conclusion: Voice as Soul?

The Portuguese anthropologist Joaquim Pais de Brito links the sound of the fado voice to a sense of the eternal. "The voice is in its transparency or huskiness, limpidity or hoarseness a vital principle which negates by its absolute and impressive existence the ephemeral bodies which produce it. No fadista can ever be alone within his body, he is his voice" (Brito 1994: 34). The story of musical sound and the singing voice as reflecting an interior soul or essence has been told over and over again. It is part and parcel of discourses about music and voicing that date back to the Greeks (Cavarero 2004). Its modern logic, in which the nation itself as a collectivity of individuals imagined as privy to a culturally specific shared inner feeling comes to be invested with "soul," underlies countless European nation-building projects that collected, promoted, and shaped the sounds of the "folk" as essence of nation (Bendix 2000; Bohlman 2011), as well as the new forms of collecting in which "national" musical genres are declared and marketed as heritage or patrimony (Ochoa-Gautier 2006). "Soul" is given voice; is commodified as music, as heritage. It finds its way onto maps drawn by the discipline of ethnomusicology and by the international industry for "world music," where an implicit assumption has sometimes been that musical genre reveals or constructs the soul or voice of a nation, a people, a diaspora. This assumption often undergirds gatekeeping arguments about authenticity that are sometimes employed by musicians and fans themselves. *You can't really sing that or play that because you aren't from here. You aren't like us. You don't have our soul.* This is a musical identity politics whose tune is familiar. In her work on intimacy in some of the settler colonies of empire, Elizabeth Povinelli (2006: 36) asks, "In a post-essentialist theory, how do we make the body matter?" Through ethnographic analysis of the pedagogies and poetics of fado voicing, this chapter has asked, in a post-essentialist theory, within the context of fado, what is the *matter* in musical voice as soul?

Mystification is a key feature on which the equating of sung voice with interior essence relies as a meta-cultural trope. In fado discourse and practice, vocal timbre, improvisation, and a conceit of lived story are key axes on which ideologies of the unlearned and soulful voice turn. At the same time, ideologies of mystery making regarding issues of fado's soul are aesthetically and imaginatively productive. From an idea of mystery comes a wellspring of invention and storied histories that are re-spun and imagined when the fadista sings or the listener listens *com alma* (with soul). In fado (as in all musical worlds), gestures, timbres, modes of styling, and ways of listening are shot through with feeling that is shared (Valverde 1999), transmitted through agreed on cultural codes that are both implicitly and explicitly taught and learned through the social relations of voicing and hearing (Cavarero 2004; Fox 2004). At the same time, these are ways of feeling that are physically located, rooted in a particular phenomenology of the local, saturated through and through with the sensual particularities of place (Feld and

Basso 1996), and gathered and released in fado as genre. To reverse the maxim with which I began the chapter, one is not born knowing how to sing fado. Rather, one *learns* how to listen, sing, feel, and talk about fado. Through fado's implicit and explicit pedagogies, one develops tools for a sensuous understanding of "emotion as a quality of sound" (Cumming 2000: 3). One develops a vocabulary (gestural, sonic, performative) through which to express and to "craft" (Kondo 1990) a particular kind of feeling self, a repertoire that enables participation in a particular socio-musical world of the soulful. These ways of figuring the soulful in fado have their own local genealogies and histories even as they are connected to more widely circulating (transnational) cultural forms. One of the most salient aspects of the soulful in fado is its link to a sense of the past of place, to an imagination of history. *Fado was more fado in the past. The guitarras cried more in the past.* It is to the past as sounded as a feeling, and continuously reimagined through fado's present, that the next chapter turns.

TWO

Affects of History

[Fado's] father was a foundling
Who embarked
On the caravels of Gama [Vasco da Gama]
In tatters and dirty
With more swagger [*gingão*] than a seaman
From the old alleys of Alfama
—"BIOGRAFIA DO FADO"

In the times when the sea was a secret
Challenged only by its own storms
Some heroes departed without fear
On the docile caravel of saudade
And on the high seas far from the shore
Surrounded by faith from far and wide
There was always a cry of the guitarra
And the sobbing of a fado on the deck.
—"CARAVELA DA SAUDADE"

A miniaturized colonial sailing ship, which was once a bottle of liquor, sits atop the television set at the Tasca do Jaime. Olga stands to one side of it, a golden pendant of a caravel around her neck, singing the fado lyrics "Caravela da Saudade" on a Saturday afternoon in 2003. Just like the images on a sign that hung gleaming above an old tea and coffee shop in 2010 in the Lisbon neighborhood of Baixa—a caricature of a "native" African man, a large hoop through one ear, holding a cup of coffee, and

FIGURE 2.1 • Signage in the Baixa district. Lisbon, January 2010. Photograph by the author.

another of an "Oriental" man, in a triangular hat, looming over him holding a cup of tea (figure 2.1)—images that go unnoticed in the bustle of the day to day, this performance of "Caravela da Saudade" is an example of what I think of as the "everyday colonial."

These are symbolic remainders of the colonial naturalized in contemporary Lisbon, almost invisible, inaudible in their repetition and oversaturation. I am not suggesting an easy homology between Lisbon's everyday colonial and contemporary practices and ideologies in Lisbon with respect to race and difference. Rather, this chapter works with the everyday colonial as attached to fado as genre, as a starting point for asking questions about relationships between historical "background" and political foreground, for understanding how a "historicity of affect" might be "mapped" (Flatley 2008) with respect to musical experience.

What might history feel like when rendered and experienced in musical sound? What kinds of forces might come together when history "flashes" affectively to the fore for a musical instant and is recognized as something, named, marked?[1] How might musical experience and talk, practice, performance, and discourse come together in a musical *genre* in such a way that the genre itself functions as a sensitive node, at once capable of containing, liberating, reinforcing, and transforming story—the sound of a vocal turn capable of releasing tales and the multiple desires that order the stuff of history, where story's valences are dependent on the aesthetic of sonic form and sound's affective sensuality?

Fado as genre absorbs and releases the storied mess of history: self stories and state stories; fascist, communist, and revolutionary stories; stories of the intimately quotidian; stories that order the history of Portugal in its place in the world. Stories intermingle and overlap; variants are retold, and particular core stories emerge, stories of former glory, victorious conquest that might recur, stories that speak of the illicitness of Arab influence in hushed tones, stories that traffic in dreams of Africa or mythologies of a Lusotropicalist past. Then there are the stories of the past that are whispered or that well up in bodies unspoken, unsung—the lowered voice, the sideways glance over the shoulder before speaking, or a silence—all forces of habit, remainders of a way of being in the world enacted as common sense.[2] This chapter tacks back and forth between talk about history in the present and a historicization of the ideas and sentiments presented in that talk, sometimes displacing historical chronology. This is not to deny the importance of official chronologies but, rather, to examine moments of poetic compression, moments in which history as felt becomes unmoored from its precise chronologies as officially told. It argues for fado as a genre in the widest sense (including its overlapping socio-musical scenes, musical aesthetics, poetics, venues, meta-discourses) as a field around which particular affects; ways of feeling and talking about history, the past, belonging, and nation; and ways of marking one's relationship to that history coalesce.

Narrating Empire's Remainders through Fado's Stories
Many people who guided me through fado's worlds took it upon themselves to educate me about fado's story: where it came from, what it is, what can be known about it, and what will be forever mysterious. These tellings were invariably saturated with stories of Portugal and the Portuguese, with fragments of recycled historical, academic, and nation-building discourses. These fragments in circulation, they swirl, they land upright, sometimes emerging as the same old story and sometimes as a new twist on an old tale. Some are emotionally coherent and passionately delivered narratives woven from a tangle of incongruous historical threads, gendered, raced, classed, and affectively charged.

The setting for the first story was a conversation with one of Lisbon's organic intellectuals of fado in 2003. He was a fadista, poet, and guitarrista, as well as a thoughtful university-educated man in his late forties who had served in the Portuguese colonial war in Angola. Mariza had just won the BBC World Music prize for best musician in the "Europe" category. I asked what he thought about Mariza's new fame, drawing comparisons with Amália Rodrigues's career, noting that Amália's success abroad had been critical to her subsequent fame in Portugal. Might this need for star fadistas to be validated abroad have anything to do with a Portuguese inferiority complex that so many people had spoken to me about? *It is a geographical question. We are surrounded by Spain and the sea. We are the westernmost, farthest-away point in Europe. We feel out of the heart of where the action is. We marvel at the Discoveries, the courage of those men setting out on those boats and reaching India, reaching Japan, turning the bend around South Africa without motors. Those men had just boats, ingenuity, willpower, and their bodies. We Portuguese are unique in that we colonized through love, the act of love, through the body, while other countries, such as England, colonized with weapons, through violence.* His narrative, which had the tenor of a lecture whose "facts" are well worn, combined multiple enduring tropes of Portuguese nation building and identity from different historical moments under the central plot of "the Discoveries." Portugal is marginal, isolated, and peripheral yet brave, seafaring, ingenious, and cosmopolitan. The Portuguese mode of colonization is "unique," for it was powered by "love," through intimacy.

My entrances into fado were often marked by elaborate origin stories and historical narratives like this. Many of the recorded interviews I conducted with fadistas, instrumentalists, and music industry professionals to learn more about fadistas' lives, fado aesthetics, or the fado recording industry contain Portuguese history lessons embedded within them. Sometimes, as in this narrative, Lusotropicalist strains figured overtly; more than one man explained to me that the Portuguese "invented" the "mulatto race"; miscegenation in these cases signified tolerance, an open-mindedness toward race that the speakers used to distinguish Portuguese identity from other types of European identities that were perceived as being marked by differing attitudes to race in relation to colonization. In other stories, Lusotropicalist tropes figured covertly—as in narratives about Portuguese tolerance and exposure to other cultures—and in some stories, Lusotropicalism did not figure at all. But in these unsolicited tellings of history, discourses about Portuguese identity or "national character" in relation to official Portuguese histories and reference to the colonial Discoveries were ubiquitous.

GENEALOGIES OF A PARTICULAR CIRCUM-ATLANTIC SOUL

Portuguese scholars across multiple disciplines (Almeida 2004; Gil 2007; Leal 2000b, 2008; Lourenço 2001) have noted a tendency among the Portuguese to comment reflexively and indefatigably on the subject of Portuguese "identity." The literary critic and philosopher Eduardo Lourenço (1994, cited in Castelo 1998: 140) argues for "hyperidentity" itself as a distinguishing mark of Portuguese society. In writing about the "hidden empire" in the history of Portuguese anthropology—both in nation-building folkloric anthropology focused on Portugal and in the anthropology that was explicitly directed at the study of "natives" in the Portuguese colonies—the anthropologist João Leal (2008: 49) describes "hyperamnesia" and "excessive remembering" in relation to the colonial Discoveries as being among the "major agreements upon which Portuguese national identity seems to rest," as an "important element in Portuguese cultural literacy" writ large, as well as an implicit foundation for "the daily discourses and practices of Portuguese national identity."[3]

I was struck by how often white Portuguese people born in Portugal, traversing a range of class positions and occupations and with varying degrees of formal education, spoke to me in similar terms about tenets they perceived as essentially constitutive of Portuguese identity and presented them as geographically and historically determined. Simplified versions of recurrent identity-making narratives might run like this: *We Portuguese are a deeply emotional people, but we interiorize emotion. Unlike the Spanish, Brazilians, and the Italians, we don't exteriorize our emotion so much.* Or, *We are adaptable to new cultural situations and are tolerant of people who are different from us. We learn new languages easily. For centuries, we have been exploring, migrating, and adapting to new situations. We gave new worlds to the world.* Or, *We Portuguese are special. We invented the mulatos.* These redundant claims to self and identity are also claims about nation, where the projects of nation building shape subjects on affective levels. These kinds of history lessons and discourses about identity increased in number, intensity, and detail when I was interacting with people within the realm of fado, gathering a particular force within the context of fado, foregrounding some of what implicitly lies in the background of everyday assumptions about what it might mean to be Portuguese.

Tracking a social history of the most recurrent and resilient strains of these contemporary public discourses that I heard in the context of fado in the early 2000s reveals their genesis and circulation to lie at a nexus of earlier circuitous collusions among academe (most notably, a triangulation of U.S., Portuguese, and Brazilian anthropology), a Portuguese intellectual and literary elite, the popular press, and strategic (and shifting) uses of "history" and attitudes about race promulgated by the Estado Novo.

An essentialized Portuguese soul was shaped partly by anthropology and ethnology itself, a formulation of soul that as Leal (2008) shows was always "haunted by empire." Ethnic-psychology studies of the mid-twentieth century in Portugal figured against a ground that had already been established by folkloristics of the late nineteenth century, which in turn were already saturated with the colonial Discoveries as a central trope in the formation of Portuguese identity (Leal 2000b, 2008). Leal notes that in the late 1800s, the Portuguese ethnologist Teófilo Braga drew on elements of Portuguese "folk" culture in his formulation of what typified the Portuguese "spirit." One such defining element for Braga was "an intensely passionate and naively affective character" (Braga 1867, as cited in Leal 2000b: 4); others were an "adventurous character" and a "special inclination towards overseas exploration" (Braga 1985 [1885]: 73, as quoted in Leal 2008: 43).[4] Leal (2008: 42) argues for the influence that early twentieth-century Portuguese writing on saudade and late nineteenth-century work on Portuguese national identity, along with U.S. anthropological "national character" studies of the 1940s, like those by Ruth Benedict and Margaret Mead (which were also influential elsewhere in Europe), had on the Portuguese anthropologist Jorge Dias (1990 [1953]). In "Os Elementos Fundamentais da Cultura Portuguesa" (The Fundamental Elements of Portuguese Culture), Dias argues for a Portuguese "personality" based on "a series of conflicting psychological traits": "It combined 'a remarkable capacity of adapting to different surroundings'—allegedly expressed in a process of colonisation, through assimilation or miscegenation, distinct from that of other European countries—with 'a strong capacity for keeping its own character'" (Leal

2000b: 8–9). Dias (like Braga) finds in geography a motivated history that lends nation "soul." "The attraction towards the Atlantic Ocean," he wrote, "was the soul of the nation and the driving force behind Portugal's history" (Dias 1990 [1953]: 141, as quoted in Leal 2008: 44).

Leal (2008: 42) claims that this work is "one of the most influential essays ever produced by a Portuguese anthropologist." Miguel Vale de Almeida (2004: 51) refers to it as a "cult essay," noting that it was reprinted in Portugal in a mass-market pocket edition in the 1990s and argues that "the ideas in the essay circulate in Portugal with the same vigor as [Gilberto] Freyre's theses do in Brazil: they are both texts whose main theses coincide with national self-representations." Indeed, in Dias's emphasis on the unique character of Portuguese colonization through miscegenation there are echoes of Freyre's Lusotropicalism, which was circulated in Portugal by the Estado Novo and by some sectors of the Portuguese social sciences beginning in the 1950s.[5] But this is the point in the story at which the genealogies of the ideas at play become increasingly circuitous and difficult to track. As Almeida (2004: 50) suggests, there may well have been a "happy coincidence between Freyre's ideas and something that was already effective in Portuguese national representations."[6]

In the early 1920s, the Brazilian Gilberto Freyre studied under Franz Boas at Columbia University while pursuing a master's degree in political science. Freyre later credited Boas as a primary influence in his work, particularly with respect to Boas's theories on race and culture (Castelo 1998; Freyre 1961). Freyre returned to Brazil and went on to publish widely on issues of Brazilian identity and race theory in relation to Portuguese colonialism. Freyre's work has had markedly different reception histories in Brazil and in Portugal (Almeida 2004; Arenas 2003; Castelo 1998), and the Lusotropicalism adopted in Portugal was inflected with a notably Portuguese nationalist bent (Castelo 1998: 107). Unlike in Brazil, where Freyre's work was politically influential as early as the 1930s, it was not until the 1950s and 1960s that the Estado Novo adopted strains of Freyre's Lusotropicalism. It did so in response to increasing international pressure regarding its "colonial situation" and thereby reversed decades of justifying a negative stance on miscegenation on moral and biological terms (with the assistance of Portuguese biological anthropology) by celebrating miscegenation as a sign of racial tolerance and diversity (Castelo 1998: 109–15). Freyre links miscegenation to "love" and this Portuguese proclivity for love to early contact with "difference" vis-à-vis the five-hundred-year presence of the Moors in Portugal:

> Portuguese contacts with the tropics have nearly always had a
> different configuration: convenience achieved through love.
> Drama, conflict, pain, anguish, and suffering have not been
> lacking in these contacts; but they have seldom been without love:
> the love of a man for a coloured woman and for a hot country, to
> ease and sweeten bitterness in clashes of interests which sheer
> convenience however great, cannot avoid or mitigate in relations
> between human groups, any more than between individuals. . . .
> I am one of those who attribute the ability of the Portuguese to
> unite themselves with the tropics for love, not convenience, to the
> close contacts between the Portuguese in Europe and the Moors.
> The Portuguese must have absorbed values from the Moors. . . . In
> the hot countries overseas the Portuguese were to find exaggerated
> or intensified the colours and forms of women and landscapes,
> flavours, scents, sensations, qualities in the soil and culture values
> that they knew already in less intense, lively and less crude forms
> in the parts of Portugal most deeply marked by Moorish occupa-
> tion. (Freyre 1961: 46)

Thus, the Estado Novo, in light of Salazar's will to maintain the vestiges of a rapidly fracturing empire, adopted strains of Freyre's theories
of Lusotropicalism (or the unique mode of Luso colonization), whose
discourse of racial tolerance; cultural hybridity; and the superior, hu-
manizing mode of Portuguese colonization "sociologically" and "scien-
tifically" helped to justify and to lend the colonial project credence. The
particular strain of Lusotropicalism publicly circulated by the Estado
Novo argued that the Portuguese propensity for racial mixing—or the
willingness of Portuguese men to engage in sexual relations with "native" women—was a sign of racial tolerance that resulted in a more har-
monious culturally diverse society (Castelo 1998; Freyre 1961), empire's
libidinous drives inscribing a cartography at the "margins" as feminine.[7]
This colonialist ideology of race was bolstered by the tight linkage of
Portuguese regime-era nation building and Catholicism.[8] This relationship provided the moral underpinning for the "civilizing" mission that
was empire (Vakil 2003).[9] Saudade, as a topos of feeling, mystically sutured state, nation, "history," and colonialist longing.

What do I make of Lusotropicalist fragments, the overdetermined symbolism of the Discoveries, the pedagogies of history (which are simultaneously pedagogies of the soul) delivered through an affective conduit of saudade that at every turn met me in my encounters with fado talk and practice? These are pedagogies of history that sometimes sat uneasily with the lived reality of the racial politics of black and white, of "Africa" and "Portugal," in Lisbon in the early 2000s—a Lisbon where spray-painted on walls in Alfama was graffiti that read "Pretos Fora" (Blacks Out) and "Morte aos Pretos" (Death to the Blacks); where I heard some white people blame black people for an increase in crime on the commuter train that goes from Lisbon to Sintra; where a Cape Verdean *morna* musician I met at a bar in Alfama (where a paper sign tacked on the wall read, "The Anti-Racial Hatred Restaurant") told me, "My dreams for the future are not here. They are there [in Cape Verde]. The Portuguese were horrible to us there. They cut our fingers. Yes, we have saudade; we have much more saudade than the Portuguese."[10]

Four years after the fall of the dictatorship and the official end of colonialism, Gerald Bender (1978: 3), writing about Angola under the Portuguese, commented, "To most non-Portuguese, lusotropicalism is a romantic myth (at best) or an invidious lie (at worst) used to obscure the realities of Portuguese colonialism." He noted that "even today . . . many of the Portuguese who now consider themselves 'anti-colonial' continue to believe in a number of the basic tenets of lusotropicalism." Contemporary anthropological work has argued that in EU Portugal, strands of Lusotropicalist ideologies of *mestiçagem* are recycled to bolster an idea of "multiculturalism" that occludes both colonial and postcolonial realities of race (Fikes 2009) and is deployed in multiple ways in the service of "identity redefinition in an era of globalization" (Almeida 2004: 46).[11]

Strains of Lusotropicalist and ethnic-psychology discourses still formed part of the commonsense dialogue I heard on identity and race from many white Portuguese, particularly within the context of fado. This speaks not only to the circuitous means through which academic and state discourses interanimated one another in twentieth-century Portugal, still in the early twenty-first century, saturating the fabric of public culture, or to the tenacious object ("Portugueseness") that international circuits of anthropology made and remade in dialogue with national and international politics. It speaks also to fado as a site, as a practice, as a genre through which these discourses are gathered, voiced, and rendered public, in no matter how fragmentary a fashion, with a particular salience.

What I am *not* arguing for here is a direct correspondence between Lusotropicalist narratives in the context of fado talk and implicit or explicit beliefs in these same actors regarding (racially, ethnically, culturally) hybrid "origins" in fado. Hermano Vianna (1999: 2) demonstrates how the samba in Brazil was shaped, partly via the influence of Freyre's work and a cross-Atlantic circulation of ideas, as an allegory of a *mestiço* cultural and racial Brazilian national identity beginning in the 1930s.[12] In twentieth-century Portugal, as Almeida (2004: 66) argues, concepts of hybridity or mestiçagem in official discourse (even when positively cast) were usually directed *outward*, to the colonies or Brazil. Within Portugal, the national in part was shaped around tropes of the supposed "purity" of Portuguese blood (Almeida 2004; Castelo 1998; Fikes 2009).[13]

One strain of recurrent talk regarding fado's identity and origins, voiced by some practitioners, was that it is "purely" Portuguese, "from Lisbon." I heard a distilled version of this discourse during the first "international" fado conference, which was held in Lisbon in November 2001. The majority of the panelists and audience members were Portuguese. The Brazilian historian José Ramos Tinhorão spoke on a panel about fado's origins, echoing the thesis of his book *Fado, Dança do Brasil, Cantar de Lisboa* (1994), that the sung Lisbon fado is linked to song and dance forms of Afro-Brazilian influence. A Moroccan vocalist argued for the Arab roots of the poetic ethos of saudade.[14] A heated argument broke out during a round-table discussion that followed with professional fadistas. One fadista, a man in his fifties, shouted, "Fado is our music! Fado is not Arab! Fado is not from Brazil! Fado is Portuguese! Brazil was Portuguese before it was Brazilian!" He attacked Tinhorão's research on the grounds of his "non-Portugueseness": "How can a Brazilian understand our music?"

Strains of highly nationalist talk that rely explicitly on tropes of "purity" fall at an extreme end of a continuum of discourse on fado's origins. At the other end are the multiple arguments I heard from fans, instrumentalists, and fadistas, in both amateur and professional spheres, that celebrated fado's tangled past as Arab, as African, and as Brazilian or that cited Lisbon's position as a port city as a factor that has contributed to fado's mysterious and likely mixed beginnings. But I never once heard anyone correlate fado's potentially mixed origins with Portuguese identity within Portugal. Never once did I hear speculation about hybridity in fado's roots translate into a valuing of mestiçagem outside the context of an outwardly inflected variant of Lusotropicalism. "Fado runs in our [Portuguese] DNA," said a fan at O Jaime. The phrase "Trago fado nas veias" (I carry fado in my veins) recurs in fado lyrics and fado talk.

ANXIETIES: "PORTUGAL AS EUROPE'S AFRICA"

Two black boys wearing white swimming trunks dive into an expanse of blue sea in the Portuguese Algarve above a caption that reads "Hidden Portugal," on the cover of the February 2002 issue of *Condé Nast Traveler* magazine. One of Lisbon's major daily newspapers, *O Diário de Notícias* (February 3, 2002), runs a miniature version of the cover along with an editorial note that complains, "Do they [*Condé Nast*] think Portugal is in Africa?"

During an interval of a fado session at O Jaime, I speak with a Scottish expatriate who sits across the table from me. We talk about the expansion of the European Union into eastern Europe; whether Turkey should belong to the European Union; and the growing population of eastern European immigrants in Lisbon. He leans toward me and under his breath he says, "[Eastern European immigration] is good for them [the Portuguese]. It will improve their blood. One of my students tells me that the Portuguese are just a bunch of North Africans." A well-known journalist later tells me, "We [the Portuguese] are to Europeans what the blacks in the United States are to the whites." A Portuguese friend tells me that he hates the British because they treated him badly— "They beat me"—when he was in England. He explains this treatment by invoking a stereotype that positions Portugal as a particular "South" to Europe's "North." He tells me, "We [Portugal] are Europe's Africa."

These are undisguised anxieties of in-betweeness and marginality, anxieties that go beyond the simply geographical or economic in a place where "Europeanness" (which is always implicitly "white") is something strived for, argued for, defended. Many of Lisbon's black population live on the edge in a city already on the edge. When I asked a man in his forties educated in political science at Portugal's most illustrious university why I saw hardly any non-white Portuguese in the annual popular marches (*marchas populares*) in Lisbon, he exclaimed, "They are not Portuguese!" The reproduction of *Condé Nast Traveler*'s "Hidden Portugal" cover along with the anxious editorial evokes race's simultaneous overwhelming presence alongside its invisibility, a Portuguese attempt at self-definition in light of centuries of interrelationships in which "Africa," no matter how sensualized, how desired, how dreamt for, always but always carries a burden of undesirable marginality.

PLACING FADO'S "ARAB"

While the theory of Afro-Brazilian influence on fado has academic "objectivity" and the proof of historical research behind it, and while I occasionally heard talk from participants in fado's worlds that marked the neighborhood of Alfama as the place where freed black slaves went to live (and thus as one of the birthplaces of fado), I heard much more talk that connected fado to "Arabness" (by both Portuguese and non-Portuguese people in fado-related contexts). For many, the proof was often in vocal style. At O Jaime one Saturday afternoon, a fado-loving amateur astrologist sat next to me and listened to fado. Precisely at the moment at which the fadista sang an extended voltinha, he whispered, "Do you hear that? Fado is Arab." One quiet weekday before the after-work rush, Jaime was playing a CD of instrumental arrangements of some of Amália's popular hits on the sound system behind the bar. As I sang along with the fado "Ai Mouraria," the man across the table commented, "Fado is Arab." "Why?" I asked. "Because of the *ais*," he answered.[15] "That sounds Arab," says a British tourist sitting at the table next to mine listening to fado at the elite fado club O Senhor Vinho one evening. "I don't like it, it is too melancholy." That the practice of using extended voltinhas, or vocal ornaments, in fado was first popularized by Amália Rodrigues in the 1950s and 1960s is not generally known or commented on by listeners. Rather, for some listeners, these musical moments are marked as having an *Arab* sound and pointed to as proof of fado's Moorish origins and its birth in the neighborhood of Mouraria.[16]

Tourist literature proudly describes the Moorish street plan of Alfama and the Arab derivation of its name while also marking it as Lisbon's most "typical" and "traditional" Portuguese neighborhood. Fado fans and singers spoke much more to me about fado's associations with Arab origins than with black African or Brazilian origins. An idea of an Arab civilization, with its indelible marks on Lisbon's topography and place names, indexes both the ancient past of place and Portuguese

Christian triumph (over the "Arab"), just as "Arab" when referenced as "origin" in fado carries the weight of a classical high civilization. While "the Arab" might be exoticized in the interpretation of a vocal turn or as an affective origin for fado's sadness, this kind of exoticization necessarily contains its own alterity. In 2002, I ride in the back of a car one evening with a group of fadistas from O Jaime on the way to a special amateur fado night in the suburbs. As we wind through the narrow streets in the city center, near the neighborhood of Mouraria, one of them asks me, laughing, "Aren't you afraid to go to Mouraria? That is where the Taliban live."[17] North African immigrant men wearing turbans who stood talking outside the former Church of the Holy Inquisition (now the Church of São Domingos) in Mouraria might jokingly be labeled "Taliban." *Aren't you afraid to go to Mouraria?*

The "Arab," the "Moor," and "Islam" are mercurial and always charged signifiers in Portuguese political histories, unofficial and official, and sometimes, the three terms are conflated. During the Estado Novo, the official stance toward Islam and "Arabness" shifted radically. From the mid-1960s through the early 1970s, the Salazar regime reoriented an ideology that had previously represented Portuguese history and identity as exclusively Christian toward recognition of "Muslims" as Portuguese while also celebrating Portugal's Islamic history (Vakil 2003). AbdoolKarim Vakil demonstrates that this reorientation with respect to the Portugueseness of Islam was strategically formulated to assist in mobilizing Muslim populations in the colonies against internal Marxist insurgents: "Portuguese Muslim identities were thus forged in an ambiguous and far-from-innocent strategic collusion" (Vakil 2003: 40). He goes on to show how the official remembering of Portugal's Islamic heritage has been a project of the new democracy. The discourse on Arabness in fado has a long history. Yet it carries different valences depending on the historical moment in which it is situated, its signification always animated by a shifting and complex identity politics of nation and state, self and other.

SAUDADE AS ORIGINARY TROPE FOR FEELING

A profusion of saudades in multiple registers of feeling: saudade as a return to an unchanging pre-industrial agricultural past to serve fascism; a saudade that eclipses the mess and movement of history in favor of a story of beginnings that justifies empire; saudade for what might lie beyond that bend where the river meets the sea; saudade for a summer fruit in winter; saudade for loved ones; saudade as a sickness that physically hurts; the saudades that "gave birth" to fado; the saudade of the Cape Verdean morna musician (*We have much more saudade than the Portuguese*); saudade for saudade. Saudade exists as a way of being in the present and *feeling* the past (as history or as memory—or the often un-demarcated terrain between them) while dreaming for a future; as a philosophical-historic-poetic topos of longing. When it is expressed through fado, saudade gains affective force and lability of significance via musical sound and experience. Saudade as expressed in fado works as a trope that renders history both affective and soulful.

Throughout the twentieth century, saudade has featured as one of the most dominant tropes in both scholarly and popular writing about Portuguese identity.[18] Leal (2000b: 3–11) traces a literary genealogy of saudade to the fifteenth century and describes the ways in which it was increasingly shaped as a nationalist ideology in the early twentieth century, particularly in relation to the artistic, literary, and philosophical movement of *saudosismo* of 1912–26, which also drew on ethnological portrayals of supposed characteristics of the folk. As a backlash against cosmopolitanism, saudosismo promoted "a cult of Portuguese things reflecting the true 'Portuguese soul'" and ideologically bolstered the nationalist agenda of the First Republic. Leal argues that it was also during the early 1900s that saudade became attached to fado.[19] Later, during Salazar's Estado Novo (1926–74), saudade ideologically came to broadly signify the sense of feeling, history, uniqueness, and time of the Portuguese people and nation and the "essence" of the "Portuguese soul." If saudade lent spirit and soul to the "body" of the Portuguese nation (Leal 2000b)—a soul that contained salient aspects of the past and history while gesturing to the eternal—the expressive practice of fado articulated the link between body and soul in sound. Leal argues that in postregime Portugal, saudade (like fado) became "politically incorrect" for those in power, but saudade is now symbolically appropriated to take on different valences by different social groups as a way of "being national" (Leal 2000b: 14).[20]

In a special commemorative section of Lisbon's *O Diário de Notícias* published on the third anniversary of the death of Amália Rodrigues, the musicologist Rui Vieira Nery spoke about popularly held ideas about fado's origins: "All great genres of music create a mythology. As part of a process to legitimate the fado, it was necessary to create a myth of historically remote origins. . . . An Arab origin is out of the question, just as is a medieval origin relating to the troubadours. These are fantasies. The Portuguese navigators playing the guitarra on the high sea—these are completely invented, romantic ideas. [These refutations are based on] objective, historical data. But I am for freedom of religion. If people want to believe that Don Afonso Henriques [the first king of Portugal] sang fado, that is material of faith."[21] While some origin narratives may be the "material of faith," for some fado practitioners and fans they function as originary tropes for feeling that enable expression as fadista. In these stories of origin, feeling is emplaced; feeling that positions the singer, instrumentalist, and listener in relation to wider histories and to ideas of belonging; feeling that links imaginaries of the past to the shaping of present and future.

I met the amateur fadista Maria José Melo during weekend fado sessions at the Tasca do Jaime in 2002; at the time, she was in her early fifties. Her repertoire and her performance style stood out. When she sang, she used highly theatricalized facial expressions and hand gestures to underscore the feeling of her words. She sang two unusual fados, one in which she voiced saudade for her former home in Angola (Melo is a white Portuguese who settled in Angola and returned after the revolution) and another whose lyrics lamented changes to Lisbon's cityscape. When I interviewed Melo, she passionately narrated her version of fado's story: "Fado was born from the spirit of *ventura* (fate, destiny, risk) of the Portuguese people who through the Discoveries gave new worlds to the world. Or fado was born from the saudade of those who remained for those who left or from the saudade of those who left for those whom they left behind. And perhaps from there, fado was born as a song of tears (*choro*), a song of saudade, a song of distance. Perhaps the people who sang felt closer to those who were far away."[22] Saudade, as poetic/historical topos, here indexes a particular kind of Portuguese soulfulness; it gestures to pivotal events in the definition of an official Portuguese historical narrative (Leal 2000b) and at the same time allows for the individual expression of seemingly infinite desires, memories, and senses of loss and absence.

The fadista Olga de Sousa told me, "We are born into the fado, Fado is a state of the soul (*estado de alma*). Fados are dramas of which almost all are sad. Fado has to be sung with the heart; you need to feel nostalgia. Fado is sad because fado was born almost for certain in Mouraria. Where is Mouraria? That was the place of the Moors, and they had saudade for their *terra* (land, birthplace)."[23] While I heard this particular version of an origin narrative only from Olga—one in which fado's "essential" sadness was linked to the saudade of the displacement of the Moors—(and it was not clear whether she was referring to the five-hundred-year Moorish "occupation" or to the banishing of the Moors to Mouraria after the Christian Reconquest), this story worked as a way of situating herself and her individual expression as fadista within a long-term history in which "history" does not just signify officially remembered sequences of events with respect to nationalist projects. Rather, the primary symbolic value of history lies in its emotional valence vis-à-vis saudade. Saudade in this case refers to both spatial and temporal distance. Fado as genre often serves as a catalyst for retellings of history writ large via the soulful conduit of saudade in which "history" both stands in for feeling and gives rise to its expression. Saudade's fluid logic sutures circulating fragments of public history, senses of place, and mythologies of origins to *feeling*, feeling which is then rendered soulful through sung vocality.

REMEMBERING VASCO DA GAMA

Jaime dims the lights as we settle in to listen again after a long interval. The guitarra and viola start playing, a little tentatively, sounding slightly off key. The instrumentalists look almost bored as they try out the fado "Júlia Florista" for the fadista Maria José Melo. She stands with her feet planted to the floor, hands clasped in front of her chest, and closes her eyes. The instrumentalists finish the introduction, the viola rhythmically marking the bass line as the guitarrista strums the first statement of the melody of the refrain. As Maria José begins to sing with a low grainy voice, her hands follow the gestures of her voice and breath, furling, unfurling, rising, falling, coming again to rest in a position almost of prayer. Her eyes open, close, open again. Standing in front of the instrumentalists, she shifts her weight, sometimes taking a step forward, sometimes back. Her face twists, screws up in intensity, conveying theatrically stylized smiles, grimaces, passion. She sings to the melody of "Júlia Florista," a well-known fado canção.[24] Yet Maria

José sings different lyrics, a poem whose lament critiques current changes to the landscape of Lisbon, "Lisboa, Não Mudes Assim" (Lisbon, Don't Change like This):[25]

Mudar sim Lisboa
Mas mudar à toa
Não é bem pensado
No crescer e progresso
É um mau processo
Esquecer o passado
Do povo donzela
Tão linda tão bela
Escuta o meu recado
Não percas a raça
Vais ficar sem graça
Se não tens cuidado

O Monumental
Centro de cultura
Seguro sinal
Deste mal sem cura
Ali no Saldanha
Partido esventrado
Foi capa de manha
E logo apanha um supermercado

E fora de portas
Onde eram as hortas
Há cimento armado
Se não os detêm
De certo que vêm
Nada é poupado
Se for nossa força
Salvamos da forca
O Parque Mayer
Serão preservados costumes sagrados
Se o povo quiser

E já o comboio
Vai à outra banda

Ficam cacilheiros
Sós na corda bamba

REFRAIN
Tens a Vasco da Gama
O Parque das Nações
De tudo se esquecem que desaparecem brados e pregões.

———————

Change, Lisbon, change
But to change haphazardly
Is not a good idea
In growth and progress
It is a bad process
To forget the past
[Lisbon] maiden of the people
So beautiful, so good
Listen carefully to my reprimand
Don't lose the race
Or you will be left without grace
If you do not take care

Monumental[26]
Center of culture
A sure sign
Of this evil without cure
Here in Saldanha[27]
Broken and ripped apart
It was the cloak of cunning
And later caught a supermarket

And outdoors
Where there were the *hortas*[28]
There are cement buildings
If this does not stop
It is certain
Nothing will be saved
If but by our force
We are able to save from the gallows
The Parque Mayer[29]

Sacred customs will be preserved
If that is what the people wish

And already the train
Goes to the other side [of the Tagus River]
And the ferries between Lisbon and Cacilhas[30]
Remain alone in limbo

You have Vasco da Gama
The Park of Nations[31]
In the midst of it all, everyone forgets that *brados* and *pregões* are
disappearing.[32]

Maria José repeats the last verse twice. Between the repetitions is a refrain in which she hums, gesturing with her hands, encouraging people to sing along. The first time, she renders the last verse straight; the second time, she begins a long rubato on the name "Vasco da Gama" and ornaments the "a" in "Vasco" with vocal turns, drops her dynamic slightly, then slides luxuriously downward into the next syllable. She prolongs the word "Gama," emphasizing it by swaying her shoulders from side to side. She continues the rubato into "Parque das Nações," gathers breath, throws her head back, closes her eyes, and forcefully sings the last line. A regular at O Jaime, Iracema Oliveira, shouts, "Bem!" (Well done!), and the house erupts in applause.

The Vasco da Gama commuter bridge and shopping mall were built in 1998 in conjunction with the World Exposition in Lisbon, which commemorated the five-hundred-year anniversary of the discovery of the sea route to India. Abandoned factories and warehouses along the city's eastern waterfront were demolished to make way for hyper-futuristic, gleaming glass-and-steel structures—a commercial and recreational space named Parque das Nações that was to help revitalize the new Lisbon. In her performance, Maria José prolongs, ornaments, and foregrounds the climactic phrase "Vasco da Gama" with hand, facial, and vocal gestures. While "Vasco da Gama" in this context refers literally to the bridge over the Tagus River, it also evokes the adjacent shopping mall and the Portuguese navigator and hero. In terms of its content, "Lisboa, Não Mudes Assim" figures against a ground of at least three traditional subcategories of fado lyrics. First, it is one of many fados whose lyrics celebrate places in Lisbon—that is, fados that exist symbiotically with particular Lisbon places (see chapter 3). Second, by recalling Vasco da Gama (the person), the song references a type of fado that glorifies Lisbon as the seat of colonial prowess. Last, "Lisboa, Não Mudes Assim" participates in a long tradition of fados whose lyrics are grounded in an aesthetic ethos of saudade.

The lyrics, by Manuel Calado Tomé, refer to the destruction and transformation of specific cultural sites and anxiously lament a loss of cultural history wrought by modernization and change too quickly seized. The poet's saudade for the past is not for the regime. Rather, he uses the trope of saudade to get listeners to think about the haphazardness of current modernization, the transformation of a cityscape and consequent shaping of the historical imaginary.[33] In other words, what does it mean that Vasco da Gama's *lieux de mémoire* (Nora 1989) are a commuter bridge and a shopping mall? The moment of heightened feeling on the phrase "Vasco da Gama" simultaneously calls forth multiple historical imaginaries and ideas about history. As a vestige of Estado Novo state making, a popular recounting of Portuguese historical narrative almost always starts with the colonial Discoveries. Thus, "Vasco da Gama" is a call to origin of empire in which lies the power of nation.

Yet this stylistic moment for some, where vocal turns function as an icon of the Arab, calls on a different history: that of the five-hundred-year presence of the Moors in Portugal. In warning of the havoc that rampant building and destruction are wreaking on a sense of Lisbon's past, this call also directs attention to the material shaping of Lisbon's present sense of history. These calls are made sensate—and thus, soulful—via the strategic placement of the phrase within the structure of the song that calls Maria José to foreground the phrase through the way in which she *styles* it.

"Before being thought, saudade was sung; it is prisoner of the lyricism which first gave it voice" (Lourenço 2001: 92). Eduardo Lourenço distinguishes the power of song, the poesis of the lyric as set apart, almost granting to them a primal magic that he denies to thought (and in this way he posits yet another version of sound and music as natural, as timeless). Trapped within the confines of aesthetic form and the modulations of the sonorous voice, Lourenço's saudade cannot escape the signification of feeling. I suggest that the power of fado as genre to function as a symbol, or as a node that unleashes by association individually inflected variants of history, is symbiotically linked to the lyric—to the affective, sonic, sensual, and storied aspects of the genre as musical and poetic form and practice—but that lyricism always implies agency and possibilities for improvisation and change. The power of the lyric as aesthetic form lies in the ways in which form is at once socially and individually inflected via style. Different styles in this sense often index "competing values and ideas" (Meintjes 2003: 10; see also Bauman and Briggs 1990, 1992; Feld 1988; Hebdige 1979; Urban 1991). In fado, the temporally and emotionally multivalent force of saudade as a poetic topos fuses with the ambiguity and polysemy of the musical referent—or the polyindexicality of musical sense making (Feld et al. 2004; Samuels 2004; Turino 1999). Saudade and song, powerful when unleashed in combination, affectively fuse in fado, shaping a material, specifically *musical*, sense of history and memory in relation to place, one that is anything but straightforward or linear.

History in the Entrelinhas *(Meaning between the Lines)*

There was still a sense in Lisbon among some of the older generation, who were outside fado's scenes, in the late 1990s and early 2000s, that fado was something tired. There was still a sense that fado smelled a little of the Salazar and Caetano regimes and of the trilogy of "Fs"—fado, the religious cult of Fátima, and football—that people talked about as having bolstered the dictatorship in its late stages by mollifying "the people." The Fado Museum in Alfama had just opened, and in the 1990s the careers of Mísia and Cristina Branco had catapulted fado onto the world music stage. (However, Mariza's career, one that would amplify interest in fado both locally and internationally, was just getting under way.) Fado's candidacy for recognition by the UNESCO as "intangible cultural heritage" had not yet begun. There were the missing generations at O Jaime and at other celebrated sites for amateur fado in the early 2000s. Although there were many adults older than fifty, there were few in their thirties and forties. One Portuguese man in his late forties, a language tutor educated at the University of Coimbra, told me that his generation, who had come of age around the time of the 1974 revolution, listened to the Beatles and jazz but certainly not to fado, because "fado stood for the establishment." Some people risked their lives or went to prison for song or poetry or for party affiliation; sang fado behind closed doors or sold recordings on the black market. Then there are those whom others accuse of having had the courage to denounce policies of the Estado Novo with their music and with their voices only after it had officially ended.

There is a certain romance in writing about music (or performance) as resistance. At the same time, there is a certain seduction in the conceit of "national song," a persuasive force in the symbolic logics that so often seemingly bind nation to a particular kind of song genre or music.[34] But a musical genre as lived and performed rarely stays so cleanly within the lines as to be only about resistance, or only about the inculcation of a "national" to whatever end (and there are also multiple ways of feeling "national" that may or may not link to ideologies of a state apparatus, past or present). "History is messy for people who must live it" (Trouillot 1995: 110). No matter what the official historical documents reveal, the texture of the quotidian for most people rarely lines up with the story as officially told, particularly under a long regime of surveillance. In the stories people told me about its places, its social worlds, its affects, its banality, or its beauty, fado sustained almost impossible contradictions when it came to questions of the national, of the dictatorship, and of resistance to that dictatorship. Sometimes these contradictions were sustained within the voice of one individual.

"Fado is our national song," exclaimed a middle-age female listener in O Jaime. "Salazar hated fado," said a respected male fadista in his fifties. "He wanted fighting songs." Another male professional fadista in his fifties said in 2003, "Fado is the principal cultural music of our country, but the people with power detest it, they hate it, they are ashamed to be Portuguese (vergonha de ser português). I went to the United States to sing because they invited me. They want us there." The manager of an expensive restaurant in Alfama, that hosted fado evenings, in the early 2000s, attended by some audience members who proudly claimed bloodlines to the former Portuguese monarchy, told me that her venue began as a place for people who thought that the 25 of April Revolution was a bad thing for Portugal, and Salazar a good thing. One of fado's star professional icons of the past looked me in the eye and said, "Fado was always a revolutionary song."

Just as fado talk, practice, and venues collect both Estado Novo state-making stories and revolutionary stories, they sometimes also absorb silences. For those who are passionate about fado, silence can be a rapture of listening, an opening in a musical dialogue that renders improvisation possible, an aural marker of soulful or respectful hearing, or a qualitative marker of authenticity within a venue or a protocol of etiquette, where a silence during the performance of fado is broken only with a gasp of approval at a moment of intense musical feeling. Then there are other types of silence: those that speak in embodied gestures, gestures that contain, hold back, or cast about furtively; silences that deafen. "I don't like fado," the Cape Verdean morna musician told me in 2003. "it is fascist, all of that silence. They even make you turn off your cell phones." "Tourists: Respect the Portuguese Silence or Go to Spain!" reads graffiti along the walls at the *miradouro* (viewpoint) of Portas do Sol in Alfama, where tourists sat sipping wine in the summer of 2007 (plate 2). There are so many registers and qualities of silence, one sometimes mediating another.

I often heard Salazar and the Estado Novo muted, downplayed: "The Portuguese dictatorship was a light one, *levezinha*, and nothing compared to Mussolini's Italy, Franco's Spain, Hitler's Germany." As I waited at the bank in an endless line that weaved out into the blazing sun, I overheard an older woman say, "This kind of thing would not have happened under Salazar." I heard the same kind of sentiment expressed when people in my neighborhood talked about how the outsides of houses were going to hell or when they talked about drugs, crime, the bad economy, or even race: *There were not as many blacks here before the 25 de Abril* [1974]. I asked a listener at O Jaime—a lawyer who was twenty-two when the revolution took place—why so much silence surrounds the memory of the dictatorship. "I will tell you why," he said. "Compared with Franco, this dictatorship was really not so bad; toward the end, it was almost a democracy." Then his body and voice came closer to me and hushed as if telling a secret: "For some, Salazar was *querido* (the darling one); but the problem was the colonies."[35] I walk with João, a retired store clerk and the husband of one of O Jaime's regular fadistas, Luisa, to a fado session at the association Vai Tu in the neighborhood of Bica in 2003. Luisa and another fadista friend trail behind us, and we stop to look in a bookstore window on the corner. João sees a book on Marcelo Caetano and says to me, "Yes, some things were better then. The only thing was that we couldn't talk."[36] "During the time of the PIDE [secret police], there were ears (*ouvidos*) everywhere," says another fadista.

A professional fadista in his mid-fifties tells me, "Salazar was the Portuguese Franco, the Portuguese Hitler, the Portuguese Mussolini. We had disappearances, thousands of them. . . . Immediately after the revolution, people talked about this, but now no one is interested. The Portuguese people have no respect for their own memory." In the thick sociality of the everyday, where in Lisbon's core historic neighborhoods many people of the older generations were born in the places where they still reside, nested within neighborhood social networks forged in childhood, history recedes, only to suddenly emerge again. People still spoke about the PIDE, sometimes jokingly (to a friend, "Hey, stay out of my business, who are you anyways, the PIDE?") or in seriousness (quietly among intimates, "You know, they say that so and so was a member of the PIDE").[37] More than one interlocutor on the left who had lived through the Estado Novo expressed something along the lines of, "The problem is that, unlike in Spain, we had no war. We shed no blood. So everything still remains here, under the surface."

I asked older fadistas and listeners with diverse sets of experiences in relation to fado what fado performance was like during the Estado Novo. In the taped interviews that remain, sometimes a voice audibly lowers in answering or there is a sudden gap where the speaker asked me to stop recording when talk about censorship led to talk about the gendered mores tacitly enforced under Salazar. But mostly I am impressed by the silences. Some people in the early 2000s told me that talk about the Estado Novo still felt taboo. Even in venues like O Jaime, and in the extended amateur fado network where many people of the generation who experienced the dictatorship boasted former affiliations or sympathies with the Communist Party and where some fadistas still sang fados by revolutionary poets, I learned from people's body language and tones and dynamics of voice (as voices would inevitably quiet) that open discussion of the Estado Novo in fado's public spaces was still uncommon. One amateur fadista in his eighties told me he had been a communist during the dictatorship and had sung uncensored lyrics in Alfama within the context of amateur fado, with someone always at the door on the lookout for the PIDE. I asked him about the silence. He implied that professional fadistas had "nothing to say" because they all had just been doing what they were supposed to be doing: singing censored song. But that was not necessarily so.

The everyday worlds I came to trespass in via fado, particularly among older generations, were a tangle of multiple surfaces with multiple undersides and with stories that shifted as I traced them along their circuits. Multiple actors claimed that archival fado recordings belonging to the *Emissora Nacional* (the national radio during the Estado Novo), and to other media institutions, were destroyed in the immediate aftermath of the revolution by a sector of the political left, who at the time associated fado with the dictatorship but now champion fado. "For that reason, the young singers today have no history," said one woman. "They destroyed masters of recordings of Amália!" a man told me, holding my gaze. These statements were made with passion then just as vehemently were denied by others.

I sat with the fadista Fátima Fernandes in her living room, her speech interspersed with singing. "I am not afraid to talk. The first fado I learned was a revolutionary fado that my father taught me. I remember the way he used to put a half-filled glass of water on top of the radio to catch *Radio Moscow*. I have saudade for the days we used to sing the fado hidden behind closed doors. But I have no saudade for the regime."[38] People talked to me about lyrics written to evade the censors but that contained meanings that were *subentendidos*, heard between the lines. I heard stories of fados that started when a member of PIDE or someone sympathetic to the regime was in the room, only for the lyrics to take a sharp turn after the person left. I heard about a fadista escaping a fado session through a window, just in the nick of time, with the police on his heels. I interviewed a working-class couple in their eighties who sang every Saturday evening at Tasca do Careca's celebrated amateur fado nights, she bedecked in costume jewelry and a gown; he in a well-pressed suit. We sat in their apartment across the river from Lisbon (in the *margem sul*). An hour or so into our conversation, the man pulled a Portuguese translation of Karl Marx from a bookshelf. "Do you know who he was?" he asked. "I hid volumes by Marx and Lenin inside my piano," another fadista said to me. I found that a number of the most active fadistas of the older generation (many of them working class), who constituted the core of Lisbon's amateur fado scene in the early 2000s, identified themselves as communists during the Estado Novo. Regardless of whether they spoke to me about their political party affiliations during the regime, they often shared a sentiment that the government and those in power had *always* disrespected fado and that they still did. Some people told me, "Salazar *hated* fado!" "Salazar did not like fado," one fadista explained. "But at the same time, it wasn't a favorite of the left."

For more than a year in 2002–2003, I saw tiny pillows advertising an immensely popular musical about the life of Amália Rodrigues hanging from the rearview mirrors of Lisbon taxis. (I knew people who had seen the musical more than ten times.) One night, on the way to a fado coaching session in Marvila, I noticed that the taxi did not have a pillow and asked the driver about it. He did not want the free tickets he would get if he advertised the musical in his cab. "I don't like Amália," he told me. "She was a fascist. She helped the dictatorship. I had friends who were tortured. I have women friends who still have cigarette burns on their breasts. I lost friends; I lost members of my family."[39] I said, "But I heard that Amália secretly gave money to the Communist Party. He shook his head. "No, no. It's propaganda." His outburst disrupted the silence to which I had grown accustomed. "Things are more complicated than they seem, but none of this is important today. None of this is important now."

FADO'S AFFECTS FOR NATION?

The idea that Salazar "hated" fado has some historical substantiation in official discourses early in the Estado Novo regarding the unsuitability of fado as a "national" song. It was considered by some to be too emasculating, too weak, too sad. The frontispiece to *Fado: Canção de Vencidos* (Fado: Song of the Vanquished) (published lectures that were broadcast by the Emissora Nacional in 1936) reads: "Boys, don't sing the fado!" (Moita 1936). Two decades later, state officials still considered fado suspect (this time for its degeneracy, urbanity, for a sadness linked to "Arabness") and unsuitable as a national form.[40] But this attitude predates the Estado Novo. Writing in the late 1800s, the Portuguese ethnologist Rocha Peixoto describes a group of "emaciated" and "drunken" men he saw on the street, some playing the guitar, one singing fado. Peixoto goes on to claim that fado reflects the "temperament of the [Portuguese] people," and characterizes this temperament as "dirty," "vagabond," "hypocritical," and "idle." He concludes, "Contemplating these groups, one can come only to one sad conclusion: there goes the Nation" (Peixoto 1997 [1897]: 335–36, quoted in Leal 2008: 39). Official cultural policy toward fado shifted during the Estado Novo, and it has shifted continuously since, dependent on its perceived symbolic and financial value to projects of city and state.

Nery (2004: 187) argues that during the first half of the Estado Novo, the professionalization of fado was codified and "accelerated," manifest in the formation of *casas de fado* and the strictures put on professionals, who were required to pass an audition and carry a card.[41] At the same time, he argues, the censorship that was enforced, while somewhat unsystematic and arbitrary, had the effect of "subtly silencing" socialist and *operário* (workers' movement) lyrics that were prevalent in the early twentieth century and fixing a majority of lyrics temporally in the past, rather than in the present or future, shaping new founding mythologies and a "refoundation" of the genre (Nery 2004: 191, 238, 201).[42] But he argues that until the postwar era, the regime was ambivalent about fado. In the 1950s, the Estado Novo began to utilize fado explicitly as a means through which to mobilize the public (in a populist sense), and professional casas de fado emerged as key sites for international tourism. Only then did fado become the "national song" (Nery 2004: 228, 240).

One of Nery's most interesting claims is that the censorship enforced on fado lyrics during the early years of the Estado Novo ruptured the link between misery and social injustice that could be found in lyrics of earlier fados of social protest. Thus, the voicing of suffering through fado became about the suffering of the *singular individual*, "inevitable tragedies," evacuating the expression of suffering as a cause for sociopolitical action (Nery 2004: 192). One way to extend his argument might be to think at the symbolic level about suffering as voiced in song as moving from the realm of affect (as sociopolitical and circulatory) to the realm of emotion (as supposedly personal). However, it was precisely via the normalizing strictures the regime enforced on fado during this time that a new social affect (and a differently inflected subject) was produced, many subjects in tandem all singing lyrics about their own, individual suffering, fatalistically.

The increase in international tourism in the 1950s had a powerful effect on fado as *affect*—in reinforcing its "typical" or "folkloric" aspects at tourist sites (*casas típicas* or *casas de fado*; see Nery 2004: 229) or, in the opinion of some fadistas, making its lyrics more *choradinho* (tearful; see Costa and Guerreiro 1984: 98)—shifting the sentiment of the lyrics toward clichés about romantic intimacy and loss and away from themes that critiqued the sociopolitical status quo. António Firmino da Costa and Maria das Dores Guerreiro (1984) analyze what they term *fados de contraste* (fados of contrast), which they often heard sung in working-class amateur fado in Alfama at the time of their fieldwork in the late

1970s. These lyrics set up powerful contrasts based on social class and usually had a moral embedded within them. Costa and Guerreiro (1984: 185) describe these lyrics as expressing "the sentiment of revolt against the rich, but also an envy, and the secret or explicit hope of an individual ascending the social scale to a place of privilege." They also note that these lyrics of contrast are usually presented within a larger framework of fatalism, a lamentation of the impossibility of escaping one's social position. Armando Santos, one of the interlocutors in Costa's and Guerreiro's ethnography, speaks of a change in lyrics in relation to both censorship and the rise of international tourism in the professional casas de fado during the regime:

> When before the 25 de Abril [revolution], in the time of fascism, tourism began to interest [the government], fado began to express more indirectly. It was all kisses in the eyes, "I love you," and "You left me," and " I feel jealous." And then people started to like this kind of fado. But that [kind of fado] doesn't say anything to me . . . but they didn't let you write any other way. . . . The people involved today in amateur fado still sing these [other] lyrics [fados of contrast]. In amateur fado, you hear this [kind of fado], because the majority of people who go to the [professional] casas de fado go only to hear these "little kisses in the ears and the eyes" (*beijinhos nos ouvidos e nos olhos*). (Armando Santos, quoted in Costa and Guerreiro 1984: 98–99)

In Santos's narrative, a syrupy romantic love ("little kisses in the ears") is one of the common currencies of fado tourism under the late dictatorship, a currency that finds its way into taste preferences and is naturalized, traveling into fado circuits and repertoires. In this fado, "love" and "music" communicate "beyond language" to the universal human subject, something of the "essence" of the melancholic Portuguese soul. Fado as "love" emerges again in the tourist promotional below from 1973, in the U.S.-based *Rotarian* magazine, for an iconic luxury fado venue in Alfama: "Stay in the new Sheraton Hotel, lunch at bargain-priced A Quinta (The Farmhouse) restaurant, reached by an elevator built by Monsieur Eiffel, who erected the Tower in Paris (prepare for a breathtaking view), and at night dine and listen to *fado* at Taverna do Embuçado in the Alfama, old Moorish quarter of the city. *Fado* means fate, and as a waiter once explained to me, the songs are about 'love and other things.'"[43] "Love," in both examples, works to foreclose overt political critique as heard at the local level and as a foreign export that is "beyond translation." ("Love" and loss continue in the contemporary moment as common currencies in which fado traffics when presented outside Portugal.)

HISTORICITY OF VENUE

There are some professional fado venues and practices linked more to a memory of the Estado Novo than others. The Taverna do Embuçado, which in the early 2000s was still one of Lisbon's most elite and expensive professional fado restaurants, was hidden off a dark alleyway in Alfama, just down the street from a number of amateur fado venues and tascas. A suited valet stood off the main street helping guests park.[44] One could hear illustrious fadistas sing there, including Celeste Rodrigues, the sister of Amália. Food was fancy, served in small quantities on large, shining plates. Listening to fado at the Embuçado was prohibitively expensive for the majority of Portuguese. It was prohibitive for me. On most of the occasions I visited, the majority of listeners were foreign tourists.

The manager, Pedro Guerra, who had recently taken over in 2003 and who appeared to be in his early forties, told me that during the 1960s and '70s, the Embuçado had been symbolic of the regime and the old monarchy. Immediately after the revolution (25 de Abril), it was ransacked and occupied by workers. He continued,

> It functioned for a time as a cooperative that served light refreshments (not as a casa de fado). Then it went into bankruptcy and closed. It was only opened and renovated in 1993, under new management. When it was reopened in 1993, it was renovated to appear exactly as it had in 1966, when it first opened, with the same kind of furniture and décor. It doesn't have some of . . .
> the silver and the antique items that it had during that time, but the heart and the style of the place were maintained. When the Embuçado opened [in 1966], it offered the city a *different style of hearing fado*, with luxurious service. Maybe for this reason, or for others, the regime ended up using this venue for practically all of its international guests. In that period, it was used by the regime for events, for visits.[45]

When I tried to confirm the story of the workers' occupying the Embuçado with a professional fadista in her sixties who had sung there in its heyday, she adamantly denied its veracity and turned away, refusing to engage. The manager of another long-standing professional casa de fado told me that his venue had also been occupied in the aftermath of the regime. Fernanda Maria, one of the major fado stars on the national radio during the last decades of the dictatorship and the owner of the preeminent casa de fado Lisboa à Noite in the neighborhood of Bairro Alto, spoke to me about the difficult conditions for the business of fado in the years following the revolution.[46] An instrumentalist in his sixties, who I met at a professional casa de fado in Alfama that endured through the Estado Novo to the present, expressed how he had saudade for the days in which Portuguese people (not tourists) stayed awake listening to fado, socializing, and consuming expensive liquor at the professional fado houses until dawn. These days, he said, "they are mostly tourists who come, and we pack up before midnight and go home." Piecing together fragments of these oral histories, it is clear that one of the functions the professional casas de fado served during the Estado Novo, likely with particular force during its last two decades, was to provide sites for sociality among the ruling elites, a sociality forged in relation and in counterpoint to listening to fado. The most luxurious venues, which featured performances by the most sought-after fado stars, also served as sites for international diplomacy. It is clear also that the reopening of old casas de fado and the opening of new ones, beginning in the early 1990s, was enabled partly by the increasing success of fado in the emergent global market for world music.

Whether the stories about the occupation of symbolic fado venues in the immediate aftermath of the regime are true or false, the mere circulation of the stories as history in the present is what is important here. The behavior of the fadista who denied the veracity of the occupation story can be read as pointing to the extremely difficult position in which many professional fadistas and venues found themselves in the aftermath of the regime, trying to sustain a livelihood as fado waned from favor amid possible charges of complicity in relation to the Estado Novo. It warrants underscoring that I am not arguing for any necessary relation between fadistas and instrumentalists who had professional fado careers during the Estado Novo and their political affiliations at that time. The professional casa de fado during the dictatorship assisted in catalyzing a florescence of fado virtuosity; the socioeconomic conditions of musicians' livelihoods were necessarily complex, and politics, like music, were often lived and voiced in the spaces "between the lines."

Places like the Embuçado undoubtedly brought to the city of Lisbon a "new way of hearing the fado." The censored repertoires performed in these types of venues during the dictatorship had effects on fado's affects beyond the professional casa de fado and state-sponsored radio, on ways of hearing and feeling fado that to a certain extent have endured as remainders, finding their way into practices of writing, performing, and listening to sung lyrics and instrumental sound, into attitudes about professionalism and amateurism, into the sensorium and soundscapes of the present (a point I develop further in chapter 3).

Then there were the venues, social circles, and styles of singing that, in the early 2000s, were still actively connected to the *idea* of the regime, to an aristocracy or to the old monarchy. An upscale restaurant just down the street from the Embuçado hosted amateur style fado nights twice a week. Many professionals contracted by other houses or who had stage or recording careers went there to sing (unpaid), to unwind after work. The owner told me that the venue began as a supportive meeting place for people who felt that the revolution was not good for Portugal. The space was enclosed with stone walls, vault-like. I was shown the entranceway off a side room to ancient tunnels, which I was told link the building to the Moorish castle on the hill. Its walls were sparsely decorated, lacking the customary kitsch of the amateur venues I attended. A single antique guitarra hung over the place where the instrumentalists sit and the fadista sings. Some audience members seemed to expect that I would recognize them because they were well-known actors or members of well-to-do Lisbon families, or because they had "nobility" in their blood. Some older fadistas sang in a style that some of my fadista friends might have typed as "aristocratic fado" (*the kind of fado about bullfighting and all of that*) while mocking what they understood to be effete singing mannerisms mimicking the style's "cleaner" or more bel canto vocal sound (as opposed to a textured grittiness or nasality that I often heard in working-class amateur fado sessions). Even though there was some overlap in the repertoire sung (particularly in terms of classics from Amália's repertoire), I never heard some of the older revolutionary or explicitly working-class fados that I sometimes heard at other amateur venues.

Based on conversations with fadistas of the older generation who were active participants in Lisbon's amateur scene, along with observations by interlocutors in Costa's and Guerreiro's account two decades earlier, I would argue that fado, as a form of social protest, did not die out during the Estado Novo. One of the principal means through which the legacy of fado as social protest continued during the regime (whether carrying through a socialist, anarchist, communist, or *operário* strain from before the dictatorship) was through the practice of amateur fado, sometimes in working-class neighborhood associations (*colectividades*), away from the more rigorously monitored spaces of professionalism. One of the effects that censorship had on fado was to facilitate, from necessity, an even more nuanced poetic and gestural language that could be read between the lines.

Costa and Guerreiro also noted a diversity of opinions regarding fado's political identity, with actors in Alfama in the late 1970s identifying it as *either* "fascist" or "subversive." They read this diversity of opinion with respect to struggles over classification (*lutas de classificações*) as manifestations "captured at the level of discourse of struggles between classes and interest groups" (Costa and Guerreiro 1984: 167–68). While their argument is somewhat useful in helping to explain the contradictions I found with respect to questions of fado's relationship to nation, to the Estado Novo, or to political resistance more than twenty years later (where the discursive field around these relationships is also likely differently charged, more fractured, and diffuse), it tells only part of the story.

The Portuguese phenomenological philosopher José Gil argues that there was an "expansion of affects" during the Estado Novo. He contrasts this with an "affective subject" in contemporary democratic Portugal, who, he argues, is more of a "closed individual" (*indivíduo fechado*) than a citizen:

> During Salazarismo, and paradoxically in part *against* an affective democracy of the individual/social subject, there ended up being created another life, an expansion of affects. More than affects, it was about desire. To live clandestinely, under the moral and political regime of the Estado Novo, created distorted desire, strategies, and intensifications. . . . The urban space fractured into

two, one emerging from the clandestine, another city, with different subjects, other codes of comportment, as liberty retreated, one's love life intensified. . . . However, the dominant affective environment, the affective texture of the atmosphere between people, was so pregnant that it created an illusion of inscription. (Gil 2007: 57)

I cite Gil here not to call attention to his claim about the intensification of intrigue or of the erotic during the Estado Novo but, rather, to note fractures that still run deep under the social surface of the city of Lisbon and habits of being in the body, of voicing ideas, and of public and of private that are residual from that time. If there was an "expansion of affects" during the Estado Novo, perhaps one of the ways in which this manifested was in the amplified import of small gestures; of the covert; of seeing, hearing, and being "between the lines." Music and poetry are supremely equipped to speak "between the lines." Perhaps, following Gil, we can think about not just the intensification of the amorous under the moral and political restrictions of the Estado Novo, but also the necessary intensification of the *poetic* as a communicative mode—in Roman Jakobson's (1960: 356) sense, where the poetic foregrounds the *form* of the message—some of which is also residual today. I expand the sense of "poetic function" here to include the poetic in embodied musical performance, as well as in relation to the verbal, and with respect to all of the nuanced means through which bodies speak to one another through gestures, often a "speaking" that cannot be voiced aloud.

Gil's principal argument, and one that might be read as a political provocation, is that contemporary Portugal is a country of "non-inscription" (*país da não-inscrição*), caught in an inertia (vestigial from the Estado Novo) in which subjects' knowledge of the world does not manifest in acts, does not "transform" the world. He notes that while speaking in general terms about the category of "the Portuguese" is necessarily problematic, in so doing he adopts the same kind of speaking in generalities about Portuguese identity that he finds ubiquitous in everyday Portugal. Thus, he engages this discursive mode as a rhetorical strategy. Powerfully linked to his idea of "non-inscription" are his claims that during the Estado Novo there was no public sphere, and that today, a public sphere is more illusory than real, fostered by long-standing habits of being vestigial from the regime (Gil 2007: 23–25). I, too, am working with arguments throughout this book regarding the ways in which vestigial habits from the Estado Novo linger in the present day; the ways in which they constellate (or do not) in fado scenes and social matrices; and how they might transform, circulate, and rise to awareness in response to an ever changing present. But by emphasizing the remainder of the poetic in the present day as I find it in fado's social and aesthetic worlds, I stress that the poetic, when the message is often so overdetermined and affectively saturated, always contains within it a possibility of transformation, of *inscription*.

Inflections of "history" respond continuously to politics of the present. For years following the 1974 revolution, fado was politically incorrect among Portuguese intellectuals as members of a leftist elite rose to political power in the transition to democracy (many had been in exile in Paris during 1968, and many had been affiliated with the Communist Party).[47] It was a time during which fado's potential (and histories) as a genre of social protest demanded brave argument from its few vocal practitioners on the left. As fado increasingly gains international prominence on the world stage, as the city of Lisbon uses fado (and its history) as a resource in promoting its own cultural identity vis-à-vis the European Union, and as fado's status as UNESCO-designated "intangible cultural heritage" permeates ways in which the genre is presented, it becomes more probable that fado's histories in relation to resistance (including resistance that predates the Estado Novo) are those that are foregrounded (in museum exhibits, in historical accounts) rather than those relationships that speak to totalitarianism and empire.[48]

European cosmopolitanism and belonging hinge in part on creating a future that moves beyond the histories of colonial imperialism and fascism. At the same time, fado as a genre whose "history" has always been unofficial, has begun to accrue official histories in the form of academic texts, recorded archives, and increasing institutionalization via Lisbon's Fado Museum. Ordering the messy archaeology of fado histories and showcasing *a* history becomes a prerequisite for the granting of "patrimony" (or heritage).[49]

What is remarkable is that fado can trigger so many different kinds of sentiments and responses to the dictatorship, in which one can find both strains of a regime's ideology and its antithesis. Lines demarcating these strains can be ambiguous, even in the voice of one individual. For the same person, fado might simultaneously be predicated on an essential (national) Portugueseness (*We discovered the world* or *Only the Portu-guese feel saudade*) while at the same time he or she might imagine fado as primarily a "revolutionary" genre on the political left. Fado may inspire narratives that reveal lived memories of multiple kinds of suffering inflicted by the dictatorial regime and multiple stories of nation, race, and empire promulgated by the Estado Novo, even as it may prompt the very discourses and habits of silence through which authoritarian re-gimes themselves are enabled.

As a case study in the relationship between musical/poetic aesthetics and politics, fado is interesting precisely for the ambiguity it fore-grounds. Poetic ambiguity maps onto political ambiguity with respect to actors' ideas about resistance, feelings of the national, and official and unofficial state uses of "culture" as a resource, as articulated in relation to both the past and the present. The appropriation of a musical genre as "national" whose legends have always situated its genesis at the social margins and at the boundaries of cultures is necessarily fraught. Memo-ries and histories that surface in fado talk in relation to the Estado Novo are necessarily competing and fragmented. Actors might claim the genre as "national" while simultaneously arguing that it was always a "revolutionary song." Fado's history as a genre vis-à-vis its political situ-atedness thus reinscribes its own narrative as it appears in song lyrics and in legend—fado as misfit, fado as deviant, fado as homeless, fado as outcast, fado as always at the margins, evading facile categorization. In its elusiveness therein lies its power.

THREE

Fado's City

Lisbon, chaste princess . . .
Of the discoveries of so many deserted lands . . .
Seven hills are your breasts of satin
Where the houses have gardens strewn with daisies
In your womb one day was created and sung by the
people dreaming, our Fado.
—"LISBOA CASTA PRINCESA" (1930S)

There is a curve on the route of the number 28 trolley in Lisbon, a route that has been hailed as one of the most scenic in Europe, from which Wim Wenders shot footage for his film *Lisbon Story* (1994) to the fado-esque soundtrack of the Portuguese pop group Madredeus.[1] There is a curve where it rounds alongside the Miradouro de Santa Luzia (Viewpoint of Santa Luzia), near the top of the neighborhood of Alfama. For a moment, the view of the entrance to the discovery of the world unfolds, a shimmering view of a river so vast it appears a sea. Below, histories unfurl—houses stacked on top of houses, crumbling walls, winding alleyways, stones upon stones, bricks, dirt, rubble. On a side wall, tile displays narrate strategic moments in Lisbon's history. To the left is the viewpoint of the Gates to the Sun (Portas do Sol); directly behind is the street of São Tomé. The streets sing. A map of the street names of Lisbon reads like both a poem and a litany of colonial conquest: Rua da Saudade, Avenida do Brasil, Avenida da Índia, Rua de Angola.

There are stories Lisbon told me in graffiti: "Basta de Miséria" (Enough Misery), "Pretos Fora!" (Blacks Out!), "Estou sozinho, estou triste, etc." (I am alone, I am sad, etc.) (plate 3). There are stories that fadistas sung to me alone, hushed singing, intimate singing. *Let me tell you, let me sing to you how it goes. They don't sing these songs anymore, these are the old songs. Let me tell you, his singing made even Amália cry.* There is the singing of stories that listeners told me made their skin tremble, get cold with goose flesh (*pele de galinha*), made the body vibrate, the eyes tear, the throat catch. There are songs listened to in semidarkness, eyes closed, with listeners who are also singers, where those who know how to hear well are deemed the truest fadistas of them all. There are fados sung by girls wearing jeans and laced shawls, dreaming of stardom, reaching toward the imaginary of a voice so big that it becomes the "soul" of a nation, a nation that as local legend has it, in "discovering" Africa, "discovered the world," a world whose center was imagined as the city of Lisbon.

Lisbon's geographical positioning as colonial port city figures prominently in both popular and academic origin narratives for fado. The port city is posited as the embryonic, decadent, contaminated, and cosmopolitan ground that enables the figuring of an expressive musical genre born of cultural hybridity. The city of Lisbon exists almost symbiotically with the genre of fado; endless fados celebrate the city, literally singing it into affective sonorous being.[2] Many Lisbon fado musicians understand their fado to be deeply emplaced: from the intimately local (a fado house, a street corner, a viewpoint); to neighborhood, region, and country; to a sense of Portugal's place in relation to Europe and the rest of the world. In traveling the world as the soul of Portugal's city, fado's stylized sonic icons of instrumental and vocal weeping affectively shape circulating imaginaries of Lisbon as nostalgia, Lisbon as lament.

Fado exoticizes itself as genre, and the city of Lisbon self-reflexively, through the poetics of its lyrics. In its circulating representations, in fado documentaries and films, fado as practice and object is often exoticized through poetic and aesthetic strategies. Camera shots of the cityscape might be blurred and the narration might employ heightened poetic language, both practices marking fado and its city as poetically saturated alter-worlds. In travel literature or in CD booklets that circulate with internationally marketed fado recordings, fado is often linked to a "Mediterranean" or "Latin" feeling or marked as a sonic window onto a deeply soulful geo-temporal periphery. These representations all feed back into the sense of what fado is (and might become) back home in Portugal.

Europe's South has been shaped as Europe's backward "other" by an intellectual and literary culture of the Northern metropoles, where universalizing West–East imaginaries have been mapped in multiple forms onto Europe's North–South since at least the 1700s (Dainotto 2007; Fernandez 2008).[3] Barbara Kirshenblatt-Gimblett (1998b: 177) has suggested that Europe's Catholic South might function as a "zone of repudiation" for Europe's core (or Protestant North). In this sense, the zone of repudiation collects and holds cultural detritus and castoffs, that which was repudiated and has been elsewhere reformed, edited out: "Such processes create a large domain of cultural trash, which returns as parody, 'folklore,' or even 'heritage.'" Anthropological work on southern Europe from the 1970s and 1980s commonly posits a core–periphery economic model, with the Mediterranean (or the South) as Europe's exploited periphery.[4] This model follows Immanuel Wallerstein's (1974) theorizations of the "world system" in which the periphery is mined for raw goods crucial to production in more powerful industrial centers (Gilmore 1982: 182).[5] In relation to current narratives originating in Europe's economic center, Portugal is continuously rewritten as Europe's wayward (but feeling-filled) economic periphery, short on resources of financial capital but abundant in resources of sentiment. (A celebrity fadista tells me how a foreign friend of his claims that "Switzerland is the monetary bank of Europe but Portugal is its bank of the spirit.")[6]

How does fado as genre shape affective cartographies in relation to long-standing European North–South dialectics? What kinds of sensory labors might fado perform in shaping the ways in which Lisbon places are experienced and imagined in relation to remainders, memories, and representational practices of the Estado Novo? Central to these questions is the role of aesthetic practice and production in shaping the structures of feeling, habits of memory, and the bodily practices on which the production of localities depends. Numerous anthropological case studies have eloquently argued that the material physicality of place is often intertwined with the ways in which actors shape memory and sociality (see Feld and Basso 1996; K. Stewart 1996; Tsing 1993, 2005) and that expressive vocal practices sometimes play a key role in mediating relationships between place, memory, and sociopolitical life (Fox 2004: 248–51; Samuels 2004; Samuels et al. 2010). Just as walking through the streets of a neighborhood conditions the habits and memory of the body (de Certeau 1984), listening to music, playing music, and singing songs shapes a "habitus."[7] Steven Feld (1996b) theorizes an "acoustemology" of place; a symbiotic relationship between body, voice, place, and song; ways of knowing the world and one's place in it in relationship to sound making and practices of audition.[8] I take this symbiosis as a ground against which to figure place in the specific historical, urban, and geopolitical context of contemporary Lisbon, a city situated in a geographically and economically peripheral country that was home to one of Europe's longest dictatorships, a country marked by densely layered and often competing claims by local actors to history, to the modern, to the national, and to the European.

Fado excessively gathers stories, memories, and feelings into its generic fold and releases them with a promiscuous indexicality. It mediates a politics of both scale and of affect, an aesthetics of both the durable (the layout of a neighborhood, the structuring of a viewpoint that directs a gaze) and of the ephemeral (the seeming intangibility of the aural, of musical practice). Through poetic and discursive reflexivity, an affective sedimentation through reiteration, and a sonorous vocality whose signifying exceeds the limits of the explicitly referential and comes to stand in *for* feeling, fado gathers a surplus of meanings. I argue that through a poetics of excess gathered in fado as genre, sound and sociability, story and feeling are sutured to geographies and histories of the hyper-local and to the intimate. In fado's wider circulations, these geographies and histories take on metonymic valences (as nation, as periphery, as southern, as a sensuous premodern).[9]

Place-Name Fado

When he sings, I see the entire city stretched out before me. —MUSICAL CONSULTANT in Lisbon on listening to the fadista Carlos do Carmo in 2003

Fados whose lyrics celebrate aspects of the city of Lisbon and its neighborhoods are so common that they form a subgenre within fado lyrics. Themes might include places that hold symbolic importance in fado lore or references to places of scenic beauty. Fado neighborhoods, the river, monuments, chapels, obsolete fado houses, current fado houses, street names, and names of squares are also common references. I call this toponym-focused subgenre "place-name fado."[10] With "place-name fados," my intention is to include micro-local practices of identity making in relation to place and to open up the discussion more broadly to consider how neighborhood, city, country, and geographical region are rendered affective (for different kinds of social actors from differing place-based positions) through the aesthetics and politics of poetic and sonic representation and to experiences of listening in fado. In place-name fado, places might be linked to other expressive practices such as Lisbon's popular marches or to representations of "folklore" or rusticity. In many of these fados, places are sonically and affectively described. A place name as the focus of the song might be virtuosically ornamented by the voice (Gray 2007); an instrumentalist might improvise a response, figuring a chord with a quivering timbre or citing a motivic fragment from another fado as musical commentary. Creative singing or instrumental playing can thus foreground descriptive affective sonic markers, commenting stylistically and timbrally on place, charging it with feeling, making it cry. Lyrics often self-reflexively comment on the fado voice or timbre or the sounds of fado instruments, particularly the guitarra, as saudade-filled or pain-filled (*magoada*).

The lyrics from the classic fado song "Vielas de Alfama" (Alleys of Alfama) begin like this: "Dead hours, darkened night / A guitarra trembling, a woman singing / Her fado of bitterness / And through the windowpane / Blackened and broken / Her hurt voice / Moves those who pass by." They move into the refrain: "Alleys of Alfama / Streets of old Lisbon / There is no fado that does not speak / Things of your past / Alleys of Alfama / Kissed by the moonlight / How I wish I could live there / To live close to the fado."[11] The fado appeared as a remake on the album *Fado Curvo* (2003) by Mariza, currently the most renowned fado diva internationally, and forms part of the repertoire of many amateur and professional singers. The lyrics of "Vielas de Alfama" (as in many fado lyrics) self-reflexively comment on fado itself; these lyrics link fado as genre to the sound of a "hurt voice" (the voice of a woman), situating genre in place (Alfama), and empowering genre to "speak" and to "sing" of the past of that place.

Fados like "Vielas de Alfama," fados whose lyrics fall within the thematic genre of place-name fado, are often unabashedly celebratory via the intense invocation of nostalgia or saudade, in a style evoking a "permanent way of seeing any historical city" (Williams 1973: 152).[12] This permanence of a city suspended in time through its mode of aestheticization is sometimes echoed in fado form. Many celebratory place-name fados are in the fixed form of fado canção or scored fado song (often with a refrain), as distinguished from traditional fado that is strophic and highly improvised.[13] In a self-reflexive turn, some place-name fado lyrics refer to *miradouros*, well-known viewpoints high upon Lisbon's seven hills; in those fados, topography, landscape, and song come together in a gazing and hearing from "above."[14] Place-name fado lyrics sometimes feminize Lisbon (as in the lyrics of "Lisboa Casta Princesa," which open this chapter) or miniaturize the city, naturalizing a way of gazing onto Lisbon along with a particular politics of intimacy (S. Stewart 2003). Sentimentalizing place-name lyrics, some from the dictatorship-era (or bearing a residual place-making aesthetic of the regime), nostalgically bind place and effect temporal stasis, along with various political erasures. This aesthetic is common in the composition of new lyrics and is widely found in all of the circuits through which fado travels.

"Lisboa é Sempre Lisboa" (Lisbon Is Always Lisbon) is a scored fado canção popularized by the resonant, chesty, almost lounge-like swooning vocal style of the male fadista Tristão da Silva. The lyrics are emblematic of place-name fados composed during the dictatorship set to fado canção and that are still commonly performed and composed today.

REFRAIN
Lisboa é sempre Lisboa, dos becos e das vielas
E das casinhas singelas d'Alfama e da Madragoa, ai
Dos namorados nas janelas
Das marchas que o povo entoa
Da velha Sé, das procissões e da fé
Com seus pregões Lisboa é sempre Lisboa.

Lisbon is always Lisbon, of the little streets and alleys
And the simple little houses of Alfama and Madragoa, *ai*
Of the lovers at the windows
Of the marches that the people sing
The old cathedral, the processions and the acts of faith,
With its street cries, Lisbon is always Lisbon.[15]

The neighborhoods of Alfama and Madragoa, with their "simple" "little" houses, are referenced alongside architectural patrimony ("the old cathedral") and "invented traditions" ("the marches that the people sing").[16] Throughout, Lisbon (as Portugal's capital city) is rendered feminine—a feminine that is at once quaint and childlike, exotic and soulful. At the beginning of the first verse (not quoted above), the rustic folk is gendered female: Lisbon is a *varina* (a woman selling fish on the streets). She "loses her silly little head" (*perde a tonta cabecita*); she "wears chintz, sings the fado, and feels saudade" (*veste de chita, canta o fado e tem saudade*). In the final verse, Lisbon is "held to the guitarra" (*presa à guitarra*) and sings fado "until dawn."

"Alfama Eterna" (Eternal Alfama) conveys a similar sense of stasis focused on Lisbon's quintessential traditional neighborhood. Álvaro Rodrigues, a poet in his eighties and a longtime regular at O Jaime, who considers himself "the popular poet of Alfama," wrote the lyrics. This fado circulates in the amateur circuit and has been performed in amateur practice in Alfama since at least the 1970s. In weekend sessions I attended in 2001–2003 at the Tasca do Jaime, I heard the lyrics to Rodrigues's "Alfama Eterna" sung almost every week. (Alfama is a five-minute downhill walk from Graça, the neighborhood in which O Jaime is situated.) Often, Fernanda Proença and Ivone Dias, both Alfama-born, would sing this fado together to a densely packed audience, consisting mostly of neighborhood locals and a few tourists, taking turns singing the phrases, joining in together on the last line. In their performances, Proença and Dias almost always foregrounded the word *tradição* (tradition), particularly in its last instance, with ample voltinhas, drawing out the word, suspending it in time. Local audience members always joined in on the refrains, in sync, out of sync, singing from memory:

Segundo ouvi dizer ao fadista
E também ao velho amigo
Que em tempos fora toureiro
Que o fado, este boémio, este bairrista
Já não é o fado antigo,
Já não é o verdadeiro.

Agora é um senhor da sociedade
Até por sinal viajado que há pouco esteve em Paris
Não sei se é mentira ou se é verdade
Murmuram tanto do fado
E do fado tanto se diz.

Mas quem passar pela velha Alfama a horas mortas
Terá que ouvir uma guitarra a trinar
Em noites calmas gentinha sentada às portas
Em cada peito há uma voz para cantar
Em qualquer rua, em qualquer beco, há sempre um fado
A dar nas vistas nesta Lisboa moderna
É tradição, é recordar o passado
Ai, querida Alfama, tu és sagrada tu és eterna.

According to what I heard from a fadista
And also from an old friend
Who a long time ago was a bullfighter
Fado, this bohemian fado, fado of the neighborhood
Is no longer the old fado,
Is no longer the true fado.

Now it [fado] is a man of society
It has traveled, a little while ago it was in Paris
I don't know if this is true or false
They say so much about the fado
And of the fado, so much is said.

But those who pass through old Alfama during the dead hours of the
　　night
Will hear a guitarra trembling
On calm nights, the people sitting at their doors
In each heart there is a voice with which to sing
In every street, in every alley, there is always a fado
Present in this modern Lisbon
It is tradition, it is to remember the past
Ai, darling Alfama, you are sacred, you are eternal.[17]

These lyrics link the tremulous sound of the guitarra to the intimate
spaces of neighborhood and to the nostalgic eternal. *For even if fado has
traveled to Paris and is not the same, Alfama is eternal, and at night it
will always sound of the guitarra.* This type of reference, where the sounds
of the guitarra (as tremulous, vibrating, or weeping [*gemido*]) are poetically sutured to the past of place, is common in place-name fado. This

reference echoes the sentiment of a well-known guitarrista who told me, "The guitarras cried more in the past." Note that in each of the three excerpted fados—"Vielas de Alfama," "Lisboa é Sempre Lisboa," and "Alfama Eterna"—mention of the guitarra and the trope of the singing voice recurs ("a woman singing," "the hurt voice," "in each heart a singing voice," "tied to the guitarra she sings until dawn"), reflexively linking fado sounds to fado places.

Salazar-era propaganda famously proclaimed, "Portugal Não é um País Pequeno" (Portugal Is Not a Small Country). The slogan circulated beneath a map of Europe on which were superimposed all of Portugal's colonies, demonstrating that Portugal was larger than "Europe."[18] The sentimentalizing aesthetic of place-name lyrics and representations of fado's mythological neighborhoods in contemporary Lisbon echo a geopolitical strategy of scale employed by the state during the dictatorship that produced a Portuguese cartography of both the enormous and of the miniature, where social and geo-spatial structures of intimacy and interiority (of neighborhood, of family, of faith) symbolically stood in for the expansive reach of the nation and the imperial, corporate, totalitarian state.

State cultural policy beginning in the 1930s fostered aesthetic practices and cultural institutions with the aim of ruralizing Lisbon's neighborhoods and turning them into small villages (aldeias) within the city; such that the aldeia symbolically stood in for the nation (Holton 2005; Melo 2001).[19] This move was linked to an ideology of the rural as sanitizing urban "degeneracy" and to political and aesthetic strategies directed at "countrifying" the city. As Daniel Melo (2001: 45) argues, the Estado Novo's denigration of the urban was also about the "negation of the citizen." Fado itself was partly sanitized via a poetics of rusticity, a counterforce to neutralize the strain of fado associated with the voice of working-class opposition that predated the regime (Nery 2004: 190, 198). With the formation of professional fado houses in key "traditional" neighborhoods—particularly Bairro Alto and Alfama—in the 1930s and the explicit linking of these venues to international tourism in the 1950s through state cultural policy (Nery 2004), fado tourism and the fetishization of Lisbon's mythic fado neighborhoods converged. Censored fados that were sung at these venues and that circulated on the radio and in recordings, in turn, made affectively sonorous a politics of intimacy, often sentimentalizing the home or family and reifying fado's neighborhoods.

"Uma Casa Portuguesa" (A Portuguese Home), an upbeat fado canção that was popularized by Amália Rodrigues during the Estado Novo,
is a prototypical place-name fado celebrating the miniature and the
affectionately diminutive.[20] The lyrics celebrate the hospitality and quaintness of the Portuguese household (despite poverty), where the household
can be read as a synecdoche for multiple geopolitical and spatial con-
figurations: for neighborhood, for city, for nation. I sometimes heard this
fado invoked in conversation as a cliché marshaled in making a political
critique of the present. In these instances, "Uma Casa Portuguesa" seemingly encapsulated an essence of Estado Novo–era ideology that the
speaker felt was lingering in the present. Beginning in the 1950s, with
the rise of state-sponsored tourism in the professional fado venues, fado
was often performed alongside versions of sanitized folkloric dance. This
practice continues currently in some of Bairro Alto's tourist-oriented casas de fado, such as Café Luso (discussed later). At the same time, many
of the fado lyrics performed in these venues, night after night, are highly
sentimentalizing place-name lyrics. Indeed, a common sentiment among
some fado aficionados with whom I spoke was that tourists prefer fados
like "Uma Casa Portuguesa" to *fado fado*, or the very sad fados, and that
owing to the current boom in tourism, traditional fado and the saddest
fados were being sung less and less.

Neighborhoods

Alfama, Bairro Alto, Mouraria: these neighborhoods of fado "origin,"
"birth," and legend are rendered sonorous and given story and history in
countless fados, new and old.[21] Fetishized during the regime, these
neighborhoods are still fetishized today in different ways—through
practices such as the popular marches invented in the 1930s, that continue today in the name of "tradition"; through fado lyrics, legend, and
lore; in fado exhibits; through fado marketing locally and globally writ;
and, in the case of Bairro Alto and Alfama, through fado venues and
tourism.

Mouraria thrives in the popular fado imaginary as both the fabled
home of the nineteenth-century prostitute and fadista Maria Severa,
who "gave birth" to the genre, and as the birthplace of many renowned
fadistas. Fado lyrics sentimentalize a mythical profligate urbanity of
Mouraria from which fado hypothetically sprang alongside a rustic

FIGURE 3.1 • The neighborhood of Mouraria. Lisbon, 2003. Photograph by the author.

Mouraria, a gathering place of Lisbon's "traditions" (see Colvin 2008). My amateur fadista friends sometimes remarked on the contrast between these representations of Mouraria and its contemporary reality after a Mouraria-focused fado had been sung: *There is hardly any fado anymore in Mouraria*. For the first decade of the 2000s, there was scant fado in Mouraria.[22] Lisbon's ancient Moorish quarter was cut open, torn apart, and reconstructed in aggressive projects of urban and social planning during the Estado Novo (Colvin 2008) and is now, in a manner much more visible and pronounced than other neighborhoods in Lisbon's historic core, falling apart at the seams. Home to a large and diverse population of immigrants, many buildings abandoned and boarded up, bordering the neighborhood of Intendente (a site of heavy narco-trafficking for well over a decade), Mouraria, even though positioned within Lisbon's historic center, is mostly outside of the tourist circuit and is an "othered" place for many white Portuguese Lisbon locals (see figure 3.1). Yet the mythic charge of Mouraria as one of *the* neighborhoods of fado history is such that it is still sometimes invoked as a place-based authenticating move in fadista biography.[23]

Bairro Alto, through its nineteenth-century reputation for bohemian "low-life" and prostitution, and Alfama, as a dockside neighborhood historically bearing the "illicit" (and racially hybrid) influences of the port, are both strongly linked to fado imaginaries of origin. They are also the two Lisbon neighborhoods most visibly marked by fado venues and tourism. In Bairro Alto, a *casa típica* (typical fado house) serves traditional Portuguese food at inflated prices and usually demands a high cover charge. At these venues, fado often mixes with "folklore," which can take the form of dance numbers interspersed with the fado in which the audience may be called to participate. For example, at the notoriously touristic Café Luso in Bairro Alto, where a poster outside lures tourists in by promising (in Portuguese and English) "tradition without translation," fado is performed on a platform stage, juxtaposed with folklore-inspired dances, against an illuminated backdrop representing the city of "old Lisbon."

On any given night at Café Luso, busloads of tourists sit at long tables, chatter boisterously and rattle their silverware; fado's mandatory aesthetic of darkness is punctuated by incessant bursts of flashbulbs. All the while, one of the venue's contracted fadistas sings expressively on the platform stage with two or three instrumentalists, vying for the audience's attention. After the fadista finishes a set, brilliantly adorned dancers claim the stage, twirling, holding letters above their heads that spell out L-U-S-O, and cajoling audience members to join in. A cameraman joins the dancers on the stage and invites the tourists to be photographed for a fee. The package-deal tourists clear out before midnight, and the staff quickly rearranges the space. They close off the stage area with sliding doors and move the chairs and tables into an intimate configuration; the dancers go home; the singers and instrumentalists remain. Fado appreciated in silence, in darkness, begins.

Alexandra Klein and Vera Alves (1994: 42–43) describe décor often found in tourist-oriented casas de fado: bullfighting paraphernalia; photos of famous guests; fake cobblestone floors and street lamps; murals representing "historic" Lisbon; photographs of well-known fadistas and instrumentalists; and assortments of objects that evoke particular rural regions of Portugal or a sense of the "rustic." This hodgepodge of decontextualized objects on display, running the symbolic gamut from evocations of the aristocracy to the peasantry, become kitsch, staging a folkloric setting for the performance of "culture."[24]

Fado, when performed in this context of touristic display, often becomes "folklorized" (or "fakelorized"). Two forces of historical and political erasure come together here in relation to the "folk" and to kitsch. Indeed, both the "folk" and the kitsch aesthetic at Café Luso do some of the work of "translation" in the presentation of "tradition" to an international audience. The political and historical erasure effected by display with respect to current fado tourism in some of Lisbon's professional casas de fado plays on tourists' desire for "repudiated" cultural practices (Kirshenblatt-Gimblett 1998b: 177). Current framing and staging practices in Lisbon's tourist fado clubs rely on a habitus of erasure residual from the past: the codified sanitation of fado through the construction of official fado houses; the mixing of fado with folklore and the folk kitsch surround; and the singing of some lyrics that were shaped in response to former state censorship.[25] The residual "folk" clings to fado thirty years after the dictatorship's fall; its aura is reproduced nightly in some of Bairro Alto's folklorized casas típicas, the tangled histories perhaps invisible to the tourist and rendered through repetition as part of the everyday sense of things for staff members and regulars.

There are multiple night scenes in Bairro Alto. A sushi bar stands next to a trendy sneaker shop with a dance floor; retro wear and designer fashions are displayed in boutiques that also serve tea and advertise yoga classes. Techno music blasts from a bar; gay male couples stand outside smoking. Drugs are quickly exchanged on a dark corner. Bouncers stand outside fado restaurants trying to lure in customers. A store specializing in condoms, open only at night, stands near a forsaken fado house where only two tourists sit; the wailing of a tired fado voice can be heard pouring through the open doors. The customer who might go to the Café Luso is probably not the same customer who would seek out the bar Tasca do Chico down the street. On a fado night at Chico, a stream of European twenty-something tourists, mixed with regulars from Lisbon's amateur fan circuit, can be seen through a smoky haze, packed closely together in the small space, listening to amateur fado. Some stand outside, blocking the narrow street, craning their necks to catch a glimpse of the singer through the open door. This is a radically different scene from that of the middle-age European tour groups at Café Luso—and from that of the mostly Portuguese audiences, with the majority of participants older than forty, that constituted the primary public for amateur fado during the early 2000s.[26] Chico's audience members might have used *Rough Guide* or *Lonely Planet* tourist guidebooks; they might have purchased Chico's "live" CD (Tasca do Chico 2002), produced intentionally to retain the ambient sound of the bar (replete with chatter and shouts demanding silence). This is an audience from Europe's hub trickling out to its "repudiated margins" in search of the "real thing." Indeed, when the world music fado diva Mariza was in town, she occasionally stopped by the Tasca do Chico to give an impromptu performance.

Yet this is not to say that a foreign tourist listening to fado sung in the context of Tasca do Chico or Café Luso (or at any venue) does not experience fado in a way that is emotionally charged, felt as meaningful or personal. It is not to say that foreign tourists at places like Café Luso do not cry. And when tourists cry, fado itself as genre accrues significance by way of a discourse of musical universalism. A female fadista in her early fifties, contracted at Café Luso, explained to me in 1999, "Fado is music of the soul. When I sing, I make people from all around the world cry." Practitioners who boast of making tourists cry sometimes use talk of the tears of "outsiders" to index fado's universal emotional power and reach, fado's capacity to transcend the limits of culture, of language, and of geography (and, in the case of this fadista, to underscore her power as a singer who can make even *tourists* cry). In conversations about these tears of outsiders, the same practitioners and fans almost always stress that the foreigners cry *even though they do not understand any of the words that are sung.* Tears of linguistic and geographic outsiders, when discussed as an index of fado's universalism (vis-à-vis an implicit understanding of a universal "emotive" subject), or when referenced as a way to boast about one's communicative power as a singer, would seem to fit uneasily with the unequivocal importance in fado aesthetics placed on the necessity of "saying the words well" (*dizer bem as palavras*) in order to transmit the emotion and intention of a poem, coupled with a de-emphasis on the "musical" qualities of the voice (see chapter 1). This fado tear-based emotional universalism also fits incongruously with the micro-local, place-based, and affect-based authenticities that are part and parcel of much fado discourse (i.e., *You must be from here to truly sing fado with soul*). For many fado purists, fado fado, or "true" fado, while not quite speech, dwells far from song. "Outsider" tears in this context play out a version of the music as a universal language theme foregrounding the musical, the paralinguistic, and the sonorous without referential content, in bridging seemingly impassible divides of place, history, language, and culture. For fado to work as a universal trope of the melancholic or the soulful, fado *as music* trumps fado as poetry sung.

Alfama on Display, Alfama as Display, Alfama as Fado

At the Fado Museum, situated at the base of the neighborhood of Alfama near the riverside docks, the first exhibit reveals two views. Behind false window frames in a glass case is an imaginative miniaturized reproduction of the sociality, rusticity, and patrimony of what appears to be Lisbon's quintessential fado neighborhood writ small. A plaque labels the exhibit "Vielas" (Alleyways), stating it to be a "reconstruction of the typical environment of the historic neighborhoods of Lisbon" (plate 4). The obvious reference of this miniature neighborhood is to Alfama. The landmark Alfama church, Igreja de Santo Estêvão, is a famous site in fado lore and is the subject of fado lyrics by the same name. It forms the focal point for the diaorama's perspective. The staircases and esplanades, the sheer density of people interacting on the street, and the variety and types of social activities represented (many of them associated with "tradition") in the scene also mark the neighborhood as Alfama. Metonymically, the miniature representation of Alfama and the types of sociability it reifies stand in as "typical" for all "historical" and "popular" Lisbon neighborhoods.

On the Largo da Saudade (a play on the name of a real Lisbon street in Alfama, the Rua da Saudade), an apron-clad miniaturized clay woman is frozen in a gestural mime of what might be a performance of a traditional street cry or the performance of fado; her head is thrown back; her eyes are closed; her mouth open wide; her feet planted on the ground. Women sell produce on the narrow cobbled street, lined with colorful buildings and iron street lamps. A man gestures at his mistress, who stands sulking wearing bright lipstick and a fadista's black shawl. Laundry hangs on a line. A fat policeman struts. A woman kneels, grilling sardines. Men play cards outside a tavern. Women appear to talk to one another through open windows. A street vendor blows panpipes. A man plays the guitarra, and a child kneels playing with a porcelain doll. Sounds of traditional fado can be heard from the speaker system in the adjoining room.

Turning one's back to the exhibit reveals a large window that overlooks the neighborhood of Alfama. Men chatter by the fountain; people

FIGURE 3.2 • Urban renovation scaffolding in Alfama, "Alfama é fado" (Alfama is fado). Lisbon, 2002. Photograph by the author.

sit outside, drinking wine; a doorman at the fado club Taverna d'el Rey prepares for his shift; a cement mixer mixes; laundry hangs flying in the wind; women talk to one another through open windows. Posters spread on scaffolding mark Alfama as a zone of urban restoration, declaring, "Alfama is fado" (see figure 3.2). The museum window frames my gaze of Alfama below.[27]

In his detailed sociological study of Alfama, António Firmino da Costa (1999: 19–20) writes about the neighborhood as a research object with an "excess of visibility," a neighborhood shot through with overlapping discourses and representations from the "outside" (scholarly, popular press, the Lisbon tourist industry, Lisbon urban planning, national patrimony, cinema) that in turn become complexly implicated in a hermeneutics of identity making from those on the "inside" (neighborhood residents). Over the past three decades, Alfama and other traditional Lisbon neighborhoods have been subjected to intense sociological and anthropological scrutiny (Cordeiro 1997; A. Costa 1999; Costa and Guerreiro 1984). This work has focused primarily on the unique types of sociability and cultural practices that these neighborhoods are seen to engender or maintain and on social issues related to urban restoration, such as relationships between belonging, neighborhood, and individual dwellings; and urban flight and gentrification. Alfama appears to be caught in a play of shadows and mirrors, ever reconstructed, continuously the focal point of multiple gazes—tourist culture industry, academic, state—and like all of Lisbon's fado neighborhoods, Alfama is also gazed on self-reflexively, fetishized, and shaped by fado itself. At the same time, fado as genre, as performance practice, and as tourist and culture industry, is invigorated both by the attention given to Alfama and by the dynamism of the neighborhood, which nevertheless is almost always represented in fado lyrics as eternal and unchanging.

In addition to its status as *the* fado neighborhood in the Lisbon imaginary, Alfama is often represented—in tourist pamphlets and academic texts and in films and television documentaries—as the most typically "Lisbon" and "Portuguese" neighborhood in Lisbon (A. Costa 1999: 32–33). Alfama as the dense microcosm of the typically Portuguese in many ways was shaped architecturally, scenically, and socioculturally by the Estado Novo. "There is no doubt that [during the Estado Novo] the local space [of Alfama] was partially reconstructed in scenic terms" (A. Costa 1999: 35). Staircases, arches, tiles, "Moorish" façades, viewpoints (e.g., the Miradouro de Santa Luzia), and fountains were all parts of the Estado Novo's literal re-forming of the physical space of the neighborhood; strategic alterations accented particular aspects of Portuguese patrimony and history (A. Costa 1999: 35).[28] Many of those alterations remain today but blend so well into the landscape of the quotidian that they are forgotten. A feeling of neighborhood from the repeated hearing, singing, or playing of a fado, a feeling of intimacy wrought by a particular arrangement of staircases and alleyways, a sense of history one might feel by passing a monument that is sung about over and over again, or even the very framing of the gaze out to the river that opens into a sea all put the senses in dialogue with the residual topographies and aesthetic practices of the national imaginary of a dictatorship over thirty years officially long gone.[29]

Alfama copiously gathers surplus signification (of patrimony; of history; of race, class, and ethnicity; of the "popular"; the criminal; the touristic; the traditional; and of fado) that renders it "other" even for many residents within the city. It bears vestiges of the Arab in its name and in its labyrinthine layout; it bears vestiges of a medieval Jewish quarter, of a community of freed black slaves, of palaces of royalty, of the original city wall. For much of the twentieth century, Alfama was marked by the poverty of its inhabitants (many of whom had migrated from the rural provinces in search of work), by a decaying architectural infrastructure and difficult living conditions, as a place of urban degeneracy and crime, and by an almost constant process of urban reconstruction (A. Costa 1999). Over the first decade of the 2000s, I witnessed multiple projects of so called urban renovation in Alfama, more buildings abandoned and some expensively restored and rented or sold at prices beyond the means of many longtime Alfama dwellers. Some of these, in turn, are inhabited by Lisbon residents from outside Alfama or by foreigners who can pay premium prices. Many dwellings remain abandoned or crumble around their residents, who live in the decaying buildings as best they can, rain coming through roofs, an elderly senhora sleeping fully dressed should the ceiling fall in upon her in the night. Over and over, through multiple changes in the local government, people complain that the politicians use the urban restoration platform when it is convenient for them, but that nothing much ever gets done. Alfama's alleyscapes juxtapose the cleaned-up quaintness of a renovated and gleaming Alfama with scenes of abandonment in immediate proximity: building walls crumbling in layers of green, pink, and terra-cotta; broken and boarded-up windows of long-vacated homes where discarded objects and overgrown plants take over wobbly iron terraces; a torn lace curtain hanging from the broken window of an empty attic. This decay serves in part as an aesthetic scene of ruin for tourists who amble through Alfama in relative safety and comfort (compared with the far more broken and ruined Lisbon places that are never mentioned in tourist guides), taking photos of "lost" time and place. Fado in this scene serves as the sonorous backdrop for abandonment.[30] Just as Alfama has an "excess of visibility," fado in Alfama is marked by an excess of audibility.

FIGURE 3.3 • Exterior of a restaurant in Alfama. Lisbon, 2007. Photograph by the author.

In response to global media coverage of fado, fado's increased presence on the world stage, and a greater institutionalized presence of fado within Lisbon, there has been a veritable explosion of new fado venues in Alfama of all kinds since the mid-2000s. Suddenly, it seems that every restaurant and bar is offering fado performance (figure 3.3), and that every souvenir shop is selling fado CDs and T-shirts. Alfama literally resounds with fado (plate 5). During the day, fado bounces off of the high hills from the open doors of gift shops, filling the narrow streets with waves of sound, and at night, all but the most elite professional venues open their doors to the outside. The sounds of fado voices and instruments pour out into streets. A few restaurants have gone as far as to offer fado performances outdoors during the day. When I talk to some Alfama residents about this wave of fado occurring amid a global economic crisis that has severely affected southern Europe—and Portugal in particular— they tell me that "fado sells."

Placing Lisbon, Portugal, the "South"

On the Avenue of Brazil, Lisbon flaunted further its long encounter with the seas.
Yet the surfeit of names continued to defy the established story. There were too
many signs here for history to remain official. . . . In the monumental efforts of the
Portuguese state to catch up with a history now eclipsed by nostalgia, I saw
nostalgia of the entire West for a place that exists only in the mind. I could now
glimpse the truth of my own history: The West does not exist. I know. I've been
there. —MICHEL-ROLPH TROUILLOT, *Silencing the Past*

I walk down the busy shopping street Rua Augusta in the center of Lisbon's Baixa district on a sweltering July morning in 2003. A teenage boy
with a clipboard and pen follows me, doggedly asking, "Do you think
Portugal is a developed country? Do you?" I jump onto the number 28
tram. It breaks down in Alfama, and the tourists aboard use the twenty
minutes for a photo op while locals mutter among themselves about how
things are always the same. *This is just a party for the tourists* (festa para
os turistas). *The City Council doesn't do a damn thing.* They talk about
how Portugal is just like a Third World country. While walking in Alfama, I run into a guitarra player in front of his musical-instrument
shop. He tells me that he thinks he might move back to England. "We
are at the foot of Europe; we are isolated," he says. "Lisbon is a village
(*aldeia*). People don't know the world. We have just Spain and the sea.
We were only big before there were airplanes, before there were trains.
But to be in the center, like Belgium; they are obliged to meet the world.
I am thinking of going back to England for a while, where people have a
different vision of the world, but the business is better here." In the summer of 2002, a Slovakian tourist couple from Germany sits next to me at
an amateur fado session and listens to the fado with a raptness bordering on tears. They tell me, "The Germans have no heart, no feeling; it has
been drilled out of them. But here in a city so poor, they know how to
live. They sing from feeling; they sing from the heart." As we leave together, one of them tells me that it feels like Lisbon is twenty-five years
behind the rest of Europe—even eastern Europe. "Portugal is even poorer
than Greece! But look at the Netherlands, that is where the financial
power is. . . . [The Portuguese] were shut off from the rest of Europe for
so long. . . . But soon, world capitalism will take advantage of Portuguese
generosity and feeling and run over them all."

These narratives point to the fraught positioning of Portugal in the
European imaginary, from the perspective of anxious locals (*Do you*

think Portugal is a developed country?) to the nostalgic gaze of the Slova-kian tourist from Germany. In both examples, Lisbon is imagined as behind other European cities. For the tourist, this temporal difference is linked through an experience of listening to fado in an amateur club to feeling, an emotionality that will be taken advantage of when the time of "world capitalism" catches up to it. The Germans, evidently imagined as in the grip of "world capitalism," have had the "feeling drilled out of them." In my conversation with the guitarrista, Lisbon's geopolitical and temporal positioning was framed with the word *aldeia*, or a village that modernity has passed by. The tourist tells me, "They [the Portuguese] were shut off from the rest of Europe." The Estado Novo did its best to cordon off the state, both its real and imagined borders, and to shape an idyll of nation through a turn inward—to the "land"; to the rural, bu-colic, and backward; to a pre-industrial past, as well as to the golden age of Portuguese colonialism. One way in which nostalgia and nation were mapped onto land was through the trope of saudade, which for nation-alist ends was shaped as a specifically Portuguese sentiment of longing, with the practice of fado a key conduit.

Portugal is perhaps uniquely situated as the European nation with the sharpest contrast between its remote past as a former economic and colonial power and its status during most of twentieth century as one of the poorest countries in Europe. Yet a mythology of Portugal as former geographic and economic center is still bolstered by a deep colonialist nostalgia that formed part of the nation-building project of the Estado Novo (see chapter 2). My Portuguese interlocutors often cited Portugal's positioning on the margins of Europe, sharing borders only with Spain and the sea, as a reason for Portuguese "cultural cosmopolitanism" and as an explanation for feelings of isolation, marginality, and "backward-ness" in relation to the rest of Europe. In this context, cosmopolitanism is usually associated with the Portuguese impetus to "discover" the world, and with Lisbon as a former crossroads for world commerce thus indelibly stamped by cultural hybridity. Geographic marginality maps onto residual memories, practices, and senses of place born from almost fifty years of exclusionary tactics—the isolationism wrought through practices of censorship, political repression, travel restrictions—and current economic crisis.

Fado circulation via the world music industry reinforces core–periphery economic stereotypes of Europe's North and South.[31] The world music industry and fado tourism, the two primary circuits through which the sounds of fado enter the wider European sonic imaginary, help shape Portugal and Lisbon, from the perspective of Europe's "center," into geographical "zones of repudiation," with all of the fallout that that entails, affecting characteristics commonly associated with nostalgia: erasure of historical specificity, temporal stasis, bounded geographies (Fox and Yano forthcoming; Kirshenblatt-Gimblett 1998a; Trouillot 1995). This hearing "from afar" interanimates the hearing and musical practices from "within"—tourist casas de fado and amateur Lisbon bars, Europe's North and Europe's South, geographical and economic center and periphery, global and local, city and country—in continuous aesthetically productive dialectic (Feld 1996a; Meintjes 2003).

Fado's "World"

The fadista Mariza strategically launched her first CD and her international career with the Amsterdam-based recording label World Connection in 2001. Two years later, after BBC Radio 3 had awarded her its world music prize in the Europe category, Mariza's popularity in Portugal increased. In the late 1990s, the fadista Cristina Branco had already made her European career through her success in the Netherlands, where she released her first recording; she is still better known in the Netherlands, Belgium, and France than in Portugal.[32] Recordings by the fadista Mísia in the early 1990s were some of the first to be marketed in the world music category. Mísia began her recording career in Paris, and like Branco, she has greater notoriety in France, Belgium, the Netherlands, and Germany than in Portugal and is known for her collaborations with Europe's artistic elite, such as the French actress Isabelle Huppert.[33] Although the international and national career of the late fado diva Amália Rodrigues was launched in the 1940s and 1950s by her initial successes in Paris and in Rio de Janeiro, the current patterns for successful international fado careers since the early 2000s have been shifting, particularly by the increasing prominence of the Netherlands as its hub. While the Netherlands and France have sizable Portuguese populations, the success of Mariza, Cristina Branco, and Mísia is linked more to marketing for the category of a cosmopolitan "world" rather than to Portuguese immigrants outside Portugal.

In its packaging as "world" and for its circulation within Europe's "core," fado remains intrinsically linked to feeling and soul, to a Lisbon and Portuguese-based "essence" (as it is for the local Portuguese market and in self-reflexive fado discourse within the genre). Yet these voices "transcend" the specificity of place through "innovation" and often through the evocation of a "celestial" or a universalized melancholy.[34] On her first CD, Mariza is introduced as "planetary" with a Portuguese twist: "Mariza is an adorable extraterrestrial being, someone sent by the Great Creator to reinvent the Fado. Mariza came as a bolt of lightning from the Soul of Old Portugal, a lost and found in the Sea of Intranquility within Portuguese Music. This is the kind of music that one doesn't just play, or just sing, but more than anything else, one feels" (Fernandes 2001). The "music as a universal language" theme, in which the languages of the world's music are translated by sound that signifies "feeling," serves as the central unifying trope of the international world music industry. Yet in relation to fado, the question remains as to how the work of feeling, and of emotional excess that fado chatter cultivates around its object, play out in the "world" and at "home" and in the dynamic charge and exchange between these two spaces and places.

In the seven years of its world music awards program (2002–2008), BBC Radio 3 chose six of its seven winners in its "Europe" category from Europe's periphery (four were from southern Europe). Mariza won in 2003 and was a finalist in 2006.[35] The critical role that the music industry in Europe's North plays in the success of fado divas in both the European and the world music market suggests that core Europe is mining its periphery for emotionality and for excess and that a salient way in which this rawness of "unmediated" feeling is indexed is through the sounds of the singing "southern" voice. While practitioners classify fado into multiple subgenres based on features of poetic-musical form and performance practice, in fado's international circulation, these generic classifications are often rendered moot; music that would not be heard in Portugal as fado might be marketed generically as such. An iconic stylistic tinge (e.g., the sound of a wailing voice singing in continental Portuguese accompanied by acoustic instruments) might come to metonymically carry the affective weight of the genre as a whole. And while those who listen to fado as world music in Amsterdam or Paris might feel that they are partaking in the cosmopolitan and exotic, some young fado musicians in Lisbon spoke to me with resentment about fado's classification outside Portugal. For them, the term "world music" carried a stigma. "'World music' is for Africa, maybe for Brazil, for the Third

World," a young professional guitar player told me in 2003. "Tango isn't 'world music.' Jazz isn't 'world music.' Fado isn't 'world music.'" Fado's self-Orientalizing discourses of affect, nostalgia, and place converge with exoticisms of fado and Europe's South shaped from Europe's center.

The South within "the South"

If one thinks of an imaginary of southern Europe (as shaped by the North) as symbolically accumulative of detritus, as a sensuous premodern of olive trees, vineyards, warm sun, languor, and "slow velocity" (James W. Fernandez, in Asad et al. 1997: 725), as the Land of Feeling, then within Portugal, on the periphery of the already peripheral that is the Iberian Peninsula, how deep might the South symbolically run? Portugal itself is marked by enduring sociohistorical divisions between North and South whose stereotypes partly mirror European–North–South logics. As José Manuel Sobral (2008: 205) argues, geo-cultural distinctions between the north and the south within Portugal, as theorized by northern Portuguese intellectuals and later abandoned by the intellectual elite, are still salient in popular discourse within Portugal and are often cast in racial, ethnic, gendered, and political registers.[36]

Daniel Melo (2001: 78) uses the metaphor of Russian nesting dolls to describe the semiotics of a particular aesthetics of representation in relation to the scalar politics of the Estado Novo, where the village represented the nation, the *casa do povo* (state-sponsored educational and recreational centers within villages) stood for the village, and exhibits in an "ethnographic" museum within the casa do povo represented "traditional" life in miniature to the residents of the village.[37] A similar kind of logic can be applied to understanding how Orientalisms (from both within and outside) sediment at the symbolic level in relation to fado's positioning within the logic of North–South essentialisms and the desires that fuel them, mapping onto a sentimentalizing place-making aesthetic residual from the regime. Panning inward from southern Europe to Portugal, then to southern Portugal, to Lisbon, to Alfama, and to a tiny tasca (which sometimes contains miniaturized representations of itself or those who sing there in the form of photographs or dioramas), one might find the fado voice (sometimes singing lyrics about the sounds, protagonists, histories, and places of fado itself). In this essentialized "fado voice" the raw emotion, or soulfulness, of the singing voice comes to stand in all at once for community, for neighborhood, for city, for country, for Europe's South, and for the global South—for an imaginary of an "unmediated" sentiment and sociality lodged in a time-place that neoliberal capitalism has supposedly run over in its wake.

Yet there are multiple kinds of centers, different kinds of peripheries. In North–South logics, the "South" is affectively central precisely because it is imagined as geopolitically, economically, and temporally peripheral. Within the so-called South, these very same logics and stereotypes might be generated, appropriated, or marshaled as cultural resources for similar or different ends. "All of this saudade is keeping Portugal behind the rest of Europe," a well-educated, middle-class white Portuguese man in his late forties complained to me in 2000. But during some particularly good sessions of fado in 2003, Jaime said to me more than once (partly joking, partly serious), "This here is special. You don't have this in America, do you? But you *do* have McDonald's."

From the perspective of world music, film, and local and global tourism industries, Portugal is often cast, together with Latin America, the "Latin," or the Mediterranean, as a key player in a "political economy of passion" (Savigliano 1995), with music and dance doing much of the work of indexing that "passion." Many people I spoke to in Lisbon, ranging from bank clerks to taxi drivers, fadistas, and fans, positioned themselves as national subjects reflexively vis-à-vis their supposed capacity as Portuguese to "feel deeply" (see chapter 2). But in these conversations, "passion" or "feeling deeply" were not necessarily invoked as a sign of belonging to the "Latin" or to the Mediterranean. To the contrary: many actors made routine distinctions between themselves as Portuguese affective subjects and the supposed national "character" of people from other southern European, "Latin," or Mediterranean places. And within fado communities, unexpected affective cartographies were sometimes mapped, for example between the Portuguese and the Japanese. *The Japanese have a proclivity for fado. They like fado and understand it because they have an emotional constitution close to ours. They feel things deeply, inside, but don't always demonstrate their feelings.* In these narratives, fado listening and performance practices function as markers of an affective subject; they mark *qualities* of affective experience, predilections, and capabilities for experiencing and expressing emotions.

The "Ear within an Ear"

My friend Viriato, an activist during the Estado Novo who worked clandestinely in a factory in northern Portugal as part of a wider communist-led movement to end the dictatorship, looks over multiple close-up photographs I took of the clay-figure diorama at the Fado Museum. I ask him about possible similarities between the model and an Estado Novo aesthetics of an atemporal representation of "tradition" and sentimentalization wrought through miniaturization. He explains to me that he sees the diorama as breaking from that aesthetic. He points to the miniature rotund policeman who struts with pomp; an elderly woman, arms crossed, grimacing; the general flurry of activity represented within the still format of the diorama. "The figurines in an Estado Novo–era folk display would all be smiling, and certainly the policeman would be depicted as an authority figure, not as someone to jeer at," he tells me. He sees more of the "real" in this representation than the idealized "folk." We look at the photographs again, and I see a "realness" that is cast in the dynamic chaos of the scene presented (in relation to the excess of activities occurring simultaneously in a small space) and in the variety of emotional registers indexed through the figurines' facial expressions and bodily postures. The diorama can be read as foregrounding a friction between aesthetic idioms, an ambivalence.

In the discussion of place-name fados, I focused on those that sentimentalize fado's city and fado's places because they constituted the overwhelming majority of such fados I heard performed across wide-ranging venues during the time of my field research. They are also the place-name fados that have figured most prominently on recordings that were circulating both locally and internationally during that time. I have used the term "sentimentalize" to signify a poetic and musical rendering of nostalgia that (like all nostalgias) desires an object that is forever just beyond grasp. In most place-name fados, nostalgia renders place as impossibly "pretty" and quaint, or as the site of a vague and bittersweet longing for the past, or as both simultaneously.

Affect condenses in the very small (Bachelard 1994; S. Stewart 2003).[38] In writing about an "economy of affects" in Portugal, José Gil (2007: 48) remarks on the "Lilliput Syndrome" he understands operates in Portugal as a residual habitus of the dictatorship in relation to a politics of scale. As such, symbolic relations (and the affect they generate) with tremendous power are condensed into the very small: into small social circuits, into small gestures.[39] Discourse folds back in on itself, circulating in spaces that were also closed in on themselves. In this play of scale, where affect is made more powerful, more immense in its condensation, perhaps some of fado's gestures as genre (writ large and small) can be understood to work in a similar fashion. The duration of a fado is a small eternity; it is a miniature. Small musical gestures are endowed with immense capacity to move, reinforced by smallness as a trope of the everyday, long in place since the dictatorship. Gil (2007: 46) regards smallness as the "negation of excess." I think about it as the amplification of excess. In writing on the "poetics of space," Gaston Bachelard (1994: 166) comments on the fairy-tale character of tiny Tom Thumb, reflexively, as an "ear within an ear." Fado as genre might be understood as a kind of ear within an ear, a voice within a voice, endlessly reflecting back on itself and its ever changing city, city and genre interanimated, re-sounding. This reflexivity built into the genre *can* hyper-exoticize both fado and its city, but it can also render critique possible. Fado cannot contain its own excess, its sense of itself as affect. Against the ground of a highly sentimentalizing poetics of place making, or "soul making," but working within fado's musical and discursive tropes of reflexivity, excess, and affect, some poets and fadistas figure ambivalences or ruptures.

"ALFAMA"
Quando Lisboa anoitece
Como um veleiro sem velas
Alfama toda parece
Uma casa sem janelas
Aonde o povo arrefece

É numa água-furtada
No espaço roubado à mágoa
Que Alfama fica fechada
Em quatro paredes de água
Quatro paredes de pranto
Quatro muros de ansiedade
Que à noite fazem o canto
Que se acende na cidade
Fechada em seu desencanto
Alfama cheira a saudade

Alfama não cheira a fado
Cheira a povo, a solidão
A silêncio magoado
Sabe a tristeza com pão
Alfama não cheira a fado
Mas não tem outra canção

Alfama não cheira a fado
Mas não tem outra canção.

———

When night falls upon Lisbon
Like a sailboat without sails
All of Alfama seems
A house without windows
Where the people are chilled

It is in an attic
In a space robbed from anguish
That Alfama is closed
In by four walls of water
Four walls of weeping
Four walls of anxiety
For at night they make the song
That sets light to the city
Closed in its disenchantment
Alfama smells of saudade

Alfama does not smell of fado
It smells of the people, of loneliness
Of painful silence
It tastes of sadness with bread
Alfama does not smell of fado
But it has no other song

Alfama does not smell of fado
But it has no other song.[40]

These lyrics refer to spatial enclosure, claustrophobia, poverty, and pain.
The fado effects multiple ruptures—poetic, aesthetic, musical, and
political—and presents a version of Alfama that never would have been

sanctioned during the Estado Novo. One can hear the critique leveled by this fado without straining to listen between the lines. "Alfama," which was part of the repertoire of Amália Rodrigues, was recorded in 1977, three years after the coup of April 25, 1974.[41] Imagine these words sung by a female voice so powerful that fans talk about how the warm soulful sound of it leaves them feeling "dizzy" and "drunk" and with "no words to describe" it. Yet this is a voice that, in the years immediately following the revolution, many people in Portugal associated with the dictatorship (see chapter 6). In this recording, Amália ornaments and prolongs the last utterance of the word "Alfama" in the space of the silence the guitarra and viola momentarily make as they wait for her vocal improvisations to unfold.

Ary dos Santos, the author of the lyrics, was one of Portugal's best-known communist poets. Alain Oulman composed the music. Both figures were controversial for their political and artistic work. In "Alfama," Santos deploys many of fado's stock poetic tropes: the neighborhood, the city, a home, an attic (água-furtada), a boat (which often symbolizes the Portuguese colonial Discoveries), water, a window (through which one accesses an "interior," often the singing voice "overheard"), night, weeping, loneliness, silence, song, and fado itself. He decouples fado from a censored and sanitized version of place by inverting the common significance of these tropes, emptying them of their romanticism, at once disenchanting both fado and Alfama. The Alfama of the Estado Novo—of the eternal, of the intimate—is debunked and laid bare; the architecture of intimacy becomes claustrophobic, closed.

Disenchantment is rendered in part through a poetics of synesthesia. The neighborhood is not just heard or felt. Alfama *smells* of saudade, of loneliness, of people, of a painful silence. Silence as an aesthetic associated with fado listening here blurs with silence as politically enforced. These lyrics contrast dramatically with the refrain of "Cheira a Lisboa" (Aroma [Smell] of Lisbon), an Estado Novo–era song that is still widely performed and was also recorded by Amália Rodrigues): "A carnation in an attic/Lisbon smells good/A rose flowering in a park/Lisbon smells good/A frigate that rises in the bow/A fisherwoman who insists in passing/They smell good because they are from Lisbon/Lisbon smells like flowers and the sea."[42] Santos's and Oulman's Alfama "does not smell of fado." Fado is taken away from Alfama to be reclaimed as a genre capable of overt political critique. Yet the ethos of fado as a cultural apparatus associated with the Estado Novo lingers.

Just as Santos works lyrically with some of fado's most common poetic tropes, but shifts their meanings, Oulman's musical language borrows from some of the grammars of traditional fado. Yet this is decidedly *not* traditional fado. Like all of Oulman's fados, "Alfama" is a musical composition formed in collaboration with Amália Rodrigues, and employs a harmonic language that is far more complex than is common in either fado canção or fado tradicional. While there is a critical alteration in the third verse, "Alfama" is almost strophic, the quasi-strophic structure providing some of the affective scaffolding associated with the form of traditional fado (where affect accrues through repetition with a difference). In this recorded version from 1977, the instrumentalists cite from typical instrumental figuring of tonic and dominant harmonies of the Fado Menor at the end of the fado. In sonically invoking the Fado Menor, which many consider as the saddest, the most authentic, the "oldest" and most "traditional" fado, they comment on the authenticity of affect and meaning of this ruptured fado and this ruptured place.[43]

The Gaze from the Miradouro da Meia Laranja

Meia Laranja is a small viewpoint on a hill on the very edge of Lisbon's historical periphery that looks out on a large housing project (*bairro social*), the neighborhood of Casal Ventoso. I came to learn about Casal Ventoso in 2003 through the voice of the fadista José Manuel Osório, who sang a fado titled "Meia Laranja," written by one of Lisbon's best-known fado poets, José Luís Gordo. During the dictatorship, Osório was an actor, an outspoken political activist, and a fado singer. He sold his fado recordings, which would have been censored, on the black market. In 2002, he was active as a fado researcher, a fadista, and an AIDS activist.[44]

I hear Osório sing "Meia Laranja" for the first time, improvising to the music of the traditional fado Fado Vitória, at an amateur venue in Alfama in 2002, where on that evening there is a mix of tourists and locals. He is seated. His feet tap; his eyes close; his body quivers with the intensity of the focus in his voice as he bursts forth during a phrase after holding a silence just beyond the point of expectation or pushes a note to the timbral edge of breaking. Later, he described the neighborhood of Meia Laranja to me: "Meia Laranja opens to the view of the principal entrance to one of the most problematic neighborhoods in the city of Lisbon. There one can buy everything, sell everything: antiques (stolen), automobiles (stolen), passports (false), airplane tickets (to everywhere in the world), medications (stolen from the hospitals). It is an underworld of criminality and of marginality, a type of reality that many know only from the cinema. But this is no film. This is the most difficult reality imaginable."[45] In 1995, when the fado was written, the neighborhood of Casal Ventoso, beneath the viewpoint of "Meia Laranja," was one of Europe's most active sites of narco-trafficking. This was enabled partly by Lisbon's geographical location as port city on Europe's margins, its proximity to northern Africa, and the complicity—or, at least, lack of attention—of local police and authorities. By 1998, in response to European and state-sponsored initiatives, many of its residents had been relocated and a number of dwellings demolished in an effort to "clean up" Casal Ventoso (Chaves 1999: 23).[46]

"FADO DA MEIA LARANJA"
Ali à Meia Laranja
Meio inferno de Lisboa
Onde a morte anda a viver
Há milhares de olhos baços
E a vida tem quatro braços
Para a morte se esconder

Por entre gente perdida
Jovens entregam a vida
À loucura que se esbanja
E nas veias da tristeza
Tantas facas de pobreza
Ali à Meia Laranja

Há tanto cavalo à solta
Com chicotes de revolta
Num galopar que magoa
Há punhais de infelicidade
Ali se mata a idade
No coração de Lisboa.

There in Meia Laranja
Half hell of Lisbon
Where death lives
There are thousands of dim eyes
And life has four arms
In which death can hide

In the midst of lost souls
Young people give up their lives
To a madness that wastes them
And in the veins of sadness
There are so many needles [knives] of poverty
There in Meia Laranja

There is so much heroin (and the authorities just turn a blind eye)
With whips of revolt
In a gallop that hurts
There are daggers of unhappiness
There which kill the youth
In the heart of Lisbon.[47]

Osório accentuates the throaty and sometimes nasal grain of his voice, strategically prolongs silences, and plays with rhythmic meter and with extremes of vocal volume, affectively intensifying Gordo's lyrics and drawing his listeners into a space of intimacy. We sit on the edge of our seats in the small space in darkness, listening to this man who seems at this moment only voice and tremulous sound. The silences between vocalizations are charged; we collectively hold our breath.

By crying this particular Lisbon, Osório's "Meia Laranja" helps restore the grit of materiality to fado's city and to return the city of Lisbon back to fado. These lyrics and Osório's performance of them are striking for drawing heightened attention to harsh social realities. Not only is the dark side of Lisbon in the contemporary moment rarely a subject for fado, but social problems such as drug trafficking, racism, domestic violence, and AIDS are often eclipsed in the day to day. "Meia Laranja," while playing on fado's fetishization of neighborhood, does not marshal the folk, the nostalgic, or the colonial cosmopolitan to shape the place of Portugal, or of Lisbon. It does not erase the "real."[48]

Affects of Genre

The larger story I tell here is a story about genre, about the power of a musical genre to shape topographies of affect and public feeling: the kind of affect that binds people to places or that imbues a place with desire. It is also about a dialectic between a musical genre and the city to which it is most attached. This is not an argument that exclusively binds genre's affective potencies to narratives of the nation, the city, the country, or particular belongings or histories. Rather, I am interested in how musical genre works mercurially in its syncretic iterations; how a musical genre in its excessive formal repetitions and improvisations, along with its stereotypical affective and sonic registers, might shape feeling that becomes shared sentiment while opening new possibilities for the experience of place and subjectivity. I have granted genre some agency to try to understand it in an inter-dynamic relation both with how individuals and communities experience senses of place (Feld and Basso 1996) and with the shaping of wider representations and affective topographies that are both socially and geopolitically situated.

Lisbon is not alone as a city that is associated with, and that lays originary claim to, its own musical genre. There is often a powerful inter-dynamism between particular musical genres, specific cities, and the poetics and politics of place making.[49] The story I tell here can also be read as another anthropological case study that investigates iconic or indexical linkages between song genres of loss and longing and places, regions, or nations (Dent 2009; Fox 2004; Stokes 2010; Yano 2002). Lauren Berlant (2008: 4) writes about genre as a "form of aesthetic expectation with porous boundaries allowing complex audience identifications" and argues that genre "locates real life in the affective capacity to bracket many kinds of structural and historical antagonisms on behalf of finding a way to connect with the feeling of belonging to a larger world, however aesthetically mediated." Theorizing musical reception, circulation, and experience through the prism of genre brings to this discussion the sensuality of sound in combination with the rich and polysemous way in which the often not explicitly referential language of music interacts with meaning, memory, feeling, and place making (Feld et al. 2004; Samuels 2004). Perhaps we can think about musical genres—particularly sung vocal genres, in that singing presents "surplus articulation" (Dolar 2006: 32)—as excessively porous across different sensory domains thus supremely powerful in their potential to perform multiple kinds of affective labor.

Lisbon is overdetermined by fado, mimicking fado in its excess. Fado sets in dialogue multiple imaginaries of place, history, and feeling: Lisbon neighborhoods as Portugal's "land," fado as Portugal's lost sociality, lost place, lost time, fado as universal melancholy, fado as Lisbon's excessive feminine, fado as a residual practice of one of Europe's longest dictatorships. Or, as some fans put it to me, fado as always but always a revolutionary song that will forever slip through the cracks and resist state appropriation, at once too personal, too social, too wayward, and too powerful to belong to the country. These overlaps and discontinuities open fissures in musical, generic, and historical narratives of place and of belonging. They reveal places where geography and geopolitics, official and nonofficial Portuguese histories, the intimacy of neighborhood and politics of the state, industries of music and culture, and, finally, fado aesthetics, lyrics, and lore intersect with layered, competing, and often contradictory meanings.

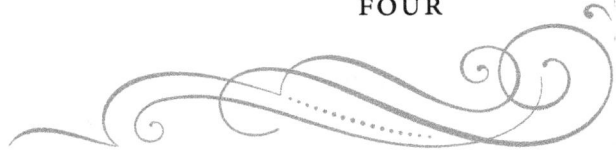

FOUR

Styling Soulfulness

How to describe the moments of improvised movement in the voice in performance so that you can imagine them? There are the shifts in pitch and rhythm; suspensions of time in a vowel drawn out or a silence prolonged; micro-timbral nuances in the voice that inflect the feeling of a word or a phrase. There are moments that hover on a continuum between speech and song—now a word declaimed, then a phrase sung. There are the variations of force behind the air as it moves out of the lungs and the throat into the air: the wails, the whispers, the falsettos, the sometimes widely oscillating vibrato. Then there is stillness, the strategic use of silence. José Manuel Osório spoke to me about the importance of hearing silences in instrumental accompaniments in order to sing into them and to style (*estilar*).[1] The guitarrista José Fontes Rocha emphasized how the most important task of the guitarra is to fill in (*preencher*) the silences opened by the fadista between vocalizations. Each guitarrista, he said, "fills this space in his own way."[2] Styling depends as much on the sensitive use and awareness of silence in performance as it does on the inventive use of sound.

There is the mutual enjoyment between the instrumentalists that one can sometimes witness—the musical jokes, the virtuosic lick, an inventive chord figuration—with pleasure signaled by an appreciative nod, a movement of the body in toward the other, a smile. While skilled instrumentalists respond musically to the fadista (and vice versa), they sometimes appear to be in their own world (particularly when, as is often the case, they are positioned behind the fadista). In fado performance, the fadista is in the limelight. But without the viola's moving bass line and the melodic and harmonic figurations and improvisations of the guitarra, there is no fado. There is the overlapping, the continuous and inventive weaving in and out of the guitarra lines, sometimes echoing the voice and sometimes harmonizing with it, playing a styled *contracanto* (countermelody), figuring harmonies, always in "dialogue" (Castelo-Branco 1994). Guitarras sometimes weep (*gemer*), they tremble and trill (*trinar*), they vibrate (*vibrar*), they sob (*soluçar*). The guitarra player has to know when to weep, how to make the instrument weep, and how to make it sing.

Listeners, and fado lyrics themselves, call attention to the importance of the guitarra—its twelve steel strings, six of them sympathetic, plucked by hard plastic fingernail extensions (*unhas*) sounding almost harpsichord-like, with specific ways of figuring chords depending on the fado at hand, and always in an inter-dynamic "styling" with the fadista and the viola—for making fado *fado*. The viola, a six-string acoustic guitar, is not as timbrally unusual as the guitarra, is not as overtly virtuosic in performance; musically its function is at the center of the triad, providing a steady bass, powering the rhythm, and propelling the harmonic movement that undergirds the fado. Sometimes, although rarely in early twenty-first century fado, one has the privilege of hearing a bass acoustic guitar (*viola baixo*) playing alongside the viola in a fado performance, lending extra depth to the harmonic line.

The guitarra mediates between the sound worlds of the fadista and of the viola. The guitarrista mediates between clearly marked diatonic harmonies of the viola and the styled vocal line of the fadista. The vocal performance of the fadista is one that at times flees diatonicism through microtonal slides and ornamentation that sometimes sounds more like speech than song. It often ruptures straight meter through rhythmic suspensions writ large and small in the silences offered by the instrumentalists or syncopates the meter marked by the viola with respect to syllabic stress and word emphasis (*dividir as palavras*). The guitarrista mediates via the twang of unhas on steel strings by his right hand and a wavering vibrato by his left, a twanging and brilliant timbre whose overtones (particularly if he pulls a note out of tune through excessive vibrato, or "weeping") can escape at times the equal tempered sound world marked by the viola.

Within the context of amateur fado, there is an enormous repertoire that the instrumentalists are expected to be able to draw on, hundreds of fados, some *fados tradicionais* (traditional fados), some *fados canção* (fado songs), all remembered in the ears, in the vocal chords, in the fingers, in the joints, in the musical memory, without recourse to notation. While many traditional fados are built around relatively straightforward chord progressions (often just I, IV, and V or I and V), there are many possibilities for how the instrumentalists choose to figure these chords, how they choose to weave the melody of the singer into their accompaniment, and how they choose to respond to the voice, affectively emphasizing key moments. At the same time, instrumentalists often employ stock figurations, or ways of figuring chords or progressions, some of which are associated with specific traditional fados.[3] Particularly in amateur fado scenes, the instrumentalists (and listeners) might vary from week to week or session to session.[4] Fadista styling is responsive to these changes.

How to give you a sense of the pleasure of saturation in listening, of feeling wrought from sedimented and layered repetitions of traditional fados? There are infinite ways to sing and to style any given traditional fado while staying within the confines of the form. There are infinite possibilities for how the guitarra and viola might accompany the voice while remaining true to the form. There are infinite possibilities regarding the lyrics the fadista (or poet) might choose to set while still adhering to the conventions of poetic meter and versification that traditional fado demands.[5] Yet the musical base of any particular traditional fado in common practice remains distinct and usually identifiable to instrumentalists, fadistas, and skilled listeners. This chapter is primarily concerned with the improvisatory stylizations of a fado voice; it is a movement toward understanding something about *acts* and *forms* of fadista styling (estilar) in relation to the performance practices that constitute the generic subcategory of *fado tradicional* (traditional fado).[6] It is an interlude, a temporary dwelling on well-worn ethnomusicological questions of relations between so-called musical/aesthetic structure and social life and questions regarding the efficacies (or colossal failures) of musical transcription to shed light on those relations. It pushes questions that were decades ago glossed in relation to "structure" into the domain of thinking about aesthetic forms in circulation and public feeling.

This chapter takes as its central focus the "Fado da Meia Laranja," the Fado Vitória, with which I concluded in chapter 3. I work here with a preliminary analysis that outlines in broad strokes the styling of the voice of José Manuel Osório against the chordal progressions and meter marked by the guitarra and the viola, focusing on three renditions of Osório performing the "Fado da Meia Laranja" set to a Fado Vitória and recorded in 2003–2004. I use this outlining of vocal gestures as the means to understand both the contours of form and styling as practiced and as a means to get at ways in which form and styling provide vehicles for fado listening *as* feeling, for the sedimentation of affect, of story, of memory and the experience of pleasure.

Fado Vitória

Fado Vitória: a traditional fado with weight, a fado for serious words in a minor key, a fado that demands verses in *sextilhas* (six-line groupings), a fado Amália Rodrigues made famous with her rendition of "Povo Que Lavas no Rio," a poem by the high-art poet Pedro Homem de Mello that tells a story of belonging to "the people," an understanding of a life of hardship. Fado Vitória: the fado to which the legendary twentieth-century male fadista of "the people," Fernando Maurício, from the neighborhood of Mouraria, sang with the lyrics "A Igreja de Santo Estêvão" (The Church of Saint Stephen), lyrics that celebrate the neighborhood of Alfama. Fado Vitória, the fado that José Manuel Osório, earlier in his career, recorded with lyrics that critiqued the politics of the Estado Novo and to which he sang later in his life, the lyrics of "Fado da Meia Laranja" (see chapter 3).

> It is a Saturday night fado session in 2003 at the Tasca do Careca, one of Lisbon's best-attended amateur fado events. The large restaurant is filled to capacity. The presenter, Sebastião de Jesus, introduces the fadista with a flourish: "Now we will dim the lights a little more to prepare for the ultimate silence. You are about to hear the voice of José Manuel Osório, a man who never sings the same way twice." As listeners hush, the guitarrista and viola begin playing the clearly recognizable introduction to a Fado Vitória, the first four pitches of the bass line steadily creeping chromatically upward. A listener, anticipating José's entrance, shouts, "Meia Laranja, José Manuel!" The instrumentalists open a silence with an

extended pause. José waits, allowing the silence in the room to accumulate. He leans forward and begins, "Ali à Meia Laranja . . ." (There in [the neighborhood of] Meia Laranja). *As he moves from strophe to strophe, over the repeated harmonic sequence of the bass line, his voice accrues intensity, dynamic, and timbral variety and covers a wider range of pitches. As he moves from strophe to strophe, the poem accrues affective power.*[7]

In contemporary practice, specific lyrics in relation to a given traditional fado are still almost always associated with the repertoire and voice of an individual fadista. However, lyrics also become coupled and associated with particular traditional fados in their circulation and are sometimes recontextualized in the voices of other singers in relation to repeated performances (or recordings) of masterful fadistas. Listeners and fadistas often link particular lyrics with the singers who first gave them voice. And because, to some extent, to sing the repertoire of another is to ventriloquize another, a degree of social risk is sometimes attached to "covering" a lyrics/traditional fado coupling, a risk of being perceived as "copying," or a risk of being perceived as presumptuous. It demands a courageous soul to get up and sing "Povo Que Lavas no Rio," a poem so infused in the aural public imagination with the voice and repertoire of Amália Rodrigues. Such "covers," in the context of amateur fado, are sometimes performed as homage to a fadista who has passed away or sometimes in imitation, as part of the learning process. Sometimes, they are simply taken on as part of a fadista's own repertoire, but this can be risky, particularly if the performance is deemed by listeners to not pass muster.

Fado Vitória: a fado in which the harmonic movement undergirding the musical phrases in each strophe consists of two sections, both repeated once with the second section also used as an instrumental introduction. There is the overarching long-drawn-out lament sigh in the bass line beginning with the vocal entrance following the introduction; this is a macro sigh, marked by the viola and filled in by the guitarra, in the downward harmonic movement emphasizing i to vii to vi to V then to i. This is a progression that musicians refer to as the *escala espanhola* (Spanish scale); it tropes the baroque lament figuration in Western art music of a descending tetrachord.[8] On top of that line are all of the possibilities for the voice to cry, in the micro sighs of a downward glissando, the approach to a note through a sigh, even between two notes only a step apart, and so many ways to style the melody.

In one of my first meetings with José, he played for me multiple renditions of a Fado Vitória, one from 1929, the hiss overlay in the recording audible, the voice and instrumentalists for the most part marking a clear duple meter, the fadista occasionally stretching out a phrase in time, just slightly, at key moments in the poem.[9] Another was the recording of Amália singing the Vitória with different lyrics, "Povo Que Lavas no Rio" from 1962; she plays with meter by holding out suspensions beyond the point of expectation in a heady melismatic virtuosity. He played me other renditions of the same fado sung by Amália: a recording of her accompanied by the saxophone player Don Byas released in the 1970s; and a live recording made at Town Hall in New York in 1990 when her tessitura had dropped and her timbre become more broken and husky, the guitarra player working to sustain pitches under her voice when she lacked the sustaining power. We took delight in the variations on a theme, the persuasive power of the voice styling—of timbre, of rhythm, of melody, of inflection, of breath, of force, of articulation, of syllable stress, of word placement—against the relatively stable marking of the time and the harmony in the bass line. That night, I went to a small amateur fado venue in Alfama where José sang the poem "Fado da Meia Laranja," written for him by José Luis Gordo, to a Fado Vitória. Over the next five years, I recorded and collected versions of José singing the Vitória with these lyrics in different performance contexts.

Styling

A man who never sings the same way twice. "Estilar" (styling) in fado, is overwhelmingly spoken about by fadistas as essentially unlearnable, as the defining characteristic of fado as genre as practice (see chapter 1) and of a fadista as an individual voice. Instrumentalists style too. Attention to styling as a musical-performance practice in fado touches on multiple murky areas of the "fuzzy fringes" (Bauman and Briggs 1992: 145) of fado as genre and raises challenging questions regarding the kinds of work musical performance does in relation to shaping the subjectivity of a performer, or a "sonic self" (Cumming 2000); questions of intellectual ownership; the importance of performance context and listeners to the

PLATE 1 • Fado diorama at the Tasca do Jaime. Lisbon, August 2012.

All photographs are by the author.

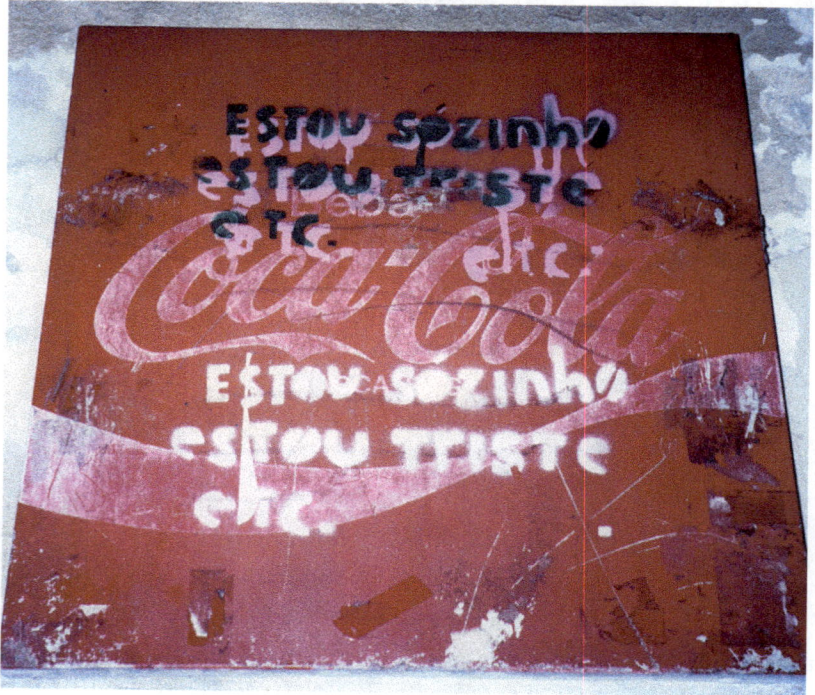

PLATE 2 • (top) "Tourists: Respect the Portuguese Silence!" Graffiti alongside the Miradouro Portas do Sol in Alfama. Lisbon, July 2007.

PLATE 3 • (bottom) "Estou sozinho, estou triste, etc." (I am alone, I am sad, etc.). Graffiti in the Chiado district. Lisbon, July 2000.

PLATE 4 • "Vielas" (Alleyways), by Rui Pimentel (1998). Collection of the Museu do Fado, Lisbon, 2009. Published by permission of Rui Pimentel and the Museu do Fado.

PLATE 5 • Fado venues in Alfama. Lisbon, June 2006.

PLATE 6 • (top) Olga Rosa de Sousa singing at the Esquina de Alfama. Lisbon, August 2007.

PLATE 7 • (bottom) Fernanda Proença singing at the Tasca do Jaime. Lisbon, July 2006.

PLATE 8 • Amália Rodrigues's grave at Prazeres Cemetery. Lisbon, July 2000.

PLATE 9 • "Rua Amália" (Rua de São Bento). Lisbon, July 2009.

PLATE 10 • "Amália Rodrigues," by the street artist MrDheo, with letters by Mosaik, 2009. Lisbon, January 2010. Published by permission of MrDheo (http://www.mrdheo.com).

forms improvisations take; as well as questions about the "responsibility of forms" (Barthes 1985) with respect to the social transmission of musical conventions and affect broadly writ. Generically at stake are questions regarding implicit understandings that listeners and musicians use to differentiate one traditional fado from another and underlying questions about the constitution of fado form.

Many practitioners agreed that the melodic line of any given traditional fado, while needing to follow the contours of the underlying harmony, is not fixed, but that the sequence of harmonic progressions figured by the instrumentalists—and, to a large extent, the basic underlying metrical structure—*is* fixed. In addition, certain aspects of poetic form in relation to which lyrics can be set to specific traditional fados are also fixed, governed by rules regarding the number of stanzas, number of lines, and, sometimes, the syllabic count and rhyme scheme.[10] However, practitioners differed in their descriptions of the extent to which *melodies* in traditional fado have underlying skeletal structures or formulas (even if they are only implicit) around which they style. For some fadistas, "to style" is precisely *to invent* the melody of a traditional fado each time anew, a melody that, while following the predicable harmonic movement and metrical base of the particular traditional fado, comes out differently in every performance. While I commonly heard references to a "musical base" that remains constant as a defining feature of any given traditional fado, the parameters delimiting this musical base had some slippage around them, both in talk about form and in the ways in which forms were musically practiced.

Fado Vitória: a traditional fado possibly heard for the first time in the 1920s, registered in the Sociedade Portuguesa de Autores (SPA) in 1967 as having been composed by Joaquim Campos. The registration is accompanied by thirty-two bars of a notated melodic line in 4/4 time consisting of a strophe in three parts; the notation bears a trace resemblance to melodies of the Fado Vitória I heard live and on recordings from the past eighty years. I saw this notated transcription only after consulting the documentation department at the SPA.[11] I never saw any musical notation used in contexts of fado performance or heard anyone speak of an "original" notation for the Fado Vitória or other traditional fados. Performance practices and implicit and explicit ideologies regarding sonic form and improvisation held by musicians and listeners with respect to traditional fado do not line up neatly with practices governing the criteria on which claims of intellectual ownership for traditional fado are based at the SPA. Fado tradicional, as a highly improvisatory, relational, and processual performance practice, complicates ideologies of a single-authored musical "composition."

Just as fado tradicional and fado canção can be thought of as existing on a continuum in terms of a "minimum of fixed elements" to "a maximum fixity of most elements" (Castelo-Branco 1994: 133), it is also productive to think about fadista styling and the idea of "melody" in the practice of fado tradicional on a continuum in terms of "fixity." The positioning of any performance on this continuum depends both on the fado in question, as some traditional fados are in practice more scripted melodically than others, and on the the creativity, musicality, skill, and risk taking of the fadista and of the instrumentalists. In practice, one hears an enormous number of traditional fados sung live and on recordings, set with different poems, sung with melodies whose primary contours and gestures are recognizable and predictable for a practiced listener.

Upon transcribing some of these different performances, an underlying "implied" or skeletal melody could be mapped.[12] Older practitioners often told me that the homogeneity of melodic styling has increased partly because of the growing reliance throughout the twentieth century on using recordings to learn fado (see chapter 1). On the other side of the spectrum are fadistas and guitarristas who take enormous risks with their styling, staying within the poetic, harmonic, and metrical outlines dictated at the most basic level of form but pushing interpretive choices to an extreme. Osório is one such musical risk taker.[13]

Most practitioners and listeners emphasized to me that styling in fado is directly related to *sentimento* (feeling); one styles as one feels, and even fadistas who were highly reflexive about their own performances did not often articulate the process of styling in terms of its techniques, its gestures, or its figures. Fado's affective power in performance often hinges on micro-level nuances of vocal and instrumental inflections and gestures. Even when sung by the same fadista, with the same words, a fado is never expressively inflected exactly the same way twice. Sentimento and estilar—feeling and styling—are coupled through an idea of spontaneity. Fadista styling in the absence of socially transmitted sentiment carries no value.

Fado voices, particularly Amália's and those that came after her (i.e., from the 1950s and onward) are difficult to chart. They are full of pitch and timbral nuance, sliding elusively between points of marking the base harmony and meter of the fado, replete with rhythmic suspensions, moments when listeners lose (then find) their bearings. Fado voices, like other voices of affectively supercharged vocal genres (e.g., blues, country, gospel) challenge the limits of standard Western art music notation, partly because vocal timbre performs so much labor of communicating affect in these genres and because conventional notation does not have a nuanced representational system with which to convey timbral variation. A discursive ideology of representational/notational elusiveness of these genres in some cases also forms part of their aura, mystique, and power. This is the case with fado.[14]

Indeed, for fado, conventional Western musical notation is not useful as a descriptive analytic with respect to some of the most—or, perhaps, the most—salient features of vocal performance and styling in terms of the way skilled listeners and fadistas talk about them. Fado aesthetics overwhelmingly dictate the primacy of the word, the expressive articulation of the words of the poem above all. Particularly challenging to notate are gradations of timbre, moments that fall on a continuum between speech and song, microtonal movement, and precise rhythm in the vocal line. In performance, the syllabic stress of the words of the fadista does not necessarily fall clearly on the beat (or on a clear subdivision of the beat) as demarcated, usually by the viola, in the bass. However, conventional notation *is* useful for my purposes here as a descriptive representation of some aspects of the melodic parameters of styling of one fadista in performance in relation to the harmonic/rhythmic outlines sounded in bass line.

In 2008, I played the multiple renditions of recordings I had made of José's "Fado da Meia Laranja" to José in order to elicit his commentary on past performances. I asked about his process of styling the melody in the moment of performance. Might not he be relying on an implicit scaffold, a "standard" version heard in the inner ear but not voiced, his actual vocal performance a riff on this internalized standard? He adamantly insisted that this was not the case. Instead, he claimed that each time he sang, he was inventing the melody anew. If José Manuel Osório falls at the far end of a spectrum of heightened risk taking and innovation as a

EXAMPLE 4.1 • "Fado da Meia Laranja," sung by José Manuel Osório, measures 3–5, strophe 1, versions A, B, and C. Transcription by Yoshiaki Onishi.

fado stylist, what might transcribing these performances illuminate about the limits of traditional fado form with respect to melodic styling? What kinds of representational work might transcriptions be able to perform in relation to conveying the sedimentation of affect, story, and feeling that an artfully styled traditional fado renders possible?[15]

The first transcription represents synchronically, the first strophes of three performances by José of "Meia Laranja," recorded in three different contexts over a two-year period (see appendix 1 for full version).[16] José's performances in these renditions sound very different from one another. He does not sing each in the same key; he radically alters the timing of his entrance and the rhythm to which he sings the words in each phrase; and his use of dynamic and timbral inflection is markedly different from one performance to another. Melodically, with respect to both pitch and rhythm, he begins each version differently (example 4.1).

However, when transcribed and transposed to the same key, similarities between melodies quickly emerge at the level of pitch as the verse

EXAMPLE 4.2 • "Fado da Meia Laranja," sung by José Manuel Osório, measures 11–13, strophe 1, versions A, B, and C. Transcription by Yoshiaki Onishi.

progresses. They include motivic patterns; clusters of pitches sung; and the interval range of pitches sung in any given phrase. In some instances, José employs smaller figures (at the same moment in the lyrics) with identical pitch and rhythm. The excerpts in examples 4.2 and 4.3 reveal instances in which Osório flexibly employs similar melodic figures in multiple performances of "Meia Laranja" in relation to specific moments in the lyrics, which he carries through the musical/poetic phrase.[17] Melodic similarities are also foregrounded at the micro level at the ends of the poetic lines or musical cadences (cadences that sometimes simultaneously mark the beginning of the following poetic line). In these instances, José concludes the phrase on one of the notes in the chord marked by the viola, favoring the root or the fifth.

When traditional fado is performed by a skilled fadista, each strophe accumulates density of signification and of affect. As José sings "Meia

EXAMPLE 4.3 • "Fado da Meia Laranja," sung by José Manuel Osório, measures 32–34, strophe 1, versions A, B, and C). Transcription by Yoshiaki Onishi.

Laranja," he ups the ante in each strophe. His voice becomes more tim- brally varied (from gritty to hoarse, whispered to shouted, then, after a moment of almost lyric bel canto, returning to a shout). In some versions he claps and stamps (atypical in fado performance), choreographically punctuating key words, the rhythms continue highly syncopated.[18] As José progresses in each of these performances through the remaining verses, the melodic lines, with respect to the relations between pitches, change (even while the underlying harmonic sequence remains almost exactly the same). The second full transcription (see appendix 2) shows melodic variation in the voice in three strophes of one entire perfor- mance of "Meia Laranja" (version A in the examples) represented over the same harmonic line.[19] In each consecutive verse, he styles different melodies. Transcription suggests that in José's s performances of "Meia Laranja," there is more melodic similarity between different renditions of the same verse than there is from one verse to another in the same

EXAMPLE 4.4 • "Fado da Meia Laranja," sung by José Manuel Osório, measures 27–29, strophe 1, versions A, B, and C. Transcription by Yoshiaki Onishi.

performance. It is likely also that, when comparing multiple performances of the same fado and lyrics sung by the same fadista, the first strophes maintain the most melodic consistency. Practitioners often sing a clearer statement of the melodic "theme" in the first strophe that they then embellish in subsequent strophes. Example 4.4 represents a moment in the phrase in which, in multiple versions of the first strophe, José sings a variation on a similar melodic figure. Example 4.5 represents this same instance in the musical phrase comparing three consecutive strophes in one single performance. Melodic invention and José's use of particular figures in each performance follows, and is largely dictated by, the specificity of utterances, the poetic lines, the word. When the poetic phrases change as he progresses from one strophe to the next, so do his melodic figurations.

EXAMPLE 4.5 • "Fado da Meia Laranja," measures 27–29, three consecutive strophes of José Manuel Osório's version A. Transcription by Yoshiaki Onishi.

Yet a transcription of the first strophe of a classic recording by Amália Rodrigues of the Fado Vitória sung with the lyrics "Povo Que Lavas no Rio" (Rodrigues [1989] 1962) reveals in a few instances loose similarities between some of the melodic figurations in José's multiple renditions of "Meia Laranja" (example 4.6). (In example 4.6 the opening melodic gesture in José's version A is somewhat similar to the gesture Amália sings in the same structural moment in the fado. Both emphasize the fifth of the tonic chord in their opening motifs through an approach from the g or g-sharp below, and both conclude their phrases on the fifth of the VII chord [a "G" in the transposed transcriptions]). But while sharing a few figures, overall, the melodies to which they style their words are strikingly different (although they are sung to the same traditional fado structure, with almost identical harmonic movement and rhythm [with the use of occasional substitution chords]). Their styles of execution of the Fado Vitória (and the words they sing) are also completely different. Amália prolongs vowels, employs ample rubati and no syncopation, and sings in an almost bel canto style, whereas José emphasizes (at times almost brutally) his attacks of consonants, the grittiness of his voice, and foregrounds syncopation.

EXAMPLE 4.6 • Fado Vitória comparison, measures 3–5 of José Manuel Osório's version A of "Fado da Meia Laranja," compared with measures 1–3 in Amália Rodrigues's recording of "Povo Que Lavas no Rio" from 1962. Transcription by Yoshiaki Onishi.

It is perhaps salient that the "composer" of the Fado Vitória submitted his registration to the SPA in 1967 (approximately forty years after the estimated date of composition; see example 4.7). In 1962, Amália Rodrigues's performance of "Povo Que Lavas no Rio" set to a Fado Vitória appeared on her high-profile LP *Busto*. By 1967, her renditions of this fado would have been widely circulated and sounded over radio and television, on records, and in live performances—her versions of the Vitória set with these lyrics saturating the aural public sphere in Portugal. While it is not possible to know for certain, some of the melodic figures in the transcription for the Fado Vitória that Campos submitted in 1967 as proof of authorship may have been influenced partly by Amália's styling in her rendition of "Povo Que Lavas no Rio" of the 1960s.[20] A loose similarity between some melodic figurations can be seen when comparing Campos's submission, the melody Amália sings in her 1962 recording of the Fado Vitória, and the transcription of Osório's second version (B) of "Meia Laranja" with respect to the melodies with which they conclude the first phrase of the fado (see example 4.8). (Note how they all emphasize the same downward motion from C, dwell on the B-flat in their movement to cadence on A, with a G or a G-sharp appearing in the last beat of the penultimate measure, foregrounding the final A.)

I emphasize details of melodic styling here, presenting the Fado Vitória as a prism through which to raise questions about seemingly conflicting, but coexisting, ideologies about musical composition in

EXAMPLE 4.7 • First eight measures of Joaquim Campos's Fado Vitória, submitted to the SPA in 1967.

EXAMPLE 4.8 • Fado Vitória comparison, last three measures of phrase 1, strophe 1: Campos (1967 notation), Amália Rodrigues (1962), José Manuel Osório (version B). Transcription of José Manuel Osório and Amália Rodrigues by Yoshiaki Onishi.

traditional fado: that of original single-authored "composition" and spontaneous styling/invention of traditional fado melodies in perfor-mance. Melody, with respect to styling in traditional fado, is dialogic and emergent in performance and, at the same time, based on prefig-ured musical structures, ideas, or "compositions." Almost all tradi-tional fados are believed by practitioners to be originally authored (i.e., composed) by an individual and styled anew (for some melodically "invented") in the moment of performance. In practice, harmonic movement and rhythm, stock instrumental figurations, and underlying metrical structures, which to some extent govern melodic choices made by performers, are remarkably consistent across performances of any given traditional fado. These similarities are found when comparing historical recordings with recordings from the present and when com-paring performances across a wide range of performers. When per-formers style melodies, they draw on shared musical grammars and conventions, some of which circulate primarily through oral/aural transmission as particular to any given particular traditional fado. Highly inventive fadistas, working within these shared conventions and performance histories, may, through repeat performances, develop their own melodic figures for specific fados in their repertoire, melodic formulas that can then be creatively refigured in their future improvisations of the same fado.

Pioneering research on orally transmitted poetry (Jakobson 1960; Lord 2003 [1960]) argued for the salience of learned and internalized formulaic patterns for scaffolding, and thus enabling, "composition in performance." While this work has been remarkably generative across disciplines for generations of scholars, of relevance to my discussion here, is its usefulness for understanding creative processes involved in musical improvisation (Berliner 1994). Paul Berliner's extensive ethnographic investigation into how jazz musicians learn to improvise argues against commonly held assumptions about improvisation as "spontaneous," "intuitive," and performed in the absence of "prefigured musical ideas" (Berliner 1994: 2). Rather, he claims that for the musicians with whom he worked, improvisation depended on gaining fluency in relation to "thinking in terms of particular [musical] figures" and that musicians, during the process of learning through performance, treat these figures with "increasing flexibility each time they perform them" (Berliner 1994: 187).

The moments of melodic similarity at the level of pitch that I noted in my discussion of repeated takes of the first verse of José Manual Osório's performances of "Meia Laranja" suggest that loosely conceived melodic figurations or formulas—which for the fadista are often attached to particular poetic phrases and undergirded by and responsive to the stable harmony of the bass line and the interaction with the instrumentalists (notably, the guitarrista)—might be at work in enabling the creative improvisatory process of styling for even the most inventive and daring fado *estilistas* (stylists). It may well be that the most adventurous styling *depends* on the fadista's flexible reuse of internalized melodic formulas that he or she has developed and experimented with over time in relation to couplings of particular fado poems with specific traditional fados and in relation to socially shared musical conventions and formulas for the performance of particular traditional fados. Formulas can also serve as a useful mnemonic (Lord 2003 [1960]); for a fadista performing traditional fado, they could serve to link the words of the poem, which are already prefigured (and exist in text form) but in performance are "sung by heart," to the harmonic structure of the fado, rendering "spontaneous" melodic composition in performance possible.

Instrumentalists, fadistas, and laypeople, amateurs and professionals, often told me that fado was musically "poor." Speakers, when making this claim, pointed to what they understood as fado's lack of harmonic complexity or its repetitive formal structures. I sometimes asked about fadistas' and instrumentalists' styling in performance, drawing attention to what I heard as a highly complex process of musical improvisation and interaction. Responses often invoked arguments about styling as "simple," about styling as being directly related to how one feels on any given day, transmitting the sentiment of the story of the poem, and about singing from the soul (see chapter 1). Sometimes actors invoked this so-called simplicity of styling as a positive value: *Fado is music of the soul, of the people. There is nothing complex about it.* At other times, actors invoked the simplicity argument disparagingly: *This is just fado. It is not jazz. Jazz has real improvisation.*

Yet the musical simplicity argument, for many actors, also implicitly supported a simultaneous claim for ontological complexity, with fado capable of birthing worlds, of expressing and provoking emotions across the full spectrum of human experience, able to move one to almost unfathomable emotional depths in part because it was, at core, "unlearned" and "soulful." Similar to the discursive context surrounding improvisatory *sana* lamentations by Warao women in the Venezuelan delta, as described by the linguistic anthropologist Charles Briggs (1993: 947), styling in fado has a "high status within the economy of truth" precisely because it is understood as "not mediated by intentionality or strategy." While the styling of fado may feel simple and spontaneous in its execution to practiced performers, all aspects of fado performance and listening rely on deeply learned, internalized behavior and rules. In fashioning melodies in performance, fadistas and instrumentalists participate in a socially emergent "intermusicality" (Monson 1996: 97).[21] Within this inter-musical context, some performers develop their own, idiosyncratic melodic figurations and formulas with respect to their particular repertoires of traditional fado, contributing to a shared vocabulary and to a continuously emergent aural imaginary with respect to any given traditional fado form.

A certain kind of affective listening, a markedly cumulative listening, is facilitated by traditional fado form and performance practices of styling. This is a listening that includes past renderings of the same traditional fado structure in the inner ear, a listening that juxtaposes the styling one hears in the present with the styling one remembers by a different performer in the past, a performance located in a specific time-place. Traditional fado structure facilitates an overdetermined relation to past listenings, a suturing of the multiple stories told by lyrics to particular musical forms, to specific traditional fado "musical bases."

The focus on inventive styling and the practice of setting multiple lyrics to the same musical structure in traditional fado (and to some extent, in fado canção) foregrounds the polysemy inherent in musical signification. In chapter 2, I argued for the multiple affects and significations that a listener might associate with a musical sign, using the example of a vocal turn (*voltinha*) on the phrase "Vasco da Gama" in the fado song "Lisboa Não Mudes Assim" (Lisbon, Don't Change like This), sung by Maria José Melo. I wrote about polysemous indexicality with respect to the ways in which actors feel history in the present through fado listening, in relation to how history is rendered affective (and public) in sound through style. I argued implicitly, through the moments of listening and performance that I described, that this "proliferation of index" (Edwards 2002: 648) with respect to fado listening is not a "free-for-all." Rather, associations that listeners voice with respect to particular musical signs are linked both to circulating fragments of public history and to shared performance conventions that govern fado styling.

Musical structures of traditional fados, in acts of listening and in acts of performing, are saturated with story and with memories of prior improvisations. Traditional fado musical form shapes a kind of palimpsest on which individuals leave their traces in the styling of their voices and the stories they sing; one performance is sedimented upon another. Fado form in performance is also saturated with the sonic excesses of affect—the wails, the whispers, the "damaged" voice, the "hurt" voice— that cannot be captured in transcription. Affect in fado is writ large (*The sadness of a nation, surrounded by the sea and bordered by Spain, that was once the center of the world*). Affect in fado is writ small, in the details of the styling of voices over a form that is known: a word emphasized with a prolonged consonant, a rubato drawn out on a vowel, a syncopation, a vibrato wavering, a word declaimed, a melodic fragment inverted and styled anew, a turn of the voice, in a sudden whisper, in a silence held, in a shout.

FIVE

The Gender of Genre

Abandoned Rose
Without a mother, without bread, without anything
What a sad and tearful life
Destiny gave to you
Abandoned Rose
Humble and perfumed
Finally, unlucky one, who are you?
Abandoned Rose
A woman who suffered.

—REFRAIN, "ROSA ENJEITADA" (ABANDONED ROSE)

Men and women sing fados of a vastly varied repertoire in multiple emotional registers: humorous, sexually raucous, proud, and strutting, or all trembling, inconsolably sad and forlorn, lovesick, homesick, *saudade* sick. They sing fados that glorify the family, the mother, the father, or illicit or officially sanctioned heterosexual romance; fados with Marian imagery; fados that romanticize prostitution, criminality, or social deviance; rebellious fados and contrite fados, and fados that celebrate empire, the city, the nation.[1] But male and female fadistas take on different kinds of labor in fado's worlds: affective, musical, pedagogical, performative, biographical, and social. The men and women I met in amateur fado moved differently through these worlds, inhabiting gendered and sexed spheres within fado that dictated the boundaries of possibility in terms of fado as social life and how one performed and was received. On the level of symbolic representation in fado, female and male are cast in different cultural forms. Forms of gendered symbolic representation that are written, painted, or drawn into historical iconographies, and legends that fado as genre has accrued and continues to generate, overlap. At times they are in tension and at other times they align with fado's gendered inflections in the everyday as sung, as listened to, as talked about, and as lived.

I argued in earlier chapters that fado as genre serves as nexus of gathering (and releasing) for historical narratives, embodied practices, for ways of feeling and remembering, for sensing place, and for affect. These are often deeply gendered forms of knowledge, habitus, and histories (which are also classed and raced). In fado, the feminine as a cultural form, or the conceit of the feminine, coupled with hetero-normative love, performs labor that is extraordinarily wide in scope. This chapter opens a conversation about the relationships between fado as genre and the feminine as form, a preamble to the last chapter of the book, which examines the synergy that occurs when both forms powerfully merge in the category of the diva and in the convention of melodrama through an extraordinary voice. What forms and practices does the feminine take in fado? How do sexed (and sexualized) histories and divisions of labor inform the genre as gendered?

Gendered Practices and Representations

Inside a dollhouse-size brothel on display at Lisbon's Fado Museum hangs a tiny gilt-framed drawing on a wall. It shows a nude woman with a Portuguese guitarra superimposed over her face, its opening overlaying her open mouth, and another guitarra framing her genitals. The miniature brothel was made by Alfredo Marceneiro, a carpenter by trade and a fado icon of the twentieth century, known for his tender declamation style in song, a voice half-spoken, half-sung. He named the dollhouse after one of his most popular fados, "A Casa da Mariquinhas," a fado about a brothel.[2] The "guitarra is a woman," some fado lyrics proclaim. Women do not play fado's instruments—the guitarra and the viola. Men do.[3]

In fado practice at large, it is men who most overtly make the rules and to whom women often turn for the final word in an argument. Once I overheard a viola player say to his male friends after someone's wife had gotten "out of hand" by arguing during a coaching session in Marvila, "In my house, it is I who command." The same maxim often applies to amateur fado social practice and, sometimes, performance practice. It is the men who take the explicit leadership roles, controlling the "house" in their roles as presenters at amateur venues. Instrumentalists, who are overwhelmingly male, play a key role in the coaching of fadistas (see Castelo-Branco 1994). They are often looked to by both male and female fadistas as more legitimate sources of musical knowledge (harmony, key relationships, possibly note-reading skills, good ears) and often have the final word in amateur contexts when the phrasing, intonation, timing of entrances, or rhythm of a performance is in question. While receiving singing lessons and observing amateur sessions and rehearsals, I noticed that the instrumentalists sometimes coached male and female fadistas differently. The instrumentalist might address a female fadista with a paternalistic inflection or a certain force behind a command. Often when boyfriends or husbands were present in the rehearsal context, they joined the male instrumentalists in giving the female singer strong advice about how to change her phrasing, breathing, entrances, timing, or intonation. I did not, however, witness a wife or girlfriend publicly giving coaching advice to her male partner. As the owner of one professional venue, who considered himself to be knowledgeable about fado, said, "There are not many women who can really talk, really think, about fado." In other words, men (usually instrumentalists), are more often considered as the theorists of fado, holding the power to frame fado, the power of meta-analysis. And while there are some women who write fado lyrics, the majority of fado poets are also men.

Within the context of fado performance, women seize and inflect their power differently than do men, through humor, with their bodies, with their voices. Masculinity and femininity, in moments of performance and listening, sometimes take the form of banter, of play. Female performers often put their bodies and sexuality on display more overtly than do men. Women and men move differently when they sing and listen. During a serious fado, a man might sing with his hands in his pockets, but the hands of a woman are more commonly in a position of prayer, or turning the fringe of her shawl as if a rosary. Both men and women sometimes cross themselves before singing (a gesture of religiosity in a space that blurs the sacred and the profane). During a raucous or humorous fado, men and women commonly employ dramatically expressive hand and facial gestures, but unlike men, women often sway their shoulders or hips from side to side. (Women listening to these fados may also sway their shoulders from side to side.) Many amateur male singers I knew seemed to model their singing styles consciously on the voices of male fadistas or icons from the past, such as Fernando Maurício and Alfredo Marceneiro, while women emulated famous female fadistas, often drawing from multiple voices and styles, but with the figure of Amália Rodrigues predominating.

Listeners might present different preferences for the style of male voices versus female; "I like a sweet voice in a man," said one listener at O Jaime. Or as a sound engineer on Lisbon's periphery, who produces recordings for the amateur circuit, said to me during a recording session for some of the star fadistas at O Jaime in 2003, "The female voice, to be the voice of fado must be a punished voice, punished by the life of fado, of the fado houses, of smoke, of drink, of late nights." In his reading of the fado voice, genre as *lived* is specifically gendered and sexed and leaves a material trace in the texture and timbre of the singing voice, a trace that is audible, value-laden.

The female fadista might be rendered symbolically (in iconography and gestures, lyrics, and popular discourse) in any of the following ways: as weepy or tearful; as sacrificial, the eternal mother, as Mary; as the victim of male betrayal; as beaten down; as a prostitute or femme fatale with cigarette in hand; as melodramatic. She readily accommodates multiple stereotypical signifiers of the essentialized feminine, including Madonna, whore, and mother. The symbolic rendering of the male fadista—at times weepy, at times fatalistic (also with a cigarette in hand)—might contain elements of machismo, bravura, and, historically, criminal deviance. But the symbol of the female fadista invites more possibilities for polysemy. One female aficionado in her late forties went as far as to both feminize and "Latinize" fado's ethos of suffering. "Fado is about the fate of suffering Latin (*latina*) women under the machismo of the Latin men," she told me. In this telling, the feminine is decoupled from the specificity of nation and linked instead to a gendered affect of so-called Latin identity (which I understood in the context of her talk to be loosely delimited to native speakers of Spanish and Portuguese, as well as encompassing southern Europe).[4]

While men and women equally participate as fadistas in Lisbon fado, it is the more sexualized or explicitly gendered voices of women that the fado star system privileges locally and internationally.[5] The roster of contemporary fado world music stars is populated almost exclusively by female fadistas; international marketing sometimes plays up the illicit gendered and sexed mythologies of fado's history. Compact disc covers, concert posters, and publicity often foreground the sexualized or fetishized body of the female fadista (in dress, facial expressions, or postures) and almost always employ visual icons that link to particular mythologies of the female fadista (black clothing, shawl iconography). The names of female fado icons of the past circulate in local fado discourse more often than do the names of their male counterparts. And the ways in which men comment on these female fadistas is more likely to be overtly sexualized: *When she was younger, my she was a looker. She could stop traffic in the streets.* Some fans and fadistas, male and female, complained to me about what they perceived as the current emphasis on the visual, on the physical appearance of the female fadista. Yet particularly in local and national contexts, an ideology also exists that values the older woman in fado, because it is believed that she is able to impart a depth of experience, a richness that comes with age, maturity of voice, and time spent living the *vida fadista* (the fadista way of life). The symbol of the older female fadista might also be linked to a public biography that renders her persona as "the woman who has led a life of suffering," "femme fatale," or "mother." The female fado voice holds greater symbolic purchase on melancholy.

The mythos and history of the nineteenth-century figure of Maria Severa, the "first" fadista, a prostitute, who, as legend has it, in the early 1800s brought fado to the aristocracy by sleeping with a count then died tragically in 1846 (in her twenties), continues to haunt fado, its lyrics, its stories, its iconographies, and an "imagined bohemia" from which fado supposedly sprung, over a century and a half after her death.[6] An official municipal plaque marks the street where Maria Severa once lived, A Rua do Capelão, in a section of Mouraria that in the early 2000s was a favored site for illicit drug transactions and that in 2012 was being renovated as a site of fado heritage. Severa was arguably fado's first diva, a figure whose celebrity was amplified posthumously in her early twentieth-century afterlife. She not only serves as the central theme for numerous fado lyrics performed in the present. She is also the focus of a well-known novel (Dantas 1901); of early twentieth-century musical theater (*revista*); and of Portugal's first sound film, *A Severa* (1931).[7] Details of her biography continue to be debated by fado aficionados and amateur historians. Specific details of her biography in these debates are often articulated in relation to, or map onto, contestations regarding fado origins writ large (or the *biography of genre*).[8] These discussions often emphasize that Severa was from the lower class, rising through an (illicit) association with royalty (just as fado as a genre "ascended" from the lower classes to the higher) and often mark her as "gypsy" (through her paternal line), thus as hybrid and exotic.

In some fado lyrics, the figure of Maria Severa "gives birth" to fado, anthropomorphizing the genre, endowing it with affect, a sadness "born" from the abandonment by the mother. In the fado canção "Maria Severa," whose subject is Severa's death, fado as genre is cast as a male child to whom Severa has given birth, but who is then hopelessly abandoned when she dies:

Deixa um filho idolatrado
Que outro afecto igual não tem
Chama-se ele o triste fado
Que vai ser desse enjeitado
Se perdeu o melhor bem
O amor de mãe.

[Maria Severa] leaves an idolized son
Who has no one else who loves him so much
He is called the sad fado
What is going to happen to that forlorn one
Who lost the best thing in life
His mother's love.[9]

"Maria Severa," in some contemporary fado talk, also stands as a loose reference to a prominent strain of originary discourse that locates fado's genesis in Lisbon's nineteenth-century taverns and brothels.[10] The mythos of the Severa figure, particularly as it gathered meaning in early to mid-twentieth-century Lisbon and Portugal, through the literary, the cinematic, and the musical and theatrical (revistas), and through fado lyrics, scaffolds a gendered/sexed biography for some versions of fado as genre (classed and ethnically hybridized via the invocation of the gypsy), one onto which would later be mapped the figure and biography of Amália Rodrigues.

The Severa narrative, or the gendered genesis story that gets retold in variation as a foundational myth of the genre of fado, assumes a particular salience in its early twentieth-century manifestations, with respect to the forging of a "new" nation during the beginning of the Estado Novo. In these remappings of Severa's musical biography, woman as mother-nation and woman as illicit siren intertwine. The Severa myth might be understood as a form of what the literary historian Ana Ferreira (2002) has noted as a "nation-sex" construct of "lusosex," or an ambivalently gendered/sexed ideology of woman promulgated in the re-foundation of the Portuguese colonial coterminous with the "regeneration" of the nation during the early years of the Estado Novo. This is an ideology of nation intimately bound to a moral reconfiguration of the place of woman and the family unit, an ideology that upheld stringent moralizing discourses celebrating women's role as "bearers" of nation and of empire vis-à-vis their supposed centrality as wives and mothers, relegating them to the domestic sphere.[11] This represented an ideological backlash against freedoms won by women during the brief First Republic (1910–26) while simultaneously propagating a masculine mythos of imperial explorer-hero ("virile seafarers") bolstered by a concomitant "uncontrollable enlightening force of sexual love [in relation to Other women]" (Ferreira 2002: 108, 110).[12]

Alone

There are so many ways of being alone. "Estou sozinho, estou triste, etc." (I am alone, I am sad, etc.) read black-and-white graffiti stenciled over a faded red Coca-Cola sign on the outside of a café door on a side street in Lisbon's neighborhood of Chiado (plate 3). The graffiti, which I first glimpsed from a trolley window in the summer of 2000 (it had been painted over by 2003) reemerged in other sites—on a crumbling wooden door in Alfama, on the side wall of the exit to a subway station near Lisbon's Saldanha shopping mall. Each time I saw it, I thought differently through the words as a way to understand multiple kinds of loneliness that surround the phenomenon of fado. Within many lyrics, within the talk about fado, and as part of a stereotype of what it means to live the fadista life, exists an ethos of melancholy, of loss, and of nostalgia in which loneliness, or being tragically alone, often figures as central. There is the loneliness of the individual and the singularity and aloneness of a nation with an island mentality—a geographical isolation heightened by the enclosures of the past dictatorship. But there is also the question of woman, what it might mean for a woman alone to be traveling through and performing in fado spaces.

While the written archive unequivocally supports claims that nineteenth-century fado flourished in tandem with and in sites of prostitution in Lisbon, there are no longer links between practices of fado and prostitution outside the symbolic realm. When prostitution appears in song lyrics, it is usually romanticized, relegated to an atemporal bohemian imaginary, and is often linked to fado's traditional neighborhoods (particularly Bairro Alto, Mouraria, and Alfama).[13] Yet fado's legendary links to prostitution and the bohemian life continue to add a gendered/sexed charge to fado as social practice. While some female fadistas, old and young, working class and middle class, told me that the stigma of fado singing for women was a thing of the past, for others—particularly for women middle-age and older—it remained important to how they narrated their biographies as fadistas. These narratives point to how critical it was in the recent past for many adolescent and young adult women to have the support of key male figures in their lives to sing fado publicly and to the precarious positioning of young female fadistas who chose to take this route alone (without male support or accompaniment). They also highlight enabling aspects of "being alone" later in life, when the death of a husband or a divorce gave them freedom to pursue their fado singing or fadista careers. At the same time, the figure of a woman "alone"—cast off, widowed, or abandoned (or waiting at the window for her seafaring lover)—is both an enduring trope in fado lyrics and a stereotype for a female fadista. Thus being widowed or divorced might lend a particular biographical authenticity to the fadista alone who has lost her man.

Ivone Dias (b. 1934), a working-class amateur fadista from Alfama, told her story like this:

> When I was a child and a teenager, my uncle never wanted me to sing. I used to love listening to Amália on the radio; I sang her fados. My mother adored it when I sang. My father, who had died when I was very young, used to sing fado and write [fado] verses. But my uncle, when I was growing up, tried to discourage me from singing, even though so many people liked hearing me sing. I even won a prize singing fado at a competition at the Café Luso.

"Fado had a bad reputation" (*má fama*), a friend at the table interjected. Ivone continued:

> Then, when I got married, my husband didn't want me to sing regularly in casas de fado. I only sang at private parties or for parties on the street (*festas na rua*).[14] I had always thought that one day I would sing with the voice that God gave me. My husband died when I was fifty-six. For three or four years, I just stayed at home. I was a widow. I never thought I would be a widow. My daughter kept encouraging me to sing fado. I wasn't well. I was crying, crying, and crying. One day I realized that I was sick from a hunger for fado (*fome de fado*). I went out and sang fado, and it was good; it was marvelous, marvelous, marvelous to sing. It was the best thing that could have happened. I became well. I am not saying that it is good that my husband died. But I had my life free. Now I sing and sing and sing. I have so much will (*vontade*) to sing. I am never tired of singing fado (*nunca estou farta*). When I sing, I don't know where I am; there is no explanation. When I sing fados that are about mothers, I am crying inside. I am remembering my mother. When I was ten, I sang for a performance (*espectáculo*) on my street. My mother was at the window, crying. My mother said, when she heard me sing, "She sounds just like her father." She adored it when I sang.[15]

Olga de Sousa was born into a middle-class Lisbon family in 1949. She has an active professional life as an interior decorator and only began singing fado in her fifties, after her marriage ended (plate 6). She told me, "I only sang when I knew people wouldn't hear me. No one knew that I sang. I was embarrassed (timid or ashamed; *tinha vergonha*). My [adult] son was perplexed the first time he heard me sing at a casa de fado; he didn't know that I sang. But he adored hearing me sing. He cried, 'How did you have this voice without me ever knowing?' My father liked fado; he sang fado very well. My father didn't let me sing fado. He said that people who were involved with fado (*andavam nos fados*) were complicated people (*pessoas complicadas*)."

I asked Olga about the gendered connotations of her father's phrase "complicated people." She confirmed that it was a way to refer to the stigma that some people associated with female fadistas. "Today, luckily we are getting past that," she continued. "But some years back, in a traditional family, if someone wanted to sing fado, that could present a very large problem. First there was my father. There was no way I could sing fado (*nem pensar*). Then I got married, and my husband was even worse. . . . I had no possibility of singing (*não tinha hipótese*)."[16]

Some older women told me that as teenagers, they sometimes snuck out of the house at night to sing fado without their parents' knowledge. One fadista in her late fifties who sings at O Jaime and freelances professionally for both local and international fado gigs explained that her father would not let her sing in casas de fado or in taverns. After she married, her husband accompanied her everywhere when she sang, but he refused to let her accept a prestigious recording contract. She is now a widow and has a more expansive professional life as a fadista.

Argentina Santos (b. 1926), a well-known professional fadista and the owner of Parreirinha de Alfama, a long-standing fado venue in Alfama, provides a similar narrative in the liner notes for a CD she made in 2003, after a recording hiatus that lasted decades. "During this time [the hiatus] I had a companion who didn't like to see me sing in public. I remarried two years after he died, and I had the same problem. Now I am free, and I accept invitations [to sing fado] when I am asked" (Santos 2003).

In these biographies, a "breakthrough" narrative features as a central trope. These women—all of whom were older than fifty and from Alfama or adjacent neighborhoods in Lisbon's historic center—were able to fully participate in fado's public spheres only after they had been freed from particular men in their lives (usually husbands or fathers). In narrating their "fado biographies" these fadistas often mentioned key figures who supported and encouraged their singing or close family members who cried (because they were moved) when hearing them sing. Some of these stories feature fathers or husbands who were involved in fado as serious listeners, fadistas, or poets. They may have encouraged their daughters or wives to sing fado within the private space of the home while prohibiting them from singing at night at casas de fado or taverns (or from signing prestigious recording contracts). These gendered strictures make some sense when understood within the context of implicit and explicit gender ideologies of the Estado Novo, the time during which these women came of age. These are not fado biographies that I heard from male fadistas from the same generation. Themes that also recur in the life stories working-class amateur female fadistas of this generation tell about themselves (or in the biographies that they choose to make public) include suffering, abandonment, loneliness, hardscrabble childhoods, and breakthroughs to a certain kind of power or well-being via singing, in which singing fado figures as "therapeutic."

These are differently gendered fado life stories from those of the working-class and middle-class girls who were learning to sing fado in Marvila in the early 2000s, with parents hovering, minidisc recorders in hand to catch every nuance of the coaching session, or actively encouraging their daughters to sing in televised competitions. Yet perhaps to sing fado as woman or girl, even in the early 2000s, was in the minds of some people to be symbolically contaminated. In the auditorium attached to the ramshackle public library in the neighborhood of Marvila in September 2002, nine-year-old Carla stepped onto the stage to compete in an amateur fado contest for children and adults. It was her first experience singing in public for a large audience, and she wore a brilliant white shawl around her shoulders. Members of the Associação Cultural o Fado in Marvila, family, and friends sat expectantly on plastic chairs packed tightly around tables, drinking beer and wine and eating *chouriço* and kale soup. The lights dimmed, and judges sat at a table to the right of the stage. After Carla sang, amid sustained applause, her nine-year-old friend Maria, who attended coaching sessions with her but who was more experienced at singing in public, ceremoniously "baptized" Carla's "loss of innocence" by walking onto the stage and exchanging her white shawl for a black one. The black shawl here could stand in as a symbolic reference to Amália Rodrigues (who some people believe, popularized the tradition of wearing black in fado), but just as easily it lends itself to a classic functionalist ritual analysis—white to black, pure to tainted—with the public exposure of the female fado *voice* as that which shifts status from girl to woman. However, if this is a symbolic contamination, the symbol (of fadista-prostitute or fadista as loose woman) has been emptied of most of its real-life signifiers and sentimentalized as an element of *castiço*. In fado parlance "castiço" refers to fado that is heard as authentic, gritty, popular, or from the neighborhood (*bairrista*). At times "castiço" invokes nineteenth-century histories of criminality and prostitution, but these are now most often sanitized histories, calling forth a sentimentalized bohemian imaginary.[17]

"Castiço" spills out into talk about fado's traditional neighborhoods and places. Neighborhoods (e.g., Bairro Alto, Alfama, and Mouraria) also figure in talk and in song lyrics as more "castiço" in the past, in nostalgic narratives in which the grittiness of neighborhood that "gave birth" to fado is cleaned up through gentrification. "Bairro Alto was better during the time of Salazar because there was more prostitution there," a taxi driver told me in 2008. "Nowadays, our girls no longer marry as virgins." His narrative (albeit extreme) presents a gendered and sexualized nostalgia for place and time, a remarkably lucid presentation of a longing for "lusosex," in which culture (and the masculine) is maintained by a feminine at once lascivious and "pure."

Fado nas Tascas (Fado in the Taverns)

Amateur fado practice explicitly foregrounds sociality and tightly linked social networks. This is a sociality with multiple implied assumptions about gender. Within the context of amateur fado practiced at present-day tascas or at working-class bars, this imagined fado bohemia overlaps with tasca culture, etiquette, and histories. During a long fado afternoon at O Jaime, when the lights dim and people at tables and listeners standing at the bar settle down for fado listening, this implied imaginary bohemia that forms a legendary historical backdrop for amateur fado practice seems to grant an implicit license for mild transgression, for behavior that might not be sanctioned in the day to day as usual. In this ambience certain social strictures loosen; others take hold, particularly those that govern fado listening and participatory practices. Wine, beer, and hard liquor flow freely at O Jaime, consumed in greater quantities generally by men than by women. Heated arguments might break out between men during intervals. Occasionally, Jaime throws someone out. Men and women might flirt with one another playfully—sometimes for real, but often in jest. More wine flows. Men become red in the face. Tears come more easily to some listeners as the afternoon moves into evening.

There is a certain reveling in the swagger (gingar). Listeners on occasion call out "Gingão!" (swaggerer), when the fado being sung borders on raucous or when a female or male singer sings with a certain lilt to the hips or shoulders. A fadista in her late sixties wearing a fake-fur miniskirt, vinyl high-heel boots, costume jewelry, and a skin-tight sweater bats her eyelashes at one of the instrumentalists as she sings. Some men (particularly those with professional fado careers and big, resonant voices) swagger off self-importantly after singing; others dedicate fados to women in the room before they sing. The oldest fadista in the house (Álvaro Rodrigues, then in his eighties) regularly sang a fado he wrote about the joys of Viagra, entitled "Praia do Meco" (Meco Beach), accompanied with hand gestures. Sometimes, he dedicated the fado to me, to the general mirth of the listeners. (The Praia do Meco is a well-known nude beach just outside Lisbon.) A male fadista in his sixties performed love-song fados, trying to catch my gaze with such earnestness that listeners occasionally were prompted to ask, "What are you doing, singing songs like that to a girl half your age?"

One single, middle-class fadista in her early fifties said to me, "I would never tell my family I come to the Tasca do Jaime. It's a tavern." Negotiating this scene as an unaccompanied woman, particularly as a newcomer, could be challenging. In general, particularly when amateur fado sessions take place at night, which is the norm, women do not attend unaccompanied either as performers or as listeners, but men often do arrive unaccompanied. Women, especially newcomers in fado circuits, have much less mobility. They are (implicitly) expected to be accompanied by husbands or boyfriends, although it is also common for women to arrive with female friends or, more often, to join a family or a couple. Within the amateur circuit, there are men whom one might term "fado husbands"—men who are not singers but who tirelessly accompany their fadista wives through the often punishing schedule of amateur fado. A fadista might attend O Jaime between 4 and 9 PM on weekend evenings, then immediately go to sing at one or more other venues from 9 PM until 3 AM or later on the same night.

During the beginning months of my attendance at O Jaime, my status as foreign, unaccompanied, unmarried, in Portugal alone, and usually (even as in my mid-thirties) one of the youngest women present at amateur venues, marked me as seemingly immediately available to advances by men (married and unmarried).[18] For the first few weeks, I arrived at O Jaime late, thinking the fado started at 6 PM, when it had really begun at 4. Thus, the tasca was already completely full when I arrived, with no empty tables. I stood at the bar counter; inevitably, the majority of people around me were men, whose manner of communicating with me almost always seemed to take into account my status as a woman alone. This type of communication ranged from mild flirtation to aggressive gazing, from haranguing to outright propositioning. Some of this was in jest, a manner of communication in which kindness was conveyed through flirtation, a jocular establishing of masculinity in relation to the female outsider. But some of it was seriously intended or insulting.

Women who dropped in to listen and who came alone were usually from the neighborhood and had good friends who were already seated and who welcomed them. Men who arrived alone freely congregated, standing, along the bar. After months of me standing at the bar, sitting alone, or squeezing in uninvited at a table already full, one of the "fado husbands" approached me and invited me to join his wife Fernanda, at what he referred to as the "women's table," a back table near the instrumentalists, where Fernanda was sitting with two other women. This brought about a critical shift in my social position both within the tasca and within larger circuits of amateur fado. Fernanda was one of the stars at O Jaime, and in amateur fado in Lisbon in general (plate 7). Eventually, she took me under her wing, referring to herself as my "mother in Portugal," granting me fictive kin status. It was Fernanda who symbolically accepted me into the amateur fado world by one night giving me a black shawl, wrapping it around my shoulders. This affiliation and friendship led eventually to a greater sense of belonging and protection both at the venue of O Jaime and in this amateur fado network at large. Through her husband's insistence that I join the table with the other women, I learned that standing at the bar exacerbated my already precarious positioning as a woman alone.[19]

Thus, my ethnographic "breakthrough" in amateur fado—from a precarious non-belonging, as outsider female foreigner, to relative social acceptance (and protection)—in part occurred through highly gendered and sexed conduits embedded in practices of fado listening and participation.[20] Some of my strongest alliances with women at O Jaime were forged by regularly sitting at the women's table and listening and participating in a specifically gendered form of "women's talk" and sociality in that context. This was a sociality marked by a certain intimacy, a sociality that was different from that at other tables (e.g., the table at the back of the room when occupied by a large group of boisterous firemen from Graça; the tables with one or two heterosexual couples; the occasional tables of tourists). At tables where women sat together, there was gossip, joke-telling (much off-color), prank playing, but most of all, there was conversation about troubles—ranging from wondering how one would find the money to pay the gas bill, to talk about deaths in the family, children, divorce, and illness. In talking about troubles there were sometimes tears, then empathy.[21] Talk was often in the context of a warm physical sociality: a hand on a hand, an arm around an arm, the stroking of another's hair, the arranging of a collar or a shawl. "A vida é assim" (Life is like that) was a common refrain of condolence among the women. All of this was interspersed with listening to fado, happening in such a way partly because of the intimacy and the atmosphere of heightened affect that went along with consecutive hours of fado listening.

My process of belonging in relation to gendered and sexed conduits in this scene had something in common with the means through which other single women (of any age) who were newcomers to amateur scenes became socially accepted by forming alliances with the female regulars. These alliances were often critical to one's socio-musical "success" in the scene. Olga de Sousa would likely have never returned to O Jaime (after the first time, when she came on a lunch invitation from neighbors) without the support of one of the female regulars. "A woman sitting close to us told me that I should keep coming back on Saturdays to sing. I told her that I couldn't come alone. I didn't know anyone there. She told me that I could sit at their table; that I already had friends there. And that is how it started."[22]

Gossip among female fadistas in the amateur circuits could be fierce, as could covert competition in relation to one's perceived status as a fadista. Another classic breakthrough narrative (albeit implicit) for female fadistas in fado lore involves a romantic attachment with a well-connected guitarra or viola player or with a male figure with fado power or connections. Just as social inclusion in these scenes often occurred around gendered and sexed lines, so did social exclusion. More than once (outside of the scene at O Jaime) I heard female fadistas refer to a particular foreign fadista as *puta* (whore). "Puta" in this case was derogatory, used to refer to an outsider fadista (with a beautiful voice) who was reportedly romantically involved with a club owner. Terms such as "castiço" or "gingão," or Marceneiro's brothel miniature at the Fado Museum, or the fado diva Mariza suggestively revealing her stockings on stage, thus evoking Maria Severa, nod to a storied, illicit past of fado as genre while sentimentalizing that past. But "puta" in this context is a word with rough edges and is not used literally here to signify "prostitute"; rather, it comments on the means by which a particular fadista outsider was perceived to have accrued status.

Yet talk of rivals as "putas" and gossip about affairs and breakups between female fadistas and instrumentalists are enabled by the backdrop, the shadow cast by fado's bohemian imaginary, indexed with words like *castiço*. In hearing a story about gendered and sexed melodramas in fado's contemporary social scenes, a listener might say with a smile, "O mundo do fado é assim" (The world of fado is like that), gendered and sexed practices in the present validating a link to, and continuously re-creating, fado's storied past.

Tristezas *(Sadnesses) and Breaking Silence*

Fado and its heteroglossia of *tristezas*. There are so many ways of being alone; so many ways of being sad. It is the Tuesday of Carnival week in 2003, and O Jaime is decorated with festive colored streamers left over from the weekend celebrations. A special holiday fado afternoon has been called at the tasca since many people have the day off from work. On Monday, some children sang fado in costumes or masks. By Tuesday, the shenanigans of Carnival have died down, and people are enjoying just being together, relaxing, and listening to fado. At one table sit two women whom nobody seems to know. They are drinking. During an interval, we start a conversation. One tells me she is a classical musician who comes from an aristocratic family of fadistas; the other (who is visibly inebriated) buys me a soda. I sit at the table next to theirs; neither sings fado. Occasionally, one of the women strokes the hand of the other. We are in the middle of a conversation when I see Luisa, a fadista friend, gesturing to me. I ignore her, not wanting to interrupt. She is insistent. "Don't have anything to do with them. You have to be careful. They are *fufas* [slang for "lesbians"]. Be careful!" A woman sitting behind me whispers in my ear, "They are lesbians."

Jaime dims the lights, signaling that the interval is over and the fado about to begin. "Because fado is like a religion, it demands that everyone be silent," he announces. A fadista takes her place in front of the instrumentalists to sing. An unprecedented scene unravels, a moment of social anxiety that calls attention to itself, rendered audible and visible through the rupturing of codes of performance in key moments. One of the women continues to stroke the other woman's hand. People whisper, giggle, point, look embarrassed, and nudge one another. The laughter dies down, and listeners try to focus on the fado. The two women hold hands. Loud laughter breaks out, coming from the table in the back corner near the singer and instrumentalists, where many regulars sit. Luisa gets up to sing. The "lesbian" woman who is very drunk gets up and kisses the hem of Luisa's skirt then her hand. In so doing, she violates an unspoken boundary between fadista and listening audience. The audience might utter exclamations at key moments, sing the refrain, or show appreciation with silence or (for women) with bodily movement (a slightly dreamy swaying body or by swinging the shoulders from side to side). But it is the fadista who chooses whether to touch someone (e.g., by placing a hand on a listener's shoulder) as a part of his or her communication while singing. Even in such close proximity, the fadista in performance, in relation to the listeners, is untouchable.

Silence ruptures. The table at the back of the room erupts with laughter and comments. The transference of the touch to Luisa's skirt hem, by a woman about whom many people are now whispering "fufa," is the last straw. The social order of fado listening—an order that is always shaped in the moment between the aesthetics of fado form, the performances of the fadista and the instrumentalists, and the listeners in the room—breaks down. Luisa, a seasoned performer, struggles to sing without laughing. A woman to my left and I stoically try to keep everyone on track by loudly singing the refrain. "In the crystal of the throat lives the soul of a country," we chant. The two "lesbian" women appear completely lost to the fado, with glazed looks of rapture on their faces. Before Luisa sings her next fado, she loudly dedicates it to these two women saying, "They appear very sad (*triste*)." (The way she says "triste" reminds me of the time we drove by a group of transvestites on the way home from a late fado night when she told me, "I am glad my son isn't a transvestite because that would be very, very sad.") Luisa sings almost as if incanting a prayer—in a way that fados are sometimes sung when dedicated to someone—to exorcise sadness and to restore health. "It is the fado that is running through our veins that is making us sad," says one of the women, ignoring the moral import behind Luisa's inflection of "triste," a moment that foregrounds tristeza's double voicings.

O Jaime and other fado places like it, amateur fado venues of the early 2000s, where primarily fadistas of the older generation who considered themselves on the political left sang, reinforced an idea of Portugueseness that, while somewhat open in terms of class, was almost always white and staunchly heteronormative in terms of the lyrics performed and the social behavior explicitly sanctioned.[23] The only time I witnessed the complete rupturing of the almost sacred rituals of silence surrounding amateur fado listening coincided with an interaction between two women that "regulars" read as signifying homosexuality. In the hundreds of amateur fado performance sessions I attended between 2001 and 2010, this was the only instance I observed of markedly erotic affection between two people of the same sex within the context of fado listening. No amount of alcohol, joking, arguing, or even displays of extreme sadness, had broken a fado silence so completely. If fado performance and sociality in the tasca in amateur fado sessions maintains an imaginary of a fado "bohemia" of the past with some license for social transgression, this is a heteronormative bohemia. This particular rupturing of fado silence, in mid-song, with the fadista breaking into laughter (while performing a struggle *not* to laugh), along with the uncontrollable laughter and uncomfortable chatter of listeners, marks a place where social strictures are for a moment denaturalized, rendered audible and named ("fufas"), within the sociality of an aesthetic. The listening conventions of fado as genre (its structures of listening), and fado itself as sung form, unravel in this moment of "transgression." Genre, in this instance, makes its parameters of social possibility felt and heard.

Concerning the "silenced world" of homosexuality during the Estado Novo, as well as the lack of political mobilizing around feminist, LGBT, and immigration issues in the two decades that followed the revolution, Miguel Vale de Almeida (2008: 5, 45) suggests that Portugal may have skipped past "a transition of mentalities.... One may even speculate that the Portuguese transition may have been a sudden leap from *ancien régime* authoritarianism to post-modern globalized capitalism, without the transition and change of mentalities that was witnessed in Northern Europe in the post–World War II period and in the 1960s."[24] In the early 2000s, fado lyrics, the amateur fado networks I followed, and fado performed in the space of tascas often presented practices and ideologies that amplified a habitus of sex, gender, and sexuality residual from the Estado Novo, strains of which I experienced in diverse social networks and scenes (outside fado) in Lisbon during this time. To be certain, some of this amplification was generational; some may have been class-based; and some was located not only in fado but also within an inter-dynamic between practices of fado and practices of living and working in Lisbon's "traditional" neighborhoods, with associated ideologies of *bairrismo* (neighborhood fealty). These practices and ideologies accrue force, are given form, and are amplified through repetition as practiced through the habits of genre: the repetition of themes in fado lyrics; the repetition of rituals of *fado amador*; the practices of listening, of singing, of playing instruments; and the practices of performing man or woman and of feeling feminine or feeling masculine.

"Forty or fifty years ago, a woman who went out alone during the day to a café for a coffee would be considered a bad girl," a man in his late sixties told me in 2002. "No self-respecting parents would let their girl out." A woman in her sixties told me during an interview in 2003, "We could never wear lipstick during the dictatorship. This wasn't an official rule, but it was tacitly enforced." She then said she felt that Portugal still lagged behind other places in the world in terms of freedoms for women and initiated a conversation about abortion (which was legalized in Portugal in 2007), asking me to turn off my recorder. The Estado Novo placed many obstacles in the way of women's full national citizenship.[25] But perhaps most suffocating for many women was a moral climate that was shaped through the regime's profound links to conservative sectors of the Roman Catholic church—a morality that placed the idea of woman as mother, even as Mary, at the symbolic center of the nation while denying women the agency of national citizenship.[26]

Fado's Feminine

During the Estado Novo, a primary symbolic conduit of the national feminine was shaped precisely through the expressive practice of fado (which, in turn, was shaped by the censorship board) and through the feminine fado voice; the latter found its apotheosis in the voice of Amália Rodrigues. Yet from the beginning of its appropriation by the state, fado has been fraught with tension between its "illicitness" (with regard to both gender and race) and its function in building nation (including normalizing gender and sexuality). In contemporary, post-Amália Lisbon, this diva figure of fado par excellence animates the fado music industry and serves as an aesthetic frame of its own that invites multiple performative renderings of the feminine that range from young girls dreaming their futures through their voices to the hyper-feminized performances of drag queens for whom Amália serves as a diva icon (an idea I develop further in chapter 6). In the case of the drag queens, these performances might be understood as invigorating the sense of an "illicit" from the margins, thus animating an illicit for fado's "center."

The nature of many of the labors of the feminine in fado (and the wide symbolic net they cast), particularly in affective realms and in relation to mappings of empire, of nation, of city, of place, of race, or of an exotic or transgressive other, is not unique to fado or to Portugal. Indeed, these labors of the feminine are mostly congruent with what other scholars of gender have found to be more widely linked to modernity, the national, and the imperial.[27] In its international circulation outside Portuguese diasporic contexts during the twentieth century and into the present, fado has depended both symbolically and literally on the feminine for the labor of its translation; this goes beyond the feminine as a player in a transnational economy of (often sexualized) passion (see Savigliano 1995). This is a feminine as form at once already transnationally shot through by multiple media and in dialogue with other forms (the imperial, the lament, the nostalgic, the nation, the sentimental, the "musical," the diva) and their attendant labors in their metacultural circulations.[28] Female fado voices are more easily translatable internationally—thus more desirable by multinational recording companies, more successful, and metonymically come to stand in for the genre outside of Portugal—*because* of their implicit linkages to multiple metacultural forms that perform labors often perceived as feminine.

Lament has been ethnographically and historically documented, through studies conducted in different areas of the world, as primarily a feminine expressive form. Scholars of lament often theorize lament performance as granting vocal and interpretive agency to women in social contexts in which women generally may not have much voice in the public sphere or in everyday life (Briggs 1993; Caraveli-Chaves 1980; Rosenberg 2004; Seremetakis 1991; Tolbert 1995). Formally, fado is not a lament. It has no link to funerary practices; not all fado lyrics are sad or melancholic. But in terms of stylized sonic-vocal characteristics and in relation to some of the meta-discursive parameters that surround it and the reflexivity built into the genre, fado shares some characteristics with formal lamentation as a metacultural form (Fox and Yano forthcoming; Wilce 2009) and partakes affectively in a cross-cultural inter-text of stylized musical lamentations, of songs of loss and longing. And even though both men and women sing fado's "sad songs," tragic lyrics of suffering and of tristeza, the female voice has a greater symbolic purchase on the *sound* of suffering, a greater indexical valence socially to sadness, to injury, to tristeza writ at once as quotidian and cosmic.[29]

This symbolic purchase is linked to a porosity in relation to the form the feminine takes in its transnational circulations, where a particular register of the female voice comes to stand in for complaint, a "female complaint": "Women live for love, and love is the gift that keeps on taking" (Berlant 2008: 1). In historicizing the "female complaint" as a pervasive trope of "U.S. public sphere femininity," and in arguing for femininity as a genre, Lauren Berlant (2008: 2) portrays U.S. "complaint genres" of "women's culture" as "foregrounding a view of power that blames flawed men and bad ideologies for women's intimate suffering, all the while maintaining some fidelity to the world of distinction and desire that produced such disappointment in the first place."[30] Her ideas are salient in thinking about the feminine that fado formalizes (both within and outside Portugal), because the so called female complaint circulated transnationally, in the nineteenth century, through the literary, the theatrical, and the operatic, and has circulated in the twentieth and twenty-first centuries, mediatized in film, soap operas (*telenovelas*), and, powerfully, in recorded song.[31] Fado's complaint of the feminine has a particular localized script, but it is a script that, since the moment of the genre's emergence, has always been shaped in dialogue with more widely circulating ideologies and conventions of the feminine. If this is an essentialized feminine implicitly marked as being in a more proximate relationship with affect, suffering, the sexual, and *life* (Berlant 2008) than the masculine, these relations of proximity are also marked and come together in the sound of the female fadista's voice, which genre itself, as a way of being in the world (*uma maneira de ser*), is understood to sonorously imprint. *The female voice, to be the voice of fado, must be a punished voice, punished by the life of fado, of the fado houses, of smoke, of drink, of late nights.* "Cantarei Até Que a Voz Me Doa" (I Will Sing until My Voice Hurts) runs the title and the first line of a fado I heard sung only by women. With this feminine purchase on the authenticity of melancholy in fado comes a certain affective power, along with the power to seize fado's conventions of spectacularized high melodrama (to which male fadistas do not have as much access)—conventions that were catalyzed and then crystallized in the middle of the twentieth century through the voice and figure of Amália Rodrigues, the subject to which the final chapter turns.[32]

SIX

Haunted by a Throat of Silver

Prime Minister Guterres spoke for many when he said:
"Amália Rodrigues was the voice of the Portuguese soul."
—BBC NEWS

I never had pretensions to express the national soul. The national soul is
something very heavy for me.
—AMÁLIA RODRIGUES

One of the ways in which Amália exists as a great creator of songs that three
generations of Portuguese listened to and learned has to do with the
sonorous involvement [with her voice] that accompanied people's lives,
more profoundly, with affects that are not spoken, the feelings or the simple
sensations that are not verbalized but are of the body.
—JOAQUIM PAIS DE BRITO

Amália Rodrigues has already been dead for eight months when I visit
her in July 2000 at her burial site at the Lisbon cemetery of Prazeres
(Pleasures). She is in a narrow locked vault, number thirty-six. The vault
is surrounded by a profusion of color and texture, making it luminous, a
place for the living in this city of white stone. Her name is writ in red
flowers on a panel of white; above, a large portrait photograph, from the
"golden age" of her voice, that appeared as an insert in the daily newspaper shortly after her death, is tacked up. There are photographs of Amália
at all stages of her career; lyrics of fados she sang; a notice for a meeting
of the Association for the Friends of Amália and for an Amália birthday

celebration; fados written in black magic marker on white paper in homage (one of which is titled "Amália Is Portugal," on which is noted beneath the title, "six months after her physical disappearance"); a piece of paper framed in wood with large, handwritten letters below a colored-in line drawing of the French flag that reads, "Amália: La France Pleure Pour Toi" (Amália: France Cries for You), along with magazine cutouts of the Eiffel Tower and Amália's photo; candles; religious items, including miniature saint and Jesus figurines, rosary beads, and crosses; a poster of the Portuguese flag; and other keepsakes. They spill out onto the walls and ledges, covering other vaults. Sunflowers, roses, geraniums, hydrangea, wildflowers, and hothouse flowers overflow into all of the space below the tomb, above and beside it. On one ledge is a white souvenir replica of the Monastery of Jerónimos.[1] Writing on a poster proclaims, "Amália is here provisionally until her burial in the Monastery of Jerónimos." A handwritten poem on another part of the wall reads, "Amália: Heteronym of Portugal / With Amália in Jerónimos / Next to Camões and Pessoa / They will be the three heteronyms / Of a country that resounds with the fado" (plate 8).[2]

When Amália Rodrigues died on October 6, 1999, the Portuguese government declared three days of national mourning. Her funeral was an elaborate theatrics of the state, her coffin wrapped in the Portuguese flag. The presiding bishop declared, "The nation is in mourning. We all turn respectfully to the mortal remains of Amália, the only artist who sang, like no one sang, the *saudade* of the Portuguese soul."[3] In an extended funeral procession, thousands of mourners weeping sang her fados. She was temporarily buried in the cemetery of Prazeres, and for almost two years debates raged in the government and among the public concerning the final burial site. Some used the fact that Amália was a woman who sang fado—a popular song form with illicit origins—to argue that she not be honored with interment at Jerónimos or in the National Pantheon. In July 2001, twenty-one months after her burial at Prazeres, her body was moved with elaborate state ceremony, which included the singing of some of her fados along with the national hymn and a speech by the President of the Republic, to the National Pantheon alongside tombs of Portuguese kings and a cenotaph for Vasco da Gama. She is the first woman to be buried there.

Many admirers continued to argue that she should have been buried in the Monastery of Jerónimos and some, that she should have remained at Prazeres, where there is no charge for admission, thus where the people can more easily come pay her homage. The move to the National Pantheon abruptly put an end to the possibilities for personal rites of memorialization around her burial site, the profuse material acts of popular remembrance made manifest in the poetry, posters, keepsakes, handwritten letters, photographs, miniature shrines, and outpourings of flowers that had previously adorned her grave. In the National Pantheon, in an echoing stone chamber dedicated to Portuguese language and culture, an official sign describes her contribution, and just a few vases of flowers rest at the foot of her tomb.

Monumentalization demands the illusion of fixity, the erasure of process. In 2009, I stand in the entrance of Amália's home, turned museum after her death. I buy a ticket from Estrela, who fell in love with Amália's voice when she heard it over the radio as a girl in Angola and later moved to Lisbon to become Amália's live-in personal assistant.[4] Now Estrela works the counter and the recently published memoir of her life with Amália is on display in a glass box along the wall (Carvas 2009). I tell her that I am visiting the house for the first time in many years just to see if anything has changed, and she looks surprised. "Nothing, nothing has changed," she says emphatically. "Everything is exactly how it was when she passed away. Nothing has changed." During the guided tour, I see books about Amália sitting on top of the piano in the living room— books that had not yet been published when she was alive. One is the reissue of her biography (see V. Santos 2005 [1987]); another is a catalogue for the exhibit commemorating the tenth anniversary of Amália's death that had just opened at the National Pantheon, *Amália in the World; The World of Amália*. Her bed is made, the covers carefully turned back. Makeup, half-used, sits organized neatly on a dressing table. The dining room table is set for a formal dinner with antique British china. Costume copies of her jewels sit in a glass box outside the bedroom. A soundtrack of her voice singing spins. I visit the National Pantheon the following day. Some of Amália's gowns, eerily illuminated, stand on their own in the upper balconies. Towering displays with blown-up photographs of Amália tell a story about her movement out into the world, how she went from being a local "Portuguese" star to international celebrity. Meticulously arranged and labeled personal objects—fetish icons— are under glass, a high-heel black pump with a golden bow, a black fadista's shawl, sunglasses, jewelry, a faded passport, a preserved plane

FIGURE 6.1 •
Newsstand in the
Baixa district.
Lisbon, August
2007. Photograph
by the author.

ticket. The controversy behind the move of Amália's body to the National Pantheon is absent, the petitions, the votes in Parliament, the out-
cry of fans who wanted her buried at Jerónimos, eclipsed in the
monument that is already made.

During the years immediately following Amália's death, the most
vociferous and public debates about memorialization concerned her final burial site, or the monumentalization of her body. Yet her death
catalyzed multiple practices and discourses of remembrance. Death amplified Amália's presence, increasing consumption of her recordings
(sales peaked in the days following her death) and foregrounded mimetic production both in performance practice and within the music
and larger culture industry (figure 6.1). Death charged her aura, her voice,
with heightened nostalgia, heightened saudade. Fado performance,

which has long borne mimetic imprints of Amália's style, continues to be haunted by her death, which has given rise to emergent practices of memorialization in ritual, in performance, and in the uses of the singing voice itself.

When I lived in Lisbon in 2001–2003, Amália's image was widely present in fado venues. Her photograph from a newspaper insert was tacked up on walls; portraits hung in ornate frames, backlit, or were presented in miniature, enshrined, on tables with flowers, or were pasted on exterior doors as lures for tourists, iconic of fado itself. Her portrait hung in the record store Valentim de Carvalho in downtown Lisbon, prominently framed near the entrance. It sat on top of a fado cart that sells CDs to tourists (operated by the Lisbon CD shop Discoteca Amália) in the neighborhood of Chiado. Her image loomed large in double in an advertisement for the musical "Amália," which played in Lisbon for almost two years to sold-out houses: Amália is pictured in the height of her career and she appears to look over her shoulder; to the right of this photograph is a copy of the first, with her face enlarged. This image hung from rearview mirrors of taxicabs on little pillows, plastered billboards next to bus stops, and revolved on stands in the arrival hall of the Lisbon airport.

Her name was everywhere, invoked as a divine musical standard, as patrimony, as culture, as nation, as place: *My daughter is a veritable Amália. You should hear her sing. The voice of Amália is the voice of national patrimony.* "Amália Rodrigues" is a TAP Portugal airplane, her name inscribed on its side—the name of a vessel, gendered after the national *she* (figure 6.2). Newspapers discussed whether a street should be officially renamed in Amália's honor and possible locations for Amália monuments and a park. In 2001, all along the winding long street where she had lived, the Rua de São Bento (the same street on which the Parliament is located), were stenciled black block graffiti letters, reading "Rua Amália." In 2009 the graffiti was still there (plate 9).

Recordings of Amália's voice surprised me from open windows sometimes on quiet neighborhood streets, from tourist shops, or blasting from outdoor speakers on busy shopping streets. At amateur fado contests and fado gala nights, every young girl and woman seemed to be singing Amália's most popular fados mimicking the vocal ornamentation Amália used. The recording company EMI-Valentim de Carvalho and Amália's fans ("Amalianos") debated how best to reinscribe her voice on disc; which recordings should be remastered, restored,

FIGURE 6.2 • Amália Rodrigues as an airliner (note her name to the right on the plane). Lisbon airport, December 2002. Photograph by the author.

rereleased, or even released for the first time. Spectacular drag queens at a late-night club lip-synced her fados, reenacting, with a swagger, her bodily gestures. Masses were held in Amália's honor, and tiny Amália dolls, singing into miniature microphones, were for sale in tourist shops. In the amateur fado community, poets wrote fados in homage, and fadistas collected keepsakes, listened to Amália's recordings as they went about their days, and sang her fados in their own ways. In 2009, public commemorations, publications, exhibits, and graffiti in Lisbon marked the ten-year anniversary of her death (plate 10). In the years since her death, the practices of individual remembrance, public discourse, and public commemoration have gradually shifted. Certain aspects of Amália's story have fallen away, while others have been foregrounded to make way for new stories, new stars, new singing styles, and differently imagined and felt histories.

The story I tell here fits into a drama already many times enacted and retold: the mourning of an icon, the theatricality of state commemorative practices magnifying an afterlife to be put to use in the service of the nation, the mourning and the afterlife of a *female* icon (Paredez 2009; D. Taylor 2003), and of an icon's seeming transparency despite (or because of) its excessively stacked redundancy.[5] This is a story whose scripts are almost invisible for their familiarity and repetition—scripts of the relationship of the feminine to the nation, of the "female complaint" (Berlant 2008), of the death of the beautiful woman (Bronfen 1992, cited in D. Taylor 2003: 145; Colvin 2008). It is a story of celebrity-icon in which a subject's encounter with the icon potentiates the "activation of intense sensations," a "tumultuous synesthesia" (Ghosh 2011: 8). But it is also a story about the mourning and afterlife of *vocal* celebrity and vocal celebrity as amplified through the affective expectations of the particular musical genre of fado.[6] As such, questions of voice, sound, listening, and the labors of musical genre become critical both to "reconstituting the complex materiality of the icon" (Ghosh 2011: 3) and to understanding the extraordinary potentiating force of vocal celebrity for shaping affective life worlds and public feeling.

This chapter is made from the overlapping re-voicing of tropes, the scrapbooking of an excessive poetics, a poetics of excess that flutter around the intangibility of the affective power of the voice of a diva. I analyze the poetics of public biography and fan discourses, commemorative practices, and performative mimesis (vocal, gestural, sartorial, biographical) to think about dialectics between the genre of celebrity and fado as genre and to theorize more broadly about relationships between singing musical superstars and their publics. I explore the excessive hauntings of a voice, a voice that so *went beyond itself* that for many it became a means of deeply shaping personal subjectivity: for some it became the soul of a nation, or a way of feeling Portuguese. What does it mean to be haunted by such a voice—a voice that during Amália's life had already become the national sonic signifier of loss and longing? How does one memorialize something as intangible as a voice? What does it mean that this voice is female, marked as feminine? I ground questions about memorialization, memory, affect, intimacy, and mimesis in multiple rememberings, representations, and performative renderings of Amália as diva.

Biography of a Voice

Amália Rodrigues was born in 1920 in Lisbon, close to the neighborhood of Mouraria, to a poor family.[7] Her parents were from a rural region of Portugal (Beira Baixa), northeast of Lisbon, but she was raised primarily by her grandparents in Lisbon. After completing primary school at twelve, she held menial jobs (including working as an embroiderer, in a cake factory, and as a fruit seller at a tourist stand) and sang informally. Her rise to public prominence as a fadista began in her late teens, with her first engagement at the *casa de fado* Retiro da Severa in Lisbon. By nineteen she was working as a professional fadista in Lisbon's fado houses, and by her mid-twenties, she had already found great success in musical-theater roles in Lisbon and had begun an international career at a time that international careers for fado singers were rare. Her most pivotal international success came during a ten-month engagement in 1945 in Brazil, where she performed and made her first commercial recordings. She starred in more than a dozen films, most with singing roles (many produced abroad and some intended for foreign audiences), and in Portugal, her voice was often broadcast over radio.[8] Her early success in Brazil led to engagements in Paris and London. Her notoriety escalated, and by the early 1950s, her career had become immensely international in scope. She gave live performances and her recordings were distributed (and in some cases, produced) in Europe, Africa, Asia, North America, and South America. She came to be known as simply "Amália."

In her public performances and recording career, she demonstrated flexibility in performing multiple genres beyond fado, including flamenco songs, Broadway hit tunes (e.g., George Gershwin's "Summertime" and Richard Rodgers and Lorenz Hart's "Blue Moon") with orchestral accompaniment, popular French songs (e.g., "La Vie en Rose"), Italian folk songs, and Mexican rancheras, as well as Portuguese folk music (*folclore*) and popular marches.[9] She also occasionally wrote poetry, some of which she sang to fado. She is widely credited with raising the artistic level of fado, particularly through her collaborations with the French Portuguese composer Alain Oulman, and for being the first to sing fado set to the work of high canonical poets such as Camões.[10] Her prolific career continued through the mid-1990s; her last public performance took place in Lisbon in 1994.

Specific biographical details about Amália's life and career recur, overlap, and commingle in contemporary talk with fadistas and fans, in historical accounts from the popular press, and in staged and mediatized representations of her life story.[11] These details often stress a rags-to-riches life narrative, her humble upbringing and subsequent working-class jobs, her lack of formal education and of formal voice training (this is always commented on in a positive light), and a personality prone to bouts of extreme sadness and fatalism that gave rise to multiple suicide attempts. Finally, they foreground a voice and a public figure who brought Portugal and fado to international attention through her role as the "ambassador of fado."

Many of these details shape a profile that is in line with common mythology surrounding what it means to be a fadista and fado mythology writ large, particularly regarding the trope of suffering and fado's gendered and classed origins (see also A. Osório 1974). In coming from a poor family with rural origins and selling oranges for a living, Amália is *do povo* (of the people). Her rise to success mimics fado's own biographical trajectory (as a genre) from the working class to the salons, accounted for in fado legend by the figure of Maria Severa, the "first fadista," a prostitute who in the early 1800s brought fado to the aristocracy by sleeping with a count (see chapter 5). Just as fado lore has it that "one does not learn to be a fadista; one is born a fadista," stories about Amália always stress her lack of formal musical education. Yet these stories also note her "genius" in that she was able to speak and sing in several languages and genres, even though she was unschooled. They often account for these talents and her intelligence as part of what marks her an *artista* (artist).

Amália as a diva who became for so many iconic of the nation (and whose national acclaim was tied to her internationalism) represents a particularly twentieth-century phenomenon of musical celebrity. Her company includes the Egyptian diva Umm Kulthum, Édith Piaf, the Japanese postwar *enka* diva Misora Hibari, and the Argentine tango singer Carlos Gardel.[12] This is a kind of musical celebrity shaped by twentieth-century nationalisms broadly writ and particular economies of feeling and state apparatuses in relation to the national. This is a version of vocal celebrity that is embedded in early to mid-twentieth century practices of recording production, distribution, and media circulation. This is a vocal celebrity enabled by the emergence of radio as a tool for nation building, along with the florescence of an international film industry (with its locus of power in the United States), with their concomitant roles in shaping celebrity literally as larger than life and in powerfully linking celebrity to commodity consumption.[13] As Portugal's most celebrated and widely travelled musician during the Estado

Novo, Amália's career was necessarily entangled with the ideologies of the regime. It was António Ferro, Salazar's director of propaganda/minister of culture in 1933–49, who brought Amália to London and to Paris for her first engagements there in 1949. In 1950, she was sent as a Portuguese representative to perform a series of European concerts under the Marshall Plan, and in the late 1960s, she would travel to Angola to sing for Portuguese troops fighting in the colonial wars. The figure of Amália as the voice of Portugal was undoubtedly appropriated by the regime in the service of nationalism, and as Maria de São José Côrte-Real (2001) argues, it was later used by the incipient Portuguese democracy in shaping national sentiment and the imaginary of Portugal abroad. As I argue, it continues to be appropriated for political ends. Amália publicly claimed that she was "apolitical," yet immediately after the fall of the dictatorship, her career in Portugal suffered because of her supposed relationship to it. In talking to fans of Amália and to singers and instrumentalists who admire her, I found a tendency to position her on neutral ground as "apolitical" or "above politics." Yet in 2003, almost thirty years after the revolution, I also spoke to people who vehemently called her "fascist." Others claimed in the months following her death that she had aided political prisoners and proclaimed that she had sent large quantities of money clandestinely to the Communist Party during her lifetime.[14]

It is possible that her figure and her voice mediated multiple political positions during the dictatorship. If so, the Amália phenomenon would bear some resemblance to the case of Umm Kulthum, who is widely known for her role as a critical mediator in Egyptian politics (Danielson 1997). The complex nuances regarding the role the regime played in Amália's rise to success and the multiple ways in which her voice may have been shaped as the conduit for Portugal's "soul" have yet to be critically examined.[15]

Biography of a Voice Continued: The Santos–Amália Collaboration
When they tell my story and I am no longer alive to say how it was, then they will be inventing things. Even here, spoken by me, many people will say that it isn't true, that the rumors are what are true. A person is in charge of [his or her] own self. If it were the truth, I wouldn't care what they said. It is the lies that irritate me. But *I know that my story is what they choose it to be*, that which is most interesting, that which isn't my story. —VÍTOR PAVÃO DOS SANTOS, AMÁLIA (emphasis added)

The most influential source for Amália's public biography over the past two decades has been Vitor Pavão dos Santos's *Amália—Uma Biografia* (2005 [1987]).[16] This text has been used as a primary source for both fictional and nonfictional biographical accounts that span many genres, including film, biopic, documentary, written narratives for commemorative exhibitions, and CD liner notes. It also figures as an internalized Ur-text biography for some of the fans with whom I spoke. One fan repeated entire lines verbatim as if they were his own; others riffed on key themes, inflecting the details to match their own imagined ideal of Amália. In terms of its enduring use value as source material over the past twenty years, the collaboration between Santos and Amália gave Amália tremendous power over how her life story would be represented and how she would be officially remembered, despite her doubts to the contrary.

Santos, an impassioned Amália fan since his childhood, trained in history, and a longtime director of Lisbon's Museu Nacional do Teatro (to which Amália was a financial donor), conducted seventy-eight hours of taped interviews with Amália between 1982 and 1986. He then edited a select portion of these interviews for the book (V. Santos 2005 [1987]: 21). With the exception of dates inserted in parentheses after key events, the "biography" reads as an autobiographical monologue spoken by Amália. Santos does not include his voice in the text, and he does not provide a rationale for how he selected portions of the narrative from the vast archive of recorded interviews he collected. He explicitly attempts to retain Amália's voice, including her vernacularisms (V. Santos 2005 [1987]: 22).[17] The biography exhibits some circularity in the genealogy of its production. During the interviews, Santos used press clippings and photographs from various moments in her career, which he had bound together in chronological order in a scrapbook, as prompts to elicit Amália's memories and narratives of her life history. From these scraps and fragments of public biography, Santos and Amália formed a cohesive story. The collaboration is a node of collecting and selective memory that gestures backward historically to the role of the press in producing Amália's celebrity biography and forward to the ways in which Amália hoped to be remembered.

Amália walks a fine line on questions of politics in the text. She elides, for the most part, the fact that the bulk of her career took place during decades of a dictatorial regime in which a culture of informing, political imprisonment, travel restrictions, censorship, and lack of a public sphere (Gil 2007), along with the social enforcement of sharply gendered behavioral mores, were de rigueur. She repeatedly positions herself as politically naïve or uninterested in politics and adamantly refutes that the regime played a pivotal role in enabling her career. "I never had subsidies," she claimed. "António Ferro never had any importance in my career. He thought I was the best linen [*melhor toalha*] in the house [the best fadista in Portugal], but he never helped me to be Amália Rodrigues" (V. Santos 2005 [1987]: 146, 99).[18] She claims not to have understood the political import of some of the lyrics she sang. Regarding the fado "Abandono," whose first line is "Because of your free thinking they locked you up far away," she states, "I was never defiant. When I sang 'Abandono,' I did not understand that it was political" (V. Santos 2005 [1987]: 98). Later in the text she claims,

> I always thought that "Abandono," by David Mourão-Ferreira, was a fado about love. I never thought about Peniche [a maximum security prison from the Estado Novo period that housed many political prisoners]. It is a fado that is so well done, with such beautiful words, with so much weight, that I don't want to say that I would have not sung it had I understood its intention. Perhaps had I sung it in a revolutionary manner, it would not have had the effect that it did. The disc [on which "Abandono" was featured] was prohibited because of "Abandono." Later, it did very well. But when I sang it, it was about a sadness of love, that is a sentiment much more beautiful and more painful than a revolutionary idea. (V. Santos 2005 [1987]: 139)

Her commentary on "Abandono" can be read as an example of how she refuses to commit to a clear-cut political positioning throughout the text and how she sidesteps the political through recourse to a discourse of sentiment. She states that she was "never defiant" and, at the same time, suggests that she might have sung the lyrics even had she realized their full political import. In one of the few moments in the narrative where she speaks overtly about censorship, she claims that she never had fixed programs, that she would turn one program in to the censorship board, then sing a different program at the actual performance (V. Santos

2005 [1987]: 141). In telling the story of how she helped her best-known and most loved collaborator, Alain Oulman (who created the music for "Abandono"), get released from prison, where he was being held for his political activities, she claims she phoned the Portuguese ambassador in France and told him, "I don't understand anything about politics. I never heard Alain talk about politics, all I know is that he spent a lot of time with poets" (V. Santos 2005 [1987]: 140). Self-reflexively commenting on this, she states, "What I told the ambassador was what I thought, because Alain was really so political that he never talked about [politics]."

Just as fado aficionados and practitioners told me that reading between the lines was critical to understanding many fado lyrics, fado also has its own argot and a history of coded and secretive poetic language that long predates the Estado Novo. Heightened listening, speaking, and reading between the lines are naturalized practices in relation to everyday discourse and reception under state regimes of censorship, practices that can linger long after speech becomes "free." Amália's biography/autobiography does call for some reading between the lines. It is challenging to understand how a singer who gave so much weight to understanding and interpreting the poetic and emotional charge of language—someone who was surrounded by a milieux of artistic collaborators on the political left—could have not understood the import of explicitly political lyrics or could have understood nothing about politics.

The rumors Amália refers to are those that circulated after the revolution, regarding her alleged complicity with the dictatorship. "Later they came up with the idea [inventaram] that I had a tunnel from my house to Salazar's, [and] that Salazar never did anything without talking first to me. They said I belonged to the PIDE [secret police], but the lie was what shocked me" (V. Santos 2005 [1987]: 146, 164). Indeed, even in the early 2000s, I found people who repeated the sentiment behind such rumors, such as the taxi driver who told me how much he hated Amália (see chapter 2). (*I have friends whose breasts are marked by cigarette burns from torture during the dictatorship.*) Amália notes that some of her intellectual friends and artistic collaborators simply dropped her after the revolution (V. Santos 2005 [1987]: 164). Some rumors that I have heard over the past decade would have it that general public sentiment turned almost completely away from Amália in the aftermath of the revolution, but that sometime later, the public returned to favoring her. Apart from her discussion of the rumors, the reasons some close friends and members of the political left would have abandoned her after the revolution are not clarified in the text. The vagueness in the Santos text on this point mirrors a similar vagueness with respect to the figuring of the contemporary historical imagination of Lisbon's fado world regarding the status that fado held in Portugal in the aftermath of the 1974 revolution.

Amália's ambiguous political positioning in Santos's biography/autobiography fits into larger metanarratives that run throughout the text. These reach beyond the particularities of the Amália phenomenon and draw on wider tropes about art and sentiment that have circulated with vigor in many Anglo and European art worlds (given heighted form beginning with eighteenth-century Romanticism) and on tropes about both the affective labor of the feminine and the enchantments of celebrity (see Berlant 2008). Ideologically, the assumption that underpins Amália's narrative, throughout Santos's book, is that art is about the sublime human and is above (or outside) the political. Amália seeks refuge from the political by drawing on a combination of sentimentalism in discourses of emotion and love; the sublimity of art, in which art is music transmitted through her voice; and a performance of gendered naiveté. She stresses that she was the one who made the choices, that she was in charge, letting her spontaneous art take her voice where it would, and that the people (*o povo*) were always with her and understood her when others did not.

Amália consistently makes claims for her uniqueness as an artist and as a fado singer. She insists not only that the state did not play an important role in her success, but also that she was not influenced artistically and stylistically or helped by other fadistas. She mentions other fadistas by name infrequently, and when she does, she almost always does so in the context of a backhanded compliment, laudatory in one breath and dismissive in another.[19] She marks her uniqueness in terms of her vocal timbre, her performance style, the trajectory of her career, her choices in lyrics and in repertoire. She specifies multiple ways in which *she* influenced fado as a genre, as a performance practice, and its publics. "Without me, had I not continued the fado of saudade, sad fado, fado would not exist today," she claims, and she extends her role as an innovator beyond the genre of fado. At the same time, she is hesitant to identify with fadista as a type; rather, she identifies with fado as sentiment (V. Santos 2005

[1987]: 141, 155, 173, 180). She promotes herself and her celebrity while claiming that she lacked ambition (which might not have been understood as an attractive feminine quality). She marks her own celebrity by making frequent references to her contact with other international celebrities of the time, showing that she moved in celebrity's social orbit, yet she keeps returning to her status as one of the people and to her humble upbringing.

Amália invokes her rural roots—the fact that her parents were from the Beira Baixa—as both a point of vocal stylistic origin and as a foundation for "proper" womanhood in relation to sexual norms. She claims that her mother's singing had the greatest influence on her own and that her unique mode of ornamentation, her way of singing *voltinhas*, owes something to the traditional vocal style of the Beira Baixa.[20] In commenting on discovering that Pedro Homem de Mello, one of the key erudite poets whose work she sang, was bisexual, she again retreats into a [properly] gendered naiveté: "I never understood these things, my family is from the Beira Baixa, *where they wear long skirts*" (V. Santos 2005 [1987]: 139; emphasis added).[21] Invoking rural origins in these two spheres does the work of loosely binding Amália's uniquely ornamental singing style (that her critics initially derided as "Spanish") to both the Portuguese rural folk and to modest feminine virtue.

Amália's narrative emphasizes the power of feeling, linking her voice and manner of singing to deeply felt shared sentiment, her own intense feeling while singing to its public physical and emotional contagion. "If the scream [*grito*] is with the kind of intensity that I like, the public feels it. No one is able to avoid feeling shivers or goose bumps [*arrepio*] when I feel it" (V. Santos 2005 [1987]: 170). She repeatedly mentions her lack of formal vocal training and her lack of technique. "I don't know how to sing," she states, offering as proof that she "never sang the same way twice" (V. Santos 2005 [1987]: 158, 161). She connects her "lack of technique" to fado's ethos of spontaneous feeling that defies learning or explanation—"Fado isn't sung, it happens" and "Fado is felt; it can't be understood or explained" (V. Santos 2005 [1987]: 60). Yet her narrative reveals a musician who is articulate about her craft and about her aesthetic, musical, and technical preferences, and she often describes specific aspects of her vocal technique and performance style. It reveals a woman, an artist, and a celebrity who is not only politically savvy in how she situates her identity as fluid with respect to politics and to fado, but who is able to theorize about the cultural phenomenon of her celebrity and her own "authenticity":

> They were speaking a lot about the cultural value of Amália. I would understand much better when they would call me the "soul of fado," because I was singing fado and it didn't come out badly and fado has that thing that comes from inside [of oneself]. I explain this idea of cultural value in the following manner: I think that all countries have something in the air that distinguishes one [country] from another, a kind of collective soul of which I am part. Because of this, I arrive someplace, and the people identify me with Portugal. *I have a truth that is so large, I have an authenticity that is so large and I am Portuguese.* (V. Santos 2005 [1987]: 181; emphasis added)

Even for Amália, "Amália Rodrigues" exceeds the boundaries of self and body. "Amália Rodrigues" is a collection and an interplay of multiple phenomena, performances, press, films, television appearances, her voice on radio, her international career, and her recordings. "My life has nothing to do with who I am as an artist," she claims (V. Santos 2005 [1987]: 140). Yet she shapes her life story in such a way that it is entangled with the genre of fado: "Fado began for me as a song and ended as a form of life that I identified with. A strange form of life" (V. Santos 2005 [1987]: 27).[22] In this narrative, as in the discourse of many fado fans and singers, fado as musical-poetic genre, as poetic and musical form, is also a form for living, one with its own biography.

I have dwelled on Santos's text because it has been influential in shaping both recent representations of Amália's life story and the ways in which some fans identify with the biography they hear in her voice. As one fan told me, "The point of departure [for me] was the Santos biography. She is speaking in the first person, Amália as artist, Amália as woman. There was sympathy between what I was reading and what I felt. I read with a hunger to know."[23] The biography's reception in circulation and performative mutations (video documentary, musical theater, biopic) foregrounds the collusion of forms, the textual (literary) and the sonic/musical (in the form of recordings), in shaping the ways in which voice as biography is mapped onto voice as sung and onto the mythological biographies, performance practices, and sedimented affects layered in fado as genre.

On Celebrity

As an overarching genre and as a phenomenon, celebrity is marked by multiple characteristics, regardless of the primary spheres of activity in which it thrives, and to some extent these spheres often overlap.[24] Celebrities have publics, are made by and through media, and have fans. Celebrity can inspire idolatry, a religious-like fervor. For the performance theorist Joseph Roach, celebrity is about having "it," a "certain quality, easy to perceive but hard to define, possessed by abnormally interesting people" (Roach 2007: 1). This "it" simultaneously embodies and projects singularity and typicality, strength alongside vulnerability, elements of the ordinary and of the extraordinary. Celebrity spawns offshoots, mimetic renderings, imitations, and aspirations; often, mimesis opens up possibilities for performative critique, satire, or subversion. Celebrities have entourages of assistants who enable them to perform their celebrity with a seeming transparency. Celebrities "absorb superlatives" and take on a "different ontological category" (Dyer 1979: 49); they are "hyper-individuals" (C. Taylor 1989, cited in Marshall 2006a: 8). Scholars of celebrity point to the ruptures between the star's public personas and private selves and between the shaping of celebrity and the shaping of public intimacy and sentiment. Celebrity exploits the desire in the subject that is born of distance and performs "significant nodal points of articulation between the social and the personal" (Rojek 2001: 16). Biography, in relation to celebrity, takes on a heightened charge in its multiple renderings, in its circulatory power and permutations, in its mercurial tensions that push the public into the private and the intimate into the public. Aspects of a celebrity's public biography may be internalized or appropriated by fans, shaping subjectivity, a sense of selfhood. The power of celebrities to hail or to interpellate subjects is a common trope in academic theorizations of celebrity (Marshall 2006a: 3). Yet there is never a one-to-one correspondence between nationalist ideologies or state apparatuses of power and the multiple ways in which people come to *feel* themselves (or not) as national subjects or come to constitute publics.[25]

The relationships between vocal celebrities and their publics are often extraordinarily powerful in shaping popular discourses and practices of belonging, sociality and affect.[26] Much generative work on celebrity was energized initially by attention to film celebrity. But popular-music celebrity does not necessary map neatly onto theorizations of celebrity concerned with film or other visual media (see Marshall 2006b: 205).

I am interested in the phenomenon of vocal celebrity, of the diva in relation to the possibilities it engenders for the "crafting of selves" (Kondo 1990).[27] How might we think about celebrity vis-à-vis the affective power of the voice in its multiple valences, the voice as mediator between exteriority and embodied interiority, the voice as simultaneously social and at once deeply intimate and physiological, its resonances standing in all at once for nature and for culture? Ross Chambers (1991) calls attention to the importance of understanding the power of *desire* as a space of opposition (where oppositional practices work within the creative, improvisational, and sometimes playful "room for maneuver" within systems, as opposed to "resistance," which openly negates the system or frameworks of power in place).[28] Michael Warner (2002) argues for the ways in which reflexivity in relation to the field of circulation enables a space of improvisation and the performance of multiple subjectivities. Here I foreground feeling in relation to subjecthood and personhood vis-à-vis musical experience as a "space of ambivalence" (Butler 1993: 124) or as "room to maneuver." The polysemous, sensuous, and often deeply interiorized nature of musical sense making that renders music such a powerful tool for shaping soulful national subjects also lends it its excessive slippage (from which multiple possibilities for self-crafting and imagining might be figured).

I am not arguing here for a concept of self that is somehow "beyond" culture or that exists outside of the nation. Neither am I offering a one-to-one model for understanding the relationship of the subject's engagement with nationalized public culture and an inculcation of an affective "national subject." Lisa Rofel argues ethnographically that engagement with "public allegories" (in her case, soap operas in China) provides a means through which people make their "inner selves"; they learn *how to long*. This self-making through interaction with public forms is never just about the inculcation of a national subject. These encounters offer sites of negotiation of the self and the social, "horizons of possibility or impossibility" (Rofel 2007: 6). In the case of soap operas in 1990s China, or mediatized fado and a mediatized Amália, these encounters are also marked by transnational traces and circulations of power, forms, styles, aesthetics, and ideas about what affectively constitutes the "human."

Understanding the social valences of vocal celebrity demands heightened attention not just to the political, the poetic, the physiological, and the sonic features of the voice but also to how publics listen and how diverse (but overlapping) listening publics coalesce around the same voice. Amália's overlapping listening publics might to some extent be productively thought through in light of Lauren Berlant's theorization of literary and cinematic "female complaint" genres in the United States in the nineteenth century and twentieth century in relation to "intimate publics." Berlant argues that cultural forms of female complaint (via their affective power) implicitly scaffold assumptions undergirding a normative gender and sexuality and an emotional subject on which discourses of liberal humanism rely. In her theorization, an intimate public is a space where affective knowledge is privileged over ideology; it is at once a "porous affective scene of identification amongst strangers" and a "space of mediation in which the personal is refracted through the general" (Berlant 2008: vii, 8). Personal biographies, framed within an intimate public sphere, take on a collective cast, where "all sorts of narratives are read as autobiographies of collective experience" (Berlant 2008: vi). Berlant asks questions about the relationships between celebrity and citizenship and about the relationships between sentimentality and antisovereignty. "Is sentimentality ultimately anti-sovereign, a discipline of the body toward assuming universal response," she asks. "How are different types of person and kinds of population hailed by the universalist icon of the person who loves, suffers and desires to survive the obstacles that bind her or him to history" (Berlant 2008: 13, 56, 89)? Just as Portuguese "soulfulness" can be understood partly as developing in conversation with a transatlantic circulation of anthropological ideas on "ethnic identity" in the early to mid-twentieth century (see chapter 2), Amália's melodramatic persona, which is critical to her "soulfulness" and based on a biography of a woman who tragically suffers, calls to be understood and historicized in relation not only to an "aesthetics of the local" but also to transnationally circulating ideologies and forms (in this case, of the feminine).[29]

It might also be important to ask how it is that we are seduced into feeling belonging, into becoming soulful or desirous subjects vis-à-vis aesthetic engagement with the singing voice. Through an excessively redundant poetics, fans, fadistas, and instrumentalists emphasize the affective power of Amália's *voice* as what enabled her to sing to the intimate, to the local, while singing to the world, reaching a "universality" of expression as "Portugal's greatest musician of the twentieth century." Through its timbre and the repertoire that it sings, this voice publicly celebrates a particular biography that carries multiple valences: as a biography that personifies fado as genre; as a framework or model for being fadista, for feeling Portuguese, or for particular ways of structuring and hearing feelings through stylized sound. I turn now to the excess of this voice and to a discussion of how the experience of this voice is refracted in invidual listeners and singers.

Amaliano Poetics

I have been listening to [Amália's] voice every day for sixteen years, at least to one song. I never get tired; every time is like the first time I am listening to her. She has this capacity to go beyond herself, to renew herself. Every time I listen to her, I find new things about her voice. She goes straight to my heart. One might think, with this identification thing, that I am sick. . . . There are very sad feelings and songs in her voice and texts; some are very mournful. But it is a good thing, because when you identify [with what she sings], you exorcise your phantoms, those thoughts that come to you once in a while. Listening to Amália, you clean yourself and you feel right afterward. You feel perfectly sane, even happy. —FERNANDO FORTE, June 13, 2002

When I was fifteen years old [in 1986], I started liking Amália. I saw one of her concerts at the [Coliseu dos Recreios] in 1990 to celebrate fifty years of her career; seven thousand people were there. From there, it was a fantastic discovery. I heard her sing "Povo Que Lavas no Rio" at seventy years old. I began to fall in love. It was a total communion between Amália and the people. —RICARDO COSTA, January 29, 2003

The second fado [by Amália] I discovered was "Maldição," and by then I was completely in love (apaixonada). It is not just the way she sings; it is also the timbre of her voice. It is hot; it is something that messes with one's soul. It is beautiful, beautiful. The power of her voice is something I don't know how to explain. It is something that one feels. I have had moments of true delirium listening to Amália, madness listening to Amália. —"ROSA," May 29, 2002

As ardent Amalianos (i.e., self-identified Amália fans), Rosa and Fernando are part of an interpretive community in which the voice and symbol of Amália, along with questions concerning her remembrance and memorialization, are central. There are multiple and overlapping interpretive communities in Lisbon that center on the phenomenon of fado, and the memory of Amália plays an implicit or explicit role in them all. Yet my fadista, musician, and fado aficionado friends did not identify as Amalianos. Their terms of engagement with Amália were different from those of her fans. For the Amalianos, Amália, rather than fado, was the object of their attention and affection, whereas for the fadistas and fado aficionados, Amália generally featured as just one figure (albeit a monumentally important one) among many fado singers and personalities that populate fado's histories and lore. The discourse of fans repeatedly marked Amália as fundamental to yet distinct from the world they perceived as belonging to fado as genre, as practice, as a type of atmosphere, and as a style of sociability. I think of these overlapping communities as *communities of affection*, communities in which belonging is predicated on shared discourses and practices of feeling that, in turn, are animated by the "object" itself (in this case, fado, Amália, or both). These are communities in which feeling and passion are explicitly foregrounded, in which particular kinds of feeling and languages about feeling are shared through "emotional contagion" (see Hatfield et al. 1994, cited in Yano 2002: 120). I draw on extended interview material with Rosa and Fernando (with a third fan, Ricardo, making cameo appearances) to understand ways in which the voice of Amália is imagined, experienced, and discursively shaped in relation to affect and musical power within the community of Amália fans. What might be particular to the identificatory practices and discourses of fans with their stars when at issue is the "form of address that is peculiar to the singing of a song" (Marshall 2006b: 205), when sound is the experientially privileged sense modality?[30]

ROSA

I met Rosa, a woman in her early twenties, at a panel I attended in the spring of 2002 on the digital remastering and recovery of recordings of Amália Rodrigues held at the Lisbon Fonoteca, a small municipal CD lending library in the basement of a shopping mall. Rosa doggedly questioned the panelists (an executive at Amália's record label and a private consultant) in detail about numerous potential rereleases of albums. She knew almost every album date, song, and public concert for which an album was never made, and every album that was out of print. She told me that she is studying law at the university but is passionate about Amália. We remained in contact through the next year, and she helped me make contact with some of the fans (in Lisbon and abroad) who identify as Amalianos. She told me:

I never connected much with fado; that is normal for people of my generation. But I remember that my grandparents had [the] CD *A Biografia do Fado*, which had a fado [sung] by Alfredo Marceneiro ("A Casa da Mariquinhas" [The Brothel]) that I liked very much and one by Amália ("Foi Deus" [It Was God]).[31] I went through this phase when I was fourteen when I would listen to Amália and sing alone in my room, imitating her. I put on a shawl and everything and sang in front of the mirror. But that [stage] passed, and I forgot about it. Then Amália died in 1999, . . . and I saw the impact that she had created, the thousands of people on the street for her funeral, and I was curious. Who was this woman? I told myself I should buy a CD, but I never did. In 2001, at the end of June, her remains were transported to the National Pantheon, and there was a lot of talk about Amália on television. There were interviews, and they played her music. Finally, I bought my first Amália CD, *O Melhor de Amália II* [The Best of Amália II]—actually, I bought it for my grandmother, who adores Amália. The first fado I listened to of hers was "Confesso" [I Confess]. I remember that moment very clearly. I walked into the room where my grandmother was listening to the song—it was in the middle of the refrain. I have no words to describe that experience. I stood there with my eyes open very wide, wondering, "What is this?" It was a divine, transcendent experience. I listened over and over again. The second fado I discovered was "Maldição" [Curse]. By then, I was completely in love [*apaixonada*]. I started to buy and buy more CDs. I went to the [Amália] musical by [Filipe] La Féria, I . . . visited [Amália's] house, went to the [Amália] musical starring Bibi [Ferreira] . . . , and now, after less than one year, I have forty CDs.[32] The first time I listen to a new Amália CD, I have to listen completely alone in my room; then I can listen with my grandmother. Amália used to say that her soul had just been waiting for Alain [Oulman] to come along to write music for her. My soul had been waiting for Amália.[33]

FERNANDO

One month after meeting Rosa, I am in the car of an Amaliano named Fernando, as he drives me back to Graça after our long interview. As soon as we get in the car, he puts a cassette in the player: an Amália mix. We sit listening in silence before beginning the drive up through

Alfama. In that contained space filled with Amália's voice, Fernando talks about what it is like for him to listen to her: "When Amália improvises, my own emotion soars to a peak. I have such a concentration on her voice. It is like I am inside a glass box with her voice, suspended on that voice, and that is the height of emotion."[34]

Fernando is a Portuguese lawyer in his mid-thirties. He speaks English elegantly and French fluently. As we sit at an outdoor café with my recorder on, he unravels his story about his relationship to the voice and figure of Amália, carefully choosing his words:

My love affair (as I call it) with Amália began when I was eighteen, when I was at university studying, and I started listening to her records a lot. I fell in love with Amália's voice in two different ways. First, there was the identification with what she sang, with her voice. Second, if you set aside the idea of identification, there is only the voice, the artistry, the talent, the soulfulness of Amália's voice, the power of her voice—a voice which completely makes one feel dizzy and drunk. Gradually, I realized that she had become a companion. That love only grew. Then I also fell in love with the kind of person she represented, who I thought she was. I always regarded Amália as someone who represented all kinds of persons. She could be a lady of the people, like the orange seller she once was. She could be a queen, a gypsy, a Spanish dancer, an opera singer, a divinity reincarnate. For me she represented all of these characters in one. She was herself a whole world—a world that is suddenly delivered to you permanently as you listen to her voice. I think that Amália represented a whole world—she was everything, you know. As I grew and got older, I found all of these women in her. She might be singing a lively, jolly song, then all of a sudden there was the more austere depth of fado as she created it—conveying all of the sadness, loneliness, all of the saudade in the world. She ran the gamut of emotions when she spoke, acted, and especially, of course, when she sang. I only saw Amália twice on stage, once on January 8th, 1990, at the fiftieth anniversary of her career. In 1990, it was a total, complete hysteria for Amália. I'll never forget that concert. I have never felt anything like it. You could feel a sort of energy that passed between people with Amália at the epicenter.

Intimacy, the Extraordinary, Excess

Rosa and Fernando mark their experiences of listening as simultaneously intensely private and intimate, but at the same time, they both call attention to a universality of affective experience rendered through Amália's voice. They use the effusive language of ecstasy, of passion, of falling in love when they talk about listening to the voice of Amália. Rosa is caught, held rapt by the sound of Amália's voice when she walks into the room where her grandmother is listening. For her, it is a voice that "messes with one's soul"; a voice capable of bringing on delirium and inarticulateness; experiences of listening that are "divine," "transcendent," that she has "no words to describe." For Fernando, it is a voice that can leave him feeling "dizzy" and "drunk." While fans may feel that language does not adequately represent their experiences (*there are no words to describe*), Amália fan talk is replete with excessive language—adjectives, superlatives, and redundancy. While Rosa's descriptions are filled with adjectives, she tells me she does not like to use them, because "they all seem insufficient."

Fans' use of heightened poetics to describe the experience of listening frames these experiences as extraordinary, where the domain of the extraordinary serves as a resource for a heightened sense of the "real" (Abrahams 1986: 66), for feeling.[35] These are narrations of extraordinary experiences fully integrated into the sonic texture of the quotidian (Amália's voice as background "Muzak" while shopping in the city center or while sipping wine at Lisbon's Port Wine Institute; her recorded voice overheard pouring out of the open window of a taxi, a house, or a fado restaurant during off-hours in Alfama or Bairro Alto). Fans' narrations of experiences of listening might be productively understood in Bilinda Straight's terms as "expansive experiences," where "expansive" marks an effort to "overcome the textual and signifying limits of phenomenological experience" and calls attention to "the most ephemeral aspects and moments of experience as a process that includes unrealized possibility" (Straight 2007: 8).[36] Just as verbal descriptions of timbre often call forth an excessive metaphorical language to name the "un-namable" (Feld 1984; Feld et al. 2004), talk about listening, for Amália fans, shares commonalities with the ways in which people might narrate experiences of altered states (a language of religiosity, of trance, of dreams), states that are marked as experientially alter from the day to day as usual, calling forth poetic excess, redundancy, and metaphoric descriptions, drawing parallels with other heightened experiences (sexual, substance-induced, religious). In fans' descriptions of listening, the heightened poetics and metaphoric language often found in talk about timbre merge in fan discourse with the excessive poetics of talk about vocal celebrity. The Amalianos with whom I spoke entered the realm of the extraordinary routinely, every day, simply by attentively listening to recordings of Amália singing. These moments of the routine extraordinary lodged in the ordinary potentiate unrealized possibilities for imagining, for feeling feelings that are larger than life, for an expansion of one's subjectivity, for experiences of intimacy in the midst of solitude.

These are experiences of intimate listening. Listening, in this context is practiced with the utmost seriousness, care, and attentiveness. Rosa must be alone with Amália's voice the first time she hears a recording; the voice of Amália keeps Fernando company. Ricardo Costa, an accountant and an Amália fan in his early thirties, told me, "One has to be careful when listening to Amália. She can sing aggressively, go to the depths, can be melancholic; one has to take care." Ricardo, like Fernando, spoke about listening to Amália's most melancholic repertoire in terms of its therapeutic effects: her voice might take one to the depths of suffering, but after listening, one emerges into the "ordinary" feeling better. Rosa described the act of listening in intimately sensual terms. She lamented that she was not ten years older; had she been older, she would have been able to hear Amália live and, she says, have had "her skin touched by her voice." Sometimes she listened to Amália with the volume very high, partly to feel as if Amália were there with her and partly to fill the gap left by the impossibility of hearing her live voice. When she listens like this, Rosa said, she sometimes feels "penetrated" by Amália's voice; it "enters" her.[37]

In her research with British female fans of 1950s Hollywood films, Jackie Stacey (1994) distinguishes between practices of identification that take place within the imagination of the spectator and "extra-cinematic" identificatory practices that involve pretending to be, copying, or trying to resemble the star.[38] The first category is predicated on a fan's perceived distance between the star and the self and includes overlapping discourses of adoration, devotion, worship, and transcendence. Like some of Stacey's subjects, Rosa and Fernando tell their stories of fan identification within these frames, drawing on generic conventions of a romantic narrative—a narrative that sometimes uses the language of religious worship and that "expresses an intense homoerotic bond between idol and worshipper" (Stacey 1994 :140, 145).[39] Unlike some of the amateur female fado singers for whom mimetic performance figured prominently in their practices of internalizing Amália, and unlike drag queens' performances of Amália, which are overtly about the power the copy seizes from the original (see Taussig 1993), externalized mimetic practices did not seem as important to the practice of Amaliano fandom, or to figure in how Amalianos spoke about identification with Amália and her voice. Rosa said that she had dressed up as Amália when she was younger, singing in front of the mirror alone in her bedroom, but she marks this as an earlier stage that she has left behind. Rosa does not sing along when listening to Amália, like she usually does when listening to other singers. Amália "takes all of the room for music and doesn't leave any for me," Rosa told me. She sings Amália's songs only in the absence of the sound of Amália's voice: "Even when I am not listening to her, *she is still inside of me, when I hear her inside of me*, then sometimes I sing" (emphasis added). When Rosa sings, it is because she feels inhabited by Amália's voice; her singing is an act of ventriloquism of a voice she hears internally rather than an act of copying or miming.

Fans fall in love with Amália "the person" through experiences of listening. This love of the "person" relies on an understanding of "person" that is principally mediated by Amália's singing voice, a voice that fans engage with primarily through recordings. In describing Amália's voice and her person, fans also use a discourse of "naturalness." "She had a voice that was so pure, so natural, that came so much from inside of her, without artifice," Rosa told me. "She sang the sea, the stars. She was another force of nature. To hear Amália for me is like hearing the sea." Fernando said, "Her voice was at the same time very powerful, very soulful, and warm, sometimes even hot. Singing with that voice intelligently, she brought to us all of the feelings in the world. She seemed to be so natural: the naturalness of her posture while singing, the immediacy of the words, the voice. That immediacy is why she was so great—really, really great." In describing the "natural" characteristics of Amália's voice, fans echo language of "non-learning" that is common in fado discourse (see chapter 1), a language that also surrounds descriptions of Amália's voice in more widely circulating discourses (including Santos's biography), where terms such as "organic," "natural," "force of nature," "soulful," and "spontaneous" are often used.

Multiplicity as a key trope in Amália discourse generally takes two forms, the first referring to her creative capacity in terms of vocal interpretation and improvisation (*She never sang the same way twice*) and the second to a perceived variety of personas she was capable of performing when singing (*I hear all of these women in her*). This capacity for endless renewal, never singing the same song the same way twice, is something that Amália herself emphasized: "I sang 'Povo Que Lavas no Rio' thousands of times and never sang it the same way twice."[40] It is also a conceit of vocal celebrity writ large. But Amália, and almost all of the discourse about her, casts improvisation in terms of spontaneity rather than in relation to acquired skill (in line with the trope that she is *a force of nature*) and in keeping with fado's ethos of naturalized soulfulness and non-learning. Multiplicity in the second sense, in relation to her personas, is something that a wide variety of listeners connected to the fact that she performed in many genres and languages and that her public biography speaks simultaneously to rurality, working-class roots, and the hyper-local along with urbanity, internationalism, cosmopolitanism, and high glamor.

For some, this multiplicity is also about hearing the sedimentation of temporality and age in her voice; age is often indexed timbrally for her listeners. "I always make reference to the decades: the '40s, the '50s, the '60s, the '70s, the '80s, the '90s. Six decades of singing; it is a lot," Ricardo told me. "I have a room where I have many [recordings and videos]. It gives me this great pleasure when I arrive home at night and think, do I want to hear a young Amália, an old Amália, or a middle-age Amália? Yesterday I heard Amália at thirty, but today I could hear her at seventy-five. At times I have the feeling that her voice is going back in time, as if she forgets she is on the stage, and her voice returns to the spirit of the '40s, the spirit of the '50s." Amália aficionados are able to move effortlessly in discussion among multiple recorded renditions of the same fado from different points in her career, precisely specifying date and place of recording. These fans hear her repertoire as layered within the context of multiple variations recorded over a long career; timbral changes in the voice that are a mark of age map onto her personal history. "She knew that people's love for her was not just for her singing," Ricardo tells me. "When she had her voice [when she was young] she didn't sing with the same soul. She said that she only began to understand the word fado as she got older, fado fado, what was fado."

Fan discourse consistently marks Amália as transcending the genre of fado, with its stigma of the intimately local, stressing that she sang expertly (and recorded) in multiple genres and languages while also standing in metonymically for fado. This discourse mimics Amália's narrative in Santos's text. Rosa tells me, "[Amália] herself was fado. Her life was fado." For Fernando, Amália is responsible not only for how people sing fado today but for how people *listen* to it. Fans stress that in singing fado, Amália voices an affect that is simultaneously local, national, international, and universal, shifting fado from the realm of vernacular culture to that of art. For Fernando, Amália is responsible for shifting fado's affect from a quotidian, particular loss, from the individual expression of sadness, to the "sadness of a whole nation" and to a "longing" that is connected to "times past." This move from particular to nation parallels discourses in which Amália is talked about as being responsible for rescuing fado from the taverns, or for dignifying fado. Linking Amália's universalism to a more heightened poetics or to abstraction marks a concept of universalism through the poetics of voice that is classed.[41] "Before Amália, fado was something for the taverns," Rosa tells me. "Amália transformed the fado, dignified it. People used to laugh at the fadistas. But today people say, 'We're going out to hear the fado.'" Or, as a young operatically trained male fadista who acted in the musical *Amália*, sang for her reburial ceremony, and recorded a CD covering some of her repertoire (a rare move for a male fadista) says to me, "[Amália] turned fado into something abstract. She made it bigger. It left behind its tiny descriptive dimension [describing specific situations or quarrels between lovers] for an absolute dimension, and it came to embrace everything."[42]

For Rosa, Ricardo, and Fernando, their practice of identifying as "Amaliano" entails consumption, collection, and listening. For Rosa, the experience of "falling in love with a voice" is directly linked to consumption vis-à-vis the Amália industry; through practices of consumption, Amália as icon is "re-auratized" (Ghosh 2011: 16). Fernando was determined to transform his mourning into something positive, toward Amália reception in the future. The Internet, Rosa said, was allowing her to turn her "platonic" passion for Amália into a "professional" passion by enabling her to establish an international group of fan contacts and to share music and lyrics. "Being Amaliano" involves attending Amália-related events and commemorative ceremonies, such as the annual memorial on the day of her death; adding to the existing knowl-

FIGURE 6.3 •
Altar to Amália
Rodrigues in the
home of Suzette
Fílipe. Lisbon,
January 2010.
Photograph by
the author.

edge about Amália's life story; establishing communication networks with other fans, locally and internationally; and sharing practices of remembrance (figure 6.3). Finally, being Amaliano involves participating in a community of affection that shares particular poetics in relation to Amália's repertoire and biography, Amália's relationship to fado and the life of a fadista to the voice of Amália, and the experience of listening to her voice (figure 6.4).

Timbral Poetics and the Capture of Voice

Listeners often link the affective power of Amália's voice to its unique sound through a poetics of synesthesia (of color or heat). The timbre of Amália's voice, a timbre that fans like Rosa and Fernando might describe as "warm" or "hot," is also often spoken of in terms of its unique color. This is a color that one of Amália's primary guitarristas, José Fontes Rocha, described to me as a "color that only comes around once, maybe once in one hundred years,"[43] and what in other terms was poetically described to me by a fan one evening at a coaching session in Marvila as "uma garganta de prata" (a throat of silver). Hugo Ribeiro, Amália's primary sound engineer throughout her career, described her voice to me as "uma voz velada" (a husky or "veiled" voice), crediting a "light veil"

FIGURE 6.4 • Stereo system adorned with a photograph of Amália Rodrigues in the home of Suzette Fílipe. Lisbon, January 2010. Photograph by the author.

on her vocal chords for her unique timbre.[44] He contrasts her timbre with that of Maria Teresa de Noronha, another well-known female fado idol of the past who, he claims, had "uma voz limpa" (a clean voice). When understood within the context of general fado discourse about authenticity, the "veiling" or covering of the vocal chords suggests a *grain* of the voice (Barthes 1977) that signifies, among other things, a voice or lived experience that bears the imprint of felt suffering, a grain that renders a biography of suffering audible.[45]

Ribeiro explained to me that Amália had *so much voice* that, "when she went for the high notes, she would saturate the microphone," and that the standard would have been to use a compressor to limit the peaks. He did not do this. Rather he worked carefully with microphone placement so he would not have to cap the highs. "I preferred to keep all of Amália, even at a greater distance, than to mechanically compress [the voice]." In one of the many passages in Santos's text in which Amália reflexively comments on the hearing of her own voice, she discusses Ribeiro's ability to capture the color and the timbre of her *gritos* (screams) and to record her voice in the way she herself heard it. In this passage, reflexive "hearing" takes on a cast of interiority, of the voice as imagined in the inner ear:

> Hugo Ribeiro . . . recorded my voice, *what I hear.* Outside Portugal, [the sound engineers] are not used to my voice. When I sing, with the screams, that needle that shouldn't pass the middle goes low and all of a sudden swings to the other end, into the red area. For those who are not used to my voice, as soon as [the needle] moves to red, they cut it. What remains is a scream that isn't a scream, without anything, without timbre, without color. Because they are scared and they cut it. . . . My voice has a color. If it is not there, it is because [the foreign sound engineers] have taken it out. (V. Santos 2005 [1987]: 154; emphasis added)[46]

Ribeiro also stressed that he avoided playback techniques when recording and that he tried to always record the instrumentalists together with Amália. David Ferreira, who in 2002 was the executive responsible for Amália's recordings at her former label, EMI-Valentim de Carvalho, spoke about Ribeiro's process in terms of producing "real sound":

> Ribeiro was very focused on producing real sound. He was fantastic at placing the mikes. It was craftsmanship. The recordings that Ribeiro made from the 1950s through the early '70s are unique. For me, that is the standard of how to record fado and Portuguese guitar. Nothing has ever been done as well. That also had to do with a sound engineer attitude, which was "I must get your voice as clean and as clear as it comes to me through my ears." What you need for fado is to reproduce it as if you were there, as live as possible. But, of course, a lot of the recordings made by studios and record companies all over the place in the 1970s, '80s, and even for a large part in the '90s were not that—live, ethnic, the real thing. But, of course, in those days [before the 1970s], if you had a voice like Amália's, what could you do but get it as it is? Just as in the early '80s, one would tend to protect her [voice] and overuse delay. It is only natural. If you have a beautiful young girl, she doesn't need any makeup.[47]

In speaking about the preferred aesthetic and technique of recording Amália's voice, Ribeiro and Ferreira mirror the larger discourses of naturalness that listeners use to talk about her voice and the tropes of liveness and naturalness found in fado practice in general. Yet to capture the "natural" required highly skilled craftsmanship. Ferreira casts the capture of Amália's voice at different points in her career in a gendered poetics: technology that audibly draws attention to its artifice (in the form of delay) is only understandable when it intervenes as "makeup" for her aging voice. Vocal timbre, where Amália's timbre is discursively linked to the natural, the warm, the hot, and the immediate, is one of the key hinges on which affect and soulfulness of the Amália phenomena turns.

Miming Amália

An immense iridescent blue guitarra forms the backdrop to the outdoor stage in the middle of Lisbon's Feira Popular, a circa 1940 urban amusement park off a busy street, with old neon glowing white, yellow, red.[48] A Ferris wheel circles, vacant, illuminated. There are bumper cars, a photo booth, cotton candy for sale that no one buys, a cheap Indian take-away with plastic chairs and tables where no one eats. Sirens and horns from park rides wail out from time to time, and videogames flash their lights around the periphery. Nine-year-old Maria from the Associação Cultural o Fado in Marvila is the invited opening singer for the final round of a city-wide amateur fado competition sponsored by Lisbon's daily newspaper *24 Horas*. It is a September evening in 2002. I am there to film Maria at her mother's request. I see people I know from Marvila and wave to Maria's mother, who smiles. I find a chair in a crowd of people sitting behind a makeshift metal fence beneath a metal roof in front of the stage above which a neon sign reads "Colónia Balnear" (Seaside Resort).

As the crowd settles, a young woman in black knee-high boots and a short black skirt waltzes onto the stage and, in the style of a 1970s U.S. game-show host, announces Maria. Maria enters wearing a white dress sewn by her mother with a black shawl draped around her shoulders, and confidently takes the microphone to audience applause: "Thank you, thank you, this is my first time here, and I hope you will like it." Any vulnerability I might have seen in her during the coaching sessions in Marvila has vanished. She moves and speaks with the poise of a miniature diva. She has the style of stardom down.

Her mother tells me, "Maria sings herself to sleep with fado." Maria sings "Que Deus Me Perdoe" (May God Forgive Me [for loving the fado]), which I heard her practicing in Marvila. She opens: "If my closed soul could show/If it could tell how I suffer in silence/Everyone would see how unhappy I am/How I feign happiness/How I cry when I sing." While this is a classic fado canção from Amália's repertoire, Mariza also recorded it on her first CD, released in 2001, and Maria would have been familiar with both versions. Maria sings with the voice of a child following the vocal gestures of a woman. She sings dramatically, her voice replete with exaggerated voltinhas, her interpretation full of extended rubatos. Her head is thrown back; the bones and muscles in her face vibrate. Her small body sways backward with the intensity of her voice. *What dream is she living when she sings?*

There are six finalists. One is a man. The five women, who range in age from their twenties to their forties, sing two fados, of which at least one is from Amália's repertoire. One repeats "Que Deus Me Perdoe." The invited celebrity of the evening announces herself by saying, "I am not a fadista. I am just a singer who sometimes sings fado," then sings two fados from Amália's repertoire, opening with one that Amália sang that is titled simply "Fado Amália."[49] Just as the fado endlessly reflects back on itself as a genre in many of its lyrics, "Fado Amália" comments reflexively on fado's diva. As the celebrity, in her sixties with a shock of lime green hair that matches her sweeping lime green shawl, breaks into a fully voiced rendering of "Fado Amália," I am bedazzled by the presence of so many Amálias, no longer able to distinguish original from copy, copy from copy. All of these women, all of these girls, are somehow Amália, somehow embodying the dream of Amália by recalling her, by miming her through their turns of voice, through the shawls they wrap around their shoulders. And somewhere, within these turns of the voice, these voltinhas—the ways in which they are sung and the ways in which they are breathed—is lodged an imaginary of the feminine.

Mimesis, Excess

Fado's performance scenes were flush with mimetic Amália production, along with explicit attempts to avoid Amália reproduction, when I was in Lisbon in the early 2000s. The enlarged aura that death brought to her person, her name, and particularly her voice catalyzed mimetic prolif-eration while also encouraging other fadistas, finally freed from the im-mensity of her shadow, to break new interpretive and stylistic ground. Every young professional female singer trying to make it big had to somehow account for Amália. *Will she be the next Amália?* Mariza, whose international career in 2001 was just beginning, was initially ac-cused by her critics of imitating Amália; in her first CD she sang almost exclusively fados from Amália's repertoire. "Amália deplored imitation," I was told by a young male professional singer who had recorded many Amália covers on an album he made in homage to her. "My CD is an homage to everything she did so that what she did would not have been in vain. But it is not copying. It is my own interpretation." A professional female fadista in her late teens said, "I hate Amália. Everything she sings sounds the same." "It is always Amália, Amália, Amália," others com-plained. "People don't pay enough attention to the other great historical figures of fado. Everyone is always in her shadow." Fados proliferated in the amateur scene whose lyrics were written for Amália, to be sung to Amália, in homage to Amália. Girls at fado coaching sessions in Mar-vila performed her fados. Drag queens lip-synced to Amália. At the Tasca do Jaime, Olga de Sousa learned to be a fadista by modeling her-self, her dress, her affect, and her vocal turns on her imaginary of Amália.

The performative mimesis I witnessed in relation to Amália calls at-tention to the soulfulness and excess of embodied mimetic contact through musical experience (the index of the soulful for fado is often in its excessive display) and the room for play and for remembering, but also for desiring and for the senses of possibilities for individual being, often gendered, that it enables. Michael Taussig (1993: 21) takes Walter Benjamin's writing on mimesis and the "withering" of the aura in the age of mechanical reproduction (Benjamin 1968b) as a point of depar-ture, and of return, for thinking through self and other in relation to colonial contact in Latin America: "Here is what is crucial in the resur-gence of the mimetic faculty, namely the two-layered notion of mimesis that is involved—a copying or imitation, and a palpable, sensuous, con-nection between the very body of the perceiver and the perceived." He draws attention to the power that the copy seizes from the original, to the power of the "bad copy" wherein replication contains both the power of magic and the power of the soulful. For Joseph Roach (1996: 4), performance constitutes the "doomed search for originals by continuously auditioning stand-ins." He uses the term "surrogation" to elucidate a tripartite relationship between performance, memory, and substitution. In the imperfect fits of surrogation lies performative excess, and within excess are memory and counter-memories: "performances so often carry within them the memory of otherwise forgotten substitutions" (Roach 1996: 5). Performative excess, the slippage between "copies" and "originals," thus spawns myths of origin and trenchant claims to authenticity.[50] In theorizing performance through the afterlife of Princess Diana, Diana Taylor (2003: 143) writes about how "performance makes visible (for an instant, live, now) that which is always already there: the ghosts, the tropes, the scenarios that structure our individual and collective life. These specters, made manifest through performance, alter future phantoms, future fantasies. . . . [Diana's] enactment left a trace." What traces of Amália do performances by others render *audible*? In the re-voicing, how are these traces and their significations reformulated, shifted?

These are mimetic performances that might be about "ironic critique" or the "bad copy" or they might not; these are performances in which, in some cases, an attempt at verisimilitude might have more to do with the desire for individual expression of personhood than for replication.[51] For the performer, imitation might be implicit or explicit, intended or not. For the novice fadista, miming Amália might be just one stage in the learning process, later to be cast aside or outgrown, a way of finding one's voice by re-voicing another's. Nor are all cases of mimesis conscious attempts in which the whole is intentionally mimicked or copied. Like all mimesis in relation to performance, it is schizoid, fragmented, a phenomenon that the circulation of sounds via recordings, or "schizophonia" (Feld 1996a; Schafer 1977), only heightens. Yet because of Amália's enormous auratic presence, even an iconic tinge in a performer who is perceived as imitating her might for the listener index the whole.

Amália's voice and the biographical narrative encoded within its style, and much of her repertoire, render audible and amplify the mythological biography of fado, with all of its links to gendered nation building, simultaneously making this biography particular to the "person" of Amália but also available as a resource for "the people." Diva as phenomenon foregrounds particular aspects of an imaginary of the feminine while catalyzing desire, imitative acts, and fantasies of identification. Fadista as category, diva as category, and woman as category overlap, coming together in the imaginary of Amália. In the fado coaching sessions I attend in Marvila, and in the performances I witness at O Jaime and other amateur venues, I am struck by the ways in which Amália's vocal style and repertoire are taken up and the manner in which they are embodied and voiced by girls and women. I am struck by how some female fadistas talked about Amália, how she figured in their daily lives, and by how some young girls seemed to be living the myth of her, embodying her, through learning to sing fado and how, through singing Amália's repertoire, they might be learning to become woman. I compliment a teenage girl I heard sing for a number of weeks at Marvila by saying, "Every week, you seem more fadista." The guitarra player responds in the girl's presence (echoing a sentiment found in a popular fado), "Every week, she becomes more woman."[52]

A pudgy twelve-year-old girl with glasses struggles every week to get the fado out. She brings with her a black cape that she wears over her shoulders, standing in for Amália's trademark black fadista shawl. She always gets the rhythm wrong, but keeps singing. Nine-year-old Maria passionately sings fados from Amália's repertoire—fados such as "Que Deus Me Perdoe," which Olga de Sousa sings at O Jaime, fados that are about a soul wrenched with fado, or a soul suffering in silence, or a soul torn in love. These are precisely the kinds of fado about which people sometimes say, "Those fados are too heavy for a young girl," or "You must be a woman to sing those! You must live first, to suffer to sing those." "That is violent," a fadista says to me about children who sing dark or heavy fados. "I call that musical prostitution!" Many amateur female singers I knew used Amália's recordings as Ur-texts for learning to imitate a fado "by heart." In the same vein, while taking "lessons" at the Fado Museum, I was encouraged to learn from recordings by Amália, rather than from the oldest recording of the same fado (recorded by a different fadista in the 1920s). As Mariza became more successful internationally toward the end of my field research, I noticed young girls imitating her recordings and sometimes even imitating Mariza covering Amália.

Four Amálias: Voicing Drag

A January evening, midnight, 2003. The club is in a zone of Lisbon informally known as the *docas* (docks), which in the early 2000s, was a relatively new area for nightlife. Discos, large franchise restaurants, and nightclubs line up along the river leading out of the city proper. I arrive with a friend at an address off a narrow, dark side street. I am carrying my tripod and a camera case. The bouncer, a large man guarding the entrance, looks at me suspiciously and asks who I am. I give him the name of the producer who invited me. The doors open to a dark, intimate space, a small stage with four rows of folding chairs set up in front of it, a dance floor, swirling colors of disco ball lights, clouds of cigarette smoke, and recorded dance music booming. Gay men in their twenties and thirties sit and stand along the bar, cruising; various kinds of negotiations for sex appear to be under way. My friend points to audience members whose faces she recognizes from television.

"The Show Must Go On" features numerous scantily clad drag beauties, lip-syncing sequences to the voices of female stars, framed by two prominently muscled men who, the program informs, are among Portugal's most "prestigious male strippers."[53] A svelte drag queen wearing a bobbed brunette wig, a plunging bikini top, a choker around her neck, and a tattoo around her upper arm, who does not resemble Amália at any stage in her career, lip-syncs to an Amália recording of the first verse of "Foi Deus" (It Was God [who gave this voice to me]), gesturing expressively with her arms and hands: "I don't know, no one knows / Why I sing the fado in this sorrow-filled key of pain and weeping."[54] At the end of the first verse, as the recorded instrumentalists strum, she turns her back to the audience and, with hips swaying, walks back to join the strippers, who are lip-syncing voices of crowd members yelling "Amália! Amália!" This first Amália remains with her back to the audience, positioned between the two men.

A second Amália enters to loud applause. She has pinned-up blonde curly hair and wears a tight sleeveless dress. She stands at the right of the stage, taking up the third verse by mouthing the words and "singing" out to the audience with her body. As she launches into the final verse, "It was God / Who gave voice to the wind / Light to the heavens / And who gave blue to the waves to the sea," the playback abruptly stops, interrupted by a third Amália—a brunette in a slinky silver dress. She moves her lips to what sounds like Amália's speaking voice in old age with the resonant acoustics of a live performance in a large hall. "I have so many saudades, saudades for my voice," she says. We then hear the sound of Amália's voice at the end of her career—guttural, raspy, and deep— singing the words to "Foi Deus" lip-synced by the drag queen. The other two Amálias pick up the words in the last verse and alternate, sometimes appearing to sing at the same time to a soundtrack of a younger Amália, and sometimes joined by the strippers. These two Amálias stop before singing the final line: "*Ai*, and he [God] gave this voice to me." Then they exit the stage.

Amália number three launches into a performance of the Amália standard, "Lágrima" (Tear). The stage lights dim, and "Lágrima" is cut short. We hear the recorded sound of the guitarra and viola playing the introduction to "Estranha Forma de Vida" (Strange Form of Life), a tour de force of Amália's repertoire. Amália number three stands with arms outstretched while another drag queen walks out from the stage door and takes her place, back to the audience, directly behind her, arms also outstretched. Amália number three exits, and as the instrumental introduction continues, a full-blown diva Amália late in her career is revealed standing in a characteristic opening-of-the-show pose: back to audience, right arm outstretched, as if in invitation. She is the only Amália of the evening who actually resembles Amália Rodrigues in appearance. She wears a wig the color and style of Amália's hair when she was in her sixties (reddish tinged, big around her face); she wears the fadista's black shawl, immense dangling earrings, a large silver brooch, and a ring with a large stone. Beneath the shawl this "Ur-Amália" is wrapped in a dress in the colors of the Portuguese flag. She turns to face the audience, keeping her right arm outstretched in Amália fashion, throws back her head, closes her eyes, and starts to sing. Rather than placing her left hand on her heart (where Amália's would have been), she cups her left breast, jutting it outward. As she sings, her hands mimic common gestures of a female fadista—furling, unfurling, clasped in front of her as in a position of prayer. When she mouths the word "saudade" in the first verse, she emphasizes it with a side-to-side inflection of her head. Then at the end of the verse, she signals to the (absent) instrumentalists with her right hand. Her eyes remain closed, and she sings (lip-syncs) the entire fado without interruption, the precise movements of her mouth led by the words, sounds, and inflections of Amália's voice in its prime resounding.

Through the magnified lens of drag, this spectacle calls attention to performative details (as all drag does) in which the style's meaning (Hebdige 1979) reveals a feminine that is specifically embodied and particularly sexualized. The female body in stylized detail is made visible in the sway of a pair of hips, revealing clothing, a cupped or accentuated breast, the feminine made more "real" precisely through its "made-up-ness." The melodramatic performance of fado is indexed by the pantomime of the face expressing stylized emotion, and fado performance in its feminized version is referenced not only by the "female" body and by costume but also by the sweeping or intimate hand and arm gestures used by Amália or by female fadistas. The feminine is set up against, and framed by, the hyper-masculinity of the strippers, who are a constant presence on stage.

This performance by the four "Amálias" presents multiple ways of experiencing, embodying, and imagining Amália and is thus in keeping with the discourse of fans regarding her capacity for dramatic and musical transformation and newness: *Every time I listen to Amália, I hear something new. She had this remarkable capability to transform herself.* Or, as the Amaliano Fernando told me, "I found all of these women in her."[55] The genre of camp provides a frame that invites the "troubling" (Butler 1990) of tropes of gender, sexuality, and nation as they are commonly construed and bound together in Amália and fado mythology. The enactment of Amália's multiplicity in this context becomes a "space of ambivalence," with fado's illicit history implicitly granting "room to maneuver."[56] Sonorously, multiplicity is rendered by using recordings of the same fado from different moments of Amália's career in playback, foregrounding different timbres of her voice.

Silently singing along is common in amateur fado listening practice (see chapter 1). The lip-syncing in this performance by cross-dressed Amálias might be understood as a fully embodied extension of this practice, in which the expressive play of the "passing" body becomes a conduit for the interiorization of the voice of Amália. With the voice of the individual actor rendered mute in this act of ventriloquism, the body becomes all voice, all hearing, the act of miming the substituted voice demanding a heightened listening of the performer. The final Amália performs the ultimate exteriorization of the interiorized voice or hearing. "She" "sings" with eyes closed and head thrown back (two icons of interiority and soulfulness in fado); she uses exaggerated hand and arm gestures. In cupping her left breast with her right hand, particularly on the word *coração* (heart), a gesture of soulfulness (putting the hand to the heart) is inflected in an act of inventive "signifying" (Gates 1988) such that soulfulness in rendering fado, of embodying Amália, is explicitly feminized and sexualized. Finally, through hyperbolic performative excess and parody, this performance calls attention to the nation–feminine complex that haunts both fado and the Amália phenomenon, destabilizing it by rendering it visible. Through her costume of Portuguese flag dress, this ultra-feminized "Ur-Amália" is linked through a gesture that camp renders satire to the soulful "voice of Portugal."

Amália at the Tasca do Jaime

There are numerous luminaries in the hallowed halls of revered female fadistas, some long gone, some old but still singing, and some retired, including Ercília Costa, Fernanda Maria, Beatriz da Conceição, Argentina Santos, Lucília do Carmo, Hermínia Silva, and Maria Teresa de Noronha. While these fadistas came up from time to time in conversation at the Tasca do Jaime, Hermínia Silva was the only one of these professional stars (besides Amália) whose photograph hung on the wall. At O Jaime, and in other amateur contexts, people did not stress (as Rosa did) how Amália "dignified the fado" or how she "rescued it from the taverns." Rather, they tended to locate fado's authenticity precisely in the sociality of the taverns. My friends at O Jaime valued the internationalism Amália brought to the genre, and many had internalized her voice, drawing on it as a resource and inspiration for their performances, self-crafting, and ways of being a female fadista. But fadistas and listeners across a wide generational and class range, professional and amateur, were far less likely than were the Amalianos to situate Amália in a metonymic relationship to fado as genre.

Yet Amália is present everywhere at the Tasca do Jaime: in the miniature photograph cut from a postcard that appears in the diorama on the back wall; in the large, illuminated photograph presiding over the house whose light is turned on before the fado starts; in a small lit-up box where, among ornaments and fado trophies, is displayed another picture of her. Sometimes people gesture to her photograph. I heard a male fadista who had once been big (as rumor had it before drugs took over his life) talking to it (*She was the only one who clapped for me. She was the only one who supported my career*), thus invoking her status to bolster his own when he was down and out. Amália is there in the black shawl that hangs on the wall. She is present in conversation. And she is present in the voices of the women singing, in the black shawls they wrap around their shoulders, in their stances, in their voltinhas, very often in their repertoire, and perhaps in the ways in which they symbolically suffer or in the ways in which some of them transcend the grit of the day to day, rising to stardom in moments of singing, exulting in the power their voices give them. Some men do sing Amália's repertoire, but rarely, and never here.

Women at the Tasca do Jaime shape their identity as fadistas vis-à-vis Amália's repertoire and style in different ways. There is Teresa, the girl-friend of the ex-professional fadista whose luck has run out, who shows up from time to time always singing at least one fado from Amália's repertoire, with sensitive, long-drawn-out rubatos, and microtonal voltinhas. She tells me she has studied music. Laurinda, who recently moved back to Portugal after raising her children, working in a factory, and singing in fado clubs in Newark, New Jersey, for many years, attends the sessions at O Jaime sometimes with her husband. She wears glittering dresses and proudly sings the fado canção "Grito" (Scream), the words written by Amália herself, to be sung at her own funeral: *Silence!, From the silence I make a scream . . . One who is dead no longer cries.* Amateur fadistas talked to me about "Grito" in terms of its beauty and the vocal challenges it presents.[57] Ivone Dias (see chapter 5) told me that as a child, she would listen to Amália's voice on the radio and learn all of the fados she sang by heart. She sings some of the fados from Amália's repertoire that are more complex, particularly those composed by Oulman, and told me that the style of this repertoire is suited to her voice. She has a voice that she thinks of as "lyric," and she prefers to sing *fado canção* (or fados that people talk about as being "more musical") rather than *fado tradicional*. She is endlessly inventive in the ways she styles these fados with her vocal ornaments and physical gestures. At times, she seems almost to dance. When we talk, the slightest mention of the name of a fado from Amália's repertoire sets her singing.

Fernanda Proença is one of the fadistas most integral to the functioning of O Jaime. (Her photograph also hangs in a prominent position on the wall.) When she sings, she seems rooted, planted. An enormous voice, a rich voice (the kind of voice that people might refer to as having the sound of the *bairro* [neighborhood], or the sound of *fado castiço* [true or authentic fado]), rises from her. She has strong ideas about what constitutes good fado singing, which she sometimes reveals to me by a glance across a table, or a muttered comment while someone is singing, or in in the way she coaches or makes fun of me, when I sing for her or perform. Yet she is generously supportive of beginning singers and young fadistas (at least one I know calls Fernanda her *madrinha* [godmother] of fado). She has appeared on fado documentaries as an "authentic fado voice," as a fadista of the neighborhood. (One documentary that aired in Japan prompted a young Japanese singer to come to Lisbon to seek her out.) She works odd jobs, cleaning stairs, ironing, and waiting tables, and sometimes is contracted for paid fado gigs.

When she appears to sing fado, she is all made up—sequined, fancy, and fine—and her voice renders us all spellbound. But with the exception of one of the less well-known fados, Fernanda does not sing Amália's repertoire publicly. She has her own repertoire, and this is one of the marks that distinguishes her from the rest and is also in keeping with star fadistas. She sings fados written just for her, often by her friend Álvaro Rodrigues, fados that tell the story of her life—a life of suffering (she was raised in an orphanage), but also a life of pride. Rarely she might sing something from Amália's repertoire on request, but only after the fado has officially ended and most people are gone or during a fado session on a weekday afternoon. She appears to take this on as something sacred, deserving all of her utmost attention, respect, and full power of her voice. When she invites me to her home for the first time, I see a book of poetry written by Amália, late in her life, by Fernanda's bedside table; a photograph of Amália hangs on the wall; she has cassettes of Amália to which she sings as she works in the kitchen. Before I leave, Fernanda shows me a special drawer where she has keepsakes and photos. She sorts through dozens of glossy photo inserts of Amália saved from newspapers and she gives me some as a gift.

Olga de Sousa, on the other hand, seems to model herself, voice, body, and soul, explicitly on Amália as she learns to perform being a fadista. For the first year that I heard her sing, Olga always sang a fado from Amália's repertoire of the two fados she sang. The other fado she often sang during this time was the highly melancholic fado "Rosa Enjeit-ada," which initially was part of the repertoire of Maria Teresa de Noronha, a twentieth-century fadista who is often talked about in terms of her "lyric" and "trained" voice and her aristocratic status. The fado from Amália's repertoire Olga most often sang was "Que Deus Me Perdoe." The lyrics of both "Rosa Enjeitada" and "Que Deus Me Perdoe" ostensibly foreground profound suffering. In the most classic recorded versions of these fados—the former by Maria Teresa de Noronha and the latter by Amália—both fados are sung with a highly ornamented vocal style. The choice of these two icons as models to emulate for Olga's start as fadista make sense, particularly as she comes from a middle-class to upper-middle-class family. She regularly attends the opera and had a piano in her house when growing up. Both Maria Te-resa de Noronha and Amália are suitably "high" enough in terms of their standing in relation to "art," and their status as *artistas*, for Olga to model herself on them.

It is Amália she talks about most, sings most. It is Amália she most enacts. Olga comes to O Jaime dressed in form-fitting black dresses, with black shoes, and wears a black shawl. When she performs, she seems all dark, all melancholy, all suffering. As I follow the process of her learn-ing, I notice that she is exaggerating certain traits characteristic of Amália's singing (extended voltinhas, rubato, and vocal glissandi), and that this exaggeration takes a musical toll. In her languorous slides into and out of notes, she often misses entrances, falls behind the beat, or becomes out of tune. With practice, she develops more precision, but her passion for ill-timed rubatos and vocal slides often results in annoyed glances from the instrumentalists, who struggle to keep her on track. But everyone comments positively on her timbre, dark and slightly husky, a timbre I would definitely call "veiled." Every week, this woman, who has recently divorced and is just beginning to find her voice in the world of *fado amador*, crosses herself before singing, enacts a rite of suf-fering stylized, but each time made more dramatic and improved by new musical/performative knowledge and increasing confidence. She tells me, "There is only one Amália but each one of us can sing her fados in our own way." But each week, it seems to me, that in becoming more "fadista," Olga becomes more "Amália."

A fifteen-year-old girl wearing jeans and a black tank top shyly goes to the front of the Tasca do Jaime on a crowded Sunday afternoon. Jaime teases her about how pretty she looks. One of the women in the room pulls a black lace shawl from her handbag, walks to the front, and wraps it around the girl's shoulders. The girl positions herself behind the instrumentalists (a classic Amália pose), throws back her head, and sings "Barco Negro" (Black Boat). "Barco Negro" is a favorite among teenage girls, one of the sultriest but also most virtuosic fados (in terms of the vocal range demanded) in Amália's repertoire, a love song where a young woman is abandoned by her lover but never loses hope for his return.[58]

This girl singing at O Jaime might be using Amália as a structure for feeling, for performing woman, while as the momentary subject of our heightened hearing and gaze she might simply be playing at being a star. Meanwhile, the performative icons she employs might index a swirl of layered and affectively charged associations for the listeners. *Did you know that "Barco Negro" was banned by the censors when it first came out? But then, it had different lyrics. It was "Mãe Preta" (Black Mother). It was Brazilian. My daughter has a recording of Mariza singing "Barco Negro," but it doesn't do much for me. Mariza lacks throat* (garganta). A woman cries silently at the back table. *My husband died five years ago today.* Or, *I know a man whose singing could make even Amália cry.* Or, *I have the recording of Amália singing that. She sang it in Japan. The Japanese love fado. Did you ever hear about a great* senhora, *a grand* fadista *named Amália Rodrigues? She was the only interpreter of fado. She sang with soul. She brought our music to the rest of the world. There will never be another Amália. There was just one.*

Turns of the Voice

[Amália] was the sort of person we thought was immortal. I think to this day many people don't believe she is dead. They keep her alive even in death. . . . *Her voice went beyond herself.* . . . When she died, a part of me died, some part of me that I shall never retrieve. Part of Portugal died also, my country. She used to say that she was a scent in Portugal to which people had grown accustomed. When she died, it was that part of Portugal—that beautiful, lovely scent—that died. And one of the many ways one might regard as being Portuguese disappeared with her.
—FERNANDO FORTE, June 13, 2002 (emphasis added)

A memorial service is held for Amália Rodrigues at the National Pantheon on Sunday, October 6, 2002, three years after her death. I attend with the twenty-two-year-old Japanese woman who sings Amália's repertoire and is trying to become an international star. The Pantheon is filled with a small group of somber Amalianos, close friends and associates, many dressed in black. I see Fernando. I see Rosa. People put flowers at the foot of the tomb, and some pause before it, incanting a prayer. Slowly we gather around; we are called to public prayer in a whispering silence. A professional male fadista in his late forties who is standing behind me ceremoniously starts to sing a fado from Amália's repertoire, without guitarra, without viola. In the middle of a rubato, while singing extended voltinhas and executing a *pianinho*, in the precise structural moment for fado's display of heightened emotion, in the phrase preceding the finale, a moment that Amália's style of singing forever amplified, crystallized for fado, his stylized crying in song breaks into a sob. Afterward, I try to talk with Amália's former secretary on the steps of the National Pantheon. She has always avoided me, believing I am a journalist, no matter how often I tell her I am not. She protects Amália still, even in death. But this time, she says a few words, appearing disgruntled. *They don't do enough for her. This city, this country. They should do more for her.*

The national memorialization of Amália hinges in part on the interiorization of the voice, figure, biography, and mythology of Amália by individuals, fans, singers, listeners. This interiorization takes multiple forms, wresting its power from a structure of longing (of saudade) already in place that links feelings of personal loss to national sentiment, from the aesthetically syncretic, reiterative structure of fado form and from the embodied "inarticulateness" of music's power to signify. The singing voice might be experienced as at once deeply intimate and simultaneously social. This interiorization is also mediated by the Amália culture industry in the form of sound and audio recordings, books, commemorative keepsakes, television documentaries, films, and large-scale performances (such as the musical *Amália*). Exteriorizations, or performative mimesis in the form of fetishization and imitation of her gestures, costumes, repertoire, vocal or interpretive style, and, sometimes, even vocal timbre, might serve as a playful critique (as in drag) or as a manner of rendering personal biographies or individual dreams and aspirations public. This interplay between memorialization and mimesis through the conduit of the figure and voice of Amália foregrounds the excess wrought by the experience of beauty and aesthetic power in relation to the shaping of subjects, subjectivity, and belonging and draws attention to the sense of possibility for individual being that it enables. This is mimesis that is animated by communities of affection and the social interstices where intimate publics meet the "national public." It is animated by the interplay of mechanical reproduction, by the performance of heightened ritual and the everyday, and also by the "nation" and the "subject" and the multifarious ways in which they are interdependently constituted.

In the figure of Amália, fado as genre, celebrity as icon, and the feminine generically overlap, providing forms for amplified feeling, feeling rendered through the sound and expression of her singing voice. Both the voice and celebrity, in this case, are shot through with more widely circulating cross-cultural and stereotypical tropes of the feminine—the voice of the feminine in relation to desire, to emotional expression and affective labor, to intimacy, to the physical and to the national body, and to complaint itself as a sentimental feminine genre (Berlant 2008). Biography as a form provides a point of articulation between Amália as celebrity, celebrity as Amália, and fado as genre. Cliché, stereotype, redundancy, and repetition—places of overlap and places of disjuncture between stories, between clichés, betweenforms—play critical roles in shaping both the identifications of listeners and the affect(s) of vocal celebrity. Recurring tropes of the natural (*She was a force of nature. Her voice was like hearing the sea*), of the soulful (*She is the voice of the Portuguese soul*), of heterogeneity (*She never sang the same way twice. I heard all of these women in her*), of being "of the people" yet transcending the limitations of class, of being a woman who suffered—all of these merge in treatments of Amália's public biography; the lyrics in her repertoire; and in the discourse of fans, singers, and listeners about her vocal timbre, style, and interpretation. The first four tropes are common tropes of vocal celebrity.[59] All five form part of the mythological biography and performative elements (fado as unlearned, fado as soul, fado as improvised styled soulfulness with infinite variation, fado as moving from low culture to high, fado as suffering, as fate) that undergird fado as a genre. Just as the form of traditional fado lends itself to the syncretic stacking of memories of prior performances, where the base pattern is the ground against which variation and invention are measured and affect is figured, fado, celebrity, and the feminine as cultural forms powerfully come together in practices of interiorizing, memorializing, and remembering Amália, providing scripts that undergird the imaginative and improvisatory shaping of selves and the structuring of public feeling.

The Tangibility of Genre

Spring 2011. Portugal's sovereign credit rating has been downgraded to one notch above junk. There is talk about a financial bailout of Portugal by the European Union. The True Finns party in Finland protests. Under the pressure to accept a bailout, the Portuguese government collapses. Portugal is bailed out. New elections are held. Spain fears "contagion." Images circulate on European television news of elderly women in Lisbon selling their jewelry, small golden trinkets passed down for generations, as scrap. That summer, the city's wealthy shopping district of Chiado gleams, bustling with tourists lining up for gelato, shopping at Diesel and two recently opened Starbucks outlets and buying fado CDs from the street cart on the Rua do Carmo where the voice of Amália Rodrigues still sounds. While the crisis is not visible in the city center, many workers have had their salaries cut, gaps between rich and poor have widened, and there is a palpable anxiety about where it all will end. Some tell me that this crisis feels manufactured from the outside. At the same time, a stoic acceptance. *Portugal is always in crisis.* In 2001, a taxi driver had told me, "Go home, girl. Go home. Portugal has no future." Crisis, a recurring lament.

This particular crisis in Portugal, intricately linked to a global state of financial emergency, stands out for its public nature. Throughout 2011–12, international media focused relentlessly on the south of the euro zone—particularly on Greece, Portugal, and Spain—where impact of the crisis in Europe has been most dramatically felt. The crisis catalyzes a return to stereotypical discourses officially voiced by Europe's North (particularly by Germany), where the southern nations are again cast as prodigal and profligate offspring of Europe "proper," reinvigorating debates about the compatibility of a European common currency given the "cultural differences" between North and South, the honor of the South publicly shamed in the international arena. These are not crises locally manifest that can be contained within the domestic housekeeping of nations. Yet these crises at Europe's southern periphery, with all of their interconnectedness to global financial crisis writ large and to one another, manifest differently at local levels both practically and in affective response. These differences are sometimes elided when the discursive net thrown by the North (or by the United States) is cast wide. "We [the United States] are not Greece! We are not Portugal!" declares President Barack Obama in a televised excerpt of a speech he gives about the U.S. economy that reaches me at a working-class restaurant in Graça in July 2011 (following a news segment about cuts in Christmas bonuses for Portuguese workers).

In the summer of 2011, amid this deepening crisis, fado and talk of fado as "patrimony" redundantly saturate Lisbon's public sphere. Amália's 1960s rendition of "Povo Que Lavas no Rio" provides the soundtrack for the "made in Portugal" section of Lisbon's upscale Spanish department store El Corte Inglés. In Alfama, fado refrigerator magnets and T-shirts are available at small shops; handwritten signs, placed in front of restaurants, reading "Hoje Há Fado" (Fado Today) are ubiquitous. There are fado specials on television, classic fado discs stamped with the word *património* (patrimony) for sale, fado films from the 1940s screened in the open air with English subtitles on an old palace rooftop in Mouraria. While fado as genre is publicly poised on the brink of "becoming" "intangible cultural heritage of humanity" in the summer of 2011, UNESCO's final decision has not yet been made. The campaigning for intangible cultural heritage (ICH) status has been already for years ongoing and is perhaps most tangibly visible in the complete remodeling of the city-sponsored Fado Museum in Alfama in 2008, where phrases from UNESCO's Convention for the Safeguarding of the Intangible Cultural Heritage of 2003 have been painted in large script in Portuguese and in English on a prominent wall that visitors see before entering the main exhibition rooms, where fado's histories, canons, and stars are presented more officially than before. "Intangible" heritage demands its own performance and documentation long before being granted as such—it demands tangibility. Heritage in one arena spills out to others. "Super Bock Classic e fado. O que é bom é para sempre (Super Bock Classic and fado. What is good is for forever) reads the bottom of a billboard promoting both a quintessential brand of Portuguese beer and Lisbon's 2011 summer festivals (which are sponsored by the same municipal business that runs the Fado Museum), fado in this instance articulating a relationship between a brand of beer and cultural patrimony.

November 2011. The Portuguese prime minister asks the former colony of Angola for financial assistance. Portugal's credit rating is downgraded to junk. Three days later, at a meeting in Bali, UNESCO awards fado ICH status. Reporters on the Portuguese RTP Internacional cable channel interview elderly working-class *senhoras* in Lisbon's historic neighborhoods about the award. Their faces are beaming; they talk about having something to feel proud of in the midst of crisis. The story of fado as patrimony captivates the Lisbon newspapers. Fado as genre as patrimony, internationally validated, restoring a bit of honor lost. That week, on a late-night Portuguese television satire, following days of televised fado specials and galas, a group of dour-faced men and women dressed in black parody fadistas, singing in an exaggerated nasal timbre about Moody financial ratings, thus bringing fado, patrimony galas, and crisis into the same frame. Crisis is Portugal's public story; patrimony is fado's. Fado as genre as cultural heritage productively labors as a resource in crisis. Nation and genre recycle their alignments, recasting their interlinked histories in new guises. The public caretakers of genre burnish its sheen.

THIS BOOK HAS ARGUED for the labor of a popular music genre in rendering feeling public, a city as sonorous, and for bringing contested histories to the present with a palpable, tangibly felt force. It has argued for fado as genre as a form of possibility for ways of being in the world, *uma maneira de ser*, ways of being in the world shot through with particularly situated ideologies of voicing, listening, subjectivity, and musical expression. Ethnographically, it has made these arguments by focusing on a genre's amateur social worlds and protagonists, not to imbue those perspectives with a greater purchase on truth than those coming from the "center" but, rather, to foreground how a genre's socio-aesthetic and political life, and the histories it calls forth, are critically and dynamically shaped by actors at its so-called margins. A popular musical genre, as living, is in movement, gesturing forward and backward in time all at once, resounding.

July 2011. I sit with Olga de Sousa in her house one evening in Graça, catching up on her news, a white linen embroidered tablecloth set out on the table, a homemade almond cake, cups of tea, and fine china. She tells me how she recently placed in an amateur fado competition and appeared on television; how she was invited to sing at an event for a well-known man, how they liked her singing, and how they arranged for her arrival in a fancy car. She reminds me how her son, when he heard her sing for the first time, how he cried when she sang and asked, "How did you have this voice without me ever knowing?"

Olga invites me to an upcoming lunch meeting of a fado and poetry association. That Saturday, in a back room of a small restaurant in Mouraria, a close-knit group of fifteen gather around a long table. One by one, people get up and perform fados. A man in his seventies recites a poem by Ary dos Santos; the instrumentalists play a medley. The presenter introduces Olga as the star celebrity of the house. Olga confidently wraps her lace shawl around her shoulders and makes her way to the front. She whispers to the instrumentalists, and they begin to play. Gathering her forces, she turns toward her listeners, throws back her head, closes her eyes, and she sings.

APPENDIXES

Fado Vitória Transcriptions

APPENDIX 1: *Three Renditions of the First Strophe of the "Fado da Meia Laranja" as Sung by José Manuel Osório*
Lyrics by José Luís Gordo, set to the structure of a Fado Vitória by Joaquim Campos: (A) January 10, 2004, live performance in a recital hall at Duke University in Durham, North Carolina; (B) August–September 2004, professional studio recording in Lisbon (J. M. Osório 2004); (C) May 3, 2003, live performance at an amateur fado session at the Tasca do Careca in Lisbon. Transcription by Yoshiaki Onishi.

= pitch is brought down by approx. 30 cents
= pitch is brought up by approx. 30 cents
= consonance only, no pitch
= gliss.
= between speech and song
≈ 110
(A = 430Hz)
Version A
A-li
à Mei-a La-ran
d: i
Version B
A-li à
M - e-ia La-ran
d: i
V
i
Version C
A-li
à Mei-a La-ra-n
d: i
A
- ja
Meio-o in fer-no de Lis-bo - a
♭VII7
VI
B
- ja
Meio in - fer - no de Lis - bo - a
♭VII
VI
C
- ja
Meio in - fer - no de Lis - bo - a
♭VII7
VI

A
On-de_a mor-te_an - da_a vi-ver
A-li
♭VII VI V i
B
On - de_a mor-te_an-da a vi - ver
A-li
iv (viiº / V) i
C
On-de_a mor-te_an - da_a vi-ver
A-li
VI V i
A
à M - ei - a La - ran - ja
M - eio in - f - er - no de Lis -
i VI ♭VII
B
à M - ei - a La-ran - ja
Mei - o in - fer - no de Lis-bo -
i ♭VII
C
à M - ei - a La-ran - ja
Meio in - fe - r - no de Lis-bo -
i ♭VII

A
boa
On-de a mor-te an-da a vi-ver
VI ♭VII VI V
B
- - a On - - - de a mor - te an - da a vi - ver
VI VI+ iv (viiº / V)
C
- - a On - de a mor - te an - da a vi - ver
VI ♭VII VI V
A
Há mi - lha - res de o - lhos ba - ços
♭VII (V / III)
B
Há mi - lha - res de o - lhos ba - ços
♭VII (V / III)
C
Hà mi - lha - res de o - lhos ba - ços
♭VII (V / III)

A
A vi - da tem qua - tro bra ços Pa-ra a mor - te se es-con-der
i VI V
B
A vi - da tem tan - tos bra - ços Pa-ra a m-or - te se es-
i VI V
C
A vi-da tem qua tro bra - ços Pa-ra a mor - te se es - con -
i V
A
Há mi - lha - res de o-lhos ba -
i
♭VII (V /
B
- con - der Há mi - lha - res de o-lhos ba -
i
♭VII (V /
C
der Há mi - lha - res de o-lhos ba - - -
i
♭VII (V /

A
ços
A vi - da tem quatro bra - ços
III) i VI V
B
ços
A vi - da tem tan - tos bra - ços
III) i VI V
C
ç - os
A vi - da tem qua - tro bra - ços
III) i VI V
A
Pa - ra a mor - te se es - con - der
i
B
Pa - ra a mor - - - te se es - con - der
i
C
Pa - ra a mor - te se es - con - der
i

Lyrics by José Luís Gordo, set to the structure of a Fado Vitória by Joaquim Campos. Live performance in a recital hall at Duke University, Durham, North Carolina, January 10, 2004. Transcription by Yoshiaki Onishi.

9
10
11
12
V1
V2
V3
A-li à M - ei - a La-
ja
Por en - t-re gen-te per-di-
go - a
Há ta - nto ca-va-lo à sol-
V
i
i
VI
13
14
15
ran - ja
M - eio in - f - er - no de Lis - bo - a
- - da
Jo-vens en - tre - gam a vi - - da
- - ta
Com chi - cotes de re - vol - ta
♭VII
VI

16
17
18
19
V 1
On- de a mor - te an-da a vi - ver
Há mi -
V 2
À lou-cu - ra que se es-ba - n - - ja
E nas
V 3
Num ga - lo - par que ma - go - a
Há pu -
♭VII VI V
♭VII
(V /
20
21
22
V 1
lha - res de o - lhos ba - - ços
A vi - da tem qua - tro
V 2
vei - as da tri - s - te za
Tan - ta-s fa - cas de po
V 3
nhais de in - feli - ci-da- - - de
A li s - e ma-ta a i -
III)
i VI

23
24
25
V 1
V 2
V 3
bra- ços
Pa-ra a mor - te se es-con - der
bre - za A-li à M - - - ei - a La-ran - - ja
da - de N - o cora - ç - ão de Li - s - bo - a
V
i

26
27
28
29
V 1
V 2
V 3
Há mi- lha - res de o - lhos ba - ços
E n - a - s vei - as da tri - ste - za
Há pu-nhais de in - fe - li - ci - da-de A-li
♭VII
(V/
III)

V 1
V 2
V 3
30
31
32
A vi-da tem qua - tro
bra - ços
Pa-ra a mor - te se es-con -
Tan-tas fa - cas de po-bre - - - - za
A - li à M - eia La -
se m - a - ta a i - da - de
N - o cora-ç - ão de Lis -
i
VI
V
1, 2.
3.
33
34
35
36
37
38
Verse 2:
Verse 3:
der
Por en - tre gen - te per
ran-ja
Há tanto ca-valo à
bo-a

Introduction

1. Following my interlocutors, throughout the book I use the terms "dictator-ship" (*ditadura*), "regime," and "Estado Novo" (New State) interchangeably to refer to the dictatorship in Portugal in the twentieth century. I refer to the Estado Novo period as beginning with the fall of the First Republic in 1926 and ending with the military coup (or Carnation Revolution) of April 25, 1974 (*25 de Abril*). All translations from the Portuguese are mine. Throughout the book, unless other-wise noted, reported speech of interlocutors that appears in quotation marks or italics without a reference to a taped interview or to personal communication has been taken from my field notes.

2. I retain the capitalization of the word "Discoveries" that is commonly used in Portugal when referring to the *Descobrimentos* (the Portuguese colonial discoveries).

3. When I include Portuguese verbs that refer to fado poetics and practice, I generally present them in the infinitive rather than conjugating them (unless doing so would obfuscate the Portuguese meaning and my translation).

4. For a narration of the "ordinary" as an assemblage of affectively charged scenes, see K. Stewart 2007.

5. *Fado Resounding* is based on twenty-one months of consecutive primary field research conducted in Lisbon between September 2001 and May 2003 and six periods of short-term research (1999, 2000, 2006–10).

6. Richard Bauman and Charles Briggs (1992: 147) articulate a model for thinking about the relationships between genre formation and negotiations of identity and power based on a theorization of generic intertextuality:

We would argue, similarly [to Bakhtin], that genre cannot fruitfully be characterized as a facet of the immanent properties of particular texts or performances. Like reported speech, genre is quintessentially intertextual. When discourse is linked to a particular genre, the process by which it is produced and received is mediated through its relationship with prior discourse. . . . When genre is viewed in intertextual terms, its complex and contradictory relationship to discourse becomes evident. We suggest that the creation of intertextual relationships through genre simultaneously renders texts ordered, unified, and bounded, on the one hand, and fragmented, heterogeneous, and open-ended, on the other. Each dimension of this process can be seen from both the synchronic and the diachronic perspective.

7. Benjamin Lee and Edward LiPuma (2002: 192) theorize circulation as a "cultural process" and stress its constitutive nature, foregrounding "structures of circulation," or the relations between "specific types of circulating forms and the interpretive communities built around them" (see also Gaonkar and Povinelli 2003).

8. On the objects of emotion as "sticky," see Ahmed 2004.

9. Sherry Ortner (1996: 12) specifies "serious games" as "a model of practice that embodies agency but does not begin with, or pivot upon, the agent, actor, or individual: "While there are very definitely in this view actors and agents, desires and intentions, plans and plots, these are embedded within—what shall we call them games? projects? dramas? stories?—in any event, motivated, organized, and socially complex ways of going about life in particular times and places."

10. "Sound, hearing, and voice mark a special bodily nexus for sensation and emotion because of their coordination of brain, nervous system, head, ear, chest, muscles, respiration and breathing. . . . Moreover, hearing and voice are connected by auditory feedback and by physical resonance, the immediate experience of one's presence through the echo-chamber of the chest and head, the reverberant sensation of sound, principally one's own voice" (Feld 1996b: 97).

11. David W. Samuels (1999, 2004) points to music's capacity for polyvalent indexicality and iconicity with reference to belonging and to senses of place and history in the experiences of listeners and musicians. He cites examples of Apache interlocutors who might feel most Apache not through the experience of listening to Apache "traditional" music but, rather, through listening to the rock band Guns N' Roses or through singing individually inflected covers from American country music.

12. As such, I build on work in the anthropology of the senses (see Howes 2007; Porcello et al. 2010; Seremetakis 1996; Stoller 1989; Taussig 1999), as well as on approaches in a thriving interdisciplinary literature in critical sound studies that argues for an examination of the aural and the sonic as salient to understanding the production of knowledge, histories, places, social identities, and publics (see, e.g., Bendix 2000; Born 2010; Corbin 1998; Feld and Brenneis 2004; Hirschkind 2006; Meintjes 2003; Ochoa-Gautier 2006; Samuels et al. 2010; Sterne 2003; Stokes 2004; Thompson 2002).

13. On "emotional contagion," see Hatfield et al. 1994, as cited in Yano 2002: 120. For affect as contagious, see also Gregg and Seigworth 2010: 4.

14. Michael Hardt (1999: 1–2) situates "affective labor" within a larger framework of "immaterial labor," with earlier precursors in feminist scholarship as "caring

labor" and "kin work." Fado musicians (and their recordings that circulate) can also be understood as performing a kind of affective labor (as transmitting "passion," "melancholy," intimacy, etc.).

15. On "public feeling," see Ann Cvetkovich's 2007 article. She writes, "Political identities are implicit within structures of feeling, sensibilities, everyday forms of cultural expression and affiliation that may not take the form of recognizable organizations or institutions" (Cvetkovich 2007: 461). See also Berlant 2008; Cvetkovich 2003; K. Stewart 2007.

16. The burgeoning interdisciplinary literature on affect, or the "affective turn" (Clough and Halley 2007), owes some of its impetus to pioneering work in queer and feminist theory (e.g., Sedgwick 1990, 2003; Warner 2002). For concise summaries of genealogies undergirding contemporary affect theory, see Flatley 2008; Gregg and Seigworth 2010. Theorists of affect differ in how they configure the relations between "emotion" and "affect" (there is sometimes slippage between them) and the degree to which they mark affect as non-discursive, as "embodied," as an "intensity" (e.g., Massumi 2002). I use affect here in co-constitutive relation to the discursive.

17. While many scholars have focused on the way in which the past is presented and made manifest through the material (de Certeau 1984; Nora 1989; S. Stewart 2003; Trouillot 1995) in working with the idea of "writing the history of the present" (Foucault 1977), fewer have substantially investigated the way in which historical traces and memory are physically carried in the body. Scholarship that accounts for the body in relation to questions of history and memory (e.g., Connerton 1989; Foucault 1977; Roach 1996; Taylor 2003) is often historically based—for instance, on historical moments, texts, or performances. Paul Connerton (1989: 104) observes that while many scholars assert that the body carries social meanings, this scholarship is often "cast in an etherealized form" by focusing on discourses about the body or the body as symbol.

18. In writing about the history of *retornados* (white Portuguese who settled in the colonies, then moved to Portugal after the 1974 revolution) in Lisbon, Stephen Lubkemann calls for the need to "unsettle" former colonial metropoles with respect to the workings of memory: "A reinvigorated examination of postcoloniality equally requires an examination of processes of selective remembering and forgetting in former colonizing societies themselves" (Lubkemann 2005: 258; see also Stoler 1995).

19. In his ethnohistory of the Afro-Brazilian Candomblé, James Lorand Matory (2005: 2) asks, "What would a culture look like, and how would an ethnography look, if we attended consciously to the transnational processes that have constantly informed the meanings and motives of its participants?"

20. *Fado Resounding* is concerned exclusively with practices and forms of the genre of Lisbon fado (*fado de Lisboa*), as differentiated from Coimbra fado (*fado de Coimbra*), a ballad genre associated with male university students in the city of Coimbra.

21. *Landum, lundu, lundum,* and *londum* refer to a specific dance of African "origin" from which the fado is often thought to have been influenced or derived. In the words of Pinto de Carvalho (1992 [1903]: 25), "The *lundum* or *lundú* was an obscene dance of blacks from the Congo imported in Brazil then in Portugal." According to the Brazilian historian José Ramos Tinhorão (1994: 39), whose book on fado is subtitled *O Fim de um Mito* (The End of a Myth), the lundum appeared in the 1700s in Brazil as a sensual dance of African origin and was danced navel to navel with a syncopated musical accompaniment; this lundum was also always sung. The first references to the lundum as sung and danced in Portugal date from 1784. As it was appropriated by the upper classes, the song component became more accepted than the dance, partly because of the lascivious nature of the dance (Tinhorão 1994: 41).

22. In the original, "Que caustica um género eminentemente nacional com uma pigmentação indesejável."

23. As such, fado shares narratives of social legitimation and upward "mobility" with numerous popular music genres (e.g., jazz, tango, samba).

24. Published writing on the Lisbon fado in Portuguese extends over one hundred years and constitutes, in fragmentary fashion, a nexus of discourse that circulates among fans, fadistas, and instrumentalists, shaping how fado's genealogies, major figures, locales, and histories are imagined and understood. Most of this literature has been written for a popular audience and has been occupied with similar themes (see Brito 1992: 14–16). Some of this writing appears in the form of popular serials published in Lisbon between 1910 and 1954, many of which contain a mixture of fado lyrics, debates, and information on figures in the fado world (see Brito 1994: 157; Brito 1992: 14). For reviews of the extant fado bibliography, see Gray 2005; Holton 2006; Nery 2004. The speculation on the theme of fado's "origins" shows no sign of abating; it was one of the most popular topics expounded to me by listeners, fadistas, and instrumentalists (see chapter 2) and has been a central focus of the fado bibliography from the early 1900s to present. For a recent example, and a distinctly national/local and non–"Black Atlantic" argument, see Sardinha 2010.

25. "The concept of a circum-Atlantic world (as opposed to a transatlantic one) insists on the centrality of the diasporic and genocidal histories of Africa and the Americas, North and South, in the creation of the culture of modernity" (Roach 1996: 4).

26. Many regard the guitarra (Portuguese guitar) as providing the quintessential instrumental timbre for fado. When describing the timbre of the guitarra to me, many listeners likened it to that of a harpsichord. Within Lisbon fado, two types of guitarra are used: the Lisbon guitarra and the Coimbra guitarra. The Coimbra guitarra is distinguished by the icon of a tear carved at the top of its neck and by a larger resonating chamber; it is tuned one tone lower than the Lisbon guitarra (but with the same intervals between strings). The Coimbra guitarra, in the opinion of some of the Lisbon guitarristas with whom I spoke, has a "warmer" sound, and currently Coimbra guitarras are sometimes used in Lisbon fado in both profes-

sional and amateur contexts. Salwa El-Shawan Castelo-Branco (1994: 131) describes the guitarra as "a type of cittern with a pear-shaped sound board, six double courses of metal strings, and seventeen frets corresponding to three-and-a-half octaves. The neck terminates in a flat fan-shaped tuning device with machine screws. It is performed with the thumb and index fingers using either fingernails (earlier this century) or false nails."

27. Many practitioners refer to traditional fado also as *fado castiço* (authentic fado) or *fado fado*.

28. José Manuel Osório, personal communication, July 4, 2008.

29. Questions concerning constitutive characteristics of the musical "base" that delimit one traditional fado from another, and the discursive murkiness around the idea of the musical base particularly in relation to ideas about fadistas' originality and improvisatory "styling," are developed in chapter 4. I estimate the most commonly used traditional fado repertoire, across all of the circuits in which fado travels and is performed, to number fewer than fifty. But as more esoteric historical recordings from fado's archives are digitized, commercialized, and circulated among musicians, the repertoire appears to be gradually expanding. Ruben de Carvalho (1999: 155) also puts the number between forty and fifty and specifies fifteen that he considers "classics," which constituted the "nucleus" of the performed traditional fado repertoire as he perceived it in the late 1990s.

30. Both the question of authorship with respect to intellectual ownership and the limits of the constitution of a "composition" in traditional fado warrant further study (see also chapter 4).

31. The fado singer and researcher José Manuel Osório preferred to dispense with the category of fado canção, splitting it into two categories: "fado with refrain" and "fado with its own music" (*fado com música própria*). In his discussion of fado with refrain, he noted that it does not necessarily have a set schema in terms of rhyme or number of strophes and that fadistas sometimes use the musical base of this type of fado with a flexibility that is similar to that one would use with traditional fado, meaning that alternative lyrics might potentially be set to a fado with refrain. He contrasted fado with refrain with fado with its own music, noting that the latter is often musically scored with the lyrics almost always circulating with the same melody (José Manuel Osório, personal communication, April 17, 2005).

32. On the social productivity of fado taxonomies and generic classifications, see Gray (forthcoming); chapter 1 in this volume.

33. While fado performance and activity is most densely concentrated in Lisbon, the genre of Lisbon fado is also performed in other parts of Portugal.

34. Casas típicas often serve "traditional" Portuguese food, have performances of fado by paid professionals, and sometimes have folkloric dance performances; they are concentrated in Lisbon's touristic neighborhoods.

35. On the reconfiguration of race in Portugal in relation to the country's 1986 accession to the European Union, see Fikes 2009.

36. For historical research on relationships between expressive culture and cultural policy in Portugal during the Estado Novo and beyond, see Côrte-Real 2001 (1960s–1980s, with a focus on music and the transition to democracy); Holton 2005 (early years of the Estado Novo through the early 2000s, with a focus on the folkloric dance practice of *ranchos folclóricos* within the frame of EU belonging); Melo 2001 (1933–58, with a focus on *cultura popular* [popular culture]).

37. For a preliminary investigation into fado's history of sound recording, see Vernon 1998.

CHAPTER ONE
Pedagogies of the Soulful in Sound

1. On the gathering power of place, see Feld and Basso 1996; K. Stewart 1996.

2. In line with the usage of my interlocutors, I use "Tasca do Jaime" and "O Jaime" interchangeably throughout the text to refer to the same venue.

3. As Michael Taussig (1999: 183) asserts, "Sound has a privileged function in stoking the dialectic of Being and Nothingness in the public secret." Referring to Ronald Berndt's work on Papua New Guinea, he states, "Again and again it seems like we are being told to listen but not look, that it is at the point where the world is presenced through unsighted sound that the labor of the negative exerts its extremity, as with the 'voice,' which emblematizes Donald Tuzin's study of what he calls the 'secret men's cult' in the East Sepik region of Papua New Guinea" (Taussig 1999: 200–201; see also Berndt 1962; Tuzin 1997). Taussig (1999: 206) goes on to comment, "How strange, given its importance to these sacred secrets that so little attention has been paid to sound and music by ethnologists!"

4. I assume here a relation between repeated externalized practices and the shaping of a sense of self and interiority. Saba Mahmood's thinking about "ethical pedagogy" in relation to habitus is useful in this respect. In her discussion, she recovers an Aristotelian genealogy of Bourdieu's "habitus," where the "Aristotelian model of ethical pedagogy [understands] external performative acts (like prayer) to create corresponding inward dispositions" (Mahmood 2005: 135).

5. José Manuel Osório, personal communication, December 7, 2002.

6. Sebastião de Jesus, interview, March 25, 2003. Practitioners (and venues) often use the designations "fado amador" and "fado vadio" (lit., vagrant or homeless fado) interchangeably. Yet some fadistas and listeners in Lisbon's amateur scenes object to "fado vadio" as a proper term, claiming it does not respect the fado.

7. For a discussion of the history of professionalization in relation to casas de fado and the Estado Novo, and for a discussion of the development of the phenomenon of fado vadio, see Klein and Alves 1994. For an ethnographic account of social practice in the amateur fado venue Guitarra da Bica in the 1990s, which has since closed, see Cordeiro 1994.

8. Jaime Candeias, who was born in the 1950s, told me how his parents sent him away from his home in the rural north (Beira Baixa) when he was eleven to work

for a family in Lisbon in return for room and board (a common practice at the time). He explained to me that in the late 1980s, after finishing a term in the army, he purchased the tasca with a loan given to him by a friend. He told me that with the loan came an extreme sense of responsibility to earn the money to pay it back. He described the state of the tasca (and Graça) in the late 1980s as "terrible." Jaime told me how the tasca was frequented by a group of men who saw the place as "theirs," many of whom were "alcoholics" and "very aggressive," some who had spent years in prison, some who were homeless. They spent the day at the tasca, thus making it difficult for Jaime to make any money with his new business. Although he liked fado, he had had no prior experience in organizing, singing, or presenting it. In the mid-1990s, however, he began to experiment with scheduling one day a week (Saturday) for fado, partly as a way to bring in a new clientele and dislodge the "regulars" (Jaime Nunes Candeias, interview, November 6, 2002). Jaime's use of fado to lend upward mobility to the tasca in this case runs contrary to the historic (1800s) stereotype of fado (and fadistas) in the tascas, brothels, or taverns as contributing to the "debauched" nature of these locales. Yet some locals complained to me that the Tasca do Jaime was "pretending" to be a tasca in the old sense, to present fado "as it used to be," while at times charging excessively for food and drink on fado afternoons.

9. For points of comparison, see Cordeiro 1994; Valverde 1999. While this chapter focuses on the practices that were most often foregrounded in Lisbon's amateur fado performance contexts, it is not my intention to suggest that professional fado practice is not also highly codified and ritualized or that there is no porosity of practice between the two domains.

10. While amateur fadistas generally keep careful track of the keys in which they sing particular fados (usually by writing them down), most fadistas and instrumentalists with whom I worked did not read musical notation. However, as a young (and more institutionally trained) generation has recently come of age, more instrumentalists are fluent in Western musical notation and music theory.

11. "Lágrima" (Tear), lyrics by Amália Rodrigues, music by Carlos Gonçalves. This popular fado canção was part of Amália's repertoire.

12. Fado sessions at O Jaime ran from 4 to 8 PM and sometimes ran over. O Jaime is one of just a few places in Lisbon in the early 2000s that I attended that held fado in the afternoon, breaking with the tradition of fado sessions almost always taking place at night, in darkness. By holding sessions during weekend afternoons, O Jaime was able to hire instrumentalists for a lower price and ensure the greatest participation of fadistas.

13. The diorama was installed by a group of domino players who frequented the bar in the years before Jaime purchased it. It forms the focal point of the small space and serves as an icon for the venue. Its image was blown up for the cover of the first CD recorded by Jaime and the house fadistas (released in 2003).

14. A *guitarrada* is an improvised instrumental piece, usually virtuosic in nature, sometimes composed of a medley of diverse fados.

15. I never witnessed a woman in the role of presenter.

16. At the time, I interpreted this as one of the many ways fado fans and practitioners give value to a fado past that is somehow always *mais fado* (more real, more fado) than the present. But by 2010, I had attended multiple fado sessions at O Jaime at which no one presented the fadistas. In one instance, this prompted tourists to ask me, "If no one announces the singer's name, how do the fadistas expect to become known?"

17. Sebastião de Jesus, personal communication, March 25, 2003. For more than a decade, until his death in 2005, Sebastião de Jesus presented fado weekly at two of Lisbon's most hallowed venues for amateur fado: the neighborhood association Grupo Excursionista Vai Tu in the neighborhood of Bica and the Tasca do Careca.

18. Fátima Fernandes, interview, November 26, 2002.

19. Ibid.

20. José Manuel Osório, personal communication, June 4, 2004.

21. Greg Urban (1991: 156) describes commonly understood characteristics of what he terms "icons of crying": cry break, voiced inhalation, creaky voice, and falsetto vowel.

22. José Fontes Rocha, interview, May 26, 2003.

23. For a discussion of emotionality and sociality in relation to the concept of *tarab* in contemporary Arab classical music in Syria as it simultaneously relates to practices of listening, performing, and the shaping of aesthetic judgment, see Shannon 2003. For a theorization of listening as performance and listening as linked to the formation of an ethical subject, see Hirschkind 2006.

24. In his formulation of "racial sincerity," John Jackson contrasts "sincerity" with "authenticity," arguing that the latter foregrounds a subject–object relation while the former foregrounds a "subject–subject interaction." Sincerity "presumes a liaison *between subjects*—not some external adjudicator and a lifeless scroll. Questions of sincerity imply social interlocutors who presume one another's humanity, interiority, and subjectivity" (Jackson 2005: 15).

25. Ethnomusicology as a discipline has historically relied on acquiring musical competence (as ethnographer/musician) by working within local musical pedagogies as a methodological key to understanding a musical "culture," or sometimes even "culture" itself (see Berliner 1978; Blacking 1973; Hood 1960).

26. I use the word "novice" here to describe fadistas who do not have much public experience performing fado. But I rarely heard fadistas use categories such as beginner or novice, perhaps reflecting the idea of fado's essential "unlearnability."

27. In professional casas de fado, it has also historically been common for older or more experienced singers and instrumentalists to offer feedback to those with less experience and status.

28. In most of the cases I witnessed, these relationships were female–female or male–male; I heard multiple female fadistas speak of having a fado madrinha and male fadistas a padrinho. It is also common (but not necessarily the norm) for fado singing and instrument playing to follow kinship lineages and to run in families and over generations (see Gonçalves in preparation).

29. Fernanda Proença, interview, January 27, 2002.

30. Fátima Fernandes, interview, November 26, 2002.

31. Sebastião de Jesus, interview, March 25, 2003.

32. Anonymous, interview, December 13, 2002.

33. This was a musical-cultural logic that only the voice of the international celebrity diva Amália Rodrigues was allowed to rupture. She was simultaneously hailed as the voice of the quintessentially Portuguese while praised for her excellence in singing non-Portuguese genres with strong place-based and national associations (e.g., Spanish flamenco, Mexican rancheras, Italian tarantella). On the role of genre in shaping Amália's celebrity, see chapter 6 in this volume.

34. The total up-front cost of 125 euros in 2002 was more than half the monthly retirement pension of a fadista friend of mine who sang at O Jaime and more than a third of the amount I paid in monthly rent for my fully equipped studio apartment in a new high-rise condominium in Graça.

35. The audition in this context was a convention possibly appropriated from both the pedagogical traditions of Western art music and from the history of professional fado. Coterminous with the professionalization of fado at the beginning of the Estado Novo was the requirement that, to perform professionally, a fadista obtain and carry a *carteira profissional* (professional card). According to former card-carrying professionals with whom I spoke, the card was procured through a singing examination for a jury of instrumentalists (and sometimes poets); one litmus test used to determine professional status was the singing of a Fado Menor. But the card was not necessarily obtained through an evaluation of performative competence alone. Social connections (*cunha*) could also be useful. The card could also be revoked. One fadista told me that during the dictatorship, his card was taken away by the secret police (PIDE) after he was discovered singing revolutionary lyrics. Even in 2003, twenty-nine years after the fall of the dictatorship, he requested that I not make that information public.

36. "Que Deus Me Perdoe," lyrics by Silva Tavares, music by Frederico Valério.

37. This is a partial and edited excerpt of my fieldnotes dated April 8, 2002. My narration of events was written after the fact and from memory.

38. At the time of this writing, the museum was advertising its lessons for singers as Gabinete de Ensaios para Intérpretes (Department of Rehearsals for Interpreters). On the website (http://www.museudofado.egeac.pt [accessed March 1, 2010]), this was included under the category "Escola do Museu" (Museum School).

39. "Perseguição," lyrics by Avelino de Sousa, music by Carlos da Maia.

40. While there is a striking timbral uniformity (often marked by nasality) in women's voices in the earliest recordings of fado, this sound is likely a result of early twentieth-century recording technology (José Manuel Osório, interview, March 26, 2003).

41. The ethnographic descriptions of lessons at the Fado Museum in this chapter are drawn from my field notes (written from memory after the event) and from my recordings of the events (the dates of which appear in the section subheadings).

42. Even before widespread ownership of personal playback equipment became financially viable, fado heard on the radio served as a pedagogical resource for fadistas. It is difficult to overstate the extraordinarily potent force of music on the radio in dictatorship-era Portugal, not just in shaping fado's aesthetics, stars, and canons, but also in forming the censored sonic, musical backdrop of the everyday. It was a revolutionary song (not a fado) played over the radio that gave the auditory signal for the military coup to begin in April 1974.

43. Fado's origin stories and contemporary marketing narratives consistently link its authenticity with "the people," and with Lisbon's "traditional" and "popular" or working-class neighborhoods (bairros populares). These fado neighborhoods historically have been populated by migrants from all over Portugal, who have different regional accents, and by displaced Africans. On Alfama, see Costa 1999. Yet in this example, the sound engineer tries to efface (or neutralize) sonic markers of (working) class or regional difference.

44. António Rocha (recorded lesson, May 10, 2002), contrasted breathing in fado with the use of breath in the Western art music tradition, saying, "Pode respirar sempre que queira desde que não corte as frases ou palavras. . . . Na música erudita as palavras cortam. . . . As palavras são um suporte para a música. . . . No fado a música é um suporte para as palavras" (You can breathe whenever you want to, as long as you don't cut the phrases or the words. In art music [música erudita], they cut the words [with the breathing]. The words support the music. In fado, the music supports the words).

45. These two traditional fados were Fado Menor do Porto and "A Perseguição," both of which are commonly sung with a melody that is relatively scripted and strongly attached to lyrics that Amália recorded.

46. An ethnographic study of instrumentalists' processes of learning and a detailed account of how they coach singers has yet to be done. For a call for researchers of fado to give more attention to the role of instrumentalists, see Castelo-Branco 1994.

47. Although it was not technically classified as a neighborhood association (in terms of eligibility for funding by the city government), ACOF fit loosely into a larger civic and social model of colectividades, associações recreativas, associações de bairro (collectives, recreational associations, and neighborhood associations), which predates the Estado Novo but also was exploited by it (see A. Costa 1999; Holton 2005; Melo 2001).

48. Through much of the twentieth century, the annual Grande Noite do Fado competition played a pivotal role in launching the careers of professional fadistas. Lisbon's neighborhood associations often sent representatives to compete, and the quantity of applause was a factor in determining winners (C. Costa 1994). Thus not just individual reputations were at stake; neighborhoods competed against one another, shaping a sense of bairrismo (neighborhood fealty) fostered by the Estado Novo (see chapter 3). When I was conducting research in the early 2000s, the professionalization function of the competition had become almost obsolete. (In

2002, the competition did not even take place.) The coaching sessions in Marvila were also included in a guide to Lisbon's fado published by the Fado Museum in 2001.

49. In 2002, my subscription payments to participate as a member were less than three euros per month.

50. Ethnographic description and reported speech draw on my video recording of the event (Associação Cultural o Fado, rehearsal, September 12, 2002).

51. Reported speech transcribed from my recording of the event (Associação Cultural o Fado, rehearsal, May 22, 2003).

52. I draw here on recorded interviews I conducted with Fátima Fernandes (November 26, 2002), Sebastião de Jesus (March 25, 2003), and António Rocha (June 5, 2002). "Dizer bem as palavras" can also signify the proper "division" of the words (the Portuguese verb used is *dividir*) of the poem in relation to the melody, with attention to syllabic stress.

53. Sebastião de Jesus, interview, March 25, 2003.

54. "Fado is a popular song and it is intuitive. You don't study to learn it, to do these modulations of the voice. If I sing a fado one time, the second time it is not the same; this is not intentional or because I studied to do it like that. It is the form that it comes out in the moment" (António Rocha, interview, June 5, 2002).

55. The renowned fadista Maria Teresa de Noronha is often spoken about in terms of the "lyric" qualities of her voice. More than once, I heard in the same breath, "She was a great lady. She had noble blood, was an aristocrat. Did you know she took singing lessons?"

56. "Cantarei Até Que a Voz Me Doa," lyrics by José Luís Gordo, music by José Fontes Rocha. This fado is in the repertoire of the professional fadista Maria da Fé and is sung widely in amateur and professional settings.

57. "Ao Fado tudo se diz / Ao Fado tudo se canta / No cristal de uma garganta / Vive a alma de um país." This phrase is popularly glossed to take on different meanings in multiple fado lyrics. The author of the phrase was most likely Avelino de Sousa (1880–1946) (José Manuel Osório, personal communications, August 15, 2005, June 9, 2006).

58. A similar discourse is found in the early controversy and outrage that surrounded the collaborations between Amália and the French Portuguese composer Alain Oulman in the early 1960s. These collaborations took the form of texts of high poetry (including work by the Renaissance epic poet Camões) set to music with a far more complex harmonic language than had ever been heard in fado. Thus, her instrumentalists nicknamed this repertoire "the operas" (Mourinha 2002: 8, quoting V. Santos 2005 [1987]). But in another sense, the Amália–Oulman controversy calls on a history of debates about class within the fado world in relation to so-called legitimate or authentic venues—that is, should fado be sung in the taverns or in the salons? Is it sacrilegious for a fadista (with all of the links to social marginality and debauchery that this term entails) to sing high poetry or for the work of high poets to be set to the "debased" form of fado?

CHAPTER TWO

Affects of History

First epigraph: "Biografia do Fado" (Biography of Fado), lyrics and music by Frederico de Brito, still common in the repertoires of male fadistas at amateur sessions:

O pai era um enjeitado
Que até andou embarcado
Nas caravelas do Gama
Um mal-andrajado e sujo
Mais gingão do que um marujo
Dos velhos becos de Alfama.

"*Gingão*" (rowdy, one who swaggers, struts), as a voiced exclamation by a listener during a fado performance is sometimes used as an expression of authenticity (see chapter 5).

Second epigraph: "Caravela da Saudade," lyrics by Carlos Zamara, commonly set to the music of the traditional fado Fado Esmeraldinha, by Júlio Proença:

Nos tempos em que o mar era um segredo
Desafiando a própria tempestade
Alguns heróis partiram sem ter medo
Na dócil caravela da saudade
E já no alto mar, longe da barra
Rodeados p'la fé de lés a lés
Havia sempre um choro de guitarra
E o soluçar de um fado no convés.

1. "The past can be seized only as an image which flashes up at the instant when it can be recognized and is never seen again" (Benjamin 1968a: 255). Flatley (2008: 4) writes about "affective mapping" as a phrase that refers to "the aesthetic technology—in the older, more basic sense of a *techne*—that represents the historicity of one's affective experience." He is particularly interested in moments of naming, or "flashes of recognition" of the "historicity of one's affective experience" in relation to melancholia (which he understands as productive).

2. For the colonial in present-day Portugal as "common sense," see Almeida 2004.

3. The literary scholar Fernando Arenas (2003: 10) notes, "It is impossible not to be overtaken by the realization that Portuguese national identity continues to be intimately and irreversibly linked to the era of maritime expansion, 'discoveries,' and colonial empire, in spite of all of the major historical, political, socioeconomic, and cultural changes that have taken place in Portugal over the last twenty-five years."

4. Leal (2008: 41, 2000b) notes that Braga was writing during a period of Portuguese history characterized by concern with the empire's state of decay, which was marked by a questioning of Portuguese identity in response to concrete

political events such as the British Ultimatum of 1890 (marked as well as by a broader fin de siècle emphasis on decline in Europe). Leal (2000b: 5) also remarks that, while Braga was noting "positive" characteristics of the Portuguese soul based on his reading of folk culture, some intellectuals were portraying the folk as decrying negative characteristics of the Portuguese soul (of which fado, as the dolorous complaint of the folk, was used as a prime example). The turn to the folk as a source of this identity, or soul, was, of course, widespread throughout Europe at this time. For a synthesis of Leal's work in the context of thinking through the "roots and ramifications" of Lusotropicalist discourses, see also Almeida 2004: 51.

5. Cláudia Castelo (1998: 101) notes that the influence of Freyre's Lusotropicalism on Portuguese academe was coterminous with the adoption of Freyre by the Estado Novo, notably in work by the politician, sociologist, and lawyer Adriano Moreira, the anthropologist Jorge Dias, and the cultural geographer Orlando Ribeiro. Also in the 1950s (in 1957), the PIDE formed international anticommunist alliances via North Atlantic Treaty Organization contacts with various Western intelligence agencies outside Portugal and with the U.S. Central Intelligence Agency (I. Pimentel 2010: 161).

6. Almeida (2004: 45, 51) argues that precursors for Lusotropicalism can be found in the second half of the nineteenth century in Portugal in the anthropological, historical, and literary movement known as "Decadentism," which he characterizes as "the complaint of the loss of past glory when the country was compared to industrialized Europe." See also Leal 2000a: 5 on Braga. I acknowledge Ana Gonçalves and João Guerra for identifying early in my research that some of the fragmentary discourse concerning miscegenation I heard from various actors in the fado world could likely be traced to Lusotropicalist ideologies.

7. "What is the meaning of this persistent gendering of the imperial unknown? As European men crossed the dangerous thresholds of their known worlds, they ritualistically feminized borders and boundaries. Female figures were planted like fetishes at the ambiguous points of contact, at the borders and orifices of the contest zone" (McClintock 1995: 24).

8. Castelo (1998: 47) argues that the first two decades of the Estado Novo were saturated with propaganda of "imperial mysticism," which strategically drew on particular aspects of a vainglorious colonial past to regenerate the "new" nation, fusing this "history" with Catholicism.

9. "The moral discourse of Catholicism lay at the core of this nationalist narrative and seamlessly wove the historical processes of nation formation, consolidation, expansion and empire, with the ideological legitimation of Salazarist regeneration and the apologia of the colonialist civilizing mission" (Vakil 2003: 37).

10. Kesha Fikes (2009: 39) notes that the first antidiscrimination law in relation to race in Portugal was passed in 1999.

11. Almeida (2004: 46) argues that Lusotropicalist strands surface in contemporary Portuguese discourses about immigrants and migrants; in relation to discourses about "lusophony," a global community of Lusophone cultures; and in

the "Portuguese struggle for a politically correct way of celebrating the Discoveries." Fikes's interest is in understanding what Lusotropicalist ideologies and their remainders potentiate or negate with regard to racial politics within Lisbon: "Rather than questioning whether this ideology [Lusotropicalism] existed at one time in practice, it is crucial to ask what its presence and absence have enabled and disabled over time. By positioning tropicalism as an authorial allowance for the white Portuguese citizen under Salazarian fascism, we can focus not only on the practices of social relationality it informed but also on the ways in which these practices effectively negated the possibility of publicly conceiving of racist practice in the metropole" (Fikes 2009: 62). Ana Paula Ferreira (2010: 280) regards the "language of inter-culturalism" as a "colonial form" of contemporary Europe: "Such politically correct terms for the era of postcolonial globalization not only do not abolish, but quite the contrary, activate a neo-colonial reminder (and are a remainder) of the nation's colonial past as well as the former territorial borders."

12. Vianna (1999: 2) locates the "foundational myth" of samba in this respect to an interaction between samba musicians (Donga, Pixinguinha, and Patrício), Gilberto Freyre, and the historian Sérgio Buarque de Holanda. Thus, in this interpretation, Freyre's ideas about mestiçagem were pivotal to the ways in which samba was shaped as a "hybrid" genre that represented national hybridity.

13. "The Portuguese nation has seldom been described as miscegenated and *mestiça* itself. In the discourses of national identity, emphasis has been placed on what the Portuguese have given to others—a gift of 'blood' and culture—not on what they have received from others" (Almeida 2004: 66). In the 1930s, these tropes were supported by "scientific" testing by ethnologists commissioned by Salazar (Castelo 1998; Fikes 2009: 37).

14. This conception of the "Arabness" of saudade echoes the work of Adalberto Alves (1995). In his work on representations of Islam in relation to postcolonial Portugal, Vakil (2003: 37) cites Alves for foregrounding an Arab Islamic past in Portuguese literature and for locating in saudade an ethos that is simultaneously of the Arab and of the Portuguese: "Where the early-twentieth-century poet-prophet Teixeira de Pascoaes had discovered in the untranslatable word *saudade* and its uniquely Portuguese sentiment the very essence of the distinctiveness of the Portuguese 'soul,' the basis of a regenerative and patriotic *Art of Being Portuguese*, Alves finds *saudade* specifically Portuguese . . . and Arabic."

15. "Ai Mouraria," a place-name fado (see chapter 3) set in a nostalgically rendered version of the neighborhood of Mouraria, is a fado canção from Amália's repertoire (lyrics by Amadeu do Vale, music by Frederico Valério). By citing "*ais*," the man was referring to expressive inflections that employ rubato, melisma (sometimes microtonal), or glissando that occur in some fados on the exclamation *ai*. Some practitioners told me that the practice of singing "*ais*" is less common now than it was in the past.

16. I thank the musicologist Rui Vieira Nery (personal communication, November 2001) for being the first to call my attention to Amália Rodrigues's role in popularizing melismatic vocal ornamentation in fado performance. Nery also

discussed the influence of a tradition of melismatic improvisation that is characteristic of the Beira Baixa region of Portugal on her vocal style (Nery, personal communication, November 10, 2006). While Amália was born in Lisbon, her parents were originally from the Beira Baixa. Amália credited her mother's singing style and the songs from the Beira Baixa as formative influences: see V. Santos (2005 [1987]: 60). At the same time, she enjoyed singing and listening to flamenco, which is highly melismatic (see chapter 6).

17. The reference was to the "war on terror" led by the United States in response to the attacks of September 11, 2001, and the subsequent U.S. campaign against the Taliban in Afghanistan. "Mouraria" originally referred to the Moorish quarter of a city. In fado lore, Mouraria figures prominently as one of the "origin" neighborhoods for fado, and in fado lyrics it is often featured as a site of nostalgia. In contemporary Lisbon, Mouraria is one of the city's most ethnically diverse neighborhoods, including Indian, Asian, African, and northern African populations, as well as white Portuguese.

18. An extensive critical literature on saudade in the Portuguese context exists in Portuguese. For recent examples, see Gil 2007; Leal 2000b; Lourenço 2001.

19. Leal's position is similar to that of Nery (2004: 193), who argues that during the first two decades of the Estado Novo, the theme *tenho saudade* (I have saudade), became ubiquitous in fado lyrics: "Insistently, fado was presented as a kind of last stronghold of an idealized historical tradition, opposed by definition, to modernity and political intervention in the present."

20. "From this point of view, *saudade* should be regarded as an example of a more widespread tendency present in other processes of construction and circulation of national symbols and stereotypes: although directed towards the whole national population, they are in fact selectively appropriated by specific cultural and social groups who reproduce them as particular symbols of their own sense of a more general feeling: that of 'being national'" (Leal 2000b: 14).

21. João Miguel Tavares, "Personalidades como Amália Não Deixam Herdeiros," interview with Rui Vieira Nery, *Diário de Notícias*, October 6, 2002, 14–15.

22. Maria José Melo, interview, January 17, 2003.

23. Olga de Sousa, personal communication, September 3, 2002.

24. Júlia Florista (1967), lyrics by Joaquim Tavares Pimentel, music by Leonel Villar and Joaquim Tavares Pimentel. This fado was recorded by numerous well-known singers, including Amália Rodrigues and Carlos do Carmo.

25. "Lisboa, Não Mudes Assim," lyrics by Manuel Calado Tomé, published by permission of Edite B. de Medeiros Tomé. The translation is mine. While it is common in traditional fado for the same fados (in terms of basic melodic and harmonic patterns) to be set to an infinite number of poems, this is less common in fado canção. "Lisboa, Não Mudes Assim," however, is an example of a well-known fado canção (e.g., "Júlia Florista") set to new lyrics.

26. The Monumental was an old theater in Lisbon that was demolished to build a shopping mall with the same name.

27. Saldanha is the name of another shopping mall that is nearby a monument of the Duke of Saldanha, a nineteenth-century Portuguese military man and statesman.

28. *Hortas* are outdoor gardens where fado was often performed.

29. The Parque Mayer is a famous old vaudeville theater that in 2003 was being restored.

30. Cacilhas is a town across the river from Lisbon.

31. The Parque das Nações is the name given to the site constructed for the 1998 World Exposition.

32. *Brados* and *pregões* are traditional street cries (between speech and song) that were used by street vendors in Lisbon (rarely they can still be heard). They are often referenced in fados as an expression of nostalgia, and some fado lyrics contain examples of old street cries, which are vocalized in performance.

33. Manuel Calado Tomé and Edite B. de Medeiros Tomé (interview, May 30, 2003) noted that these types of lyrics (i.e., as leveling critique that could be read as directed toward city policy) probably would have been censored during the regime. If Michael Colvin's (2008) thesis that during the Estado Novo, multiple fado lyrics covertly critiqued the city's urban-planning policy in relation to the demolition and reconstruction of Mouraria, is correct, then Tomé's lyrics also fit into a longer-standing subgenre of fado lyrics that critique official Lisbon urban planning.

34. I write against a popular stereotype that circulates via fado tourism and within Portugal that fado is (or was) the "national" music of Portugal, as well as tendencies in the history of ethnomusicology as a discipline to theorize relationships between song genre *as* nation or music *as* resistance.

35. In this recasting of the dictatorship, a version I heard more than once, the colonies (particularly the former African colonies) figure as belligerent offspring, with their insurgency and demands for independence draining Portuguese resources via the colonial wars.

36. In 1968, after Salazar had suffered a stroke, Marcelo Caetano was appointed prime minister.

37. There were three incarnations of the political police in Portugal during the Estado Novo: (1) the Polícia de Vigilância e Defesa do Estado (PVDE), 1933–45; (2) the Polícia Internacional e de Defesa do Estado (PIDE), 1945–69; and (3) the Direcção-Geral de Segurança (DGS), 1969–74 (I. Pimentel 2007: 24). However, when referring to the political police, the overwhelming majority of my interlocutors used only the designation "PIDE."

38. Fátima Fernandes, interview, November 26, 2002.

39. "As regards its 'investigatory' methods, the pide used what are referred to as 'continuous' interrogation methods. Such are broadly a euphemism for 'sleep' torture—preventing the prisoner from sleeping throughout many days—and 'statue' torture—preventing the prisoner from moving—as well as beatings and physical assault at the PIDE headquarters or later in its prison stronghold of the Caxias fortress" (I. Pimentel 2010: 164).

40. "Whether because of its origins or its pessimism and the lack of animation that it expresses, the excessive diffusion [of fado] was proclaimed inconvenient in relation to [questions of] the national and the folkloric, as its values contradict the most authentic and constructive sources and manifestations of the popular [folk]. . . . Fado is reminiscent of the lamenting guitarras of Alcácer, not of shouts of victory or of faith" (transcript of a meeting of the Assembleia Nacional [National Assembly] on ethnography and folklore, published in *Diário das Sessões*, June 6, 1956, 1227, cited in Melo 2001: 83–84).

41. Nery (2004: 218–19) argues that these regulations during the first part of the Estado Novo did not target fado in particular. Rather, they were directed more generally at public performance, censorship, and professionalism.

42. Some of Nery's argument regarding a propagagtion of a new mythic foundation for fado during the dictatorship runs parallel to that of some Portuguese political historians of the Estado Novo (e.g., Castelo 1998; Rosas 1992), who claim that during the early years of the regime, the Estado Novo focused on disseminating an ideology that would "re-Portugalize" Portugal, an ideology based in the glory of empire and past conquest, a fixation on the past, and on the promulgation of a mythic origin narrative for the nation that justified empire.

43. Robert Deardorff, "Playgrounds in the Sun: South to Sand, Sea, and Siesta," *Rotarian* 122, no. 1 (January 1973): 41.

44. The Taverna do Embuçado has since closed.

45. Pedro Guerra, interview, April 1, 2003; emphasis added.

46. Fernanda Maria, interview, October 30, 2002.

47. According to one interlocutor, the general distaste for fado that followed the revolution endured for approximately fifteen years.

48. In official representations of fado's histories (e.g., in the remodeled Fado Museum in Lisbon), professional fadistas and instrumentalists, particularly those who had recording careers, figure as the primary actors. Amateur practice continues to be underprivileged in historical accounts (such as those found in museum exhibits and the popular press), even though it sustains a mythos of authenticity for the genre as a whole. When political resistance is highlighted in these accounts or in generic representations, it is often in relation to professional star fadistas or highly visible fado poets and instrumentalists (generally those who wrote for or accompanied professional fadistas).

49. One of the most striking examples in recent years of the use of fado as "culture" in relation to the European Union was the contracting in 2007 by the Portuguese state (in cooperation with the Bank of Portugal) to purchase a large recorded sound archive of Portuguese music, containing hundreds of 78s of fado, from a British collector. This coincided with the year that both the European Commission and the Council of the European Union had Portuguese presidents. Fado thus acquired a sound "history" at a moment of increased Portuguese prominence in the European Union, emphasizing Portugal as a player in the game of "culture" as "resource" (Yúdice 2003), with inscribed history (a recording archive) in this instance as a qualification for "culture."

CHAPTER THREE

Fado's City

Epigraph: "Lisboa Casta Princesa," lyrics by Álvaro Leal, music by Raúl Ferrão.

Lisboa, casta princesa . . .
Lisboa das descobertas de tantas terras desertas . . .
Sete colinas são teu colo de cetim
Onde as casas são boninas
Espalhadas em jardins
E no teu seio, certo dia foi gerado e cantado pelo povo
Sonhador o nosso fado.

An earlier version of this chapter appears in Gray 2011.

1. Wim Wenders (1995: 4) claims that the way in which he explores the representation of Lisbon in this film was influenced by the soundtrack, which was made before the film was shot: "The city certainly had inspired this band and their music, now their music helped us to enter the city and find our way through it, and through our story."

2. For additional approaches to the relationship of fado to place and to the city of Lisbon, see Brito 1999; A. Costa 1999; Costa and Guerreiro 1984; Elliott 2010; Gray 2005, 2007.

3. James Fernandez (2008: 208) argues that the North–South distinction is critical to European understandings of space and identity that date back to the ancient Greeks. The disciplining machinations of anthropology have not been immune historically from a tendency to position southern Europe as "behind." Edward Banfield's study of southern Italy, *The Moral Basis for a Backward Society* (1958), is a case in point.

4. For critiques of anthropology in southern Europe during this time period, see Herzfeld 1987; Llobera 1986.

5. For a world systems influenced approach to North–South relations as they map onto Portugal's positioning within Europe, framed in the context of the current economic crisis, see Santos 2012.

6. Carlos do Carmo, interview, November 12, 2002.

7. Susan Buck-Morss (1989: 27) comments on the writing of Asja Lacis and Walter Benjamin on the city of Naples (regarding their article "Neapel," which appeared in the *Frankfurter Zeitung* in 1926): "The phenomena—buildings, human gestures, spatial arrangements—are 'read' as a language in which a historically transient truth (and the truth of historical transiency) is expressed concretely, and the city's social formation becomes legible within perceived experience."

8. "Acoustemology, acousteme: I am adding to the vocabulary of sensorial-sonic studies to argue the potential of acoustic knowing, of sounding as a condition of and for knowing, of sonic presence and awareness as a potent shaping force in how people make sense of experiences. . . . Experiencing and knowing place—the idea of place as sensed, place as sensation—can proceed through a complex interplay of

the auditory and the visual, as well as through other intersensory perceptual processes" (Feld 1996b: 97–98).

9. My thinking about genre takes its cues from recent scholarship on public sentiment that locates aesthetic genres as critical to shaping the "affective intensities" of the social (see Berlant 2008: 4); from work in linguistic anthropology that extends Mikhail Bakhtin's sociohistoric approach to speech genres to argue for genre as practice-based (Hanks 1987); and from work that foregrounds generic intertextuality in relation to verbal discourse and social power (Bauman and Briggs 1992).

10. In his sociological analysis of neighborhood identity in Alfama, António Firmino da Costa (1999: 127) notes a type of fado commonly practiced in Alfama that focuses thematically on the neighborhood itself or on important sites in the neighborhood, and where these foci are referenced in the fado's title. He categorizes these as *fados identitários* (identitarian fados).

11. "Vielas de Alfama" (excerpt), lyrics by Artur Ribeiro, music by Maximiano de Sousa:

Horas mortas noite escura
Uma guitarra a trinar
Uma mulher a cantar
O seu fado de amargura
E através da vidraça
Enegrecida e rachada
A sua voz magoada
Enternece a quem lá passa.

REFRAIN
Vielas de Alfama
Ruas da Lisboa antiga
Não há fado que não diga
Coisas de vosso passado
Vielas de Alfama
Beijadas pelo luar
Quem me dera lá morar
P'ra viver junto do fado.

The lyrics Mariza sings in her recording of 2003 employ a minor word substitution from the official version (signed by the poet) that is on record at the Sociedade Portuguesa de Autores. She substitutes *entristece* (saddens) for *enternece* (to affect, to move) in the last line of the first verse.

12. Raymond Williams (1973: 152) references Wordsworth on London—"The city now doth like a garment wear / The beauty of the morning; silent, bare / Ships, towers, domes, theatres and temples lie / Open unto the fields and to the sky"— referring to a time when the city of London was understood as "the center of civilization."

13. I am not claiming that all or even most place-name fados are in the fado canção form. I note only that I commonly heard a particular type of place-name fado canção sung in amateur practice. This type of fado is often derived in style or content from Lisbon's *revista* or musical theater era of the mid- to late 1800s through the mid-twentieth century, and is through-composed or contains a refrain. In performance, the singer often employs a vocal style that foregrounds timbral resonance (i.e., is less "grainy," strained, or nasal than is commonly heard in performances of traditional fado or perhaps in fado canção whose subject [i.e., the lyrics] is not primarily the city of Lisbon).

14. "If we attempt to describe the city from a distanced and transcendent position, to thereby miniaturize it, the tendency is to naturalize the city landscape" (S. Stewart 2003: 78).

15. "Lisboa é Sempre Lisboa," lyrics by Artur Ribeiro, music by Nóbrega e Sousa.

16. The annual *marchas populares*, in which Lisbon neighborhoods compete with one another in highly visible parades that neighborhood associations often spend the entire year preparing, are commonly held in Lisbon in June. They can be understood as "invented traditions" from the dictatorship era in that they began during the Estado Novo, but for many, this historical referent has been lost (see Hobsbawm and Ranger 1983, quoted in A. Costa 1999: 33).

17. Lyrics published by permission of Álvaro Rodrigues. The poem is set to the melody of the fado canção "A Lenda das Algas." Rodrigues is also a central interlocutor in Costa and Guerreiro 1984, and "Alfama Eterna" appears as a song text in their ethnography as part of contemporary practice in the late 1970s and early 1980s in amateur fado in Alfama. In a narrative of his life history, Rodrigues states that he wrote the lyrics approximately twenty years earlier for a fadista who was representing an association in Alfama at Lisbon's annual Grande Noite do Fado competition (Costa and Guerreiro 1984: 123). Thus, the lyrics most likely have been in circulation in Lisbon's amateur scene for approximately five decades.

18. For an expanded discussion of "Portugal não é um país pequeno," and for the relationship of Ferro's cultural policy to "invented" traditions, see Holton 2005: 9.

19. On the miniature and the gigantic as metaphors for the "interior" of the subject and the "abstract authority of the state," see S. Stewart 2003: xii.

20. "Uma Casa Portuguesa" (A Portuguese Home), lyrics by Reinaldo Ferreira, music by Vasco Matos Sequeira and Artur Fonseca.

21. All three neighborhoods bear the *bairros populares* designation within Lisbon (by both neighborhood residents and nonresidents). The term cannot be translated literally into English as it runs up against the nuanced (and sometimes contradictory) connotations of "popular" in Portuguese (where "popular" does not simply stand in for "working class"). For an explication of the "popular" in relation to how the designation played out on the ground in Alfama in the 1990s, see A. Costa 1999: 278–79.

22. The neighborhood association Grupo Desportivo da Mouraria, founded in 1936, was one of the few remaining outposts for fado activities in the area during that time. As of 2012, partly in response to the granting of "Intangible Cultural

Heritage" status to fado by UNESCO in 2011, the city was attemping to encourage more fado activity in Mouraria. At the same time, restoration and development projects that foregrounded fado's history in relation to the neighborhood (i.e., on scaffolding announcing restoration work) were under way. This phenomenon foregrounds (once again) the enduring linkage between fado and cycles of urban restoration in relation to municipal policy and politics.

23. When the fadista Mariza began her international career in 2001, her public biography stressed that she had grown up singing fado in Mouraria. Mariza came from an unorthodox lineage, for a fadista, in that she had earlier experience as a jazz singer and was born in Mozambique to an African mother.

24. "Kitsch does not emerge in a political vacuum; rather, it responds to particular kinds of historical events and indicates particular kinds of political acquiescence. The well-known German critiques of kitsch saw it as an element of the rise of fascism in Nazi Germany, and kitsch has often been associated with a totalitarian or fascist regime" (Sturken 2007: 22). Marita Sturken quotes Milan Kundera: "Kitsch is the absolute denial of shit, in both the literal and the figurative senses of the word; kitsch excludes everything from its purview that is essentially unacceptable in human existence" (Kundera 1984: 248–51; Sturken 2007: 22).

25. Fado as an urban and, according to some of its past detractors, "debauched" song form historically has stood in ambivalent relation in Portugal to the category of "folklore." Beginning in the 1950s, however, fado was often performed alongside versions of sanitized folkloric dance in professional fado houses. On folklore and the shaping of a "politics of the spirit" during the dictatorship, see Holton 2005. On fado policies in the 1950s, see Nery 2004.

26. The configuration of the typical audience for amateur fado is rapidly changing as global media outlets report on out-of-the way places where tourists can hear the "real thing," as videos shot on cell phones in amateur venues by tourists circulate on YouTube, and as new venues spring up to cater to this audience. The international release of the film *Fados*, by the Spanish director Carlos Saura, in 2007 may also have contributed to shifts in Lisbon's international fado publics. (The production of the film was financially supported by Lisbon's municipal government.)

27. This description refers to the placement of the diorama in the museum from 1998 through 2008. In 2008, the museum was remodeled, and the exhibit was moved.

28. "Physical structures were implanted in the neighborhood that were meant to pass for archaic, including fountains and engraved stones, panels of *azulejos* [Portuguese tiles], and street arches, iron grates and railings, walls and terraces, Moorish roof tiles and flower vases. At the same time, festive activities and other cultural practices with folkloric objectives, both political-ideological and touristic, were promoted" (A. Costa 1999: 35). Yet Costa also cautions against arguing for the role of the Estado Novo in shaping sociocultural and physical/architectural aspects of Alfama in too strong of a manner, as this underscores an imaginary of an "authentic" patrimony (predating the Estado Novo) and also overstates the role of the dictatorship as the creator of sociocultural reality and "identity" in Alfama.

29. For an analysis of relationships between sentimental popular song, the scenic, urban policy, and the shaping of affective citizens (in relation to twentieth-century Istanbul), see Stokes 2010.

30. In the summer of 2008, this relationship between Alfama, an aesthetics of abandonment, and fado was foregrounded in an outdoor art exhibition in which large cloth artworks were hung on Alfama's abandoned houses. Some of these works featured stereotypical fado iconography.

31. What is striking here is that a core–periphery model still holds for much fado production, circulation, and distribution within Europe, even though transnational neoliberal capitalism and economic shifts in relation to current European Union practices have greatly complicated this model's usefulness for understanding political economies of Europe's margins.

32. Branco has even recorded fados written by the Dutch poet Jan Jacob Slauerhoff.

33. These claims about Branco's and Mísia's reputations and notoriety are based on observations gathered while I was conducting fieldwork in Lisbon in the early 2000s and making regular visits to the Netherlands.

34. The cover of Mariza's CD *Terra* (Earth), released in 2008, portrays her dominating a miniaturized landscape with a famous Lisbon colonial monument, the Tower of Belém, in the background. (Thus, symbols of colonialism are recycled and reused in her "domination" of the international market.)

35. Romania won in 2002 and 2006; Portugal won in 2003; Spain won in 2004, 2005, and 2008; and France won in 2007. In 2002, Romania won under the rubric "Europe/Middle East"; by 2003, the BBC had split the rubric into two categories: see http://www.bbc.co.uk/radio3/worldmusic (accessed June 10, 2008).

36. "[These distinctions] can be found in daily conversation, when people from Porto refer to Lisbon and the south as Mourolândia (Land of the Moors) often in the context of the rivalry between the Porto Soccer Club and Lisbon soccer teams" (Seabra 1999, cited in Sobral 2008: 207). José Manuel Sobral describes the pervasive influence within Portugal of the geographer Orlando Ribeiro's *Portugal, o Mediterrâneo e o Atlântico* (1967 [1945]), which argued that Portugal was split along a northern–southern division in terms of climate, landscape, and land use based on either "Atlantic" or "Mediterranean" influences. As Sobral notes, the Portuguese anthropologist Jorge Dias, influenced by Ribeiro's work, theorizes a Mediterranean–Atlantic division within Portugal in terms of sociocultural characteristics (Dias 1961: 121–43, cited in Sobral 2008: 207; see also Leal 2008: 42).

37. "Dolls of cloth or of clay, representing and fixing models of regional clothing, miniatures of tools, of utensils, of vehicles of transport, will portray a visual image of professional activities in the village" (A. J. de Castro Fernandes 1947: 53, quoted in Melo 2001: 78).

38. "Values become condensed and enriched in miniature" (Bachelard 1994: 150).

39. "The drive of the small provides the opportunity for the formation of tiny affective worlds in which symbolic relations develop with extraordinary force. To separate for a day is an eternity, immense pain, immense saudade" (Gil 2007: 46).

40. Lyrics published by permission of Editorial Avante! (2011). Note that there is a discrepancy between the final line as it appears in the published version of this poem in an anthology of José Carlos Ary dos Santos's song lyrics (Santos 1993 [1989]: 20). The final line in the published version appears as "Mas tem outra canção" (But it has another song), while in the version Amália sang, the final line is "Mas não tem outra canção" (But it has no other song). I thank K. David Jackson and Helena Correia for suggestions on my translation.

41. I never heard "Alfama" sung at a Lisbon fado venue in the early 2000s. This is not to say that it was never sung, only that during my fieldwork in the early 2000s, it was not part of the common performance repertoire. Oulman's compositions are notoriously difficult for both singers and instrumentalists to perform, but even at amateur venues, adventurous fadistas sometimes perform his standards. Mariza covers the fado on her CD *Terra* (2008), which was produced by the Spanish producer Javier Limón and includes other world music stars from Spain and Brazil. "Alfama" appears on this diverse album without any explanation or note. What is perhaps striking is that while Mariza covered many of Amália's fados in her previous albums, she recorded "Alfama" only after both her position and that of fado had been well established on the world music stage.

42. "Cheira a Lisboa" (Aroma [Smell] of Lisbon), lyrics by César Oliveira, music by Carlos Dias:

Um craveiro numa água-furtada
Cheira bem, cheira a Lisboa
Uma rosa a florir na tapada
Cheira bem, cheira a Lisboa
A fragata que se ergue na proa
A varina que teima em passar
Cheiram bem porque são de Lisboa
Lisboa tem cheiro de flores e de mar.

The song reaches its pinnacle of repeat performances in June for Lisbon's massive outdoor party (whose epicenter is Alfama) honoring the city's patron saint, Santo António (Saint Anthony). During this time, in multiple performances and recordings, overlapping and out of sync, it bounces off the walls until the early hours of many mornings.

43. For traditional instrumental figurations for Fado Menor, see Castelo-Branco 1994: 134.

44. Multiple aspects of Osório's biography stand out as unusual in fado's genre worlds. Born in 1947 in the former Belgian Congo, Osório moved to Lisbon at ten. He trained in classical piano and voice at the conservatory in Lisbon and studied theater at the National Theater Conservatory. (His training included both piano and operatic voice.) After completing secondary-school training, he joined (and helped to found) professional theater groups, working as both an actor and a director. He recorded his first fado album in 1968; it contained fados by some of Portugal's finest leftist poets. He was in Paris, in exile, during the protests of 1968.

When he returned to Portugal, he was imprisoned on multiple occasions. Following the revolution, he recorded a disc that celebrated fado (which was politically out of favor at the time) and worked in political outreach theater, touring rural regions of Portugal. He was a member of the Communist Party for more than thirty years and a well-known producer of large-scale performance events in Portugal. In the last two decades of his life, Osório distinguished himself as a fado researcher, working on issues of fado's history and form and editing recording collections intended for a broad public. He mentored young professional fadistas and was a close friend to Amália Rodrigues. While not a formally trained scholar, he was a mediating figure between worlds of fado performance (later in life performing primarily in amateur contexts) and academic research. He died in 2011. This biographical sketch was culled from conversations I had with Osório in 2002–2008, from Osório and Osório 2003, and from official biographical information publicly accessible at Lisbon's Fado Museum.

45. José Manuel Osório, e-mail correspondence, August 14, 2004.

46. For an extended sociological/historical treatment of drug trafficking in Casal Ventoso, see Chaves 1999.

47. The lyrics to "Meia Laranja" are published by permission of José Luís Gordo. I am grateful to José Luís Gordo, to Ana Gonçalves, and to Helena Correia for suggestions on my translation.

48. Both the fado "Meia Laranja" and the fado "Alfama" might be understood as "countersentimental" (Berlant 2008), as simultaneously working within generic conventions and expectations while thematically and performatively undermining them. Berlant (2008: 55–56) identifies a "resistant strain" of the "countersentimental" within what she terms the "sentimental domain": "An author's or a text's refusal to reproduce the sublimation of subaltern struggles into conventions of emotional satisfaction and redemptive fantasy might be called 'countersentimental,' a resistant strain within the sentimental domain. The countersentimental does not involve the aesthetic destruction of the contract sentimentality makes between its texts and its readers, that proper reading will lead to more virtuous, compassionate feeling and therefore to a better self. What changes is the place of repetition in this contract, a crisis frequently thematized in formal aesthetic and generational terms." Berlant (2008: 55) introduces the notion of the "countersentimental" in relation to a discussion of recontextualizations of Harriet Beecher Stowe's *Uncle Tom's Cabin* as a form and various "textual resistance[s] to the *Uncle Tom* form itself."

49. On tango, see, e.g., Luker 2009; Savigliano 1995.

CHAPTER FOUR
Styling Soulfulness

1. José Manuel Osório, personal communication, July 4, 2008.

2. José Fontes Rocha, interview, May 26, 2003.

3. The use of stock instrumental patterns is perhaps most apparent in instrumental performance practices regarding the three anonymous traditional "root" fados: Fado Mouraria, Fado Menor, and Fado Corrido. For transcriptions of typical guitarra accompaniment figurations for these fados as demonstrated by the guitarrista Raúl Néry and for examples of contracanto formulas, see Castelo-Branco 1994: 134, 138. Two young instrumentalists with whom I spoke referred to guitarra accompaniment figurations by using the term *malhas* (lit., mesh of a net; a nautical term for a bowline knot). Salwa El-Shawan Castelo-Branco (1994: 138) translates "malhas" as "textures" and notes that Portuguese jazz musicians also use the term to differentiate stock instrumental accompaniment patterns from more personally styled figures and sonic textures.

4. I agree with Castelo-Branco (1994: 128) when she argues that fado musicians (singers and instrumentalists) and audiences do not understand the relationships between instrumentalists and fadista in terms of a "fado ensemble." Rather, guitarra, viola, and fadista are interdependent roles. In theory, each role can be subsumed by any number of individual actors, but sometimes strong working relationships or associations are forged between instrumentalists or between particular fadistas (particularly in the case of celebrities) and their instrumentalists. For more on associations between instrumentalists and between instrumentalists and fadistas, see Castelo-Branco 1994: 128–29.

5. For more on details of versification in relation to traditional fado forms, see R. Carvalho 1999; Gouveia 2010; Nery 2004.

6. Processes, histories, and figurations of fado styling in relation to fado voices, poetry, and instrumentalists deserve extended scholarly treatment and could benefit from a wide range of methodologies and approaches, including historical, ethnographic, ethno-poetic, ethnomusicological, and linguistic.

7. Ethnographic description culled from field recording of performance (José Manuel Osório, Tasca do Careca, Lisbon, May 3, 2003).

8. In reference to the Fado Vitória, Amália Rodrigues makes claims for the improvisatory and affective potential of the structure of the escala espanhola: "[It is] a music that gives me freedom, because it allows me to change, I am able to go there, inside [of myself]" (Amália Rodrigues, quoted in V. Santos 2005 [1987]: 96). The traditional fado, Fado Menor do Porto, also uses the escala espanhola. For an extensive compilation of recordings of traditional fados organized by name, see Osório 2005.

9. An edited archival collection dates this recording of a Fado Vitória, sung by the fadista José Porfírio, June 6, 1929 (Porfírio 1994).

10. In practice, fadistas sometimes make their own minor changes to the lyrics when singing. One example found in some of Osório's performances of "Meia Laranja" is a substitution of the word *tantos* (many) for *quatro* (four) in the first verse.

11. This notation was included in the file as "proof" of original composition. It includes no indications as to underlying harmonic progressions. In July 2011, a staff member at the SPA's center for documentation explained to me that if a

composer could not read or write music, he or she might have someone else notate the composition for submission.

12. On the salience of understanding an "unplayed" melody to enabling musical creativity and improvisation for practitioners in the Javanese Gamelan, see Perlman 2004. Marc Perlman's work is also relevant for my purposes here in its elucidation of the importance of both implicit and explicit knowledge in music pedagogy and improvisation.

13. I am not arguing in this chapter that Osório (or any fadista) represents a "typical" voice or figure in fado. Osório's manner of styling fado falls at a far end of a continuum of musical risk taking and innovation.

14. On W. E. B. Du Bois's musical transcriptions of "sorrow songs" in *The Souls of Black Folk* as "shadows of echoes," see Flatley 2008: 141–57. Jonathan Flatley historicizes a discourse regarding the untranscribability of the voice in African American spirituals (see Zora Neale Hurston, as quoted in Cunard 1996, and Radano 2003, both cited in Flatley 2008: 237).

15. The initial challenge in these projects of transcription was determining the underlying metrical structure *in relation to* the pitches accentuated rhythmically in the voice. In the first transcriptions, which were primarily concerned with pitch relations in the voice, I used the words of the poem as a means to mark visually the rhythmic movement of the voice. I later consulted with a colleague, the pianist Matthew Goodrich, who heard these performances with a contrapuntally trained ear. Together we mapped the harmonic and melodic contours of one of the "straightest" performances (the only performance recorded in a studio). The next step was to work with a composer sympathetic to the challenges fado voices present to standard notation. My research assistant, Yoshiaki Onishi, meticulously listened to and transcribed the versions presented in this chapter and in the appendixes, into Finale software; we then collaboratively finessed them. The elaborate styling and figurations of the guitarra are mostly absent, not because they do not deserve attention, but because I wished to foreground the vocal line, and extended treatment of the interrelationship between fadista styling and guitarra styling is beyond the purview of this chapter. These transcriptions begin two bars before the vocal entrance (and omit approximately seven bars of the standard instrumental introduction). The rhythmic values in the vocal lines reflect our closest approximation of Osório's performances using conventional notation. Please note that when notating syllabic division, we privilege a performative version (representing Osório's actual use of vocal sound in different performances) of syllabic division over a standard, or "correct," version.

16. These recordings are as follows: (A) a live performance in a recital hall at Duke University in Durham, North Carolina, on January 10, 2004; (B) a professional studio recording made in Lisbon in August–September 2004 (see Osório 2004); and (C) a live performance at an amateur fado session at the Tasca do Careca in Lisbon on May 3, 2003. For full text of the poem and my translation, see chapter 3.

17. For a legend to special symbols used in the musical transcriptions, see the appendixes.

18. Osório noted that while he often stamps (and sometimes claps) while singing without being consciously aware of it, the performances we recorded in the recital hall at Duke University in 2004 and 2005 probably included more stamping and clapping than is customary for him because he was using embodied emphasis as a mode of translation (since most listeners in these contexts were unfamiliar with the genre and did not understand Portuguese) (José Manuel Osório, personal communication, July 4, 2008).

19. Since the harmonic movement and rhythm were almost identical as performed in each of three strophes, I include only the bass line of the first strophe to facilitate a simultaneous viewing of the three vocal lines.

20. My speculation here is in line with Castelo-Branco's (1994: 130) more general argument that in some cases, the "improvised melodic glosses" of some of the most well-known fadistas "have been incorporated as fixed elements within the fados to which they were initially added."

21. In her ethnographic study of jazz interaction and improvisation, Monson (1996: 97) develops the concept of "intermusicality" to refer to a kind of "intertextuality in sound as a way to begin thinking about the particular ways in which music and, more generally, sound itself can refer to the past and offer social commentary," foregrounding how "music functions in a relational or discursive rather than an absolute manner."

CHAPTER FIVE
The Gender of Genre
Epigraph: "Rosa Enjeitada" (Abandoned Rose), lyrics by José Galhardo, music by Raul Ferrão:

Rosa enjeitada
Sem mãe sem pão sem ter nada
Que vida triste e chorada
O teu destino te deu
Rosa enjeitada
Rosa humilde e perfumada
Afinal desventurada quem és tu?
Rosa enjeitada
Uma mulher que sofreu.

The fado canção "Rosa Enjeitada" was recorded by Hermínia Silva and Maria Teresa de Noronha, female fado icons of the mid-twentieth century, and currently circulates in the repertoires of contemporary amateur and professional female fadistas. The lyrics that appear here are as I commonly heard them sung in Lisbon in the 2000s. They are significantly modified from the lyrics attributed to Galhardo that are on file at the SPA.

1. I refer here to the diversity of the repertoire I heard sung during amateur fado sessions. Professional fado performance is often more limited in terms of the breadth of lyrics.

2. "Casa da Mariquinhas," lyrics by Silva Tavares, music by Alfredo Marceneiro.

3. While there are a few exceptions to this stereotype, female instrumentalists, in the genre of Lisbon fado, remain extraordinarily uncommon.

4. This usage of *latina* bore no resemblance to the term as used in the contemporary United States (or in Latin American studies).

5. With rare exceptions, Coimbra fado (from the city of Coimbra) features only men as fadistas.

6. For more on Severa, see Colvin 2008; Sousa e Costa 1936. In her performances on international tours in the early and mid-2000s, Mariza sometimes called attention to the iconography of prostitution in fado by connecting herself indirectly to this genealogy via costume and gesture. Before the performance of a particular fado, she sometimes put her foot up on a stool and raised her skirt suggestively to reveal a striped stocking while telling the audience about the story of fadista and prostitute Maria Severa.

7. Júlio Dantas's novel was adapted for the film *A Severa* (dir. Leitão de Barros, 1931).

8. For an example of an attempt to wrest nuances of "history" from "legend" in relation to both Severa and fado in the early twentieth century, see A. Pimentel 1989 (1904).

9. "Maria Severa," lyrics by José Galhardo, music by Raúl Ferrão.

10. The prostitution "giving birth" to a child metaphor also appears in some scholarly accounts of fado's history: "O fado pode ser considerado como filho da prostituição e das baiucas. Daí que no bordel estivesse sempre presente uma guitarra" (The fado could be considered a son of [coming from] prostitution and the taverns. In the bordello, a guitarra was always present) (Pais 1985: 45).

11. "It can be asserted that the discursive currency given to woman and the family throughout the making of the New State puts into motion a specific construct of nation-sex that structurally binds and yet threatens the process of national reimagining and imperial rebuilding" (Ferreira 2002: 110). Ferreira argues that new literary practices and canons were part of the gendered propaganda of the Estado Novo (within a general national context of high illiteracy). She reads the lusosex construct as running through Camões's Renaissance epic poem *Os Lusíadas*. This text was taken up as the national literary text par excellence during the Estado Novo.

12. Ferreira (2002: 110, citing Baptista 1986: 193) argues that non-reproductive sex during the Estado Novo, even between married couples, was highly discouraged. At the same time, there was a Foucauldian "incitement" to "tell about the bodily pleasures of the 'nation's various definitional others'" (Ferreira 2002: 110, citing Parker et al. 1992: 5). She claims that during the early twentieth century, as

part of larger discourses about "national degeneration" in Portugal, the "hysterical" or sexualized woman came to stand internally for a Luso "other" and that this contradictory ideology of woman and sex in relation to the nation—or of lusosex—endured and took stronger form during the Estado Novo (Ferreira 2002: 111).

13. This is not to say that prostitution does not thrive in contemporary Lisbon. However, it is not associated in practice with fado venues.

14. Fadistas of this generation often refer to singing on the street during the yearly summer festivals in Lisbon for the popular saints (*santos populares*).

15. Ivone Dias, interview, February 27, 2003.

16. Olga Rosa de Sousa, interview, January 25, 2010.

17. Practitioners also use "castiço" in reference to the subgenre of *fado tradicional* (i.e., *fado castiço*) as differentiated from fado canção.

18. For a discussion of erotic subjectivity in relation to her field research in Greece, see Jill Dubish's (1995) work. Dubish (1995: 33–34) notes the inverted nature of sexual Orientalism for the female fieldworker from northern Europe or the United States who is working on Europe's southern periphery: "The threat [of exoticizing or eroticizing a female anthropological 'other'] however, is usually for the Western *male*. The muted, generally unacknowledged side of erotic Orientalism is the exotic male Other's potential attraction for the Western female."

19. As tourists have increasingly sought out amateur fado in the past decade, and as more Portuguese young people flock to amateur fado as singers, gendered and sexed dynamics of fado in the tasca are changing. In 2012, numerous international tourists routinely attended fado sessions at O Jaime (many of them young men and women from European metropoles). In 2009, Jaime's wife, Laura, asked for my assistance in writing the English translations for new signs on the walls that direct those who do not intend to order food to stand at the bar counter.

20. Six months after I started attending amateur fado, I began making regular audio and visual recordings of performances, sitting with studio headphones on and a microphone set up or positioned behind a camcorder. I realized that the recording equipment, for some people, functioned symbolically as my "man," dignifying me with a recognizable, socially acceptable (if albeit strange) activity.

21. For "trouble talk" as a woman's genre, see Berlant 2008.

22. Olga Rosa de Sousa, interview, January 25, 2010.

23. Homosexuality among men in Portugal was officially criminalized in the Penal Code of 1852. It was not decriminalized until 1982. Lesbianism was not mentioned in the Penal Code (Almeida 2008: 6).

24. Almeida historicizes debates about abortion (which was legalized in 2007) and same-sex marriage (legalized in 2010) in contemporary Portugal within larger European North–South politics and stereotypes. As he notes, gender equity in terms of citizenship rights was instantiated soon after the fall of the dictatorship, but many other social movements (including those around LGBT, feminist, and immigration issues) lacked energy and force in the wake of a predominant political focus on class politics in which competing Marxist groups vied for power following the revolution (Almeida 2008: 5).

25. "Under Salazar, a woman could not vote unless she were literate and head of a household and could not sell family property or enter into any economic arrangement, obtain a passport or even open a separate bank account without the consent of her husband. Women were considered the moral backbone of the all-important family" (Anderson 2000: 14). "The famous proviso to article 5 of the 1933 constitution withdraws women from the sphere of citizenship and the (supposed) 'igualdade de direitos perante a lei' (the equality of rights before the law) on the grounds of 'differences' resulting from 'a natureza da mulher e o bem da família' (women's nature and the good of the family) (*Constituição Política da República Portuguesa e Acto Colonial* [Lisbon: Livraria Moraes, 1936], 4–5, cited in Ferreira 2002: 126). During the Estado Novo, the Portuguese family was ideologically shaped as a "microcosm of nation" (Ferreira 2002: 108). In part, this focus on the nuclear family was seen as necessary "national therapy" to recover from the "democratic excesses of the First Republic" (Martins 1986, cited in Ferreira 2002: 108).

26. "Women are typically construed as the symbolic bearers of the nation, but are denied any direct relation to national agency" (McClintock 1993: 62). See also *The Three Marias*, the seminal poetic, erotic, and feminist Portuguese text of early 1970s feminism (Barreno et al. 1975). The authors were arrested for "abuses of the press" when the book was published in 1972 (Barreno et al. 1975: translator's preface).

27. On feminine forms of the imperial and the national, see Berlant 2008; Chatterjee 1993; McClintock 1995; Ramaswamy 2010.

28. On "metaculture," see Urban 2001. On music itself in Western cultures marked as effeminate or feminine, see, e.g., Leppert 1993; McClary 1991. On the "voice" as ontologically feminine (in the West) vis-à-vis a feminist reading of classical mythology and philosophy, see Cavarero 2004.

29. Mariza collaborated in a pan-Mediterranean recording project of exclusively women's voices from different parts of the Mediterranean (see Limón 2010). The recording, titled *Mujeres de Agua*, was an act of protest explicitly dedicated to women in Iran, who are prohibited from singing in public. The singing voice of an international female fadista in this context comes to stand in for the "inalienable human" as part of a larger (Western) global discourse on rights.

30. "For femininity to be a genre *like* an aesthetic one means that it is a structure of conventional expectation that people rely on to provide certain kinds of affective intensities and assurances" (Berlant 2008: 4).

31. In an interesting case of postcolonial circulation, some of the most popular soap operas in contemporary Portugal are telenovelas produced in Brazil. They were popular with some of my female amateur fadista interlocutors.

32. For a historicization of the emergence of melodrama in tandem with European modernity, for a critical intervention into the labor of melodrama in the Latin American context, and for melodrama as a phenomenon that "organizes an aesthetic assimilation or functioning of codes, and narrative and performative elements of other media"—that is, an organizational labor of *intermedialidade* (intermedia-ness)—see Herlinghaus 2002: 39.

CHAPTER SIX

Haunted by a Throat of Silver

First epigraph: BBC News, October 9, 1999, available online at http://news.bbc.co. uk/1/hi/world/europe/469679.stm (accessed December 19, 2009). Second epigraph: Amália Rodrigues, quoted in Bruno de Almeida, dir., *Amália: Uma Estranha Forma de Vida*, documentary (Portugal: Arco Films with Valentim de Carvalho, 1995). Third epigraph: Joaquim Pais de Brito, quoted in "Amália e as Nossas Mães," *O Público*, October 8, 1999, 35.

1. The Monastery of Jerónimos, from the late fifteenth century, is Lisbon's grandest monastery and one of its most celebrated architectural masterpieces. It was built with money from the spice trade from early colonial expeditions and sits near the river across from Salazar's monument dedicated to the Portuguese Discoveries. Vasco da Gama and Portugal's two most enshrined writers, Fernando Pessoa and Luís Vaz de Camões, have tombs there.

2. The Portuguese reads: "Amália: Heterónimo de Portugal / Com Amália nos Jerónimos / Junto a Camões e Pessoa / Eram os três heterónimos / Dum país que a fado soa." It is dated July 23, 2000. The phrase "Amália: heterónimo de Portugal" was coined by David Mourão-Ferreira, a fado poet and former secretary of culture, and became known after the commemoration of the fiftieth anniversary of Amália's career in 1990 (see Côrte-Real 2001: 326). As it is used here, *heterónimo* (heteronym) transcends its literal meaning to refer to the literary techniques of Fernando Pessoa in relation to concepts of identity. *Pessoa* translates as "person." One of Pessoa's trademarks was to write under multiple "heteronyms" in different styles.

3. José Alves, "Sermon for the Funeral of Amália Rodrigues, November 8, 1999," http://www.patriarcado-lisboa.pt/ . . . /vc3_III_5_amalia_rodrigues.doc (accessed October 4, 2010).

4. After her death, in accord with her wishes, Amália's home on the Rua de São Bento in Lisbon was turned into a private museum. Even after death, her name serves formally to validate or commemorate stars in the professional fado community: the Fundação Amália Rodrigues regularly awards prizes to fado singers.

5. "As with all overloaded icons, these women [Diana, Mother Teresa] look so transparent" (D. Taylor 2003: 152).

6. For genre as affective expectation, see Berlant 2008.

7. This is not the place for extended biographical treatment of Amália Rodrigues. The strictly biographical material in this paragraph and the one following is summarized from V. Santos 2005 (1987); from Almeida's *Amália: Uma Estranha Forma de Vida* (1995) which includes extensive footage of video interviews of Amália from the 1980s; and from archival research I conducted at Lisbon's Museu Nacional do Teatro in 2003.

8. For a filmography, see V. Santos 2005 (1987).

9. Her singing of the ballad "Coimbra" (lyrics by José Galhardo, music by Raúl Ferrão) in the 1950s inspired numerous cover versions as "April in Portugal" (by,

among others, Louis Armstrong, Les Baxter, Dorothy Collins, and Liberace). Amália sang "April in Portugal/Coimbra" (starting the song in English, then switching to Portuguese) during an appearance on the U.S. television program *Coke Time*, sponsored by the Coca-Cola Company, in a segment hosted by Eddie Fisher in 1953. *April in Portugal* is also the title of a film in which Amália starred that was produced in London and premiered there in 1955 (V. Santos 2005 [1987]: 245).

10. For a recent gloss on Amália's repertoire and stylistics of voice, see Nery 2009.

11. For examples, see Filipe La Féria's musical *Amália* (which played to sold-out houses in Lisbon in 2000–2003); the film *Fado: História D'Uma Cantadeira* (Fado: The Story of a Singer; 1947), whose fictional plot is loosely based on Amália's life; the semi-fictional biopic *Amália: O Filme* from 2008; and Almeida's five-hour *Amália: Uma Estranha Forma de Vida* and his one-hour version, *Amália*, for English-speaking audiences. "Amália: Coração Independente" (Amália: Independent Heart), the large-scale exhibit commemorating the tenth anniversary of Amália's death that ran at Lisbon's Museu Berardo in 2009–10, followed Santos's text for its underlying organization and narrative exposition. (The phrase "Coração Independente" is from the fado "Uma Estranha Forma de Vida.")

12. I am grateful for ongoing conversation about vocal celebrity with Virginia Danielson (on Umm Kulthum) and Christine Yano (on Misora Hibari). Some fruitful cross-diva thinking came from our collaboration for the panel "Theorizing Musical Celebrity across Disciplines," presented at the 2008 Annual Meeting for the Society for Ethnomusicology, and from the American Anthropological Association panel I organized in 2007 on vocal celebrity for which Yano provided incisive critique.

13. See the discussion of Lux soap (the international "soap of the stars") in Stacey 1994: 279. Amália endorsed Lux in the 1950s.

14. "Reality is always more difficult than it appears: the same Amália of whom it is said was celebrated by *salazarismo* [Salazar's Estado Novo], I am able to say that sometimes this same Amália enabled money to be delivered via other people, money that she knew was going to the PCP [Portuguese Communist Party], then clandestine" (Nobel laureate José Saramago as quoted in Ana Navarro Pedro, "José Saramago em Paris: 'Amália fez chegar dinheiro ao PC,'" *O Público*, October 9, 1999, 9).

15. For additional discussion of Amália's ambivalent political positioning framed within the catalogue for the commemorative exhibit at the Museu Berardo in 2009, see Chougnet 2009.

16. A critical historical biography at the level of Virginia Danielson's work on the Egyptian diva Umm Kulthum (Danielson 1997) remains to be done.

17. I work with the text assuming that its narration (with minor editing) was based directly on the interview transcripts.

18. She denies the importance of António Ferro to her career after noting that he took her to sing for the first time in Paris and London in 1949 and commenting that she she liked him (V. Santos 2005 [1987]: 99).

19. Amália mentions a wide range of artists and types of music she enjoyed listening to, many from outside Portugal. In multiple passages in Santos's text, Amália self-identifies as *cigana* (gypsy).

20. "When I began singing fado, I had never heard any Spanish person sing, but [the Portuguese critics] said that I was singing fado in a Spanish style. Some of the turns of the voice [*voltas*] I used, I had learned from the songs of the Beira Baixa, with my mother and my aunts. They didn't have anything Spanish in them" (V. Santos 2005 [1987]: 60). Beira Baixa borders Spain.

21. At the same time, she includes details of her personal life (e.g., an early divorce, living alone in Lisbon in her thirties, a second marriage in her forties) that mark her as an uncharacteristically modern woman for her day, particularly for a Catholic in dictatorship-era Portugal.

22. "Uma Estranha Forma de Vida" (A Strange Form of Life) is the title of celebrated fado lyrics that Amália wrote and sang set to the traditional fado, Fado Bailado (music by Alfredo Duarte Marceneiro).

23. Ricardo Costa, interview, January 29, 2003. All quotes from Ricardo Costa in this chapter are from this interview.

24. The past two decades have witnessed a surge of interest in the discipline of sociology, as well as in literary, film, cultural, and theater studies, in theorizing celebrity and publics, sometimes in tandem with a renewed interest in charisma, reworking the Weberian formulation (see, e.g., Hughes-Freeland 2007). In a sweeping review of celebrity, Chris Rojek (2001) divides the literature into three categories: "subjectivist" accounts, which uncritically celebrate the supposed uniqueness and singularity of a star; structuralist theorizations, which were common in the 1960s–80s, often working from a culture industry paradigm influenced by the Frankfurt School; and poststructuralist models, which are concerned with the inter-textual shaping of stardom involving dynamism among multiple parameters, including the relationships between media and its publics, consumption and production, and the "actual" body and persona of the star.

25. Judith Butler (1993: 122, 125) points to parody, mime, or the performative as a way to figure *disobedience*, as nuancing Louis Althusser's "bad subjects" to open a range of possibilities for rupture, re-signifying, disobeying, a "space of ambivalence which opens up the possibility of a reworking of the very terms by which subjectivation proceeds—and fails to proceed." Jackie Stacey (1994) argues, through ethnographic work with fans, against an idea of spectator identification that she claims as overly rigid, where the fans are understood as pawns or as "being duped." Rather, her work demonstrates the rich practices of self-making that occur in fans' multifaceted engagements with celebrities. More recent work on media icons also insists on nuancing critiques of celebrity reception and consumption, moving beyond "mass stupefaction" (see Ghosh 2011: 5).

26. Yet in ethnomusicology and in its related disciplines, these relationships are under-studied, and ethnomusicology rarely takes musical celebrity as a locus of study. "Ethnomusicologists have rarely studied individuals; perhaps this tendency represents an effort to avoid interpretations of culture based on the works of 'great

men,' so long in vogue in the history of European classical music. When individuals appear at the forefront of ethnomusicological or folkloric studies, they are rarely musical stars" (Danielson 1997: 15).

27. On the enabling relationship between divas and their queer fans, see Koestenbaum 1993. On "Selenidad," or Selena fans in relation to the afterlife of their diva, see Paredez 2009. And on the afterlife of Zeki Müren, the queer Turkish nightclub vocal star, in relation to cultural intimacy, see Stokes 2010.

28. However, Chambers (1991: 12) acknowledges the fragility of these distinctions between "resistance" and "opposition." He further distinguishes between "'oppositional behavior' which does not have change as its outcome, and discursive, or 'narrative' opposition which has as its distinguishing feature the power of 'authority' to affect people, mentally and emotionally, and by that means to change states of affairs in general."

29. It could be argued that Amália's melodramatic persona and public biography were shaped, at least to some extent, in relation to gendered melodramatic conventions that were given a particular form and amplified by Hollywood. Berlant (2008) analyzes multiple examples of the female complaint genre of the "weepy" in U.S. cinema from the 1930s–1950s in relation to the shaping of intimate publics. In a curious case of transatlantic cultural circulation in which the ethos of Hollywood "weepy" and melodrama meets the "soul" of the Portuguese fado, Amália discusses attending the cinema as a young person and being moved by *Camille* and *You Only Live Once*, both released in 1937. "When I was a girl, I wanted to be Sylvia Sidney," she said. "The film that impressed me the most was the one where at the end, Henry Fonda is holding her dead in his arms [*You Only Live Once*]. Later, when I saw Greta Garbo in *Dama das Camélias* [*Camille*], I drank vinegar and placed myself in a draft so I could have tuberculosis like she did" (V. Santos 2005 [1987]: 43).

30. On performance codes in contemporary U.S. popular song genres, see Marshall 2006b: 202: "The mode of address, unlike in the play or the film, is constructed to be direct. The directness of the address of the musical performer has always constructed the relationship between performer and audience at a very personal level. In the attempt to express the emotions of the musical and lyrical content of the song, the contemporary popular music performer has worked to authenticate his or her performance through acknowledgment of the direct nature of the address. The personal sentiments expressed in the song's lyrics are freely exposed in action and voice."

31. *A Biografia do Fado* (The Biography of Fado) is a CD collection of fado greats from the twentieth century that was produced in 1994 in conjunction with the exhibit *Fado: Voices and Shadows* at the Museu Nacional de Etnologia. Marceneiro is one of the most celebrated male fado singers of the twentieth century, and "A Casa da Mariquinhas" is one of the most popular fados in his repertoire. (It was also sung by Amália.) Fans reported to me that "Foi Deus" (It Was God) was played at masses in Amália's honor after her death.

32. Bibi Ferreira is a Brazilian actress who at the time of the interview was starring in *Bibi Vive Amália*, a musical about Amália's life that was in production in Brazil.

33. "Rosa" (pseudonym), interview, May 29, 2002. All subsequent quotes by Rosa in this chapter are from this interview.

34. Fernando Forte, interview, June 13, 2002. All subsequent quotes by Forte in this chapter are from this interview.

35. "Our continuing fascination with those who openly perform, especially if they are willing to take on the role of the eccentric or the vagrant spirit—from Hell's Angels and punkers to hoboes and spielers at carnivals—reminds us that those who appear to speak and act on the basis of extreme experience often seem more real to us than those involved in more mundane pursuits. In fact, in many situations we seem to judge what "the real thing" is by how fully such others are able to make us recognize the range of experiential possibilities, whether or not we go through such experiences ourselves" (Abrahams 1986: 66).

36. I understand the "extraordinary" to be a porous category that is animated by and is on a spectrum or dynamic continuum with the ordinary. On the extraordinary, see Abrahams 1986; Straight 2007. On performance moving on a continuum of markedness and formality, see Bauman and Briggs 1990; Goffman 1959.

37. For different perspectives on how musical listening might be understood in relation to the intimate or erotic, see Cusick 1994; Dolar 2006; Frith 1996; Goldin-Perschbacher 2007; Koestenbaum 1993; McClary 1991.

38. "Psychoanalytic theories of identification used within film criticism have led to very narrow conceptualizations of *cinematic* identification, which have ignored the broader meanings of spectator/star relations and indeed have led to some overly pessimistic conclusions about the pleasures of popular cinema. How might we conceptualize cinematic identification, not solely as analogous to early psychic developments, but as a cultural process with social meanings beyond the cinema?" (Stacey 1994: 135).

39. "The memory of the first 'meeting,' or rather 'sighting,' is retold within the structure of a romantic narrative whose sequence of events culminates in the moment of seeing her favourite star on the cinema screen. Its structure is built around a series of gaps, enigmas or absences which is typical of the romance narrative" (Stacey 1994: 141). For a discussion of the relationship between the construction of stardom and heterosexual love plots, see Dyer 1979.

40. Amália Rodrigues, quoted in Almeida, *Amália*.

41. Joaquim Pais de Brito (1999: 33) notes that during the last quarter of the nineteenth century, fado had already begun to shift along class lines with regard to the content of its lyrics. Upper-class fado was performed in salons linked to the aristocracy and came to use a poetic language separated from the narrative dimension (*linguagem poética mais separada da dimensão narrativa*), and this aspect can be found in the late twentieth century in fadistas such as Maria Teresa de Noronha and Vicente da Câmara.

42. Gonçalo Salgueiro, interview, September 23, 2002.

43. José Fontes Rocha, interview, May 26, 2003.

44. Hugo Ribeiro, interview, October 25, 2002. All quotes from Hugo Ribeiro in this chapter are from this interview.

45. Yet Amália's voice contrasts strikingly with the stereotypical timbre of the "authentic" working-class female fadista from one of Lisbon's traditional fado neighborhoods. Within the context of amateur fado performance, Amália's voice is marked as "clean," "more musical" or "lyric" in relation to the gritty, nasal, and highly textured timbre of the traditional fadista.

46. "Hugo Ribeiro . . . é que grava aquela que eu acho que é a minha voz, aquela que eu oiço. No estrangeiro, não estão habituados à minha voz. Quando eu canto, com os gritos que dou, aquela agulha, que não deve passar do meio, vem de baixo e, de repente, passa para o outro lado, para o encarnado. Tenho uma maneira de cantar que a quem for estranha, quando chega ao encarnado, corta. E fica o grito, que não é grito, nem coisa nenhuma, sem timbre, sem cor. Porque eles têm medo e cortam. . . . A minha voz tem uma cor. Se não aparece lá é porque eles a tiram." When Amália uses *grito*, which I translate as "scream," I think she is referring to sudden shifts and swells in tessitura and volume from low to high.

47. David Ferreira, interview, June 12, 2002.

48. The park has since closed. The set follows a visual tradition of enlarged guitarras as stage scenery. For example, in the set for a performance in *O Fado: História D'Uma Cantadeira* (Fado: The Story of a Singer; 1947), one of Amália's first films, a guitarra forms the stage backdrop, and Amália sings as she walks out of its opening.

49. "Fado Amália," lyrics by José Galhardo, music by Frederico Valério.

50. As the long sweep of literature on performative mimesis from a range of disciplinary perspectives reminds us, to mimic can be about gaining a repertoire to express the self by inhabiting the repertoire of another. It can be about being seemingly inhabited by another as a way to transcend the self. It can be about creative inflection, "signifying," parody, satire, and subversion—and also about admiration, about desire, and about love.

51. Butler (2004: 201) objects to the idea that "ironic mimesis is not a critique": "The voice [of Irigaray] that emerges 'echoes' the master discourse, but this echo nevertheless establishes that there is a voice, that some articulatory power has not been obliterated, and that it is mirroring the words by which its own obliteration was to have taken place."

52. "Mostrando ser mais fadista / Provando ser mais mulher (Demonstrating that she is more fadista / Proving that she is more woman)": "Foi na Travessa da Palha," lyrics by Gabriel de Oliveira, music by Frederico de Brito).

53. "The Show Must Go On" was written and directed by Carlos Castro.

54. "Foi Deus," lyrics and music by Alberto Janes.

55. For a discussion of how the concept of transformation works in relation to divas with large gay followings (here with reference to Maria Callas), see Koestenbaum 1993: 139, 145; emphasis added): "Careers with gay followings often have moments of rupture and reinvention: moments when the star's body or persona

radically shifts and proves the former self to have been a fabrication. The gay fan, schooled in the gap between public manner and private feeling, may identify less with Callas' newfound glamour than with her former plainness; or he may identify with the *rift between the two*. . . . We love her because she incarnated vocal multiplicity and heterogeneity."

56. I agree with Butler (1993: 125) that "there is no necessary relation between drag and subversion. . . . [Drag] may well be used in the service of both the denaturalization and reidealization of hyperbolic heterosexual gender norms."

57. "Grito" (Scream), music by Carlos Gonçalves.

58. "Barco Negro," lyrics by David Mourão-Ferreira, music by Caco-Velho/ Piratini. The transformation of "Mãe Preta" into "Barco Negro" can be understood as another example from the Estado Novo period of the political (in this case, lyrics that treated the issue of race) being eclipsed by a romantic love narrative (see chapter 2).

59. "Initially, I found the explanations and evaluations attached to Umm Kulthum's repertory redundant to the point of seeming incomprehensible: it was as though listeners had learned the talk along with the tunes. . . . 'She sang naturally.' . . . 'Her voice was full of our everyday life.' . . . 'It wasn't just her voice—her *character* was the reason for her success'" (Danielson 1997: 4). Similar rhetoric circulates around Maria Callas: "Here lay the danger, the lure: she was a mess *and* she was a goddess" (Koestenbaum 1993: 136). It might be useful to investigate parallelism in discursive tropes about national divas and how these tropes are attached to specific repertoires among varied listeners (i.e., the link between repertoire and public biography). How much would tropes of "naturalness," "rags-to-riches" life narratives, the idea that the diva can sing to the "everyday" but also at the level of "high" art, and the tendency to value the *character* or the *person* of the diva feature in them all? How many of these tropes are necessary in sustaining an imaginary that links a particular female voice to the so-called soul of a nation? How much are they imbricated in age-old discourses (some of which span East and West) that connect music to soulfulness or that situate the female singer/performer in complex relation to ideas of the public and the private and to sexuality?

REFERENCES

Abrahams, Roger D. 1986. "Ordinary and Extraordinary Experience." In *The Anthropology of Experience*, ed. Victor W. Turner and Edward M. Bruner, 45–72. Urbana: University of Illinois Press.

Ahmed, Sara. 2004. *The Cultural Politics of Emotion*. New York: Routledge.

Almeida, Miguel Vale de. 2004. "*Tristes Luso-tropiques*: The Roots and Ramifications of Luso-tropicalist Discourses." In *An Earth-Colored Sea: "Race," Culture, and the Politics of Identity in the Post-colonial Portuguese-Speaking World*, 45–64. New York: Berghahn.

———. 2008. "Gender and Sexuality in Contemporary Portugal: The Case of Same-Sex Marriage or Hopeful News from a Silenced World." Keynote address presented at the Sixth Congress of the American Portuguese Studies Association, Yale University, New Haven, Conn., October 11.

Alves, Adalberto. 1995. *Portugal, Ândalus e Magrebe: Um Contexto de Tolerância*. Lisbon: Edições Universitárias Lusófonas.

Anderson, James Maxwell. 2000. *The History of Portugal*. Westport, Conn.: Greenwood.

Appadurai, Arjun. 1996. *Modernity at Large*. Minneapolis: University of Minnesota Press.

Arenas, Fernando. 2003. *Utopias of Otherness: Nationhood and Subjectivity in Portugal and Brazil*. Minneapolis: University of Minnesota Press.

Asad, Talal, James W. Fernandez, Michael Herzfeld, Andrew Lass, Susan Carol Rogers, Jane Schneider, and Katherine Verdery. 1997. "Provocations of European Ethnology." *American Anthropologist* 99, no. 4: 713–30.

Bachelard, Gaston. 1994. *The Poetics of Space*. Boston: Beacon.

Bakhtin, Mikhail. 1986. "The Problem of Speech Genres." In *Speech Genres and Other Late Essays*, ed. Caryl Emerson and Michael Holquist, 60–102. Austin: University of Texas Press.

Banfield, Edward. 1958. *The Moral Basis of a Backward Society*. New York: Free Press.

Baptista, Luís Vicente. 1986. "Valores e Imagens da Família em Portugal nos Anos 30: O Quadro Normativo." In *A Mulher na Sociedade Portuguesa: Visão Histórica e Perspectivas Actuais*, 191–219. Coimbra: Instituto de História Económica e Social, Faculdade de Letras da Universidade de Coimbra.

Barreno, Maria Isabel, Maria Teresa Horta, and Maria Velho da Costa. 1975. *The Three Marias: New Portuguese Letters*, trans. Helen R. Lane. Garden City, N.Y.: Doubleday.

Barthes, Roland. 1977. *Image–Music–Text*, trans. Stephen Heath. New York: Hill and Wang.

———. 1985. *The Responsiblity of Forms: Critical Essays on Music, Art, and Representation*. New York: Hill and Wang.

Bauman, Richard, and Charles Briggs. 1990. "Poetics and Performance as Critical Perspectives on Language and Social Life." *Annual Review of Anthropology* 19:59–88.

———. 1992. "Genre, Intertextuality, and Social Power." *Journal of Linguistic Anthropology* 2, no. 2: 131–72.

———. 2003. *Voices of Modernity: Language Ideologies and the Politics of Inequality*. Cambridge: Cambridge University Press.

Bender, Gerald J. 1978. *Angola under the Portuguese: The Myth and the Reality*. Berkeley: University of California Press.

Bendix, Regina. 2000. "The Pleasures of the Ear: Toward an Ethnography of Listening." *Cultural Analysis* 1:1–9.

Benjamin, Walter. 1968a. "Theses on the Philosophy of History." In *Illuminations*, ed. Hannah Arendt, 253–64. New York: Schocken.

———. 1968b. "The Work of Art in the Age of Mechanical Reproduction." In *Illuminations*, ed. Hannah Arendt, 217–51. New York: Schocken.

Berlant, Lauren. 2008. *The Female Complaint: The Unfinished Business of Sentimentality in American Culture*. Durham: Duke University Press.

Berliner, Paul. 1978. *The Soul of Mbira: Music and Traditions of the Shona People of Zimbabwe*. Berkeley: University of California Press.

———. 1994. *Thinking in Jazz: The Infinite Art of Improvisation*. Chicago: University of Chicago Press.

Berndt, Ronald M. 1962. *Excess and Restraint: Social Control among a New Guinea Mountain People*. Chicago: University of Chicago Press.

Blacking, John. 1973. *How Musical Is Man?* Seattle: University of Washington Press.

Bohlman, Philip Vilas. 2011. *Music, Nationalism, and the Making of the New Europe*. New York: Routledge.

Born, Georgina. 2010. "Listening, Mediation, Event: Anthropological and Sociological Perspectives." *Journal of the Royal Musical Association* 135, no. 1: 79–89.

Braga, Teófilo. 1867. *Cancioneiro Popular Coligido da Tradição*. Coimbra: Imprensa da Universidade.

‎

———. 1985 (1885). *O Povo Português nos Seus Costumes, Crenças e Tradições.* Lisbon: Publicações Dom Quixote.

Briggs, Charles L. 1993. "Personal Sentiments and Polyphonic Voices in Warao Women's Ritual Wailing: Music and Poetics in a Critical and Collective Discourse." *American Anthropologist* 95:929–57.

Brito, Joaquim Pais de. 1992. "Sobre o Fado e a História do Fado." In *História do Fado*, Pinto de Carvalho (Tinop), 9–20. Lisbon: Publicações Dom Quixote.

———. 1994. "Fado: Voices and Shadows." In *Fado: Voices and Shadows*, ed. Joaquim Pais de Brito, 15–36. Lisbon: Electa.

———. 1999. "O Fado: Etnografia na Cidade." In *Antropologia Urbana: Cultura e Sociedade no Brasil e em Portugal*, ed. Gilberto Velho, 24–42. Rio de Janeiro: J. Zahar Editor.

Bronfen, Elisabeth. 1992. *Over Her Dead Body: Death, Femininity, and the Aesthetic.* New York: Routledge.

Buck-Morss, Susan. 1989. *The Dialectics of Seeing: Walter Benjamin and the Arcades Project.* Cambridge: MIT Press.

Butler, Judith. 1990. *Gender Trouble.* New York: Routledge.

———. 1993. *Bodies That Matter: On the Discursive Limits of "Sex."* New York: Routledge.

———. 2004. *Undoing Gender.* New York: Routledge.

Caraveli-Chaves, Anna. 1980. "Bridge between Worlds: The Greek Women's Lament as Communicative Event." *Journal of American Folklore* 368, no. 93: 129–57.

Carvalho, Pinto de (Tinop). 1992 (1903). *História do Fado.* Lisbon: Publicações Dom Quixote.

Carvalho, Ruben de. 1999. *Um Século de Fado.* Amadora: Ediclube.

Carvas, Estrela. 2009. *Os Meus 30 Anos Com Amália.* Lisbon: Guerra e Paz, Editores.

Castelo, Cláudia. 1998. *O Modo Português de Estar no Mundo: O Luso-tropicalismo e a Ideologia Colonial Portuguesa (1933–1961).* Porto: Edições Afrontamento.

Castelo-Branco, Salwa El-Shawan. 1994. "The Dialogue between Voices and Guitars in Fado Performance Practice." In *Fado: Voices and Shadows*, ed. Joaquim Pais de Brito, 125–40. Lisbon: Electa.

Cavarero, Adriana. 2004. *For More Than One Voice: Toward a Philosophy of Vocal Expression.* Palo Alto, Calif.: Stanford University Press.

Chambers, Ross. 1991. *Room for Maneuver: Reading (the) Oppositional (in) Narrative.* Chicago: University of Chicago Press.

Chatterjee, Partha. 1993. *The Nation and Its Fragments: Colonial and Postcolonial Histories.* Princeton: Princeton University Press.

Chaves, Miguel. 1999. *Casal Ventoso: Da Gandaia ao Narcotráfico, Marginalidade Económica e Dominação Simbólica em Lisboa.* Lisbon: Imprensa de Ciências Sociais.

Chougnet, Jean-François. 2009. "Um Livro Pensamento." In *Amália: Coração Independente*, ed. Jean-François Chougnet, 57–65. Lisbon: Museu Colecção Berardo.

Clough, Patricia Ticineto, and Jean O'Malley Halley, eds. 2007. *The Affective Turn: Theorizing the Social.* Durham: Duke University Press.

Colvin, Michael. 2008. *The Reconstruction of Lisbon: Severa's Legacy and the Fado's Rewriting of Urban History*. Lewisburg, Penn.: Bucknell University Press.

Connerton, Paul. 1989. *How Societies Remember*. Cambridge: Cambridge University Press.

Corbin, Alain. 1998. *Village Bells: Sound and Meaning in the 19th-Century French Countryside*. New York: Columbia University Press.

Cordeiro, Graça Índias. 1994. "The Fado in the Bica Neighborhood: The House of Milú." In *Fado: Vocies and Shadows*, ed. Joaquim Pais de Brito, 57–72. Lisbon: Electa.

———. 1997. *Um Lugar na Cidade: Quotidiano, Memória e Representação no Bairro da Bica*. Lisbon: Publicações Dom Quixote.

Côrte-Real, Maria de São José. 2001. "Cultural Policy and Musical Expression in Lisbon in the Transition from Dictatorship to Democracy (1960s–1980s)." PhD diss., Columbia University, New York.

Costa, António Firmino da. 1999. *Sociedade de Bairro: Dinâmicas Sociais da Identidade Cultural*. Oeiras: Celta Editora.

Costa, António Firmino da, and Maria das Dores Guerreiro. 1984. *O Trágico e o Contraste: O Fado no Bairro de Alfama*. Lisbon: Publicações Dom Quixote.

Costa, Catarina Alves da. 1994. "Fado Gala Night." In *Fado: Voices and Shadows*, ed. Joaquim Pais de Brito, 107–24. Lisbon: Electa.

Cumming, Naomi. 2000. *The Sonic Self: Musical Subjectivity and Signification*. Bloomington: Indiana University Press.

Cunard, Nancy, ed. 1996. *The Negro*. New York: Continuum International Publishing Group.

Cusick, Suzanne. 1994. "On a Lesbian Relationship with Music: A Serious Effort Not to Think Straight." In *Queering the Pitch: The New Gay and Lesbian Musicology*, ed. Philip Brett, Elizabeth Wood, and Gary C. Thomas, 67–83. New York: Routledge.

Cvetkovich, Ann. 2003. *An Archive of Feelings: Trauma, Sexuality, and Lesbian Public Cultures*. Durham: Duke University Press.

———. 2007. "Public Feelings." *South Atlantic Quarterly* 106, no. 3: 459–68.

Dainotto, Roberto. 2007. *Europe in Theory*. Durham: Duke University Press.

Danielson, Virginia. 1997. *The Voice of Egypt: Umm Kulthum, Arabic Song, and Egyptian Society in the Twentieth Century*. Chicago: University of Chicago Press.

Dantas, Júlio. 1901. *A Severa*. Lisbon: M. Gomes.

de Certeau, Michel. 1984. *The Practice of Everyday Life*, trans. Steven F. Rendall. Berkeley: University of California Press.

Dent, Alexander. 2009. *River of Tears: Country Music, Memory, and Modernity in Brazil*. Durham: Duke University Press.

Dias, Jorge. 1961. *Ensaios Etnológicos*. Lisbon: Junta de Investigações do Ultramar.

Dias, Jorge A. 1990 (1953). "Os Elementos Fundamentais da Cultura Portuguesa." In *Estudos de Antropologia*, vol. 1, 135–57. Lisbon: Imprensa Nacional-Casa da Moeda.

Dolar, Mladen. 1996. "The Object Voice." In *Gaze and Voice as Love Objects*, ed. Renata Salecl and Slavoj Žižek, 7–31. Durham: Duke University Press.

———. 2006. *A Voice and Nothing More*. Cambridge: MIT Press.

Dubish, Jill. 1995. "Lovers in the Field: Sex, Dominance, and the Female Anthropologist." In *Taboo: Sex, Identity, and Erotic Subjectivity in Anthropological Fieldwork*, ed. Don Kulick and Margaret Willson, 29–50. London: Routledge.

Dyer, Richard. 1979. *Stars*. London: British Film Institute.

Edwards, Brent Hayes. 2002. "Louis Armstrong and the Syntax of Scat." *Critical Inquiry* 28, no. 3: 618–49.

Elliott, Richard. 2010. *Fado and the Place of Longing: Loss, Memory and the City*. Farnham, Surrey: Ashgate.

Feld, Steven. 1982. *Sound and Sentiment*. Philadelphia: University of Pennsylvania Press.

———. 1984. "Communication, Music, and Speech about Music." *Yearbook for Traditional Music* 16:1–18.

———. 1988. "Aesthetics as Iconicity of Style, or 'Lift-Up-Over Sounding': Getting into the Kaluli Groove." *Yearbook for Traditional Music* 20:74–113.

———. 1996a. "Pygmy POP: A Genealogy of Schizophonic Mimesis." *Yearbook for Traditional Music* 28:1–35.

———. 1996b. "Waterfalls of Song: An Acoustemology of Place Resounding in Bosavi, Papua New Guinea." In *Senses of Place*, ed. Steven Feld and Keith H. Basso, 91–135. Santa Fe, N.M.: School of American Research Press.

Feld, Steven, and Keith H. Basso, eds. 1996. *Senses of Place*. Santa Fe, N.M.: School of American Research Press.

Feld, Steven, and Donald Brenneis. 2004. "Doing Anthropology in Sound." *American Ethnologist* 31:461–74.

Feld, Steven, and Aaron A. Fox. 1994. "Music and Language." *Annual Review of Anthropology* 23:25–53.

Feld, Steven, Aaron A. Fox, Thomas Porcello, and David Samuels. 2004. "Vocal Anthropology: From the Music of Language to the Language of Song." In *A Companion to Linguistic Anthropology*, ed. Alessandro Duranti, 321–45. Oxford: Blackwell.

Fernandes, António Júlío de Castro. 1947. *Enfrentando o Destino das Casas do Povo*. Lisbon: Junta Central das Casas do Povo.

Fernandez, James. 2008. "Displacements: The Experience of Vectored Spaces in Pennisular Places." In *Recasting Culture and Space in Iberian Contexts*, ed. Sharon R. Roseman and Shawn S. Parkhurst, 271–90. Albany: State University of New York Press.

Ferreira, Ana Paula. 2002. "Loving in the Lands of Portugal: Sex in Women's Fictions and the Nationalist Order." In *Lusosex: Gender and Sexuality in the Portuguese-Speaking World*, ed. Susan Canty Quinlan and Fernando Arenas, 107–29. Minneapolis: University of Minnesota Press.

———. 2010. "The 'Colonial Form' in the Postcolonial Portuguese Metropolis." In *Conflict, Memory Transfers, and the Reshaping of Europe*, ed. Helena Gonçalves da Silva, Adriana Alves de Paula Martins, Filomena Viana Guarda, and José Miguel Sardica, 274–90. Newcastle upon Tyne: Cambridge Scholars.

Fikes, Kesha. 2009. *Managing African Portugal: The Citizen–Migrant Distinction*. Durham: Duke University Press.

Flatley, Jonathan. 2008. *Affective Mapping: Melancholia and the Politics of Modernism*. Cambridge: Harvard University Press.

Foucault, Michel. 1977. *Discipline and Punish*. New York: Random House.

Fox, Aaron A. 2004. *Real Country: Music and Language in Working-Class Culture*. Durham: Duke University Press.

Fox, Aaron, and Christine Yano, eds. Forthcoming. *Songs out of Place: Global Country*. Durham: Duke University Press.

Freyre, Gilberto. 1961. *The Portuguese and the Tropics*. Lisbon: Executive Committee for the Commemoration of the Fifth Centenary of the Death of Prince Henry the Navigator.

Frith, Simon. 1996. *Performing Rites: On the Value of Popular Music*. Cambridge: Harvard University Press.

Frow, John. 2005. *Genre*. London: Routledge.

Gaonkar, Dilip Parameshwar, and Elizabeth A. Povinelli. 2003. "Technologies of Public Forms: Circulation, Transfiguration, Recognition." *Public Culture* 15, no. 3: 385–97.

Gates, Henry Louis. 1988. *The Signifying Monkey*. New York: Oxford University Press.

Ghosh, Bishnupriya. 2011. *Global Icons*. Durham: Duke University Press.

Gil, José. 2007. *Portugal, Hoje: O Medo de Existir*. Lisbon: Relógio D'Água.

Gilmore, David D. 1982. "Anthropology of the Mediterranean Area." *Annual Review of Anthropology* 11:175–207.

Gilroy, Paul. 1993. *The Black Atlantic: Modernity and Double Consciousness*. Cambridge: Harvard University Press.

Goffman, Erving. 1959. *The Presentation of Self in Everyday Life*. New York: Doubleday.

Goldin-Perschbacher, Shana. 2007. "'Not With You but Of You': 'Unbearable Intimacy' and Jeff Buckley's Transgendered Vocality." In *Oh Boy! Masculinities and Popular Music*, ed. Freya Jarman-Ivens, 213–33. New York: Routledge.

Gonçalves, Ana. In preparation. "Famílias do Fado: Tipos e Casos de Transmissão Familiar de uma Forma Musical Urbana." PhD diss., Instituto de Ciências Sociais, Universidade de Lisboa.

Gouveia, Daniel. 2010. *Ao Fado Tudo se Canta*. Linda-a-Velha: DG Edições.

Gray, Lila Ellen. 2005. "Re-sounding History, Embodying Place: Fado Performance in Lisbon, Portugal." PhD diss., Duke University, Durham, N.C.

———. 2007. "Memories of Empire, Mythologies of the Soul: *Fado* Performance and the Shaping of *Saudade*." *Ethnomusicology* 51, no. 1: 106–30.

———. 2011. "Fado's City." *Anthropology and Humanism* 36, no. 2: 141–63.

———. Forthcoming. "Fado Taxonomies, Fado Fado: Toward an Anthropology of Fado Genre." In *Fado: Percursos e Perspectivas*, ed. Salwa Castelo-Branco and Rui Vieira Nery, Lisbon: Museu do Fado.

Gregg, Melissa, and Gregory J. Seigworth. 2010. "An Inventory of Shimmers." In *The Affect Theory Reader*, ed. Melissa Gregg and Gregory J. Siegworth, 1–28. Durham: Duke University Press.

Hanks, William. 1987. "Discourse Genres in a Theory of Practice." *American Ethnologist* 14, no. 4: 668–92.

Hardt, Michael. 1999. "Affective Labor." *Boundary* 26, no. 2: 89–100.

Hatfield, Elaine, John T. Cacioppo, and Richard L. Rapson. 1994. *Emotional Contagion.* Cambridge: Cambridge University Press.

Hebdige, Dick. 1979. *Subculture: The Meaning of Style.* London: Routledge.

Herlinghaus, Hermann. 2002. "La imaginación melodramática: Rasgos intermediales y heterogéneos de una categoría precaria." In *Narraciones Anacrónicas de la Modernidad: Melodrama e Intermedialidad en América Latina*, ed. Hermann Herlinghaus, 21–59. Santiago: Editorial Cuarto Proprio.

Herzfeld, Michael. 1987. *Anthropology through the Looking Glass: Critical Ethnography in the Margins of Europe.* New York: Cambridge University Press.

Hirschkind, Charles. 2006. *The Ethical Soundscape: Cassette Sermons and Islamic Counterpublics.* New York: Columbia University Press.

Hobsbawm, Eric, and Terence Ranger, eds. 1983. *The Invention of Tradition.* Cambridge: Cambridge University Press.

Holt, Fabian. 2007. *Genre in Popular Music.* Chicago: University of Chicago Press.

Holton, DaCosta Kimberly. 2005. *Performing Folkore: Ranchos Folclóricos from Lisbon to Newark.* Bloomington: Indiana University Press.

———. 2006. "Fado Historiography: Old Myths and New Frontiers." *P: Journal of Portuguese Cultural Studies* 0 (winter): 1–17.

Hood, Mantle. 1960. "The Challenge of Bi-musicality." *Ethnomusicology* 4, no. 2: 55–59.

Howes, David. 2007. *Sensual Relations: Engaging the Senses in Culture and Social Theory.* Ann Arbor: University of Michigan Press.

Hughes-Freeland, Felicia. 2007. "Charisma and Celebrity in Indonesian Politics." *Anthropological Theory* 7, no. 2: 177–200.

Ivy, Marilyn. 1995. *Discourses of the Vanishing: Modernity, Phantasm, Japan.* Chicago: University of Chicago Press.

Jackson, John L. 2005. *Real Black: Adventures in Racial Sincerity.* Chicago: University of Chicago Press.

Jakobson, Roman. 1960. "Closing Statement: Linguistics and Poetics." In *Style in Language*, ed. Thomas A. Sebeok, 350–77. Cambridge: MIT Press.

Jerónimo, Rita, and Teresa Fradique. 1994. "The Fadista as Artist." In *Fado: Voices and Shadows*, ed. Joaquim Pais de Brito, 91–106. Lisbon: Electa.

Kirshenblatt-Gimblett, Barbara. 1998a. *Destination Culture: Tourism, Museums, and Heritage.* Berkeley: University of California Press.

———. 1998b. "The Ethnographic Burlesque." *Drama Review* 42, no. 2: 175–80.

Klein, Alexandra, and Vera Alves. 1994. "Fado Houses." In *Fado: Voices and Shadows*, ed. Joaquim Pais de Brito, 37–57. Lisbon: Electa.

Koestenbaum, Wayne. 1993. *The Queen's Throat: Opera, Homosexuality, and the Mystery of Desire.* New York: Poseidon.

Kondo, Dorinne K. 1990. *Crafting Selves: Power, Gender, and Discourses of Identity in a Japanese Workplace*. Chicago: University of Chicago Press.

Kundera, Milan. 1984. *The Unbearable Lightness of Being*, trans. Michael Henry Heim. New York: Harper and Row.

Leal, João. 2000a. *Etnografias Portuguesas (1870–1970): Cultura Popular e Identidade Nacional*. Lisbon: Publicações Dom Quixote.

———. 2000b. "The Making of Saudade: National Identity and Ethnic Psychology in Portugal." In *Roots and Rituals: The Construction of Ethnic Identities*, ed. Ton Dekker, John Helsloot, and Carla Wijers, 267–87. Amsterdam: Het Spinhuis.

———. 2008. "The Hidden Empire: Peasants, Nation Building, and the Empire in Portuguese Anthropology." In *Recasting Culture and Space in Iberian Contexts*, ed. Sharon R. Roseman and Shawn S. Parkhurst, 35–53. Albany: State University of New York Press.

Lee, Benjamin, and Edward LiPuma. 2002. "Cultures of Circulation: The Imaginations of Modernity." *Public Culture* 14, no. 1: 191–214.

Leppert, Richard. 1993. *The Sight of Sound: Music, Representation, and the History of the Body*. Berkeley: University of California Press.

List, George. 1963. "The Boundaries of Speech and Song." *Ethnomusicology* 7, no. 1: 1–16.

Llobera, Josep R. 1986. "Fieldwork in Southwestern Europe: Anthropological Panacea or Epistemological Straitjacket?" *Critique of Anthropology* 6:25–33.

Lord, Albert B. 2003 (1960). *The Singer of Tales*. Cambridge: University of Massachusetts Press.

Lourenço, Eduardo. 1994. *Nós e a Europa, ou as Duas Razões*. Lisbon: Imprensa Nacional-Casa da Moeda.

———. 2001. *Portugal Como Destino: Seguido de, Mitologia da Saudade*. São Paulo: Gradiva.

Lubkemann, Stephen C. 2005. "Unsettling the Metropole: Decolonization, Migration and National Identity in Postcolonial Portugal." In *Settler Colonialism in the Twentieth Century: Projects, Practices, Legacies*, ed. Caroline Elkins and Susan Pedersen, 257–70. New York: Taylor and Francis.

Luker, Morgan. 2009. "The Tango Machine: Musical Practice and Cultural Policy in Post-crisis Buenos Aires." PhD diss., Columbia University, New York.

Mahmood, Saba. 2005. *Politics of Piety: The Islamic Revival and the Feminist Subject*. Princeton: Princeton University Press.

Marshall, P. David. 2006a. "Introduction." In *The Celebrity Culture Reader*, ed. P. David Marshall, 1–16. New York: Routledge.

———. 2006b. "The Meanings of Popular Music Celebrity: The Construction of Distinctive Authenticity." In *The Celebrity Culture Reader*, ed. P. David Marshall, 196–222. New York: Routledge.

Martins, Moisés de Lemos. 1986. "Uma Solidão Necessária à Ordem Salazarista: A Família Como Terapêutica Nacional." *Cadernos de Ciências Sociais* 4 (April): 77–83.

Massumi, Brian. 2002. *Parables for the Virtual: Movement, Affect, Sensation*. Durham: Duke University Press.

Matory, James Lorand. 2005. *Black Atlantic Religion: Tradition, Transnationalism, and Matriarchy in the Afro-Brazilian Candomblé*. Princeton: Princeton University Press.

McClary, Susan. 1991. *Feminine Endings: Music, Gender and Sexuality*. Minneapolis: University of Minnesota Press.

McClintock, Anne. 1993. "Family Feuds: Gender, Nationalism and the Family." *Feminist Review* 44:61–80.

———. 1995. *Imperial Leather: Race, Gender, and Sexuality in the Colonial Conquest*. New York: Routledge.

Meintjes, Louise. 2003. *Sound of Africa! Making Music Zulu in a South African Studio*. Durham: Duke University Press.

Melo, Daniel. 2001. *Salazarismo e Cultura Popular (1933–1958)*. Lisbon: Imprensa de Ciências Sociais.

Moita, Luiz. 1936. *O Fado: Canção de Vencidos: Oito Palestras na Emissora Nacional*. Lisbon: Empresa do Anuário Comercial.

Monson, Ingrid. 1996. *Saying Something: Jazz Improvisation and Interaction*. Chicago: University of Chicago Press.

Nery, Rui Vieira. 2004. *Para uma História do Fado*. Lisbon: Público-Comunicação Social and Corda Seca, Edições de Arte.

———. 2009. *Pensar Amália*. Lisbon: Tugaland.

Nora, Pierre. 1989. "Between Memory and History: *Les Lieux de Mémoire*." *Representations* 26 (spring): 7–25.

Ochoa-Gautier, Ana Maria. 2006. "Sonic Transculturation, Epistemologies of Purification, and the Aural Public Sphere in Latin America." *Social Identities* 12, no. 6: 803–25.

Ortner, Sherry B. 1996. *Making Gender: The Politics and Erotics of Culture*. Boston: Beacon.

Osório, António. 1974. *A Mitologia Fadista*. Lisbon: Livros Horizonte.

Osório, José Manuel. 2005. *Todos os Fados*. Lisbon: Visão.

Osório, José Manuel, and Luís Osório. 2003. *Quanto Tempo: Uma Criança No Olhar*. Lisbon: Oficina do Livro.

Pais, José Machado. 1985. *A Prostituição e a Lisboa Boémia do Século XIX aos Inícios do Século XX*. Lisbon: Editorial Querco.

Paredez, Deborah. 2009. *Selenidad: Selena, Latinos, and the Performance of Memory*. Durham: Duke University Press.

Parker, Andrew, Mary Russo, Doris Sommer, and Patricia Yaeger. 1992. "Introduction." In *Nationalisms and Sexualities*, ed. Andrew Parker, Mary Russo, Doris Sommer, and Patricia Yaeger, 1–18. New York: Routledge.

Peixoto, Rocha. 1997 (1897). "O Cruel e Triste Fado." *Etnográfica* 1, no. 2: 331–36.

Perlman, Marc. 2004. *Unplayed Melodies: Javanese Gamelan and the Genesis of Music Theory*. Berkeley: University of California Press.

Pimentel, Alberto. 1989 (1904). *A Triste Cançao do Sul: Subsídios para a História do Fado*. Lisbon: Publicações Dom Quixote.

Pimentel, Irene Flunser. 2007. *A História da PIDE*. Lisbon: Círculo de Leitores.

———. 2010. "The PIDE/DGS Political Police in the Portuguese *Estado Novo*: History and Memory." In *Conflict, Memory Transfers and the Reshaping of Europe*, ed. Helena Gonçalves da Silva, Adriana Alves de Paula Martins, Filomena Viana Guarda, and José Miguel Sardica, 155–75. Newcastle upon Tyne: Cambridge Scholars.

Porcello, Thomas, Louise Meintjes, Ana Maria Ochoa, and David W. Samuels. 2010. "The Reorganization of the Sensory World." *Annual Review of Anthropology* 39:51–66.

Povinelli, Elizabeth A. 2006. *The Empire of Love: Toward a Theory of Intimacy, Genealogy, and Carnality*. Durham: Duke University Press.

Radano, Ronald. 2003. "Magical Writing: The Iconic Wonders of the Slave Spiritual." In *Lying Up a Nation: Race and Black Music*, 164–229. Chicago: University of Chicago Press.

Ramaswamy, Sumathi. 2010. *The Goddess and the Nation: Mapping Mother India*. Durham: Duke University Press.

Ribeiro, Orlando. 1967 (1945). *Portugal, o Mediterrâneo e o Atlântico*. Lisbon: Livraria Sá da Costa Editora.

Roach, Joseph R. 1996. *Cities of the Dead: Circum-Atlantic Performance*. New York: Columbia University Press.

———. 2007. *It*. Ann Arbor: University of Michigan Press.

Rofel, Lisa. 2007. *Desiring China: Experiments in Neoliberalism, Sexuality, and Public Culture*. Durham: Duke University Press.

Rojek, Chris. 2001. *Celebrity*. London: Reaktion.

Rosas, Fernando, ed. 1992. *Portugal e o Estado Novo (1930–1960)*, vol. 12. Lisbon: Editorial Presença.

Rosenberg, Ruth. 2004. "A Voice Like Thunder: Corsican Women's Lament as Cultural Work." *Current Musicology* 78:31–51.

Samuels, David W. 1999. "The Whole and the Sum of the Parts, or, How Cookie and the Cupcakes Told the Story of Apache History in San Carlos." *Journal of American Folklore* 112, no. 445: 464–74.

———. 2004. *Putting a Song on Top of It: Expression and Identity on the San Carlos Apache Reservation*. Tucson: University of Arizona Press.

Samuels, David W., Louise Meintjes, Ana Maria Ochoa, and Thomas Porcello. 2010. "Soundscapes: Toward a Sounded Anthropology." *Annual Review of Anthropology* 39:329–45.

Santos, Boaventura de Sousa. 2012. *Portugal: Ensaio Contra a Autoflagelação*. Coimbra: Almedina.

Santos, José Carlos Ary dos. 1993 (1989). *As Palavras das Cantigas*. Lisbon: Editorial Avante!

Santos, Vítor Pavão dos. 2005 (1987). *Amália—Uma Biografia*. Lisbon: Editorial Presença.

Sardinha, José Alberto. 2010. *A Origem do Fado*. Vila Verde: Tradisom.

Savigliano, Marta. 1995. *Tango and the Political Economy of Passion*. Boulder: Westview.

Schafer, R. Murray. 1977. *The Tuning of the World*. New York: Alfred A. Knopf.

Seabra, Daniel. 1999. "Mágico Porto, Vence Por Nós." Master's thesis, University of Minho.

Sedgwick, Eve Kosofsky. 1990. *Epistemology of the Closet*. Berkeley: University of California Press.

———. 2003. *Touching Feeling: Affect, Pedagogy, Performativity*. Durham: Duke University Press.

Seremetakis, C. Nadia. 1991. *The Last Word: Women, Death, and Divination in Inner Mani*. Chicago: University of Chicago Press.

———. 1996. *The Senses Still: Perception and Memory as Material Culture in Modernity*. Chicago: University of Chicago Press.

Shannon, Jonathan H. 2003. "Emotion, Performance and Temporality in Arab Music: Reflections on Tarab." *Cultural Anthropology* 18, no. 1: 72–99.

Sobral, José Manuel. 2008. "Race and Space in Interpretations of Portugal: The North–South Division and Representations of Portuguese National Identity in the Nineteenth and Twentieth Centuries." In *Recasting Culture and Space in Iberian Contexts*, ed. Sharon R. Roseman and Shawn S. Parkhurst, 205–24. Albany: State University of New York Press.

Sousa e Costa, Júlio de. 1936. *Severa*. Lisbon: Livraria Bertrand.

Stacey, Jackie. 1994. *Star Gazing: Hollywood Cinema and Female Spectatorship*. London: Routledge.

Sterne, Jonathan. 2003. *The Audible Past: Cultural Origins of Sound Reproduction*. Durham: Duke University Press.

Stewart, Kathleen. 1996. *A Space on the Side of the Road: Cultural Poetics in an "Other" America*. Princeton: Princeton University Press.

———. 2007. *Ordinary Affects*. Durham: Duke University Press.

Stewart, Susan. 2003. *On Longing: Narratives of the Miniature, the Gigantic, the Souvenir, the Collection*. Durham: Duke University Press.

Stokes, Martin. 2004. "Music and the Global Order." *Annual Review of Anthropology* 33:47–72.

———. 2010. *The Republic of Love: Cultural Intimacy in Turkish Popular Music*. Chicago: University of Chicago Press.

Stoler, Ann Laura. 1995. *Race and the Education of Desire: Foucault's History of Sexuality and the Colonial Order of Things*. Durham: Duke University Press.

Stoller, Paul. 1989. *The Taste of Ethnographic Things: The Senses in Anthropology*. Philadelphia: University of Pennsylvania Press.

Straight, Bilinda. 2007. *Miracles and Extraordinary Experience in Northern Kenya*. Philadelphia: University of Pennsylvania Press.

Sturken, Marita. 2007. *Tourists of History: Memory, Kitsch, and Consumerism from Oklahoma City to Ground Zero*. Durham: Duke University Press.

Taussig, Michael. 1993. *Mimesis and Alterity: A Particular History of the Senses*. New York: Routledge.

———. 1999. *Defacement: Public Secrecy and the Labor of the Negative*. Stanford, Calif.: Stanford University Press.

Taylor, Charles. 1989. *Sources of the Self.* Cambridge: Harvard University Press.

Taylor, Diana. 2003. *The Archive and the Repertoire.* Durham: Duke University Press.

Thompson, Emily Ann. 2002. *The Soundscape of Modernity: Architectural Acoustics and the Culture of Listening in America, 1900–1933.* Cambridge: MIT Press.

Tinhorão, José Ramos. 1994. *Fado, Dança do Brasil, Cantar de Lisboa: O Fim de um Mito.* Lisbon: Caminho (da Música).

Tolbert, Elizabeth. 1995. "The Voice of Lament: Female Vocality and Performative Efficacy in the Finnish-Karelian Itkuvirsi." In *Embodied Voices: Representing Female Vocality in Western Culture*, ed. Leslie C. Dunn and Nancy A. Jones, 179–96. Cambridge: Cambridge University Press.

Trouillot, Michel-Rolph. 1995. *Silencing the Past: Power and the Production of History.* Boston: Beacon.

Tsing, Anna Lowenhaupt. 1993. *In the Realm of the Diamond Queen.* Princeton: Princeton University Press.

———. 2005. *Friction: An Ethnography of Global Connection.* Princeton: Princeton University Press.

Turino, Thomas. 1999. "Signs of Imagination, Identity, and Experience: A Peircian Semiotic Theory for Music." *Ethnomusicology* 43, no. 2: 221–55.

Tuzin, Donald F. 1997. *The Cassowary's Revenge: The Life and Death of Masculinity in a New Guinea Society.* Chicago: University of Chicago Press.

Urban, Greg. 1991. *A Discourse-Centered Approach to Culture.* Austin: University of Texas Press.

———. 2001. *Metaculture: How Culture Moves through the World.* Minneapolis: University of Minnesota Press.

Vakil, AbdoolKarim. 2003. "The Crusader Heritage: Portugal and Islam from Colonial to Post-colonial Identities." In *Rethinking Heritage: Cultures and Politics in Europe*, ed. Robert S. Peckham, 29–44. London: I. B. Tauris.

Valverde, Paulo. 1999. "O Fado é o Coração: O Corpo, As Emoções e a Performance no Fado." *Etnográfica* 3, no. 1: 5–20.

Vernon, Paul. 1998. *A History of the Portuguese Fado.* Sydney: Ashgate.

Vianna, Hermano. 1999. *The Mystery of Samba.* Chapel Hill: University of North Carolina Press.

Wallerstein, Immanuel Maurice. 1974. *The Modern World-System.* New York: Academic Press.

Warner, Michael. 2002. *Publics and Counterpublics.* New York: Zone Books.

Weidman, Amanda J. 2006. *Singing the Classical, Voicing the Modern: The Postcolonial Politics of Music in South India.* Durham: Duke University Press.

Wilce, James MacLynn. 2009. *Crying Shame: Metaculture, Modernity, and the Exaggerated Death of Lament.* Malden, Mass.: Oxford: Wiley-Blackwell.

Williams, Raymond. 1973. *The Country and the City.* London: Chatto and Windus.

——. 1977. *Marxism and Literature*. Oxford: Oxford University Press.

Yano, Christine Reiko. 2002. *Tears of Longing: Nostalgia and the Nation in Japanese Popular Song*. Cambridge: Harvard University Press.

Yúdice, George. 2003. *The Expediency of Culture: Uses of Culture in the Global Era*. Durham: Duke University Press.

Interviews (Conducted by the Author)

Anonymous. Lisbon, December 13, 2002. Digital audio tape.

Candeias, Jaime Nunes. Lisbon, November 6, 2002. Digital audio tape.

Carmo, Carlos do. Lisbon, November 12, 2002. Digital audio tape.

Costa, Ricardo. Lisbon, January 29, 2003. Digital audio tape.

Dias, Ivone. Lisbon, February 27, 2003. Digital audio tape.

Fernandes, Fátima. Lisbon, November 26, 2002. Digital audio tape.

Ferreira, David. Lisbon, June 12, 2002. Digital audio tape.

Forte, Fernando. Lisbon, June 13, 2002. Digital audio tape.

Guerra, Pedro. Lisbon, April 1, 2003. Digital audio tape.

Jesus, Sebastião de. Lisbon, March 25, 2003. Digital audio tape.

Maria, Fernanda. Lisbon, October 30, 2002. Digital audio tape.

Melo, Maria José. Lisbon, January 17, 2003. Digital audio tape.

Osório, José Manuel. Lisbon, March 26, 2003. Digital audio tape.

Proença, Fernanda. Lisbon, January 27, 2002. Digital audio tape.

Ribeiro, Hugo. Lisbon, October 25, 2002. Digital audio tape.

Rocha, António. Lisbon, June 5, 2002. Digital audio tape.

Rocha, José Fontes. Lisbon, May 26, 2003. Digital audio tape.

"Rosa" (pseudonym). Lisbon, May 29, 2002. Digital audio tape.

Salgueiro, Gonçalo. Lisbon, September 23, 2002. Digital audio tape.

Sousa, Olga Rosa de. Lisbon, January 25, 2010. Digital.

Tomé, Manuel Calado and Edite B. de Medeiros Tomé. Póvoa, Portugal, May 30, 2003. Digital audio tape.

Fado Lessons and Rehearsals (Recorded by the Author)

Associação Cultural o Fado. Lisbon, September 12, 2002.

——. Lisbon, May 22, 2003.

Rocha, António. Museu do Fado, Lisbon, April 19, 2002.

——. Museu do Fado, Lisbon, May 10, 2002.

Noncommercial Recordings of Live Performances

Osório, José Manuel. "Fado da Meia Laranja." Tasca do Careca, Lisbon, May 3, 2003. Recorded by the author.

——. "Fado da Meia Laranja." Duke University, Durham, N.C., January 10, 2004. Recorded by Thom Limbert.

Liner Notes and Commercial Recordings (Compact Disc)

Biografia do Fado. 1994. EMI-Valentim de Carvalho Música Lda., Portugal.

Fernandes, Nuno Nazareth. 2001. "Liner Notes." On Mariza, *Fado em Mim.* WC 43028. Times Square Records, New York, and World Connection, Haarlem, the Netherlands.

Limón, Javier. 2010. *Mujeres de Agua.* Universal Music, Spain.

Mariza. 2001. *Fado em Mim.* WC 43028. Times Square Records, New York, and World Connection, Haarlem, the Netherlands.

———. 2003. *Fado Curvo.* WC 9033. Times Square Records, New York, and World Connection, Haarlem, the Netherlands.

———. 2008. *Terra.* WC 29423. EMI Music, Portugal, and World Connection, Haarlem, the Netherlands.

Mourinha, Jorge. 2002. "Liner Notes." On Amália Rodrigues, *O Disco do Busto/For Your Delight/As Óperas,* 1962. 7243 5 80376 2 3. EMI-Valentim de Carvalho Música Lda., Lisbon.

Osório, José Manuel. 2004. "Fado da Meia Laranja." On *O Fado do Público (Fado, a Canção de Lisboa),* vol. 19, CSCD 19. Corda Seca, Edições de Arte, Público, Comunicação Social Lisbon.

Porfírio, José. 1994. "Fado Vitória." On *Arquivos do Fado 1: Fado de Lisboa (1928–1936).* Tradisom, Macau.

Rodrigues, Amália. 1989 (1962). "Povo Que Lavas no Rio." On *Busto.* 792671 2. EMI-Valentim de Carvalho Música Lda., Portugal.

———. 2000 (1985). *O Melhor de Amália, Volume II: Tudo Isto é Fado.* EMI-Valentim de Carvalho Música Lda., Portugal.

Santos, Argentina. 2003. "Liner Notes." On *Argentina Santos.* CNM100CD. Companhia Nacional de Música, Lisbon.

Tasca do Chico. 2002. *Ó Vadio: Fado na Tasca do Chico.* O Circo a Vapor, Lisbon.

Wenders, Wim. 1995. "Liner Notes." On Madredeus, *Ainda.* 7243 8 32636 2 2. EMI-Valentim de Carvalho Música Lda., Portugal, and Metro Blue Records, Hollywood, Calif.

Note: page numbers in *italics* refer to illustrations.

breathing in fado vs. Western art music, 252n44

Briggs, Charles, 156, 243n6

Brito, Frederico de, 254, 278n52

Brito, Joaquim Pais de, 67, 179, 277n41

Buck-Morss, Susan, 260n7

Butler, Judith, 275n25, 278n51, 279n56

Byas, Don, 144

Caetano, Marcelo, 20, 258n36

Café Luso, Bairro Alto, 114, 116–17

Callas, Maria, 64, 278n55, 279n59

Câmara, Vicente da, 277n41

Camões, Luís Vaz de, 180, 186, 253n58, 270n11, 273n1

camp, 217–18

Campos, Joaquim, 145, 153–54, 231, 237

Candeias, Jaime, 32, 34, 221–22, 248n8. *See also* Tasca do Jaime

Candeias, Laura, 32, 33, 36, 37

"Cantarei Até Que a Voz Me Doa" (I Will Sing until My Voice Hurts), 65, 178, 253n56

"Caravela da Saudade" (Caravel of Saudade), 70, 254

Carmo, Carlos do, 108

carteira profissional (professional card), 251n35

cartographies, affective. *See* place making and scale, poetics and politics of

Carvalho, Pinto de, 12, 246n21

Carvalho, Ruben de, 247n29

"Casa da Mariquinhas" (The Brothel), 159, 200, 270n2, 276n31

casa do povo, 128

Casal Ventoso, 134–35

"Casa Portugesa, Uma" (A Portuguese Home), 114, 262n20

casas de fado (fado houses): décor in, 116; during and after dictatorship, 98–100; effects of censorship and tourism on lyrics in, 97; feedback in, 250n25; folkloric dance in, 263n25. *See also* professional fado (*fado profissional*)

casas típicas, 18, 96, 117, 247n34

Castelo, Cláudia, 255n5, 255n8

Castelo-Branco, Salwa El-Shawan, 17, 247n26, 267nn3–4, 269n20

Catholicism, 176, 255nn8–9

celebrity: Amália and, 187, 193, 194, 197–98, 224; theorization of, 195–97, 275n24

censorship: *casas de fado* and, 100; Estado Novo and, 21–22; lyrics, impact on, 96; nuance and, 101; *saudade* and, 18

Chambers, Ross, 196, 276n28

"Cheira a Lisboa" (Aroma [Smell] of Lisbon), 133, 265n42

children: Carnival and, 173; fado age-appropriateness and, 214; at fado association, 58, 59–60, 168

circulation: Amália biography and, 194; of emotion, 8–9; gender and international translation, 177–78; genre and stickiness of fado and, 5; of historical narratives, 9; Lee and LiPuma on, 244n7; of lyrics, 15; origin discourses and, 13; *saudade* and, 257n20; world music and, 126–27; of writing on Lisbon fado, 246n24

circum-Atlantic world, 13, 74–80, 246n25

class: Amália and, 187, 206, 253n58; *casas de fado* and, 99; fado shift along lines of, 277n41; lyrics of contrast and, 97

coaching. *See* learning, coaching, and pedagogies

"Coimbra" (fado), 273n9

Coimbra fado (*fado de Coimbra*), 245n20, 270n5

Coimbra guitarras, 246n26

colonialism and empire: the everyday colonial, 71; "imperial mysticism," 255n8; Lusotropicalism, 73–74, 76–80; mimesis and, 212; nostalgia and, 125; remainders of empire in fado stories, 72–74; Vasco da Gama and, 89. *See also* Discoveries, the

Colvin, Michael, 258n33

communism, 21, 94, 130, 133

Communist Party, Portuguese (PCP), 20, 93, 95, 103, 188, 266n44, 274n14

"composition," complication of, 146, 153–54

Connerton, Paul, 245n17

consumption, 187, 206, 275n24

contamination, symbolic, 168–69

contrast, fados of, 96–97

core-periphery model, 107, 127, 129, 264n31. *See also* European North–South dialectics

European North–South dialectics: Fernandez on, 260n3; financial crisis and, 227–28; narratives of, 124–26; within Portugal, 128–29; Portugal as Europe's "Africa," 80–81; sexual Orientalism, 271n18; "zone of repudiation" and core-periphery model, 107

European Union, 80, 227, 259n49, 264n31

evaluation, aesthetic, 20, 47–49, 51, 56. *See also* learning, coaching, and pedagogies

excess: Amália and, 185, 202–7, 211–14, 212–13; Lisbon and, 138; origin discourses and, 13; place and, 108; smallness and, 131; of visibility, in Alfama, 120–22; world music and, 127

exclamations, vocal, 39–41

exclusion, social, 172–76

exteriority and interiority, 28, 113, 196

extraordinary, the, 202, 277n36

eyes, closing of: by fadistas, 29, 36, 37, 43, 85, 216, 217; by listeners, 38, 39, 43. *See also* weeping

"fadista," meaning of, 7, 38

fadistas. *See specific persons and topics, such as* soulfulness

fado amador. See amateur fado

"Fado Amália," 211, 278n49

Fado Bailado, 275n22

fado canção (fado song): coaching and subgenre of, 56–57; continuum with *fado tradicional*, 17; as genre category, 16–17; musicalness of, 67; Osório's "fado with refrain" vs. "fado with its own music," 247n31; place-name fado and, 110; refrains, joining in, 39

fado castiço ("authentic" fado), 247n27, 271n17. See also *fado tradicional*

Fado Corrido, 16, 267n3

"Fado da Meia Laranja" (Fado of Meia Laranja): Casal Ventoso neighborhood and, 134–35; Osório's performances of, 134–36, 142–43, 144, 266n47; text and translation, 135–36; transcription, and Osório's melodic styling in, 147–53, 231–41

fado de Coimbra, 245n20, 270n5

fado de Lisboa, 245n20, 246n24

Fado Esmeraldinha, 254

fado fado ("true" fado), 18, 65, 67. See also *fado tradicional* (traditional fado)

Fado: História D'Uma Cantadeira (Fado: The Story of a Singer) (film), 274n11, 278n48

fado houses. See *casas de fado*

Fado Menor, 16, 53, 134, 267n3

Fado Menor do Porto, 252n45, 267n8

Fado Mouraria, 16, 267n3

fado profissional. See professional fado

Fados (film), 263n26

fados de contraste (fados of contrast), 96–97

fados identitários (identitarian fados), 261n10

fado tradicional (traditional fado): continuum with *fado canção*, 17; as genre category, 15–16; lyrics linked to, 143; names of, 16; repertoire, 247n29; syncretic stacking in, 224–25. See also Fado Vitória; styling (*estilar*)

fado vadio (vagrant or homeless fado), 248nn6–7. *See also* amateur fado (*fado amador*)

Fado Vitória, 142–45, 152–54, 231, 237. *See also* "Fado da Meia Laranja"

Fado: Voices and Shadows (Museu Nacional de Etnologia), 276n31

fan discourses on Amália, 198–207

fazer um bonito (to make a beauty), 40

Fé, Maria da, 253n56

feedback in fado venues, 45–47

feeling and emotion: affective musical subjectivity, 8–9; Amália and, 193; exclamations and, 39–40; feeling, defined, 9; history rendered as, 9; loneliness and melancholy, 164–65; music as "universal language" and, 127; origin stories, emplaced feeling in, 83–84; political economy of passion, 129; *saudade* as originary trope for feeling, 82–85; sound and hearing linked to, 6; stickiness and circulation of emotion, 8–9; "structures of feeling," 8, 43; tear-based emotional universalism, 118–19. *See also* affect; public feeling; *saudade*

Feira Popular, Lisbon, 210

Feld, Steven, 108, 244n10, 261n8

"female complaint," 178, 185, 197, 276n29

Fernandes, A. J. de Castro, 264n37
Fernandes, Fátima, 34, 37, 40, 46, 63, 94
Fernandez, James, 260n3
Ferrão, Raúl, 260, 269, 270n9, 273n9
Ferreira, Ana Paula, 164, 256n11,
  270nn11–12
Ferreira, Bibi, 200
Ferreira, David, 209–10
Ferreira, Reinaldo, 262n20
Ferro, António, 188, 190, 274n18
Fikes, Kesha, 255n10, 256n11
financial crisis in Portugal (2011), 227–28
Flatley, Jonathan, 254n1, 268n14
flirtation, 170–71
"Foi Deus" (It Was God), 200, 215–16,
  276n31, 278n54
"Foi na Travessa da Palha" (It Was on Palha
  Lane), 278n52
"folk" culture, 75, 116–17, 255n4
folkloric dance, 114, 263n25
Fonseca, Artur, 262n20
foreignness: accents, 55–56; *fado canção* vs.
  fado fado and, 67; "foreign voice" and
  soulfulness, 61–62; learning fado and,
  48, 51; tears of outsiders, 118. *See also*
  colonialism and empire; tourism
form: affective listening and, 156–57;
  "Alfama" and, 134; emotional expression
  in confines of, 42; of *fado canção*, 16–17;
  of Fado Vitória, 143–44; feeling and,
  8–9; genre and, 5, 14; melodic figurations,
  flexible reuse of, 155; melodic fixity
  continuum and musical base, 145;
  memory and, 17–18; ownership vs.
  improvisation and, 145–46; risk taking
  and, 146; *saudade* and, 89–90; simplicity
  argument, vs. ontological complexity,
  156; soulfulness and, 44, 62; transcription
  and, 148; variations within, 141. *See also*
  genre
Forte, Fernando, 198, 200–206, 217, 222
Freyre, Gilberto, 76–77, 255n5, 256n12
Fundação Amália Rodrigues, 273n4

Galhardo, José, 269, 270n9, 273n9, 278n49
Gama, Vasco da, 88–89, 273n1
garganta (throat), 66–67
garganta de prata (throat of silver), 66, 207

gay fandom, 278n55. *See also* drag performances
gay men, 271n23
gender: aloneness and, 164–67, 170; Amália
  and tropes of, 192–93, 224; Coimbra
  fado and, 270n5; drag performance and,
  217–18; Estado Novo and, 164, 176, 271n25;
  fado's worlds and, 158–59; "female
  complaint," 178, 185, 197, 276n29; imperial
  unknown, gendering of, 255n7; labors of
  the feminine in fado, 176–78; Lisbon as
  feminine, 111; Maria Severa mythos and,
  162–64; Mariza's pan-Mediterranean
  recording project, 272n29; melodrama
  and, 276n29; practice and representations, gendered and sexualized, 159–62;
  stigma and fadista biographies, 165–67;
  tasca bohemian imaginary and socialities
  of, 169–73; *tristezas* (sadnesses),
  heteronormativity, and, 173–76
genre: accrued affect and memory and, 17–18;
  affect and, 137–38; affective labor and, 8;
  definitional contours, 14–15; discourse
  on, 13–14; dynamic model of, 5–6; *fado
  tradicional* vs. *fado canção*, 15–16; history,
  stories, and, 72; ideological force through
  habits of, 176; international circulation
  and, 127; Lusotropicalism and, 78–79;
  national heritage, collectivity, and, 68;
  opera vs. fado as, 64–65; place and, 106–7,
  108; reflexivity and critique in, 131–34
geographies. *See* place making and scale,
  poetics and politics of
Gil, José, 101–2, 130–31, 264n39
Gonçalves, Carlos, 249n11, 279n57
Goodrich, Matthew, 268n15
Gordo, José Luis, 134, 144, 231, 237, 253n56,
  266n47
gossip, 172–73
Graça neighborhood. *See* Tasca do Jaime
Grande Noite do Fado (Grand Night of
  Fado) competition, 59, 252n48
"Grito" (Scream), 219, 279n57
gritos (screams), 208–9, 278n46
Grupo Desportivo da Mouraria, 262n22
Grupo Excursionista Vai Tu, 250n17
Guerra, Pedro, 98
Guerreiro, Maria da Dores, 96–97, 101

national identity and nationalism, Portuguese: Amália and, 179, 188; celebrity and, 195; Dias on Portuguese "personality," 75–76; the Discoveries and, 73, 74, 254n3; divas, national, 187, 279n59; identity-making narratives, circum-Atlantic, 74–80; lusosex construct and nation-sex, 164; re-Portugalization, 259n42. *See also* patrimony and national heritage; Portugueseness

National Pantheon, 180–82, 222–23

national song, fado as resistance vs., 90–95

nation–feminine complex, 218

nation-sex, 164, 270nn11–12

naturalness: Amália and, 204, 209–10; divas and, 279n59; opera vs. fado and, 65; pronunciation and, 55; timbre and, 55, 64; unlearned soulfulness and, 67

neighborhood associations: Grande Noite do Fado and, 252n48; Grupo Desportivo da Mouraria, 262n22; Grupo Excursionista Vai Tu, 250n17; *marchas populares* and, 262n16; social protest and, 101; as venue, 19. *See also* Marvila Associação Cultural o Fado (ACOF)

neighborhoods. *See* Alfama; Lisbon; Mouraria; place making and scale, poetics and politics of

Nery, Rui Vieira, 83–84, 95–96, 256n16, 257n19, 259nn41–42

networks and amateur vs. professional fado, 19, 20

Noronha, Maria Teresa de, 32, 208, 221, 253n55, 269, 277n41

North–South dialectics. *See* European North–South dialectics

notation, musical: fado as genre and, 14–15; Fado Vitória and, 145; inability to read, 249n10; representational elusiveness of fado, 147; transcription, 148, 268n15

O Jaime. *See* Tasca do Jaime

Oliveira, César, 265n42

Oliveira, Gabriel de, 278n52

Onishi, Yoshiaki, 268n15

opera, 64–65

opposition, 196, 276n28. *See also* Estado Novo (New State)

Orientalism, sexual, 271n18

Orientalisms, 128

origin narratives: academic accounts, 3, 12–13; Amália Rodrigues on Fado Menor as "mother and father of fado," 16; discourses and polemic around, 4, 12–13; empire's remainders in, 72–73; emplaced feeling in, 83–84; examples of, 1; Lisbon as port city in, 106; prostitution, 163, 270n10; purity, tropes of, 79–80

Ortner, Sherry, 244n9

Osório, José Manuel: on *casas de fado* as schools, 30; "Fado da Meia Laranja," 134–36, 142–43, 147–53, 231–41; Fado Vitória and, 144; on "fado with refrain" vs. "fado with its own music," 247n31; on hearing silences, 139; life of, 265n44; as musical risk taker, 146, 268n13; on number of traditional fados, 15–16; stamping and clapping by, 150, 269n18

Oulman, Alain, 133–34, 186, 191, 253n58, 265n41

outsider status and *puta* label, 172–73

ownership, intellectual, 14–15, 146

padrinhos (godfathers) of fado, 45–46, 250n28

Parreirinha de Alfama, 167

participant observation, 44

Pascoaes, Teixeira de, 256n14

patrimony and national heritage: fado as genre as patrimony and international validation, 229; financial crisis, UNESCO campaign, and, 228–29; ordering of history and, 103; soul and, 68. *See also* histories; national identity and nationalism, Portuguese

pedagogies. *See* learning, coaching, and pedagogies

Peixoto, Rocha, 95

performance: intertextuality and, 7; lyrics, substitution and variation in, 15; number of consecutive fados, customary, 37–38; Rocha on history of, 52–53; silence, norm of, 38–41; soul and styling linked to variation in, 10; weeping, practices of, 41–43

periphery and core, 107, 127, 129, 264n31. *See also* European North–South dialectics

"Que Deus Me Perdoe" (May God Forgive Me), 36, 49, 57, 211, 221, 251n36

race: colonialist ideology of, 77; Lusotropicalism, 73–74, 76–80, 255nn5–6, 255n11; miscegenation and racial tolerance narratives, 73, 76–77; *saudade* and, 77–78
radio: BBC Radio 3, 126, 127, 264n35; role of, 252n42
raízes do fado ("roots of fado"), 16
recording technology: Amália, timbral poetics, and sound engineering, 207–10; destroyed recordings, narratives of, 94; difference, neutralization of, 252n43; homogeneity in melody stying and, 146; learning and, 53–54; nasality in early recordings, 251n40; sound archive purchase from British collector, 259n49; as symbolic "man," 271n20
reflexivity: Chambers on, 196; critique rendered possible by, 131–34; self-reflexivity, 109, 110
refrains, joining in, 39, 40–41
rehearsals (*ensaios*), 50, 59
release, stylized, 42
repetition of fados, norms against, 38
resistance, 91, 101. *See also* Estado Novo (New State)
revista theater, 262n13
Ribeiro, Artur, 261n11
Ribeiro, Hugo, 207–9
Ribeiro, Orlando, 255n5, 264n36
risk taking, musical, 146, 268n13
Roach, Joseph, 13, 195, 213
Rocha, António, 49–57, 64, 252n44, 253n54
Rocha, José Fontes, 42, 139, 207, 253n56
Rodrigues, Álvaro, 34, 111, 170, 220, 262n17
Rodrigues, Amália: affective labor and gendered naiveté of, 192–93; "Amália: Coração Independente" (Amália: Independent Heart) (Museu Berardo), 274n11; Amaliano fan discourses, 198–207; Amália Rodrigues (mural) (MrDheo), *plate 10*; Beira Baixa influence on, 193, 257n16, 275n20; biography and life-story representations, 185–88, 194; celebrity and, 187, 193, 194, 195–98, 224; on cinema, 276n29; death, funeral, and

burial sites of, 179–81, 222, *plate 8*; dislike of, 95; drag performances and, 204, 215–18; on *escala espanhola*, 267n8; Estado Novo and, 22, 187–88; "Estranha Forma de Vida," 275n22; excess and, 202–7, 211–14; fadista, diva, and woman categories overlapping in imaginary of, 214; *fado canção*, impact on, 16–17; on Fado Menor as "mother and father of fado," 16; in film, 274n9, 274n11; gendered emulation of, 161, 176; home turned museum, 181, 273n4; identification with, 203–4; international career of, 126, 186; learning from recordings of, 52, 54–55, 214; as lyricist, 249n11; *O Melhor de Amália II* (The Best of Amália II), 200; memorialization and commemoration of, 83–84, 181–85, *182*, *184*, 206–7, *207*, *208*, 222–23, 276n31, *plate 10*; multiplicity and, 205; musicals about, 95, 183, 200, 206, 274n11, 277n32; on national soul, 179; non-Portuguese genres and, 186, 251n33; Oulman collaborations, 134, 186, 253n58; performative mimesis and, 210–14, 223–24; political positionings of, 188, 189–92; "Povo Que Lavas no Rio," 142, 143, 144, 152–53; repertoire of, 49, 114, 133, 256n15; "Rua Amália," *plate 9*; Santos's biography/autobiography, 188–94; style of, as now classic, 54–55; Tasca do Jaime and, 33, 218–22; "throat of silver" of, 66; timbral poetics, sound engineering, and, 207–10; *voltinhas* and, 81, 193, 219, 275n20
Rodrigues, Celeste, 98
Rofel, Lisa, 196
Rojek, Chris, 275n24
Roman Catholic Church, 176, 255nn8–9
"Rosa Enjeitada" (Abandoned Rose), 158, 221, 269
"Rua Amália," *plate 9*
rubato at heightened moments, 40
rural, ideology of the, 113

sadness. See *saudade*; *tristezas* (sadnesses)
Salazar, António de Oliveira: dates of rule, 20; downplayed, 92–93; as hating fado, 91, 94, 95. *See also* Estado Novo (New State)
Samuels, David W., 244n11

universalism, 118–19, 206
Urban, Greg, 250n21
urban planning, fado lyrics critiquing, 258n33
urban renovation, 122, 263n22

Vakil, AbdoolKarim, 82, 255n9, 256n14
Vale, Amadeu do, 256n15
Valério, Frederico, 251n36, 256n15, 278n49
Vasco da Gama bridge and mall, 88–89
venues for fado: *casas de fado*, 97, 98–100, 116, 250n25, 263n25; *casas típicas*, 18, 96, 117, 247n34; elite, 20, 40–41, 66; explosion of, in Alfama, 123, *123, plate 5*; historicity of, 98–100; professional vs. amateur, 19–20; types of, 1–2, 18–19. *See also* Tasca do Jaime
Vianna, Hermano, 256n12
"Vielas de Alfama" (Alleys of Alfama), 109, 113, 261n11
"Vielas" (Alleyways) exhibit, Museu do Fado (R. Pimentel), 119, 130, *plate 4*
village (*aldeia*), 113, 124, 125
Villar, Leonel, 257n24
viola baixo (bass acoustic guitar), 140
violas and styling, 140
vocal celebrity. *See* celebrity
vocal exclamations, 39–41
voice: of Amália, affective power of, 197–98; celebrity and affective power of, 196; Feld on sound, hearing, and, 244n10; "foreign," 61–62; ideologies of voicing, 62–64; injured or punished voice icon, 65–66, 109, 161, 178; listening in

continuum with, 7–8; "lyric," 61–62, 65, 253n55; opera vs. true fado and, 65; as soul, 67–69; symbolic contamination of female voice, 168–69; *voz do bairro* (voice of the neighborhood), 65
voltinhas (vocal ornamentations): Amália and, 81, 193, 219, 275n20; at heightened moments, 40; as natural, intuitive act, 64; origin narratives, 4, 81; soulfulness and, 27–28, 43; use of, 111, 157, 211, 223. *See also* melismas
Vuillermoz, Emílio, 12

Wallerstein, Immanuel, 107
Warner, Michael, 196
"war on terror," 82, 257n17
weeping: *gemido* in guitarras, 42, 112, 140; "icons of crying," 41, 250n21; "outsiders" and tear-based emotional universalism, 118–19; practices of, 41–43, 140
Wenders, Wim, 105, 260n1
widows, 165–66
Williams, Raymond, 8, 261n12
women. *See* gender
Wordsworth, William, 261n12
world music: authenticity and, 68; *casas de fado* and, 99; core–periphery and North–South dialectics and, 125–26; emotional excess and, 127; international fado careers, 126–27; "Latin" or Mediterranean as passionate, 129; stigma of, 127–28

Zamara, Carlos, 254

www.ingramcontent.com/pod-product-compliance
Lightning Source LLC
Chambersburg PA
CBHW071014280326
41935CB00011B/1351